C INTERFACES AND IMPLEMENTATIONS

Techniques for Creating Reusable Software

Addison-Wesley Professional Computing Series

Brian W. Kernighan, Consulting Editor

Ken Arnold/John Peyton, *A C User's Guide to ANSI C*

Tom Cargill, *C++ Programming Style*

William R. Cheswick/Steven M. Bellovin, *Firewalls and Internet Security: Repelling the Wily Hacker*

David A. Curry, *UNIX® System Security: A Guide for Users and System Administrators*

Erich Gamma/Richard Helm/Ralph Johnson/John Vlissides, *Design Patterns: Elements of Reusable Object-Oriented Software*

David R. Hanson, *C Interfaces and Implementations: Techniques for Creating Reusable Software*

John Lakos, *Large Scale C++ Software Design*

Scott Meyers, *Effective C++: 50 Specific Ways to Improve Your Programs and Designs*

Scott Meyers, *More Effective C++: 35 New Ways to Improve Your Programs and Designs*

Robert B. Murray, *C++ Strategies and Tactics*

David R. Musser/Atul Saini, *STL Tutorial and Reference Guide: C++ Programming with the Standard Template Library*

John K. Ousterhout, *Tcl and the Tk Toolkit*

Craig Partridge, *Gigabit Networking*

J. Stephen Pendergrast Jr., *Desktop KornShell Graphical Programming*

Radia Perlman, *Interconnections: Bridges and Routers*

David M. Piscitello/A. Lyman Chapin, *Open Systems Networking: TCP/IP and OSI*

Stephen A. Rago, *UNIX® System V Network Programming*

Curt Schimmel, *UNIX® Systems for Modern Architectures: Symmetric Multiprocessing and Caching for Kernel Programmers*

W. Richard Stevens, *Advanced Programming in the UNIX® Environment*

W. Richard Stevens, *TCP/IP Illustrated, Volume 1: The Protocols*

W. Richard Stevens, *TCP/IP Illustrated, Volume 3: TCP for Transactions, HTTP, NNTP, and the UNIX Domain Protocols*

Gary R. Wright/W. Richard Stevens, *TCP/IP Illustrated, Volume 2: The Implementation*

C INTERFACES AND IMPLEMENTATIONS

Techniques for Creating Reusable Software

David R. Hanson
Princeton University

ADDISON-WESLEY

An imprint of Addison Wesley Longman, Inc.

Reading, Massachusetts • Harlow, England • Menlo Park, California
Berkeley, California • Don Mills, Ontario • Sydney
Bonn • Amsterdam • Tokyo • Mexico City

This book was prepared from camera-ready copy supplied by the author.

Many of the designations used by manufacturers and sellers to distinguish their products are claimed as trademarks. Where those designations appear in this book and Addison Wesley Longman, Inc. was aware of a trademark claim, the designations have been printed in initial caps or all caps.

The authors and publishers have taken care in the preparation of this book, but make no expressed or implied warranty of any kind and assume no responsibility for errors or omissions. No liability is assumed for incidental or consequential damages in connection with or arising out of the use of the information or programs contained herein.

The publisher offers discounts on this book when ordered in quantity for special sales.

For more information, please contact:

> Corporate & Professional Publishing Group
> Addison Wesley Longman, Inc.
> One Jacob Way
> Reading, Massachusetts 01867

Library of Congress Cataloging-in-Publication Data

Hanson, David R.
    C interfaces and implementations : techniques for creating
reusable software / David R. Hanson.
        p.   cm. -- (Addison-Wesley professional computing series)
    Includes bibliographical references and index.
    ISBN 0-201-49841-3 (pbk.)
    1. C (Computer program language)   2. Computer software-
-Reusability   I. Title.   II. Series.
    QA76.73.C15H37   1996
    005.13'3--dc20   96-28817
                                                          CIP

Printed in the United States of America. Published simultaneously in Canada.

Text design by Wilson Graphics & Design (Kenneth J. Wilson).
Text printed on recycled and acid-free paper.

ISBN 0-201-49841-3
123456789-MA-99989796
First Printing, August 1996

CONTENTS

Preface   xi
   Organization   xiii
   Instructional Use   xiv
   How to Get the Software   xvi
   Acknowledgments   xvii

1 Introduction   1
   1.1 Literate Programs   2
   1.2 Programming Style   8
   1.3 Efficiency   11
   Further Reading   12
   Exercises   13

2 Interfaces and Implementations   15
   2.1 Interfaces   15
   2.2 Implementations   18
   2.3 Abstract Data Types   21
   2.4 Client Responsibilities   24
   2.5 Efficiency   30
   Further Reading   30
   Exercises   31

3 Atoms   33
   3.1 Interface   33
   3.2 Implementation   34
   Further Reading   42
   Exercises   42

4 Exceptions and Assertions 45

4.1 Interface 47

4.2 Implementation 53

4.3 Assertions 59

Further Reading 63

Exercises 64

5 Memory Management 67

5.1 Interface 69

5.2 Production Implementation 73

5.3 Checking Implementation 76

Further Reading 85

Exercises 86

6 More Memory Management 89

6.1 Interface 90

6.2 Implementation 92

Further Reading 98

Exercises 100

7 Lists 103

7.1 Interface 103

7.2 Implementation 108

Further Reading 113

Exercises 114

8 Tables 115

8.1 Interface 115

8.2 Example: Word Frequencies 118

8.3 Implementation 125

Further Reading 132

Exercises 133

9 Sets 137

9.1 Interface 138

9.2 Example: Cross-Reference Listings 140

9.3 Implementation 148

    9.3.1 Member Operations 150

    9.3.2 Set Operations 154

    Further Reading 158

    Exercises 158

10 Dynamic Arrays 161

10.1 Interfaces 162

10.2 Implementation 165

    Further Reading 169

    Exercises 169

11 Sequences 171

11.1 Interface 171

11.2 Implementation 174

    Further Reading 180

    Exercises 180

12 Rings 183

12.1 Interface 183

12.2 Implementation 187

    Further Reading 196

    Exercises 197

13 Bit Vectors 199

13.1 Interface 199

13.2 Implementation 202

    13.2.1 Member Operations 204

    13.2.2 Comparisons 209

    13.2.3 Set Operations 211

    Further Reading 213

    Exercises 213

14 Formatting   215

14.1 Interface   216

    14.1.1 Formatting Functions   216

    14.1.2 Conversion Functions   219

14.2 Implementation   224

    14.2.1 Formatting Functions   225

    14.2.2 Conversion Functions   232

    Further Reading   238

    Exercises   239

15 Low-Level Strings   241

15.1 Interface   243

15.2 Example: Printing Identifiers   249

15.3 Implementation   251

    15.3.1 String Operations   252

    15.3.2 Analyzing Strings   258

    15.3.3 Conversion Functions   263

    Further Reading   264

    Exercises   265

16 High-Level Strings   269

16.1 Interface   269

16.2 Implementation   276

    16.2.1 String Operations   281

    16.2.2 Memory Management   285

    16.2.3 Analyzing Strings   288

    16.2.4 Conversion Functions   293

    Further Reading   293

    Exercises   294

17 **Extended-Precision Arithmetic**   297

17.1 Interface   297

17.2 Implementation   303

17.2.1 Addition and Subtraction   305

17.2.2 Multiplication   307

17.2.3 Division and Comparison   309

17.2.4 Shifting   315

17.2.5 String Conversions   319

Further Reading   321

Exercises   322

18 **Arbitrary-Precision Arithmetic**   323

18.1 Interface   323

18.2 Example: A Calculator   327

18.3 Implementation   334

18.3.1 Negation and Multiplication   337

18.3.2 Addition and Subtraction   338

18.3.3 Division   342

18.3.4 Exponentiation   343

18.3.5 Comparisons   346

18.3.6 Convenience Functions   347

18.3.7 Shifting   349

18.3.8 String and Integer Conversions   350

Further Reading   353

Exercises   354

19 Multiple-Precision Arithmetic   357

19.1 Interface   358

19.2 Example: Another Calculator   365

19.3 Implementation   373

    19.3.1 Conversions   377

    19.3.2 Unsigned Arithmetic   380

    19.3.3 Signed Arithmetic   383

    19.3.4 Convenience Functions   388

    19.3.5 Comparisons and Logical Operations   395

    19.3.6 String Conversions   399

    Further Reading   402

    Exercises   402

20 Threads   405

20.1 Interfaces   408

    20.1.1 Threads   409

    20.1.2 General Semaphores   413

    20.1.3 Synchronous Communication Channels   417

20.2 Examples   418

    20.2.1 Sorting Concurrently   418

    20.2.2 Critical Regions   423

    20.2.3 Generating Primes   426

20.3 Implementations   431

    20.3.1 Synchronous Communication Channels   431

    20.3.2 Threads   434

    20.3.3 Thread Creation and Context-Switching   446

    20.3.4 Preemption   454

    20.3.5 General Semaphores   457

    20.3.6 Context-Switching on the MIPS and ALPHA   459

    Further Reading   463

    Exercises   465

Interface Summary   469

Bibliography   497

Index   505

PREFACE

Programmers are inundated with information about application programming interfaces, or APIs. Yet, while most programmers use APIs and the libraries that implement them in almost every application they write, relatively few create and disemminate new, widely applicable, APIs. Indeed, programmers seem to prefer to "roll their own" instead of searching for a library that might meet their needs, perhaps because it is easier to write application-specific code than to craft well-designed APIs.

I'm as guilty as the next programmer: lcc, a compiler for ANSI/ISO C written by Chris Fraser and myself, was built from the ground up. (lcc is described in *A Retargetable C Compiler: Design and Implementation*, Addison-Wesley, 1995.) A compiler exemplifies the kind of application for which it is possible to use standard interfaces and to create interfaces that are useful elsewhere. Examples include interfaces for memory management, string and symbol tables, and list manipulation. But lcc uses only a few routines from the standard C library, and almost none of its code can be used directly in other applications.

This book advocates a design methodology based on interfaces and their implementations, and it illustrates this methodology by describing 24 interfaces and their implementations in detail. These interfaces span a large part of the computing spectrum and include data structures, arithmetic, string processing, and concurrent programming. The implementations aren't toys — they're designed for use in production code. As described below, the source code is freely available.

There's little support in the C programming language for the interface-based design methodology. Object-oriented languages, like C++ and Modula-3, have language features that encourage the separation of an interface from its implementation. Interface-based design is independent of any particular language, but it does require more programmer willpower and vigilance in languages like C, because it's too easy to pollute an interface with implicit knowledge of its implementation and vice versa.

Once mastered, however, interface-based design can speed development time by building upon a foundation of general-purpose interfaces that can serve many applications. The foundation class libraries in some C++ environments are examples of this effect. Increased reuse of existing software — libraries of interface implementations — reduces initial development costs. It also reduces maintenance costs, because more of an application rests on well-tested implementations of general-purpose interfaces.

The 24 interfaces come from several sources, and all have been revised for this book. Some of the interfaces for data structures — abstract data types — originated in lcc code, and in implementations of the Icon programming language done in the late 1970s and early 1980s (see R. E. Griswold and M. T. Griswold, *The Icon Programming Language*, Prentice Hall, 1990). Others come from the published work of other programmers; the "Further Reading" sections at the end of each chapter give the details.

Some of the interfaces are for data structures, but this is not a data structures book, per se. The emphasis is more on algorithm engineering — packaging data structures for general use in applications — than on data-structure algorithms. Good interface design does rely on appropriate data structures and efficient algorithms, however, so this book complements traditional data structure and algorithms texts like Robert Sedgewick's *Algorithms in C* (Addison-Wesley, 1990).

Most chapters describe one interface and its implementation; a few describe related interfaces. The "Interface" section in each chapter gives a concise, detailed description of the interface alone. For programmers interested only in the interfaces, these sections form a reference manual. A few chapters include "Example" sections, which illustrate the use of one or more interfaces in simple applications.

The "Implementation" section in each chapter is a detailed tour of the code that implements the chapter's interface. In a few cases, more than one implementation for the same interface is described, which illustrates an advantage of interface-based design. These sections are most useful for those modifying or extending an interface or designing related interfaces. Many of the exercises explore design and implementation alternatives. It should not be necessary to read an "Implementation" section in order to understand how to use an interface.

The interfaces, examples, and implementations are presented as *literate* programs; that is, the source code is interleaved with its explanation in an order that best suits understanding the code. The code is extracted automatically from the text files for this book and assembled into the order dictated by the C programming language. Other book-length examples of literate programming in C include *A Retargetable C Compiler* and *The Stanford GraphBase: A Platform for Combinatorial Computing* by D. E. Knuth (Addison-Wesley, 1993).

Organization

The material in this book falls into the following broad categories:

Foundations	1. Introduction
	2. Interfaces and Implementations
	4. Exceptions and Assertions
	5. Memory Management
	6. More Memory Management
Data Structures	7. Lists
	8. Tables
	9. Sets
	10. Dynamic Arrays
	11. Sequences
	12. Rings
	13. Bit Vectors
Strings	3. Atoms
	14. Formatting
	15. Low-Level Strings
	16. High-Level Strings
Arithmetic	17. Extended-Precision Arithmetic
	18. Arbitrary-Precision Arithmetic
	19. Multiple-Precision Arithmetic
Threads	20. Threads

Most readers will benefit from reading all of Chapters 1 through 4, because these chapters form the framework for the rest of the book. The remaining chapters can be read in any order, although some of the later chapters refer to their predecessors.

Chapter 1 covers literate programming and issues of programming style and efficiency. Chapter 2 motivates and describes the interface-based design methodology, defines the relevant terminology, and tours two simple interfaces and their implementations. Chapter 3 describes the prototypical Atom interface, which is the simplest production-quality interface in this book. Chapter 4 introduces exceptions and assertions, which are used in every interface. Chapters 5 and 6 describe the memory management interfaces used by almost all the implementations. The rest of the chapters each describe an interface and its implementation.

Instructional Use

I assume that readers understand C at the level covered in undergraduate introductory programming courses, and have a working understanding of fundamental data structures at the level presented in texts like *Algorithms in C*. At Princeton, the material in this book is used in systems programming courses from the sophomore to first-year graduate levels. Many of the interfaces use advanced C programming techniques, such as opaque pointers and pointers to pointers, and thus serve as nontrivial examples of those techniques, which are useful in systems programming and data structure courses.

This book can be used for courses in several ways, the simplest being in project-oriented courses. In a compiler course, for example, students often build a compiler for a toy language. Substantial projects are common in graphics courses as well. Many of the interfaces can simplify the projects in these kinds of courses by eliminating some of the grunt programming needed to get such projects off the ground. This usage helps students realize the enormous savings that reuse can bring to a project, and it often induces them to try interface-based design for their own parts of the project. This latter effect is particularly valuable in team projects, because that's a way of life in the "real world."

Interfaces and implementations are the focus of Princeton's sophomore-level systems programming course. Assignments require students to be interface clients, implementors, and designers. In one assignment, for example, I distribute Section 8.1's Table interface, the object code for its implementation, and the specifications for Section 8.2's word frequency program, wf. The students must implement wf using only my object code for Table. In the next assignment, they get the object code for wf, and they must implement Table. Sometimes, I reverse these assignments, but both orders are eye-openers for most students. They are unaccustomed to having only object code for major parts of their program, and these assignments are usually their first exposure to the semiformal notation used in interfaces and program specification.

Initial assignments also introduce checked runtime errors and assertions as integral parts of interface specifications. Again, it takes a few assignments before students begin to appreciate the value of these concepts. I forbid "unannounced" crashes; that is, crashes that are not announced by an assertion failure diagnostic. Programs that crash get a grade of zero. This penalty may seem unduly harsh, but it gets the students' attention. They also gain an appreciation of the advantages of safe languages, like ML and Modula-3, in which unannounced crashes are impossible. (This grading policy is less harsh than it sounds, because in multipart assignments, only the offending part is penalized, and different assignments have different weights. I've given many zeros, but none has ever caused a course grade to shift by a whole point.)

Once students have a few interfaces under their belts, later assignments ask them to design new interfaces and to live with their design choices. For example, one of Andrew Appel's favorite assignments is a primality testing program. Students work in groups to design the interfaces for the arbitrary-precision arithmetic that is needed for this assignment. The results are similar to the interfaces described in Chapters 17 through 19. Different groups design interfaces, and a postassignment comparison of these interfaces, in which the groups critique one anothers' work, is always quite revealing. Kai Li accomplishes similar goals with a semester-long project that builds an *X*-based editor using the Tcl/Tk system (J. K. Ousterhout, *Tcl and the Tk Toolkit*, Addison-Wesley, 1994) and editor-specific interfaces designed and implemented by the students. Tk itself provides another good example of interface-based design.

In advanced courses, I usually package assignments as interfaces and give the students free rein to revise and improve on them, and even to change the goals of the assignment. Giving them a starting point reduces the time required for assignment, and allowing substantial changes encourages creative students to explore alternatives. The unsuccessful alternatives are often more educational than the successful ones. Students invariably go down the wrong road, and they pay for it with greatly increased development time. When, in hindsight, they understand their mistakes, they come to appreciate that designing good interfaces is hard, but worth the effort, and they almost always become converts to interface-based design.

How to Get the Software

The software in this book has been tested on the following platforms:

processor	operating systems	compilers
SPARC	SunOS 4.1	lcc 3.5 gcc 2.7.2
Alpha	OSF/1 3.2A	lcc 4.0 gcc 2.6.3 cc
MIPS R3000	IRIX 5.3	lcc 3.5 gcc 2.6.3 cc
MIPS R3000	Ultrix 4.3	lcc 3.5 gcc 2.5.7
Pentium	Windows 95 Windows NT 3.51	Microsoft Visual C/C++ 4.0

A few of the implementations are machine-specific; they assume that the machine has two's-complement integer and IEEE floating-point arithmetic, and that unsigned longs can hold object pointers.

The source code for everything in this book is available for anonymous ftp at ftp.cs.princeton.edu in pub/packages/cii. Use an ftp client to connect to ftp.cs.princeton.edu, change to the directory pub/packages/cii, and download the file README, which describes the contents of the directory and how to download the distribution.

The most recent distributions are usually in files with names like ciixy.tar.gz or ciixy.zip, where xy is the version number; for example, 10 is version 1.0. ciixy.tar.gz is a UNIX tar file compressed with gzip, and ciixy.zip is a ZIP file compatible with PKZIP version 2.04g. The files in ciixy.zip are DOS/Windows text files; that is, their lines end with carriage returns and linefeeds. ciixy.zip may also be available on America Online, CompuServe, and other online services.

Information is also available on the World Wide Web at the URL http://www.cs.princeton.edu/software/cii/. This page includes instructions on reporting bugs.

Acknowledgments

I have been using some of the interfaces in this book for my own research project and in courses at the University of Arizona and Princeton University since the late 1970s. Students in these courses have been guinea pigs for my drafts of these interfaces. Their feedback over the years has been an important contribution to both the code in this book and its explanation. The Princeton students in several offerings of COS 217 and COS 596 deserve special thanks, because they suffered unknowingly through the drafts of most of what's in this book.

Interfaces are a way of life at Digital's System Research Center (SRC), and my 1992 and 1993 summers at SRC working on the Modula-3 project erased any doubts I may have harbored about the efficacy of this approach. My thanks to SRC for supporting my visits, and to Bill Kalsow, Eric Muller, and Greg Nelson for many illuminating discussions.

My thanks to IDA's Centers for Communications Research in Princeton and La Jolla for their support during the summer of 1994 and during my 1995–96 sabbatical. The CCRs provided ideal hideouts at which to plan and complete this book.

Technical interactions with colleagues and students have contributed to this book in many ways. Even seemingly unrelated discussions have provoked improvements in my code and in its explanation. Thanks to Andrew Appel, Greg Astfalk, Jack Davidson, John Ellis, Mary Fernández, Chris Fraser, Alex Gounares, Kai Li, Jacob Navia, Maylee Noah, Rob Pike, Bill Plauger, John Reppy, Anne Rogers, and Richard Stevens. Careful readings of my code and prose by Rex Jaeschke, Brian Kernighan, Taj Khattra, Richard O'Keefe, Norman Ramsey, and David Spuler made a significant contribution to the quality of both.

David R. Hanson

1

INTRODUCTION

A big program is made up of many small modules. These modules provide the functions, procedures, and data structures used in the program. Ideally, most of these modules are ready-made and come from libraries; only those that are specific to the application at hand need to be written from scratch. Assuming that library code has been tested thoroughly, only the application-specific code will contain bugs, and debugging can be confined to just that code.

Unfortunately, this theoretical ideal rarely occurs in practice. Most programs are written from scratch, and they use libraries only for the lowest level facilities, such as I/O and memory management. Programmers often write application-specific code for even these kinds of low-level components; it's common, for example, to find applications in which the C library functions `malloc` and `free` have been replaced by custom memory-management functions.

There are undoubtedly many reasons for this situation; one of them is that widely available libraries of robust, well designed modules are rare. Some of the libraries that are available are mediocre and lack standards. The C library has been standardized since 1989, and is only now appearing on most platforms.

Another reason is size: Some libraries are so big that mastering them is a major undertaking. If this effort even appears to be close to the effort required to write the application, programmers may simply reimplement the parts of the library they need. User-interface libraries, which have proliferated recently, often exhibit this problem.

Library design and implementation are difficult. Designers must tread carefully between generality, simplicity, and efficiency. If the routines and data structures in a library are too general, they may be too hard to use or inefficient for their intended purposes. If they're too simple, they run the risk of not satisfying the demands of applications that might use them. If they're too confusing, programmers won't use them. The C library itself provides a few examples; its `realloc` function, for instance, is a marvel of confusion.

Library implementors face similar hurdles. Even if the design is done well, a poor implementation will scare off users. If an implementation is too slow or too big — or just perceived to be so — programmers will design their own replacements. Worst of all, if an implementation has bugs, it shatters the ideal outlined above and renders the library useless.

This book describes the design and implementation of a library that is suitable for a wide range of applications written in the C programming language. The library exports a set of modules that provide functions and data structures for "programming-in-the-small." These modules are suitable for use as "piece parts" in applications or application components that are a few thousand lines long.

Most of the facilities described in the subsequent chapters are those covered in undergraduate courses on data structures and algorithms. But here, more attention is paid to how they are packaged and to making them robust. Each module is presented as an *interface* and its *implementation*. This design methodology, explained in Chapter 2, separates module specifications from their implementations, promotes clarity and precision in those specifications, and helps provide robust implementations.

1.1 Literate Programs

This book describes modules not by prescription, but by example. Each chapter describes one or two interfaces and their implementations in full. These descriptions are presented as literate programs. The code for an interface and its implementation is intertwined with prose that explains it. More important, each chapter is the source code for the interfaces and implementations it describes. The code is extracted automatically from the source text for this book; what you see is what you get.

A literate program is composed of English prose and labeled *chunks* of program code. For example,

⟨*compute* x • y⟩≡
```
    sum = 0;
```

```
for (i = 0; i < n; i++)
    sum += x[i]*y[i];
```

defines a chunk named ⟨*compute* x • y⟩; its code computes the dot product of the arrays x and y. This chunk is used by referring to it in another chunk:

```
⟨function dotproduct⟩≡
    int dotProduct(int x[], int y[], int n) {
        int i, sum;

        ⟨compute x • y⟩
        return sum;
    }
```

When the chunk ⟨*function* dotproduct⟩ is extracted from the file that holds this chapter, its code is copied verbatim, uses of chunks are replaced by their code, and so on. The result of extracting ⟨*function* dotproduct⟩ is a file that holds just the code:

```
int dotProduct(int x[], int y[], int n) {
    int i, sum;

    sum = 0;
    for (i = 0; i < n; i++)
        sum += x[i]*y[i];
    return sum;
}
```

A literate program can be presented in small pieces and documented thoroughly. English prose subsumes traditional program comments, and isn't limited by the comment conventions of the programming language.

The chunk facility frees literate programs from the ordering constraints imposed by programming languages. The code can be revealed in whatever order is best for understanding it, not in the order dictated by rules that insist, for example, that definitions of program entities precede their uses.

The literate-programming system used in this book has a few more features that help describe programs piecemeal. To illustrate these features and to provide a complete example of a literate C program, the rest of this section describes double, a program that detects adjacent identical words in its input, such as "the the." For example, the UNIX command

```
% double intro.txt inter.txt
intro.txt:10: the
inter.txt:110: interface
inter.txt:410: type
inter.txt:611: if
```

shows that "the" occurs twice in the file intro.txt; the second occurrence appears on line 10; and double occurrences of "interface," "type," and "if" appear in inter.txt at the lines shown. If double is invoked with no arguments, it reads its standard input and omits the file names from its output. For example:

```
% cat intro.txt inter.txt | double
10: the
143: interface
343: type
544: if
```

In these and other displays, commands typed by the user are shown in a *slanted typewriter* font, and the output is shown in a regular type-writer font.

Let's start double by defining a *root* chunk that uses other chunks for each of the program's components:

⟨*double.c* 4⟩≡
    ⟨*includes* 5⟩
    ⟨*data* 6⟩
    ⟨*prototypes* 6⟩
    ⟨*functions* 5⟩

By convention, the root chunk is labeled with the program's file name; extracting the chunk ⟨*double.c* 4⟩ extracts the program. The other chunks are labeled with double's top-level components. These components are listed in the order dictated by the C programming language, but they can be presented in any order.

The 4 in ⟨*double.c* 4⟩ is the page number on which the definition of the chunk begins. The numbers in the chunks used in ⟨*double.c* 4⟩ are the page numbers on which their definitions begin. These page numbers help readers navigate the code.

The main function handles double's arguments. It opens each file and calls doubleword to scan the file:

⟨*functions* 5⟩≡

```c
int main(int argc, char *argv[]) {
    int i;

    for (i = 1; i < argc; i++) {
        FILE *fp = fopen(argv[i], "r");
        if (fp == NULL) {
            fprintf(stderr, "%s: can't open '%s' (%s)\n",
                argv[0], argv[i], strerror(errno));
            return EXIT_FAILURE;
        } else {
            doubleword(argv[i], fp);
            fclose(fp);
        }
    }
    if (argc == 1) doubleword(NULL, stdin);
    return EXIT_SUCCESS;
}
```

⟨*includes* 5⟩≡

```c
#include <stdio.h>
#include <stdlib.h>
#include <errno.h>
```

The function doubleword needs to read words from a file. For the purposes of this program, a word is one or more nonspace characters, and case doesn't matter. getword reads the next word from an opened file into buf[0..size-1] and returns one; it returns zero when it reaches the end of file.

⟨*functions* 5⟩+≡

```c
int getword(FILE *fp, char *buf, int size) {
    int c;

    c = getc(fp);
    ⟨scan forward to a nonspace character or EOF 6⟩
```

```
        ⟨copy the word into buf[0..size-1] 7⟩
        if (c != EOF)
            ungetc(c, fp);
        return ⟨found a word? 7⟩;
    }
```

⟨*prototypes* 6⟩≡
```
    int getword(FILE *, char *, int);
```

This chunk illustrates another literate programming feature: The +≡ that follows the chunk labeled ⟨*functions* 5⟩ indicates that the code for get-word is *appended* to the code for the chunk ⟨*functions* 5⟩, so that chunk now holds the code for main and for getcode. This feature permits the code in a chunk to be doled out a little at a time. The page number in the label for a continued chunk refers to the *first* definition for the chunk, so it's easy to find the beginning of a chunk's definition.

Since getword follows main, the call to getword in main needs a prototype, which is the purpose of the ⟨*prototypes* 6⟩ chunk. This chunk is something of a concession to C's declaration-before-use rule, but if it is defined consistently and appears before ⟨*functions* 5⟩ in the root chunk, then functions can be presented in any order.

In addition to plucking the next word from the input, getword increments linenum whenever it runs across a new-line character. double-word uses linenum when it emits its output.

⟨*data* 6⟩≡
```
    int linenum;
```

⟨*scan forward to a nonspace character or EOF* 6⟩≡
```
    for ( ; c != EOF && isspace(c); c = getc(fp))
        if (c == '\n')
            linenum++;
```

⟨*includes* 5⟩+≡
```
    #include <ctype.h>
```

The definition of linenum exemplifies chunks that are presented in an order different from what is required by C. linenum is given here, when it is first used, instead at the top of the file or before the definition of getword, which is where C insists that it be defined.

The value of size is the limit on the length of words stored by get-word, which discards the excess characters and folds uppercase letters to lowercase:

⟨*copy the word into* buf[0..size-1] 7⟩≡

```
    {
        int i = 0;
        for ( ; c != EOF && !isspace(c); c = getc(fp))
            if (i < size - 1)
                buf[i++] = tolower(c);
        if (i < size)
            buf[i] = '\0';
    }
```

The index i is compared to size - 1 to guarantee there's room to store a null character at the end of the word. The if statement protecting this assignment handles the case when size is zero. This case won't occur in double, but this kind of defensive programming helps catch "can't happen" bugs.

All that remains is for getword to return one if buf holds a word, and zero otherwise:

⟨*found a word?* 7⟩≡

```
    buf[0] != '\0'
```

This definition shows that chunks don't have to correspond to statements or to any other syntactic unit of C; they're simply text.

doubleword reads each word, compares it with the previous word, and complains about duplicates. It looks only at words that begin with letters:

⟨*functions* 5⟩+≡

```
    void doubleword(char *name, FILE *fp) {
        char prev[128], word[128];

        linenum = 1;
        prev[0] = '\0';
        while (getword(fp, word, sizeof word)) {
            if (isalpha(word[0]) && strcmp(prev, word)==0)
                ⟨word is a duplicate 8⟩
            strcpy(prev, word);
```

```
        }
   }
```

⟨*prototypes* 6⟩+≡
```
   void doubleword(char *, FILE *);
```

⟨*includes* 5⟩+≡
```
   #include <string.h>
```

Emitting the output is easy, but the file name and its trailing colon are printed only if name isn't null:

⟨word *is a duplicate* 8⟩≡
```
   {
       if (name)
           printf("%s:", name);
       printf("%d: %s\n", linenum, word);
   }
```

This chunk is defined as a compound statement so that it can appear as the consequent of the if statement in which it is used.

1.2 Programming Style

double illustrates many of the stylistic conventions used for the programs in this book. It is more important for programs to be read easily and understood by people than it is for them to be compiled easily by computers. The compiler doesn't care about the names chosen for variables, how the code is laid out, or how the program is divided into modules. But these kinds of details can have enormous impact on how easily programmers can read and understand a program.

The code in this book follows established stylistic conventions for C programs. It uses consistent conventions for naming variables, types, and routines, and, to the extent permitted by the typographical constraints imposed by this book, a consistent indentation style. Stylistic conventions are not a rigid set of rules that must be followed at all costs; rather, they express a philosophical approach to programming that seeks to maximize readability and understanding. Thus, the "rules" are broken whenever varying the conventions helps to emphasize important facets of the code or makes complicated code more readable.

In general, longer, evocative names are used for global variables and routines, and short names, which may mirror common mathematical notation, are used for local variables. The loop index i in ⟨*compute* x • y⟩ is an example of the latter convention. Using longer names for indices and variables that are used for similarly traditional purposes usually makes the code harder to read; for example, in

```
sum = 0;
for (theindex = 0; theindex < numofElements; theindex++)
    sum += x[theindex]*y[theindex];
```

the variable names obscure what the code does.

Variables are declared near their first use, perhaps in chunks. The declaration of linenum near its first use in getword is an example. Locals are declared at the beginning of the compound statements in which they are used, when possible. An example is the declaration of i in ⟨*copy the word into* buf[0..size-1] 7⟩.

In general, the names of procedures and functions are chosen to reflect what the procedures do and what the functions return. Thus getword returns the next word in the input and doubleword finds and announces words that occur two or more times. Most routines are short, no more than a page of code; chunks are even shorter, usually less than a dozen lines.

There are almost no comments in the code because the prose surrounding the chunks that comprise the code take their place. Stylistic advice on commenting conventions can evoke nearly religious wars among programmers. This book follows the lead of classics in C programming, in which comments are kept to a minimum. Code that is clear and that uses good naming and indentation conventions usually explains itself. Comments are called for only to explain, for example, the details of data structures, special cases in algorithms, and exceptional conditions. Compilers can't check that comments and code agree; misleading comments are usually worse than no comments. Finally, some comments are just clutter; those in which the noise and excess typography drown out the content do nothing but smother the code.

Literate programming avoids many of the battles that occur in comment wars because it isn't constrained by the comment mechanisms of the programming language. Programmers can use whatever typographical features are best for conveying their intentions, including tables, equations, pictures, and citations. Literate programming seems to encourage accuracy, precision, and clarity.

The code in this book is written in C; it uses most of the idioms commonly accepted — and expected — by experienced C programmers. Some of these idioms can confuse programmers new to C, but they must master them to become fluent in C. Idioms involving pointers are often the most confusing because C provides several unique and expressive operators for manipulating pointers. The library function strcpy, which copies one string to another and returns the destination string, illustrates the differences between "idiomatic C" and code written by newcomers to C; the latter kind of code often uses arrays:

```c
char *strcpy(char dst[], const char src[]) {
    int i;

    for (i = 0; src[i] != '\0'; i++)
        dst[i] = src[i];
    src[i] = '\0';
    return dst;
}
```

The idiomatic version uses pointers:

```c
char *strcpy(char *dst, const char *src) {
    char *s = dst;

    while (*dst++ = *src++)
        ;
    return s;
}
```

Both versions are reasonable implementations of strcpy. The pointer version uses the common idiom that combines assignment, incrementing a pointer, and testing the result of the assignment into the single assignment expression. It also modifies its arguments, dst and src, which is acceptable in C because all arguments are passed by value — arguments are just initialized locals.

A good case can be made for preferring the array version to the pointer version. For example, the array version is easier for *all* programmers to understand, regardless of their fluency in C. But the pointer version is the one most experienced C programmers would write, and hence the one programmers are most likely to encounter when reading existing code. This book can help you learn these idioms, understand C's strong points, and avoid common pitfalls.

1.3 Efficiency

Programmers seem obsessed with efficiency. They can spend hours tweaking code to make it run faster. Unfortunately, much of this effort is wasted. Programmers' intuitions are notoriously bad at guessing where programs spend their time.

Tuning a program to make it faster almost always makes it bigger, more difficult to understand, and more likely to contain errors. There's no point in such tuning unless measurements of execution time show that the program is too slow. A program needs only to be fast enough, not necessarily as fast as possible.

Tuning is often done in a vacuum. If a program is too slow, the only way to find its bottlenecks is to measure it. A program's bottlenecks rarely occur where you expect them or for the reasons you suspect, and there's no point in tuning programs in the wrong places. When you've found the right place, tuning is called for only if the time spent in that place is a significant amount of the running time. It's pointless to save 1 percent in a search routine if I/O accounts for 60 percent of the program's running time.

Tuning often introduces errors. The fastest program to a crash isn't a winner. Reliability is more important than efficiency; delivering fast software that crashes is more expensive in the long run than delivering reliable software that's fast enough.

Tuning is often done at the wrong level. Straightforward implementations of inherently fast algorithms are better than hand-tuned implementations of slow algorithms. For example, squeezing instructions out of the inner loop of a linear search is doomed to be less profitable than using a binary search in the first place.

Tuning can't fix a bad design. If the program is slow everywhere, the inefficiency is probably built into the design. This unfortunate situation occurs when designs are drawn from poorly written or imprecise problem specifications, or when there's no overall design at all.

Most of the code in this book uses efficient algorithms that have good *average-case* performance and whose *worst-case* performance is easy to characterize. Their execution times on typical inputs will almost always be fast enough for most applications. Those cases where performance might pose problems in some applications are clearly identified.

Some C programmers make heavy use of macros and conditional compilation in their quests for efficiency. This book avoids both whenever possible. Using macros to avoid function calls is rarely necessary. It pays only when objective measurements demonstrate that the costs of the calls in question overwhelm the running times of the rest of the code. I/O is one of the few places where macros are justified; the standard I/O functions `getc`, `putc`, `getchar`, and `putchar`, for example, are often implemented as macros.

Conditional compilation is often used to configure code for specific platforms or environments, or to enable or disable debugging code. These problems are real, but conditional compilation is usually the easy way out of them and always makes the code harder to read. And it's often more useful to rework the code so that platform dependencies are selected during execution. For example, a single compiler that can select one of, say, six architectures for which to generate code at execution time — a cross compiler — is more useful than having to configure and build six different compilers, and it's probably easier to maintain.

If an application must be configured at compile time, version-control tools are better at it than C's conditional-compilation facilities. The code isn't littered with preprocessor directives that make the code hard to read and obscure what's being compiled and what isn't. With version-control tools, what you see is what is executed. These tools are also ideal for keeping track of performance improvements.

Further Reading

The ANSI standard (1990) and the technically equivalent ISO standard (1990) are the definitive references for the standard C library, but Plauger (1992) gives a more detailed description and a complete implementation. Similarly, the standards are the last word on C, but Kernighan and Ritchie (1988) is probably the most widely used reference. The latest edition of Harbison and Steele (1995) is perhaps the most up-to-date with respect to the standards, and it also describes how to write "clean C" — C code that can be compiled with C++ compilers. Jaeschke (1991) condenses the essence of Standard C into a compact dictionary format, which is a useful reference for C programmers.

Software Tools by Kernighan and Plauger (1976) gives early examples of literate programs, although the authors used ad hoc tools to include code in the book. WEB is the one of the first tools designed explicitly for literate programming. Knuth (1992) describes WEB and some of its variants and uses; Sewell (1989) is a tutorial introduction to WEB. Simpler tools (Hanson 1987; Ramsey 1994) can go a long way to providing much of WEB's essential functionality. This book uses `notangle`, one of the programs in Ramsey's `noweb` system, to extract the chunks. `noweb` is also used by Fraser and Hanson (1995) to present an entire C compiler as a literate program. This compiler is also a cross compiler.

`double` is taken from Kernighan and Pike (1984) where it's implemented in the AWK programming language (Aho, Kernighan, and Weinberger 1988). Despite its age, Kernighan and Pike remains one of the best books on the UNIX programming philosophy.

The best way to learn good programming style is to read programs that use good style. This book follows the enduring style used in Kernighan and Pike (1984) and Kernighan and Ritchie (1988). Kernighan and Plauger (1978) is the classic book on programming style, but it doesn't include any examples in C. Ledgard's brief book (1987) offers similar advice, and Maguire (1993) provides a perspective from the world of PC programming. Koenig (1989) exposes C's dark corners and highlights the ones that should be avoided. McConnell (1993) offers sound advice on many aspects of program construction, and gives a balanced discussion of the pros and cons of using goto statements.

The best way to learn to write efficient code is to have a thorough grounding in algorithms and to read other code that is efficient. Sedgewick (1990) surveys all of the important algorithms most programmers need to know, and Knuth (1973a) gives the gory details on the fundamental ones. Bentley (1982) is 170 pages of good advice and common sense on how to write efficient code.

Exercises

1.1   `getword` increments `linenum` in ⟨*scan forward to a nonspace or EOF* 6⟩ but not after ⟨*copy the word into* `buf[0..size-1]` 7⟩ when a word *ends* at a new-line character. Explain why. What would happen if `linenum` were incremented in this case?

1.2   What does `double` print when it sees three or more identical words in its input? Change `double` to fix this "feature."

1.3   Many experienced C programmers would include an explicit comparison in `strcpy`'s loop:

```
char *strcpy(char *dst, const char *src) {
    char *s = dst;

    while ((*dst++ = *src++) != '\0')
        ;
    return s;
}
```

The explicit comparison makes it clear that the assignment isn't a typographical error. Some C compilers and related tools, like Gimpel Software's PC-Lint and LCLint (Evans 1996), issue a warning when the result of an assignment is used as a conditional, because such usage is a common source of errors. If you have PC-Lint or LCLint, experiment with it on some "tested" programs.

2
INTERFACES AND IMPLEMENTATIONS

A module comes in two parts, its interface and its implementation. The interface specifies *what* a module does. It declares the identifiers, types, and routines that are available to code that uses the module. An implementation specifies *how* a module accomplishes the purpose advertised by its interface. For a given module, there is usually one interface, but there might be many implementations that provide the facilities specified by the interface. Each implementation might use different algorithms and data structures, but they all must meet the specification given by the interface.

A *client* is a piece of code that uses a module. Clients *import* interfaces; implementations *export* them. Clients need to see only the interface. Indeed, they may have only the object code for an implementation. Clients share interfaces and implementations, thus avoiding unnecessary code duplication. This methodology also helps avoid bugs — interfaces and implementations are written and debugged once, but used often.

2.1 Interfaces

An interface specifies only those identifiers that clients may use, hiding irrelevant representation details and algorithms as much as possible. This helps clients avoid dependencies on the specifics of particular implementations. This kind of dependency between a client and an implementation — *coupling* — causes bugs when an implementation changes; these bugs can be particularly hard to fix when the dependencies are buried in hidden or implicit assumptions about an implementation. A well-designed and precisely specified interface reduces coupling.

C has only minimal support for separating interfaces from implementations, but simple conventions can yield most of the benefits of the interface/implementation methodology. In C, an interface is specified by a header file, which usually has a `.h` file extension. This header file declares the macros, types, data structures, variables, and routines that clients may use. A client imports an interface with the C preprocessor `#include` directive.

The following example illustrates the conventions used in this book's interfaces. The interface

⟨*arith.h*⟩≡
```
extern int Arith_max(int x, int y);
extern int Arith_min(int x, int y);
extern int Arith_div(int x, int y);
extern int Arith_mod(int x, int y);
extern int Arith_ceiling(int x, int y);
extern int Arith_floor  (int x, int y);
```

declares six integer arithmetic functions. An implementation provides definitions for each of these functions.

The interface is named `Arith` and the interface header file is named `arith.h`. The interface name appears as a prefix for each of the identifiers in the interface. This convention isn't pretty, but C offers few alternatives. All file-scope identifiers — variables, functions, type definitions, and enumeration constants — share a single name space. All global structure, union, and enumeration tags share another single name space. In a large program, it's easy to use the same name for different purposes in otherwise unrelated modules. One way to avoid these *name collisions* is use a prefix, such as the module name. A large program can easily have thousands of global identifiers, but usually has only hundreds of modules. Module names not only provide suitable prefixes, but help document client code.

The functions in the `Arith` interface provide some useful pieces missing from the standard C library and provide well-defined results for division and modulus where the standard leaves the behavior of these operations undefined or implementation-defined.

`Arith_min` and `Arith_max` return the minimum and maximum of their integer arguments.

Arith_div returns the quotient obtained by dividing x by y, and Arith_mod returns the corresponding remainder. When x and y are both positive or both negative, Arith_div(x, y) is equal to x/y and Arith_mod(x, y) is equal to x%y. When the operands have different signs, however, the values returned by C's built-in operators depend on the implementation. When y is zero, Arith_div and Arith_mod behave the same as x/y and x%y.

The C standard insists only that if x/y is representable, then $(x/y) \cdot y + x\%y$ must be equal to x. These semantics permit integer division to truncate toward zero or toward minus infinity when one of the operands is negative. For example, if $-13/5$ is -2, then the standard says that $-13\%5$ must be equal to $-13 - (-13/5) \cdot 5 = -13 - (-2) \cdot 5 = -3$. But if $-13/5$ is -3, then the value of $-13\%5$ must be $-13 - (-3) \cdot 5 = 2$.

The built-in operators are thus useful only for positive operands. The standard library functions div and ldiv take two integers or long integers and return the quotient and remainder in the quot and rem fields of a structure. Their semantics are well defined: they always truncate toward zero, so div(-13, 5).quot is always equal to -2. Arith_div and Arith_mod are similarly well defined. They always truncate toward the left on the number line; toward zero when their operands have the same sign, and toward minus infinity when their signs are different, so Arith_div(-13, 5) returns -3.

The definitions for Arith_div and Arith_mod are couched in more precise mathematical terms. Arith_div(x, y) is the maximum integer that does not exceed the real number z such that $z \cdot y = x$. Thus, for $x = -13$ and $y = 5$ (or $x = 13$ and $y = -5$), z is -2.6, so Arith_div(-13, 5) is -3. Arith_mod(x, y) is defined to be equal to $x - y \cdot$ Arith_div(x, y), so Arith_mod(-13, 5) is $-13 - 5 \cdot (-3) = 2$.

The functions Arith_ceiling and Arith_floor follow similar conventions. Arith_ceiling(x, y) returns the *least* integer not less than the real quotient of x/y, and Arith_floor(x, y) returns the *greatest* integer not exceeding the real quotient of x/y. Arith_ceiling returns the integer to the right of x/y on the number line, and Arith_floor returns the integer to the left of x/y for all operands. For example:

```
Arith_ceiling( 13,5) =   13/5 =   2.6  =   3
Arith_ceiling(-13,5) =  -13/5 =  -2.6  =  -2
Arith_floor  ( 13,5) =   13/5 =   2.6  =   2
Arith_floor  (-13,5) =  -13/5 =  -2.6  =  -3
```

This laborious specification for an interface as simple as `Arith` is unfortunately both typical and necessary for most interfaces. Most programming languages include holes in their semantics where the precise meanings of some operations are ill-defined or simply undefined. C's semantics are riddled with such holes. Well-designed interfaces plug these holes, define what is undefined, and make explicit decisions about behaviors that the language specifies as undefined or implementation-defined.

`Arith` is not just an artificial example designed to show C's pitfalls. It is useful, for example, for algorithms that involve modular arithmetic, like those used in hash tables. Suppose i is to range from zero to N-1 where N exceeds 1 and incrementing and decrementing i is to be done modulo N. That is, if i is N-1, i+1 is 0, and if i is 0, i-1 is N-1. The expressions

```
i = Arith_mod(i + 1, N);
i = Arith_mod(i - 1, N);
```

increment and decrement i correctly. The expression i = (i+1)%N works, too, but i = (i-1)%N doesn't work because when i is 0, (i-1)%N can be -1 or N-1. The programmer who uses (i-1)%N on a machine where (-1)%N returns N-1 and counts on that behavior is in for a rude surprise when the code is ported to a machine where (-1)%N returns -1. The library function div(x, y) doesn't help either. It returns a structure whose `quot` and `rem` fields hold the quotient and remainder of x/y. When i is zero, div(i-1, N).rem is always –1. It is possible to use i = (i-1+N)%N, but only when i-1+N can't overflow.

2.2 Implementations

An implementation exports an interface. It defines the variables and functions necessary to provide the facilities specified by the interface. An implementation reveals the representation details and algorithms of its particular rendition of the interface, but, ideally, clients never need to see these details. Clients share object code for implementations, usually by loading them from libraries.

An interface can have more than one implementation. As long as the implementation adheres to the interface, it can be changed without affecting clients. A different implementation might provide better performance, for example. Well-designed interfaces avoid machine dependencies, but may force implementations to be machine-dependent, so different implementations or parts of implementations might be needed for each machine on which the interface is used.

In C, an implementation is provided by one or more .c files. An implementation must provide the facilities specified by the interface it exports. Implementations include the interface's .h file to ensure that its definitions are consistent with the interface's declarations. Beyond this, however, there are no linguistic mechanisms in C to check an implementation's compliance.

Like the interfaces, the implementations described in this book have a stylized format illustrated by arith.c:

⟨*arith.c*⟩≡
```
#include "arith.h"
⟨arith.c functions 19⟩
```

⟨*arith.c functions* 19⟩≡
```
int Arith_max(int x, int y) {
    return x > y ? x : y;
}

int Arith_min(int x, int y) {
    return x > y ? y : x;
}
```

In addition to ⟨*arith.c functions* 19⟩, more involved implementations may have chunks named ⟨*data*⟩, ⟨*types*⟩, ⟨*macros*⟩, ⟨*prototypes*⟩, etc. File names in chunks, such as *arith.c*, are omitted when no confusion results.

Arith_div must cope with the two possible behaviors for division when its arguments have different signs. If division truncates toward zero and y doesn't divide x evenly, then Arith_div(x,y) is x/y - 1; otherwise, x/y will do:

⟨*arith.c functions* 19⟩+≡
```
int Arith_div(int x, int y) {
    if ((⟨division truncates toward 0 20⟩
    &&  ⟨x and y have different signs 20⟩ && x%y != 0)
        return x/y - 1;
    else
        return x/y;
}
```

The example from the previous section, dividing –13 by 5, tests which way division truncates. Capturing the outcomes of testing whether x and y are less than zero and comparing these outcomes checks the signs:

⟨*division truncates toward 0* 20⟩≡
```
  -13/5 == -2
```

⟨x *and* y *have different signs* 20⟩≡
```
  (x < 0) != (y < 0)
```

Arith_mod could be implemented as it's defined:

```
    int Arith_mod(int x, int y) {
        return x - y*Arith_div(x, y);
    }
```

Arith_mod can also use the % operator if it tests for the same conditions as Arith_div. When those conditions are true,

```
    Arith_mod(x,y)   = x - y*Arith_div(x, y)
                     = x - y*(x/y - 1)
                     = x - y*(x/y) + y
```

The underlined subexpression is the Standard C definition of x%y, so Arith_mod is

⟨*arith.c functions* 19⟩+≡
```
    int Arith_mod(int x, int y) {
        if ((⟨division truncates toward 0 20⟩
        && ⟨x and y have different signs 20⟩ && x%y != 0)
            return x%y + y;
        else
            return x%y;
    }
```

Arith_floor is just Arith_div, and Arith_ceiling is Arith_div plus one, unless y divides x evenly:

⟨*arith.c functions* 19⟩+≡
```
    int Arith_floor(int x, int y) {
```

```
        return Arith_div(x, y);
}

int Arith_ceiling(int x, int y) {
        return Arith_div(x, y) + (x%y != 0);
}
```

2.3 Abstract Data Types

An *abstract data type* is an interface that defines a data type and operations on values of that type. A *data type* is a set of values. In C, built-in
data types include characters, integers, floating-point numbers, and so
forth. Structures themselves define new types and can be used to form
higher-level types, such as lists, trees, lookup tables, and more.

A high-level type is *abstract* because the interface hides the details of
its representation and specifies the only legal operations on values of the
type. Ideally, these operations don't reveal representation details on
which clients might implicitly depend. The canonical example of an
abstract data type, or ADT, is the stack. Its interface defines the type and
its five operations:

⟨*initial version of stack.h*⟩≡
```
  #ifndef STACK_INCLUDED
  #define STACK_INCLUDED

  typedef struct Stack_T *Stack_T;

  extern Stack_T Stack_new  (void);
  extern int     Stack_empty(Stack_T stk);
  extern void    Stack_push (Stack_T stk, void *x);
  extern void   *Stack_pop  (Stack_T stk);
  extern void    Stack_free (Stack_T *stk);

  #endif
```

The typedef defines the type Stack_T, which is a pointer to a structure
with a tag of the *same* name. This definition is legal because structure,
union, and enumeration tags occupy a name space that is separate from
the space for variables, functions, and type names. This idiom is used
throughout this book. The typename — Stack_T — is the name of inter-

est in this interface; the tag name may be important only to the implementation. Using the same name avoids polluting the code with excess names that are rarely used.

The macro STACK_INCLUDED pollutes the name space, too, but the _INCLUDED suffix helps avoid collisions. Another common convention is to prefix an underscore to these kinds of names, such as _STACK or _STACK_INCLUDED. However, Standard C reserves leading underscores for implementors and for future extensions, so it seems prudent to avoid leading underscores.

This interface reveals that stacks are represented by pointers to structures, but it says nothing about what those structures look like. Stack_T is an *opaque pointer type*; clients can manipulate such pointers freely, but they can't *dereference* them; that is, they can't look at the innards of the structure pointed to by them. Only the implementation has that privilege.

Opaque pointers hide representation details and help catch errors. Only Stack_Ts can be passed to the functions above; attempts to pass other kinds of pointers, such as pointers to other structures, yield compilation errors. The lone exception is a void pointer, which can be passed to any kind of pointer.

The conditional compilation directives #ifdef and #endif, and the #define for STACK_INCLUDED, permit stack.h to be included more than once, which occurs when interfaces import other interfaces. Without this protection, second and subsequent inclusions would cause compilation errors about the redefinition of Stack_T in the typedef.

This convention seems the least offensive of the few available alternatives. Forbidding interfaces to include other interfaces avoids the need for repeated inclusion altogether, but forces interfaces to specify the other interfaces that must be imported some other way, such as in comments, and forces programmers to provide the includes. Putting the conditional compilation directives in a client instead of the interface avoids reading the interface unnecessarily, but litters the directives in many places instead of only in the interface. The convention illustrated above makes the compiler do the dirty work.

By convention, an interface *X* that specifies an ADT defines it as a type named *X*_T. The interfaces in this book carry this convention one step further by using a macro to abbreviate *X*_T to just T within the interface. With this convention, stack.h is

⟨*stack.h*⟩≡

```
#ifndef STACK_INCLUDED
#define STACK_INCLUDED

#define T Stack_T
typedef struct T *T;

extern T     Stack_new  (void);
extern int   Stack_empty(T stk);
extern void  Stack_push (T stk, void *x);
extern void *Stack_pop  (T stk);
extern void  Stack_free (T *stk);

#undef T
#endif
```

This interface is semantically equivalent to the previous one. The abbreviation is just syntactic sugar that makes interfaces a bit easier to read; T always refers to the primary type in the interface. Clients, however, must use Stack_T because the #undef directive at the end of stack.h removes the abbreviation.

This interface provides unbounded stacks of arbitrary pointers. Stack_new manufactures new stacks; it returns a value of type T that can be passed to the other four functions. Stack_push pushes a pointer onto a stack, Stack_pop removes and returns the pointer on the top of a stack, and Stack_empty returns one if the stack is empty and zero otherwise. Stack_free takes a *pointer* to a T, deallocates the stack pointed to by that pointer, and sets the variable of type T to the null pointer. This design helps avoid *dangling pointers* — pointers that point to deallocated memory. For example, if names is defined and initialized by

```
#include "stack.h"
Stack_T names = Stack_new();
```

the statement

```
Stack_free(&names);
```

deallocates the stack assigned to names and sets names to the null pointer.

When an ADT is represented by a opaque pointer, the exported type is a pointer type, which is why `Stack_T` is a typedef for a *pointer* to a `struct Stack_T`. Similar typedefs are used for most of the ADTs in this book. When an ADT reveals its representation and exports functions that accept and return structures *by value*, it defines the structure type as the exported type. This convention is illustrated by the `Text` interface in Chapter 16, which declares `Text_T` to be a typedef for `struct Text_T`. In any case, T always abbreviates the primary type in the interface.

2.4 Client Responsibilities

An interface is a contract between its implementations and its clients. An implementation must provide the facilities specified in the interface, and clients must use these facilities in accordance with the implicit and explicit rules described in the interface. The programming language provides some implicit rules governing the use of types, functions, and variables declared in the interface. For example, C's type-checking rules catch errors in the types and in the numbers of arguments to interface functions.

Those rules that are not specified by C usage or checked by the C compiler must be spelled out in the interface. Clients must adhere to them, and implementations must enforce them. Interfaces often specify *unchecked runtime errors*, *checked runtime errors*, and *exceptions*. Unchecked and checked runtime errors are not expected user errors, such as failing to open a file. Runtime errors are breaches of the contract between clients and implementations, and are program bugs from which there is no recovery. Exceptions are conditions that, while possible, rarely occur. Programs may be able to recover from exceptions. Running out of memory is an example. Exceptions are described in detail in Chapter 4.

An unchecked runtime error is a breach of contract that implementations do not guarantee to detect. If an unchecked runtime error occurs, execution might continue, but with unpredictable and perhaps unrepeatable results. Good interfaces avoid unchecked runtime errors when possible, but must specify those that can occur. `Arith`, for example, must specify that division by zero is an unchecked runtime error. `Arith` could check for division by zero, but leaves it as an *unchecked* runtime error so that its functions mimic the behavior of C's built-in division operators, whose behavior is undefined. Making division by zero a checked runtime error is a reasonable alternative.

A checked runtime error is a breach of contract that implementations *guarantee* to detect. These errors announce a client's failure to adhere to its part of the contract; it's the client's responsibility to avoid them. The Stack interface specifies three checked runtime errors:

1.   passing a null Stack_T to any routine in this interface;

2.   passing a null pointer to a Stack_T to Stack_free; or

3.   passing an empty stack to Stack_pop.

Interfaces may specify exceptions and the conditions under which they are raised. As explained in Chapter 4, clients can *handle* exceptions and take corrective action. An *unhandled* exception is treated as a checked runtime error. Interfaces usually list the exceptions they raise and those raised by any interface they import. For example, the Stack interface imports the Mem interface, which it uses to allocate space, so it specifies that Stack_new and Stack_push can raise Mem_Failed. Most of the interfaces in this book specify similar checked runtime errors and exceptions.

With these additions to the Stack interface, we can proceed to its implementation:

⟨*stack.c*⟩≡
```
#include <stddef.h>
#include "assert.h"
#include "mem.h"
#include "stack.h"

#define T Stack_T
```
⟨*types* 25⟩
⟨*functions* 26⟩

The #define directive reinstantiates T as an abbreviation for Stack_T. The implementation reveals the innards of a Stack_T, which is a structure with a field that points to a linked list of the pointers on the stack and a count of the number of these pointers.

⟨*types* 25⟩≡
```
struct T {
    int count;
```

```
        struct elem {
            void *x;
            struct elem *link;
        } *head;
    };
```

Stack_new allocates and initializes a new T:

⟨*functions* 26⟩≡

```
    T Stack_new(void) {
        T stk;

        NEW(stk);
        stk->count = 0;
        stk->head = NULL;
        return stk;
    }
```

NEW is an allocation macro from the Mem interface. NEW(p) allocates an instance of the structure pointed to by p, so its use in Stack_new allocates a new Stack_T structure.

Stack_empty returns one if the count field is 0 and zero otherwise:

⟨*functions* 26⟩+≡

```
    int Stack_empty(T stk) {
        assert(stk);
        return stk->count == 0;
    }
```

assert(stk) implements the checked runtime error that forbids a null T to be passed to any function in Stack. assert(*e*) is an assertion that *e* is nonzero for any expression *e*. It does nothing if *e* is nonzero, and halts program execution otherwise. assert is part of the standard library, but Chapter 4's Assert interface defines its own assert with similar semantics, and provides for graceful program termination. assert is used for all checked runtime errors.

Stack_push and Stack_pop add and remove elements from the head of the linked list emanating from stk->head:

⟨*functions* 26⟩+≡
```
  void Stack_push(T stk, void *x) {
      struct elem *t;

      assert(stk);
      NEW(t);
      t->x = x;
      t->link = stk->head;
      stk->head = t;
      stk->count++;
  }

void *Stack_pop(T stk) {
      void *x;
      struct elem *t;

      assert(stk);
      assert(stk->count > 0);
      t = stk->head;
      stk->head = t->link;
      stk->count--;
      x = t->x;
      FREE(t);
      return x;
  }
```

FREE is Mem's deallocation macro; it deallocates the space pointed to by its pointer argument, then sets the argument to the null pointer for the same reasons that Stack_free does — to help avoid dangling pointers. Stack_free also calls FREE:

⟨*functions* 26⟩+≡
```
  void Stack_free(T *stk) {
      struct elem *t, *u;

      assert(stk && *stk);
      for (t = (*stk)->head; t; t = u) {
          u = t->link;
          FREE(t);
      }
```

```
        FREE(*stk);
}
```

This implementation reveals one unchecked runtime error that *all* ADT interfaces in this book suffer and that thus goes unspecified. There's no way to guarantee that the Stack_Ts passed to Stack_push, Stack_pop, Stack_empty, and the Stack_T* passed to Stack_free are valid Stack_Ts returned by Stack_new. Exercise 2.3 explores partial solutions to this problem.

There are two more unchecked runtime errors whose effects can be more subtle. Many the ADTs in this book traffic in void pointers; that is, they store and return void pointers. It is an unchecked runtime error to store a *function* pointer — a pointer to a function — in any such ADT. A void pointer is a *generic* pointer; a variable of type void * can hold any pointer to an *object*, which includes the predefined types, structures, and pointers. Function pointers are different, however. While many C compilers permit assignments of function pointers to void pointers, there's no guarantee that a void pointer can hold a function pointer.

Any object pointer can travel through a void pointer without loss of information. For example, after executing

```
S *p, *q;
void *t;
...
t = p;
q = t;
```

p and q will be equal, for any nonfunction type *S*. Void pointers must not, however, be used to subvert the type system. For example, after executing

```
S *p;
D *q;
void *t;
...
t = p;
q = t;
```

there's no guarantee that q will be equal to p, or, depending on the alignment constraints for the types *S* and *D*, that q will be a valid pointer to an object of type *D*. In Standard C, void pointers and char pointers have the same size and representation. But other pointers might be smaller or have different representations. Thus, it is an unchecked runtime error to store a pointer to *S* in an ADT but retrieve it into a variable of type *D*, where *S* and *D* are different object types.

It is tempting to declare an opaque pointer argument const when an ADT function doesn't modify the referent. For example, `Stack_empty` might be written as follows.

```
int Stack_empty(const T stk) {
    assert(stk);
    return stk->count == 0;
}
```

This use of const is incorrect. The intent here is to declare `stk` to be a "pointer to a constant `struct T`," because `Stack_empty` doesn't modify `*stk`. But the declaration `const T stk` declares `stk` to be a "*constant pointer* to a `struct T`" — the typedef for T wraps the `struct T *` in a single type, and this entire type is the operand of const. `const T stk` is useless to both `Stack_empty` and its callers, because all scalars, including pointers, are passed by value in C. `Stack_empty` can't change the value of a caller's actual argument, with or without the const qualifier.

This problem could be avoided by using `struct T *` in place of T:

```
int Stack_empty(const struct T *stk) {
    assert(stk);
    return stk->count == 0;
}
```

This usage illustrates why const should not be used for pointers to ADTs: const reveals something about the implementation and thus constrains the possibilities. Using const isn't a problem for *this* implementation of Stack, but it precludes other, equally viable, alternatives. Suppose an implementation delayed deallocating the stack elements in hope of reusing them, but deallocated them when `Stack_empty` was called. That implementation of `Stack_empty` needs to modify `*stk`, but it can't because `stk` is declared const. None of the ADTs in this book use const.

2.5 Efficiency

Most of the implementations for the interfaces in this book use algorithms and data structures for which the average-case running times are no more than linear in N, the size of their inputs, and most can handle large inputs. Interfaces that cannot deal with large inputs or for which performance might be an important consideration specify *performance criteria*. Implementations must meet these criteria and clients can expect performance as good as but no better than these criteria specify.

All the interfaces in this book use simple but efficient algorithms. More complicated algorithms and data structures may have better performance when N is large, but it is usually small. Most implementations stick to basic data structures such as arrays, linked lists, hash tables, and trees, and combinations of these.

All but a few of the ADTs in this book use opaque pointers, so functions such as `Stack_empty` are used to access fields hidden by the implementations. The performance impact on real applications due to the overhead of calling functions instead of accessing the fields directly is almost always negligible. The improvements in reliability and in the opportunities for catching runtime errors are considerable and outweigh the slight costs in performance.

If objective measurements show that performance improvements are really necessary, they should be made without changing the interface, for example, by defining macros. When this approach is not possible, it's better to create a new interface that states its performance benefits rather than changing an existing interface, which invalidates all of its clients.

Further Reading

The importance of libraries of procedures and functions has been recognized since the 1950s. Parnas (1972) is a classic paper on how to divide programs into modules. This paper is over two decades old, yet it still addresses issues that face programmers today.

C programmers use interfaces daily: the C library is a collection of 15 interfaces. The standard I/O interface, `stdio.h`, defines an ADT, `FILE`, and operations on pointers to `FILE`s. Plauger (1992) gives a detailed description of these 15 interfaces and suitable implementations in much the same way that this book tours a set of interfaces and implementations.

Modula-3 is a relatively new language that has linguistic support for separating interfaces from implementations, and it originates the interface-based terminology used in this book (Nelson 1991). The notions of unchecked and checked runtime errors, and the T notation for ADTs, are taken from Modula-3. Harbison (1992) is a textbook introduction to Modula-3. Horning et al. (1993) describe the core interfaces in their Modula-3 system. Some of the interfaces in this book are adapted from those interfaces. The text by Roberts (1995) uses interface-based design as the organizing principle for teaching introductory computer science.

The importance of assertions is widely recognized, and some languages, such as Modula-3 and Eiffel (Meyer 1992), have assertion mechanisms built into the language. Maguire (1993) devotes an entire chapter to using assertions in C programs.

Programmers familiar with object-oriented programming may argue that most of the ADTs in this book can be rendered, perhaps better, as objects in object-oriented programming languages, such as C++ (Ellis and Stroustrup 1990) and Modula-3. Budd (1991) is a tutorial introduction to the object-oriented programming methodology and to some object-oriented programming languages, including C++. The principles of interface design illustrated in this book apply equally well to object-oriented languages. Rewriting the ADTs in this book in C++, for example, is a useful exercise for programmers making the switch from C to C++.

The C++ Standard Template Library — the STL — provides ADTs similar to those described in this book. STL makes good use of C++ templates to instantiate ADTs for specific types (Musser and Saini 1996). For example, STL provides a template for a vector datatype that can be used to instantiate vectors of ints, strings, and so on. STL also provides a suite of functions that manipulate template-generated types.

Exercises

2.1 A preprocessor macro and conditional compilation directives, such as `#if`, could have been used to specify how division truncates in `Arith_div` and `Arith_mod`. Explain why the explicit test $-13/5 == -2$ is a better way to implement this test.

2.2 The $-13/5 == -2$ test used in `Arith_div` and `Arith_mod` works as long as the compiler used to compile `arith.c` does arithmetic the same way as `Arith_div` and `Arith_mod` do when they are called. This condition might not hold, for example, if `arith.c` were compiled by a cross-compiler that runs on machine *X* and generates code for machine *Y*. Without using conditional compilation directives, fix `arith.c` so that such cross compilations produce code that is guaranteed to work.

2.3 Like all ADTs in this book, the `Stack` interface omits the specification "it is an *unchecked* runtime error to pass a foreign `Stack_T` to any routine in this interface." A *foreign* `Stack_T` is one that was not manufactured by `Stack_new`. Revise `stack.c` so that it can check for *some* occurrences of this error. One approach, for example, is to add a field to the `Stack_T` structure that holds a bit pattern unique to `Stack_Ts` returned by `Stack_new`.

2.4 It's often possible to detect certain invalid pointers. For example, a nonnull pointer is invalid if it specifies an address outside the client's address space, and pointers are often subject to alignment restrictions; for example, on some systems a pointer to a double must be a multiple of eight. Devise a system-specific macro `isBadPtr(p)` that is one when `p` is an invalid pointer so that occurrences of `assert(ptr)` can be replaced with assertions like `assert(!isBadPtr(ptr))`.

2.5 There are many viable interfaces for stacks. Design and implement some alternatives to the `Stack` interface. For example, one alternative is to specify a maximum size as an argument to `Stack_new`.

3

ATOMS

An *atom* is a pointer to a unique, immutable sequence of zero or more arbitrary bytes. Most atoms are pointers to null-terminated strings, but a pointer to any sequence of bytes can be an atom. There is only a single occurrence of any atom, which is why it's called an atom. Two atoms are identical if they point to the same location. Comparing two byte sequences for equality by simply comparing pointers is one of the advantages of atoms. Another advantage is that using atoms saves space because there's only one occurrence of each sequence.

Atoms are often used as keys in data structures that are indexed by sequences of arbitrary bytes instead of by integers. The tables and sets described in Chapters 8 and 9 are examples.

3.1 Interface

The Atom interface is simple:

⟨*atom.h*⟩≡
```
#ifndef ATOM_INCLUDED
#define ATOM_INCLUDED

extern        int   Atom_length(const char *str);
extern const char *Atom_new   (const char *str, int len);
extern const char *Atom_string(const char *str);
extern const char *Atom_int   (long n);

#endif
```

Atom_new accepts a pointer to a sequence of bytes and the number of bytes in that sequence. It adds a copy of the sequence to the table of atoms, if necessary, and returns the atom, which is a pointer to the copy of the sequence in the atom table. Atom_new never returns the null pointer. Once an atom is created, it exists for the duration of the client's execution. An atom is always terminated with a null character, which Atom_new adds when necessary.

Atom_string is similar to Atom_new; it caters to the common use of character strings as atoms. It accepts a null-terminated string, adds a copy of that string to the atom table, if necessary, and returns the atom. Atom_int returns the atom for the string representation of the long integer n — another common usage. Finally, Atom_length returns the length of its atom argument.

It is a checked runtime error to pass a null pointer to any function in this interface, to pass a negative len to Atom_new, or to pass a pointer that is not an atom to Atom_length. It is an *unchecked* runtime error to modify the bytes pointed to by an atom. Atom_length can take time to execute proportional to the number of atoms. Atom_new, Atom_string, and Atom_int can each raise the exception Mem_Failed.

3.2 Implementation

The implementation of Atom maintains the atom table. Atom_new, Atom_string, and Atom_int search the atom table and possibly add new elements to it, and Atom_length just searches it.

⟨*atom.c*⟩≡
  ⟨*includes* 34⟩
  ⟨*macros* 37⟩
  ⟨*data* 36⟩
  ⟨*functions* 35⟩

⟨*includes* 34⟩≡
  #include "atom.h"

Atom_string and Atom_int can be implemented without knowing the representation details of the atom table. Atom_string, for example, just calls Atom_new:

⟨*functions* 35⟩≡
```
const char *Atom_string(const char *str) {
    assert(str);
    return Atom_new(str, strlen(str));
}
```

⟨*includes* 34⟩+≡
```
#include <string.h>
#include "assert.h"
```

Atom_int first converts its argument to a string, then calls Atom_new:

⟨*functions* 35⟩+≡
```
const char *Atom_int(long n) {
    char str[43];
    char *s = str + sizeof str;
    unsigned long m;

    if (n == LONG_MIN)
        m = LONG_MAX + 1UL;
    else if (n < 0)
        m = -n;
    else
        m = n;
    do
        *--s = m%10 + '0';
    while ((m /= 10) > 0);
    if (n < 0)
        *--s = '-';
    return Atom_new(s, (str + sizeof str) - s);
}
```

⟨*includes* 34⟩+≡
```
#include <limits.h>
```

Atom_int must cope with the asymmetrical range of two's-complement numbers and with the ambiguities of C's division and modulus operators. Unsigned division and modulus *are* well defined, so Atom_int can avoid the ambiguities of the signed operators by using unsigned arithmetic.

The absolute value of the most negative signed long integer cannot be represented, because there is one more negative number than positive number in two's-complement systems. Atom_new thus starts by testing for this single anomaly before assigning the absolute value of its argument to the unsigned long integer m. The value of LONG_MAX resides in the standard header limits.h.

The loop forms the decimal string representation of m from right to left; it computes the rightmost digit, divides m by 10, and continues until m is zero. As each digit is computed, it's stored at --s, which marches s backward in str. If n is negative, a minus sign is stored at the beginning of the string.

When the conversion is done, s points to the desired string, and this string has &str[43] - s characters. str has 43 characters, which is enough to hold the decimal representation of any integer on any conceivable machine. Suppose, for example, that longs are 128 bits. The string representation of any 128-bit signed integer in octal — base 8 — fits in $128/3 + 1 = 43$ characters. The decimal representation can take no more digits than the octal representation, so 43 characters are enough.

The 43 in the definition of str is an example of a "magic number," and it's usually better style to define a symbolic name for such values to ensure that the same value is used everywhere. Here, however, the value appears only once, and sizeof is used whenever the value is used. Defining a symbolic name might make the code easier to read, but it will also make the code longer and clutter the name space. In this book, a symbolic name is defined only when the value appears more than once, or when it is part of an interface. The length of the hash table buckets below — 2,048 — is another example of this convention.

A hash table is the obvious data structure for the atom table. The hash table is an array of pointers to lists of entries, each of which holds one atom:

⟨*data* 36⟩≡

```
static struct atom {
    struct atom *link;
    int len;
    char *str;
} *buckets[2048];
```

The linked list emanating from buckets[i] holds those atoms that hash to i. An entry's link field points to the next entry on the list, the len field holds the length of the sequence, and the str fields points to the sequence itself. For example, on a little endian computer with 32-bit words and 8-bit characters, Atom_string("an atom") allocates the struct atom shown in Figure 3.1, where the underscore character (_) denotes a space. Each entry is just large enough to hold its sequence. Figure 3.2 shows the overall structure of the hash table.

Atom_new computes a hash number for the sequence given by str[0..len-1] (or the empty sequence, if len is zero), reduces this hash number modulo the number of elements in buckets, and searches the list pointed to by that element of buckets. If it finds that str[0..len-1] is already in the table, it simply returns the atom:

⟨*functions* 35⟩+≡
```
const char *Atom_new(const char *str, int len) {
    unsigned long h;
    int i;
    struct atom *p;

    assert(str);
    assert(len >= 0);
    ⟨h ← hash str[0..len-1] 39⟩
    h &= NELEMS(buckets)-1;
    for (p = buckets[h]; p; p = p->link)
        if (len == p->len) {
            for (i = 0; i < len && p->str[i] == str[i]; )
                i++;
            if (i == len)
                return p->str;
        }
    ⟨allocate a new entry 39⟩
    return p->str;
}
```

⟨*macros* 37⟩≡
```
#define NELEMS(x) ((sizeof (x))/(sizeof ((x)[0])))
```

The definition of NELEMS illustrates a common C idiom: The number of elements in an array is the size of the array divided by the size of each element. sizeof is a compile-time operator, so this computation applies only to arrays whose size is known at compile time. As this definition illustrates, macro parameters are italicized to highlight where they are used in the macro body.

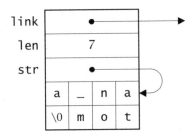

Figure 3.1 Little endian layout of a struct atom for "an atom"

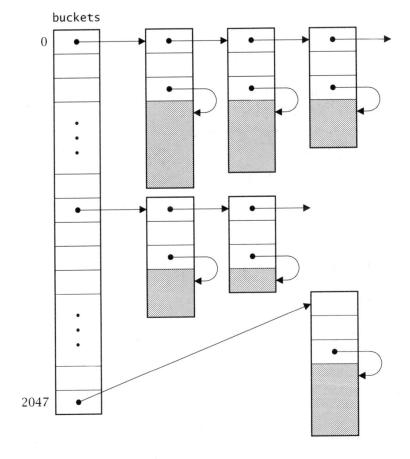

Figure 3.2 Hash table structure

If str[0..len-1] isn't in the table, Atom_new adds it by allocating a struct atom and enough additional space to hold the sequence, copying str[0..len-1] into the additional space and linking the new entry onto the beginning of the list emanating from buckets[h]. The entry could be appended to the end of the list, but adding it at the front of the list is simpler.

⟨*allocate a new entry* 39⟩≡
```
p = ALLOC(sizeof (*p) + len + 1);
p->len = len;
p->str = (char *)(p + 1);
if (len > 0)
    memcpy(p->str, str, len);
p->str[len] = '\0';
p->link = buckets[h];
buckets[h] = p;
```

⟨*includes* 34⟩+≡
```
#include "mem.h"
```

ALLOC is Mem's primary allocation function, and it mimics the standard library function malloc: its argument is the number of bytes needed. Atom_new cannot use Mem's NEW, which is illustrated in Stack_push, because the number of bytes depends on len; NEW applies only when the number of bytes is known at compile time. The call to ALLOC above allocates the space for both the atom structure and for the sequence, and the sequence is stored in the immediately succeeding bytes.

Hashing the sequence passed to Atom_new involves computing an unsigned number to represent the sequence. Ideally, these hash numbers should be distributed uniformly over the range zero to NELEMS(buckets)–1 for N sequences. If they are so distributed, each list in buckets will have N/NELEMS(buckets) elements, and the average time to search for a sequence will be $N/2 \cdot$ NELEMS(buckets). If N is less than, say, $2 \cdot$ NELEMS(buckets), the search time is essentially a constant.

Hashing is a well-studied subject, and there are many good hash functions. Atom_new uses a simple table-lookup algorithm:

⟨h ← *hash* str[0..len-1] 39⟩≡
```
for (h = 0, i = 0; i < len; i++)
    h = (h<<1) + scatter[(unsigned char)str[i]];
```

scatter is a 256-entry array that maps bytes to random numbers, which
were generated by calling the standard library function rand. Experience
shows that this simple approach helps to more uniformly distribute the
hash values. Casting str[i] to an unsigned character avoids C's ambigu-
ity about "plain" characters: they can be signed or unsigned. Without the
cast, values of str[i] that exceed 127 would yield negative indices on
machines that use signed characters.

⟨*data* 36⟩+≡

```
static unsigned long scatter[] = {
2078917053, 143302914, 1027100827, 1953210302, 755253631, 2002600785,
1405390230, 45248011, 1099951567, 433832350, 2018585307, 438263339,
813528929, 1703199216, 618906479, 573714703, 766270699, 275680090,
1510320440, 1583583926, 1723401032, 1965443329, 1098183682, 1636505764,
980071615, 1011597961, 643279273, 1315461275, 157584038, 1069844923,
471560540, 89017443, 1213147837, 1498661368, 2042227746, 1968401469,
1353778505, 1300134328, 2013649480, 306246424, 1733966678, 1884751139,
744509763, 400011959, 1440466707, 1363416242, 973726663, 59253759,
1639096332, 336563455, 1642837685, 1215013716, 154523136, 593537720,
704035832, 1134594751, 1605135681, 1347315106, 302572379, 1762719719,
269676381, 774132919, 1851737163, 1482824219, 125310639, 1746481261,
1303742040, 1479089144, 899131941, 1169907872, 1785335569, 485614972,
907175364, 382361684, 885626931, 200158423, 1745777927, 1859353594,
259412182, 1237390611, 48433401, 1902249868, 304920680, 202956538,
348303940, 1008956512, 1337551289, 1953439621, 208787970, 1640123668,
1568675693, 478464352, 266772940, 1272929208, 1961288571, 392083579,
871926821, 1117546963, 1871172724, 1771058762, 139971187, 1509024645,
109190086, 1047146551, 1891386329, 994817018, 1247304975, 1489680608,
706686964, 1506717157, 579587572, 755120366, 1261483377, 884508252,
958076904, 1609787317, 1893464764, 148144545, 1415743291, 2102252735,
1788268214, 836935336, 433233439, 2055041154, 2109864544, 247038362,
299641085, 834307717, 1364585325, 23330161, 457882831, 1504556512,
1532354806, 567072918, 404219416, 1276257488, 1561889936, 1651524391,
618454448, 121093252, 1010757900, 1198042020, 876213618, 124757630,
2082550272, 1834290522, 1734544947, 1828531389, 1982435068, 1002804590,
1783300476, 1623219634, 1839739926, 69050267, 1530777140, 1802120822,
316088629, 1830418225, 488944891, 1680673954, 1853748387, 946827723,
1037746818, 1238619545, 1513900641, 1441966234, 367393385, 928306929,
946006977, 985847834, 1049400181, 1956764878, 36406206, 1925613800,
2081522508, 2118956479, 1612420674, 1668583807, 1800004220, 1447372094,
523904750, 1435821048, 923108080, 216161028, 1504871315, 306401572,
```

```
2018281851, 1820959944, 2136819798, 359743094, 1354150250, 1843084537,
1306570817, 244413420, 934220434, 672987810, 1686379655, 1301613820,
1601294739, 484902984, 139978006, 503211273, 294184214, 176384212,
281341425, 228223074, 147857043, 1893762099, 1896806882, 1947861263,
1193650546, 273227984, 1236198663, 2116758626, 489389012, 593586330,
275676551, 360187215, 267062626, 265012701, 719930310, 1621212876,
2108097238, 2026501127, 1865626297, 894834024, 552005290, 1404522304,
48964196, 5816381, 1889425288, 188942202, 509027654, 36125855,
365326415, 790369079, 264348929, 513183458, 536647531, 13672163,
313561074, 1730298077, 286900147, 1549759737, 1699573055, 776289160,
2143346068, 1975249606, 1136476375, 262925046, 92778659, 1856406685,
1884137923, 53392249, 1735424165, 1602280572
};
```

Atom_length can't hash its argument because it doesn't know its length. But the argument must be an atom, so Atom_length can simply scream through the lists in buckets comparing pointers. If it finds the atom, it returns the atom's length:

⟨*functions* 35⟩+≡
```
    int Atom_length(const char *str) {
        struct atom *p;
        int i;

        assert(str);
        for (i = 0; i < NELEMS(buckets); i++)
            for (p = buckets[i]; p; p = p->link)
                if (p->str == str)
                    return p->len;
        assert(0);
        return 0;
    }
```

assert(0) implements the checked runtime error that Atom_length must be called only with an atom, not just a pointer to a string. assert(0) is also used to signal conditions that are not supposed to occur — so-called "can't-happen" conditions.

Further Reading

Atoms have long been used in LISP, which is the source of their name, and in string-manipulation languages, such as SNOBOL4, which implemented strings almost exactly as described in this chapter (Griswold 1972). The C compiler lcc (Fraser and Hanson 1995) has a module that is similar to Atom and is the predecessor to Atom's implementation. lcc stores the strings for *all* identifiers and constants that appear in the source program in a single table, and never deallocates them. Doing so never consumes too much storage because the number of distinct strings in C programs is remarkably small regardless of the size of the source programs.

Sedgewick (1990) and Knuth (1973b) describe hashing in detail and give guidelines for writing good hash functions. The hash function used in Atom (and in lcc) was suggested by Hans Boehm.

Exercises

3.1 Most texts recommend using a prime number for the size of buckets. Using a prime and a good hash function usually gives a better distribution of the lengths of the lists hanging off of buckets. Atom uses a power of two, which is sometimes explicitly cited as a bad choice. Write a program to generate or read, say, 10,000 typical strings and measure Atom_new's speed and the distribution of the lengths of the lists. Then change buckets so that it has 2,039 entries (the largest prime less than 2,048), change the statement

```
h &= NELEMS(buckets)-1;
```

to

```
h %= NELEMS(buckets);
```

and repeat the measurements. Does using a prime help? How much does your conclusion depend on your specific machine?

3.2 Scour the literature for better hash functions; likely sources are Knuth (1973b), similar texts on algorithms and data structures and the papers they cite,' and texts on compilers, such as Aho, Sethi, and Ullman (1986). Try these functions and measure their benefits.

3.3 Explain why `Atom_new` doesn't use the standard C library function `strncmp` to compare sequences.

3.4 Here's another way to declare the atom structure:

```
struct atom {
    struct atom *link;
    int len;
    char str[1];
};
```

A `struct atom` for a string of `len` bytes is allocated by `ALLOC(sizeof (*p) + len)`, which allocates space for the `link` and `len` fields, and a `str` field long enough to hold `len + 1` bytes. This approach avoids the time and space required for the extra indirection induced by declaring `str` to be a pointer. Unfortunately, this "trick" violates the C standard, because clients access the bytes beyond `str[0]`, and the effect of these accesses is undefined. Implement this approach and measure the cost of the indirection. Are the savings worth violating the standard?

3.5 `Atom_new` compares the `len` field of `struct atoms` with the length of the incoming sequence to avoid comparing sequences of different lengths. If the hash numbers (not the indices into `buckets`) for each atom were also stored in `struct atoms`, they could be compared, too. Implement this "improvement" and measure the benefits. Is it worthwhile?

3.6 `Atom_length` is slow. Revise `Atom`'s implementation so that `Atom_length`'s running time is approximately the same as that of `Atom_new`.

3.7 The `Atom` interface evolved to its present form because its functions were the ones that clients used most often. There are other functions and designs that might be useful, which this exercise and those that follow explore. Implement

```
extern void Atom_init(int hint);
```

where `hint` estimates the number of atoms the client expects to create. What checked runtime errors would you add to constrain when `Atom_init` could be called?

3.8 There are several functions to deallocate atoms that extensions to the `Atom` interface might provide. For example, the functions

```
extern void Atom_free (char *str);
extern void Atom_reset(void);
```

could deallocate the atom given by `str` and deallocate all atoms, respectively. Implement these functions. Don't forget to specify and implement appropriate checked runtime errors.

3.9 Some clients start execution by installing a bunch of strings as atoms for later use. Implement

```
extern void Atom_vload(const char *str, ...);
extern void Atom_aload(const char *strs[]);
```

`Atom_vload` installs the strings given in the variable length argument list up to a null pointer, and `Atom_aload` does the same for a null-terminated array of pointers to strings.

3.10 Copying the strings can be avoided if the client promises not to deallocate them, which is trivially true for string constants. Implement

```
extern Atom_add(const char *str, int len);
```

which works like `Atom_new` but doesn't make a copy of the sequence. If you provide `Atom_add` and `Atom_free` (and `Atom_reset` from Exercise 3.8), what checked runtime errors must be specified and implemented?

4
EXCEPTIONS AND ASSERTIONS

Three kinds of errors occur in programs: user errors, runtime errors, and exceptions. User errors are expected because they're likely to occur as the result of erroneous user input. Examples include naming nonexistent files, specifying badly formed numbers in spreadsheets, and presenting source programs with syntax errors to compilers. Programs must plan for and deal with such errors. Usually, functions that must cope with user errors return error codes — the errors are a normal part of the computation.

The checked runtime errors described in previous chapters are at the other end of the error spectrum. They are not user errors. They are never expected and always indicate program bugs. Thus, there is no way to recover from these kinds of errors; the application must be terminated gracefully. The implementations in this book use assertions to catch these kinds of errors. Handling assertions is described in Section 4.3. Assertions always cause the program to halt, perhaps in a way that depends on the machine or the application.

Exceptions occupy the middle ground between user errors and program bugs. An exception is an error that may be rare and perhaps unexpected, but from which recovery may be possible. Some exceptions mirror the cababilities of the machine; examples are arithmetic overflow and underflow and stack overflow. Other exceptions indicate conditions detected by the operating system, perhaps initiated by the user, such as hitting an "interrupt" key or getting a write error while writing a file. These kinds of exceptions are often delivered by signals in UNIX systems and processed by signal handlers. Exceptions may also occur when limited resources are exhausted, such as when an application runs out of memory, or a user specifies a spreadsheet that's too big.

Exceptions don't happen often, so functions in which they might occur don't usually return error codes; this would clutter the code for the rare cases and obscure the common cases. Applications *raise* exceptions, which are handled by recovery code, if recovery is possible. The scope of an exception is dynamic: when an exception is raised, it is handled by the handler that was most recently instantiated. Transferring control to a handler is like a nonlocal goto — the handler may have been instantiated in a routine far from the one in which the exception was raised.

Some languages have built-in facilities for instantiating handlers and raising exceptions. In C, the standard library functions `setjmp` and `longjmp` form the basis for building a structured exception facility. The short story is that `setjmp` instantiates a handler and `longjmp` raises an exception.

An example illustrates the long story. Suppose the function `allocate` calls `malloc` to allocate n bytes, and returns the pointer returned by `malloc`. If, however, `malloc` returns the null pointer, which indicates that the space requested cannot be allocated, `allocate` wants to raise the `Allocate_Failed` exception. The exception itself is declared as a `jmp_buf`, which is in the standard header `setjmp.h`:

```
#include <setjmp.h>

int Allocation_handled = 0;
jmp_buf Allocated_Failed;
```

`Allocation_handled` is zero unless a handler has been instantiated, and `allocate` checks `Allocation_handled` before raising the exception:

```
void *allocate(unsigned n) {
    void *new = malloc(n);

    if (new)
        return new;
    if (Allocation_handled)
        longjmp(Allocate_Failed, 1);
    assert(0);
}
```

`allocate` uses an assertion to implement a checked runtime error when allocation fails and no handler has been instantiated.

A handler is instantiated by calling `setjmp(Allocate_Failed)`, which returns an integer. The interesting feature of `setjmp` is that it can return *twice*. The call to `setjmp` returns zero. The call to `longjmp` in `allocate` causes the *second* return of the value given by `longjmp`'s second argument, which is one in the example above. Thus, a client handles an exception by testing the value returned by `setjmp`:

```
char *buf;
Allocation_handled = 1;
if (setjmp(Allocate_Failed)) {
    fprintf(stderr, "couldn't allocate the buffer\n");
    exit(EXIT_FAILURE);
}
buf = allocate(4096);
Allocation_handled = 0;
```

When `setjmp` returns zero, execution continues with the call to `allocate`. If the allocation fails, the `longjmp` in `allocate` causes `setjmp` to return *again*, this time with the value one, so execution continues with the calls to `fprintf` and `exit`.

This example doesn't cope with nested handlers, which would occur if the code above called, say, `makebuffer`, which itself instantiates a handler and called `allocate`. Nested handlers must be provided because clients can't know about the handlers instantiated by an implementation for its own purposes. Also, the `Allocation_handled` flag is awkward; failing to set it or clear it at the right times causes chaos. The `Except` interface, described in the next section, handles these omissions.

4.1 Interface

The `Except` interface wraps the `setjmp`/`longjmp` facility in a set of macros and functions that collaborate to provide a structured exception facility. It isn't perfect, but it avoids the errors outlined above, and the macros clearly identify where exceptions are used.

An exception is a global or static variable of type `Except_T`:

⟨*except.h*⟩≡
```
#ifndef EXCEPT_INCLUDED
```

```
#define EXCEPT_INCLUDED
#include <setjmp.h>

#define T Except_T
typedef struct T {
    char *reason;
} T;
```

⟨*exported types* 53⟩
⟨*exported variables* 53⟩
⟨*exported functions* 48⟩
⟨*exported macros* 48⟩

```
#undef T
#endif
```

Except_T structures have only one field, which can be initialized to a string that describes the exception. This string is printed when an unhandled exception occurs.

Exception handlers manipulate the *addresses* of exceptions. Exceptions must be global or static variables so that their addresses identify them uniquely. It is an unchecked runtime error to declare an exception as a local variable or as a parameter.

An exception e is raised by the RAISE macro or by the function Except_raise:

⟨*exported macros* 48⟩≡
```
    #define RAISE(e) Except_raise(&(e), __FILE__, __LINE__)
```

⟨*exported functions* 48⟩≡
```
    void Except_raise(const T *e, const char *file,int line);
```

It is a checked runtime error to pass a null e to Except_raise.

Handlers are instantiated by the TRY-EXCEPT and TRY-FINALLY statements, which are implemented with macros. These statements handle nested exceptions and manage exception-state data. The syntax of the TRY-EXCEPT statement is

```
TRY
      S
EXCEPT(e₁)
```

$$S_1$$
EXCEPT(e_2)
$$S_2$$
...
EXCEPT(e_n)
$$S_n$$
ELSE
$$S_0$$
END_TRY

The TRY-EXCEPT statement establishes handlers for exceptions named e_1, e_2, ..., e_n, and executes the statements S. If no exceptions are raised by S, the handlers are dismantled and execution continues at the statement after the END_TRY. If S raises an exception e where e is one of e_1–e_n, the execution of S is interrupted and control transfers immediately to the statements following the relevant EXCEPT clause. The handlers are dismantled, the handler statements S_i in the EXCEPT clause are executed, and execution continues after the END_TRY.

If S raises an exception that is not one of e_1–e_n, the handlers are dismantled, the statements following ELSE are executed, and execution continues after the END_TRY. The ELSE clause is optional.

If S raises an exception that is not handled by one of the S_i, the handlers are dismantled, and the exception is passed to the handlers established by the previously executed TRY-EXCEPT or TRY-FINALLY statement.

TRY-END_TRY is syntactically equivalent to a statement. TRY introduces a new scope, which ends at the next EXCEPT, ELSE, FINALLY, or END_TRY.

Rewriting the example at the end of the previous section illustrates the use of these macros. Allocate_Failed becomes an exception, which allocate raises if malloc returns the null pointer:

```
Except_T Allocate_Failed = { "Allocation failed" };

void *allocate(unsigned n) {
    void *new = malloc(n);

    if (new)
        return new;
    RAISE(Allocate_Failed);
```

```
        assert(0);
    }
```

If the client code wants to handle this exception, it calls allocate from within a TRY-EXCEPT statement:

```
extern Except_T Allocate_Failed;
char *buf;
TRY
    buf = allocate(4096);
EXCEPT(Allocate_Failed)
    fprintf(stderr, "couldn't allocate the buffer\n");
    exit(EXIT_FAILURE);
END_TRY;
```

TRY-EXCEPT statements are implemented with setjmp and longjmp, so Standard C's caveats about the use of these functions apply to TRY-EXCEPT statements. Specifically, if S changes an automatic variable, the change may not survive if an exception causes execution to continue in any of the handler statements S_i or after the closing END_TRY. For example, the fragment

```
static Except_T e;
int i = 0;
TRY
    i++;
    RAISE(e);
EXCEPT(e)
    ;
END_TRY;
printf("%d\n", i);
```

can print 0 or 1, depending on the implementation-dependent details of setjmp and longjmp. Automatic variables that are changed in S must be declared volatile; for example, changing the declaration for i to

```
volatile int i = 0;
```

causes the example above to print 1.

The syntax of the TRY-FINALLY statement is

```
TRY
     S
FINALLY
     S₁
END_TRY
```

If no exceptions are raised by S, S_1 is executed and execution continues at the statement after the END_TRY. If S raises an exception, the execution of S is interrupted and control transfers immediately to S_1. After S_1 is executed, the exception that caused its execution is *reraised* so that it can be handled by a previously instantiated handler. Note that S_1 is executed in both cases. Handlers can reraise exceptions explicitly with the RERAISE macro:

⟨*exported macros* 48⟩+≡
```
    #define RERAISE Except_raise(Except_frame.exception, \
        Except_frame.file, Except_frame.line)
```

The TRY-FINALLY statement is equivalent to

```
TRY
     S
ELSE
     S₁
     RERAISE;
END_TRY;
S₁
```

Note that S_1 is executed whether S raises an exception or not.

One purpose of the TRY-FINALLY statement is to give clients an opportunity to "clean up" when an exception occurs. For example,

```
FILE *fp = fopen(...);
char *buf;
TRY
     buf = allocate(4096);
     ...
FINALLY
     fclose(fp);
END_TRY;
```

closes the file opened on fp whether allocation fails or succeeds. If allocation does fail, another handler must deal with Allocate_Failed.

If S_1 in a TRY-FINALLY statement or any of the handlers in a TRY-EXCEPT statement raises an exception, it is handled by the previously instantiated handler.

The degenerate statement

```
TRY
     S
END_TRY
```

is equivalent to

```
TRY
     S
FINALLY
     ;
END_TRY
```

The final macro in the interface is

⟨*exported macros* 48⟩+≡
```
#define RETURN switch (⟨pop 56⟩,0) default: return
```

The RETURN macro is used instead of return statements inside TRY statements. It is a unchecked runtime error to execute the C return statement inside a TRY-EXCEPT or TRY-FINALLY statement. If any of the statements in a TRY-EXCEPT or TRY-FINALLY must do a return, they must do so with this macro instead of with the usual C return statement. This switch statement is used in this macro so that both RETURN and RETURN e expand into one syntactically correct C statement. The details of ⟨*pop* 56⟩ are described in the next section.

The macros in the Except interface are admittedly crude and somewhat brittle. Their unchecked runtime errors are particularly troublesome, and can be particularly difficult bugs to find. They suffice for most applications because exceptions should be used sparingly — only a handful in a large application. If exceptions proliferate, it's usually a sign of more serious design errors.

4.2 Implementation

The macros and functions in the Except interface collaborate to maintain a stack of structures that record the exception state and the instantiated handlers. The env field of this structure is a jmp_buf, which is used by setjmp and longjmp; this stack thus handles nested exceptions.

⟨*exported types* 53⟩≡
```
typedef struct Except_Frame Except_Frame;
struct Except_Frame {
    Except_Frame *prev;
    jmp_buf env;
    const char *file;
    int line;
    const T *exception;
};
```

⟨*exported variables* 53⟩≡
```
extern Except_Frame *Except_stack;
```

Except_stack points to the top exception frame on the exception stack, and the prev field of each frame points to its predecessor. As suggested by the definition of RERAISE in the previous section, raising an exception stores the address of the exception in the exception field, and stores the exception coordinates — the file and line number where the exception was raised — in the file and line fields.

The TRY clause pushes a new Except_Frame onto the exception stack and calls setjmp. Except_raise, which is called by RAISE and RERAISE, fills in the exception, file, and line fields in the top frame, pops the Except_Frame off the exception stack, and calls longjmp. EXCEPT clauses test the exception field of this frame to determine which handler applies. The FINALLY clause executes its clean-up code and reraises the exception stored in the popped frame.

If an exception occurs and control reaches an END_TRY clause without handling it, the exception is reraised.

The macros TRY, EXCEPT, ELSE, FINALLY, and END_TRY collaborate to translate a TRY-EXCEPT statement into a statement of the form

```
do {
    create and push an Except_Frame
```

```
      if (first return from setjmp) {
          S
      } else if (exception is e₁) {
          S₁
      ...
      } else if (exception is eₙ) {
          Sₙ
      } else {
          S₀
      }
      if (an exception occurred and wasn't handled)
          RERAISE;
  } while (0)
```

The do-while statement makes the TRY-EXCEPT syntactically equivalent to a C statement so that it can be used like any other C statement. It can, for example, be used as the consequent of an if statement. Figure 4.1 shows the code generated for the general TRY-EXCEPT statement The shaded boxes highlight the code resulting from the expansion of the TRY and END_TRY macros; boxes surround the code from the EXCEPT macro, and the double-lined box surrounds the ELSE code. Figure 4.2 shows the expansion of the TRY-FINALLY statement; the box surrounds the FINALLY code.

The space for an Except_Frame is allocated simply by declaring a local variable of that type inside the compound statement in the body of the do-while begun by TRY:

⟨*exported macros* 48⟩+≡
```
  #define TRY do { \
      volatile int Except_flag; \
      Except_Frame Except_frame; \
      ⟨push 56⟩ \
      Except_flag = setjmp(Except_frame.env); \
      if (Except_flag == Except_entered) {
```

There are four states within a TRY statement, as suggested by the following enumeration identifiers.

⟨*exported types* 53⟩+≡
```
  enum { Except_entered=0, Except_raised,
         Except_handled,  Except_finalized };
```

```
do {
    volatile int Except_flag;
    Except_Frame Except_frame;
    Except_frame.prev = Except_stack;
    Except_stack = &Except_frame;
    Except_flag = setjmp(Except_frame.env);
    if (Except_flag == Except_entered) {
```
S
```
        if (Except_flag == Except_entered)
            Except_stack = Except_stack->prev;
    } else if (Except_frame.exception == &(e_1)) {
        Except_flag = Except_handled;
```
S_1
```
        if (Except_flag == Except_entered)
            Except_stack = Except_stack->prev;
    } else if (Except_frame.exception == &(e_2)) {
        Except_flag = Except_handled;
```
S_2
```
        if (Except_flag == Except_entered)
            Except_stack = Except_stack->prev;
    } ...
    } else if (Except_frame.exception == &(e_n)) {
        Except_flag = Except_handled;
```
S_n
```
        if (Except_flag == Except_entered)
            Except_stack = Except_stack->prev;
    } else {
        Except_flag = Except_handled;
```
S_0
```
        if (Except_flag == Except_entered)
            Except_stack = Except_stack->prev;
    }
    if (Except_flag == Except_raised)
        Except_raise(Except_frame.exception,
            Except_frame.file, Except_frame.line);
} while (0)
```

Figure 4.1 Expansion of the TRY-EXCEPT statement

The first return from `setjmp` sets `Except_flag` to `Except_entered`, which indicates that a TRY statement has been entered and an exception frame has been pushed onto the exception stack. `Except_entered` must be zero, because the initial call to `setjmp` returns zero; subsequent returns from `setjmp` set it to `Except_raised`, which indicates that an

```
do {
    volatile int Except_flag;
    Except_Frame Except_frame;
    Except_frame.prev = Except_stack;
    Except_stack = &Except_frame;
    Except_flag = setjmp(Except_frame.env);
    if (Except_flag == Except_entered) {
        S
        if (Except_flag == Except_entered)
            Except_stack = Except_stack->prev;
    } {
        if (Except_flag == Except_entered)
            Except_flag = Except_finalized;
        S₁
        if (Except_flag == Except_entered)
            Except_stack = Except_stack->prev;
    }
    if (Except_flag == Except_raised)
        Except_raise(Except_frame.exception,
            Except_frame.file, Except_frame.line);
} while (0)
```

S

S_1

Figure 4.2 Expansion of the TRY-FINALLY statement

exception occurred. Handlers set `Except_flag` to `Except_handled` to indicate that they've handled the exception.

The `Except_Frame` is pushed onto the exception stack by adding it to the head of the linked list of `Except_Frame` structures pointed to by `Except_stack`, and the top frame is popped by removing it from that list:

⟨*push* 56⟩≡
```
    Except_frame.prev = Except_stack; \
    Except_stack = &Except_frame;
```

⟨*pop* 56⟩≡
```
    Except_stack = Except_stack->prev
```

The EXCEPT clauses become the else-if statements shown in Figure 4.1.

⟨*exported macros* 48⟩+≡
```
    #define EXCEPT(e) \
```

```
        ⟨pop if this chunk follows S 57⟩ \
    } else if (Except_frame.exception == &(e)) { \
        Except_flag = Except_handled;
```

⟨*pop if this chunk follows S* 57⟩≡
```
   if (Except_flag == Except_entered) ⟨pop 56⟩;
```

Using macros for exceptions leads to some contorted code, as the chunk ⟨*pop if this chunk follows S* 57⟩ illustrates. This chunk, which appears *before* the else-if in the definition of EXCEPT above, pops the exception stack only in the *first* EXCEPT clause. If no exception occurs while executing *S*, Except_flag remains Except_entered, so when control reaches the if statement, the exception stack is popped. The second and subsequent EXCEPT clauses follow handlers in which Except_flag has been changed to Except_handled. For these, the exception stack has already been popped, and the if statement in ⟨*pop if this chunk follows S* 57⟩ protects against popping it again.

The ELSE clause is like an EXCEPT clause, but the else-if is just an else:

⟨*exported macros* 48⟩+≡
```
   #define ELSE \
           ⟨pop if this chunk follows S 57⟩ \
       } else { \
           Except_flag = Except_handled;
```

Similarly, the FINALLY clause is like an ELSE clause without the else: Control falls into the clean-up code.

⟨*exported macros* 48⟩+≡
```
   #define FINALLY \
           ⟨pop if this chunk follows S 57⟩ \
       } { \
           if (Except_flag == Except_entered) \
               Except_flag = Except_finalized;
```

Except_flag is changed from Except_entered to Except_finalized here to indicate that an exception did *not* occur but that a FINALLY clause *did* appear. If an exception occurred, Except_flag is left at Except_raised so that it can be reraised after the clean-up code has been executed. The exception is reraised by testing whether Except_flag is equal to Except_raised in the expansion for END_TRY.

If an exception did not occur, `Except_flag` will be `Except_entered` or `Except_finalized`:

⟨*exported macros* 48⟩+≡
```
#define END_TRY \
        ⟨pop if this chunk follows S 57⟩ \
        } if (Except_flag == Except_raised) RERAISE; \
} while (0)
```

The implementation of `Except_raise` in `except.c` is the last piece of the puzzle:

⟨*except.c*⟩≡
```
#include <stdlib.h>
#include <stdio.h>
#include "assert.h"
#include "except.h"
#define T Except_T

Except_Frame *Except_stack = NULL;

void Except_raise(const T *e, const char *file,
    int line) {
    Except_Frame *p = Except_stack;

    assert(e);
    if (p == NULL) {
        ⟨announce an uncaught exception 59⟩
    }
    p->exception = e;
    p->file = file;
    p->line = line;
    ⟨pop 56⟩;
    longjmp(p->env, Except_raised);
}
```

If there is an `Except_Frame` at the top of the exception stack, `Except_raise` fills in the `exception`, `file`, and `line` fields, pops the exception stack, and calls `longjmp`. The corresponding call to `setjmp` will return `Except_raised`; `Except_raised` will be assigned to `Except_flag` in the TRY-EXCEPT or TRY-FINALLY statement, and the appropriate handler will be executed. Except_raise pops the exception stack so that if an exception occurs in one of the handlers, it will be handled by the TRY-EXCEPT statement whose exception frame is now exposed at the top of the exception stack.

If the exception stack is empty, there's no handler, so Except_raise has little choice but to announce the unhandled exception and halt:

⟨*announce an uncaught exception* 59⟩≡
```
fprintf(stderr, "Uncaught exception");
if (e->reason)
    fprintf(stderr, " %s", e->reason);
else
    fprintf(stderr, " at 0x%p", e);
if (file && line > 0)
    fprintf(stderr, " raised at %s:%d\n", file, line);
fprintf(stderr, "aborting...\n");
fflush(stderr);
abort();
```

abort is the standard C library function that aborts execution, sometimes with machine-dependent side effects. It might, for example, start a debugger or simply write a dump of memory.

4.3 Assertions

The standard requires that header assert.h define assert(*e*) as a macro that provides diagnostic information. assert(*e*) evaluates *e* and, if *e* is zero, writes diagnostic information on the standard error and aborts execution by calling the standard library function abort. The diagnostic information includes the assertion that failed (the text of *e*) and the coordinates (the file and line number) at which the assert(*e*) appears. The format of this information is implementation-defined. assert(0) is a good way to signal conditions that "can't happen." Alternatively, assertions like

```
assert(!"ptr==NULL -- can't happen")
```

display more meaningful diagnostics.

assert.h also uses, but does not define, the macro NDEBUG. If NDEBUG is defined, then assert(*e*) must be equivalent to the vacuous expres-

sion ((void)0). Thus, programmers can turn off assertions by defining
NDEBUG and recompiling. Since *e* might not be executed, it's important
that it never be an essential computation that has side effects, such as an
assignment.

assert(*e*) is an expression, so most versions of assert.h are logically equivalent to

```
#undef assert
#ifdef NDEBUG
#define assert(e) ((void)0)
#else
extern void assert(int e);
#define assert(e) ((void)((e)|| \
    (fprintf(stderr, "%s:%d: Assertion failed: %s\n", \
    __FILE__, (int)__LINE__, #e), abort(), 0)))
#endif
```

(A "real" version of assert.h differs from this one because it's not
allowed to include stdio.h in order to use fprintf and stderr.) An
expression like $e_1 || e_2$ usually appears in conditional contexts, such as
if statements, but it can also appear alone as a statement. When it does,
the effect is equivalent to the statement

```
if (e₁) e₂;
```

The definition of assert uses $e_1 || e_2$ because assert(*e*) must expand
to an expression, not a statement. e_2 is a comma expression whose
result is a value, which is required by the || operator, and the entire
expression is cast to void because the standard stipulates that
assert(*e*) returns no value. In a Standard C preprocessor, the locution
#*e* generates a string literal whose contents are the characters in the text
for the expression *e*.

The Assert interface defines assert(*e*) as specified by the standard,
except that an assertion failure raises the exception Assert_Failed
instead of aborting execution, and does not provide the text of the assertion *e*:

⟨*assert.h*⟩≡
```
#undef assert
#ifdef NDEBUG
#define assert(e) ((void)0)
```

```
#else
#include "except.h"
extern void assert(int e);
#define assert(e) ((void)((e)||(RAISE(Assert_Failed),0)))
#endif
```

⟨*exported variables* 53⟩≡
```
extern const Except_T Assert_Failed;
```

Assert mimics the standard's definitions so that the two `assert.h` headers can be used interchangeably, which is why `Assert_Failed` appears in `except.h`. The implementation of this interface is trivial:

⟨*assert.c*⟩≡
```
#include "assert.h"

const Except_T Assert_Failed = { "Assertion failed" };

void (assert)(int e) {
    assert(e);
}
```

The parentheses around the name `assert` in the function definition suppress expansion of the macro `assert` and thus define the function, as required by the interface.

If clients don't handle `Assert_Failed`, then an assertion failure causes the program to abort with a message like

```
Uncaught exception Assertion failed raised at stmt.c:201
aborting...
```

which is functionally equivalent to the diagnostics issued by machine-specific versions of `assert.h`.

Packaging assertions so that they raise exceptions when they fail helps solve the dilemma about what to do with assertions in production programs. Some programmers advise against leaving assertions in production programs, and this advice is supported by the standard's use of `NDEBUG` in `assert.h`. The two reasons most often cited for omitting assertions are efficiency and the possibility of cryptic diagnostics.

Assertions do take time, so removing them can only make programs faster. The difference in execution time with and without assertions can be measured, however, and that difference is usually tiny. Removing assertions for efficiency reasons is like making any other change to improve execution time: The change should be made only when objective measurements support it.

When measurements do show that an assertion is too costly, it's sometimes possible to move the assertion to reduce its cost without losing its benefit. For example, suppose h contains an assertion that costs too much, that both f and g call h, and that measurements show most of the time is due to the call from g, which calls h from within a loop. Careful analysis may reveal that the assertion in h can be moved to both f and g, and placed before the loop in g.

The more serious problem with assertions is that they can cause diagnostics, such as the assertion-failure diagnostic above, that will mystify users. But omitting assertions replaces these diagnostics with a greater evil. When an assertion fails, the program is wrong. If it continues, it does so with unpredictable results and will most likely crash. Messages like

```
General protection fault at 3F60:40EA
```

or

```
Segmentation fault -- core dumped
```

are no better than the assertion-failed diagnostic shown above. Worse, a program that continues after an assertion failure would have stopped it may corrupt user data; for example, an editor may destroy a user's files. This behavior is inexcusable.

The problem with cryptic assertion-failure diagnostics can be handled with a TRY-EXCEPT statement at the top level of the production version of the program that catches *all* uncaught exceptions and issues a more helpful diagnostic. For example:

```
#include <stdlib.h>
#include <stdio.h>
#include "except.h"

int main(int argc, char *argv[]) {
    TRY
        edit(argc, argv);
    ELSE
```

```
        fprintf(stderr,
    "An internal error has occurred from which there is "
    "no recovery.\nPlease report this error to "
    "Technical Support at 800-777-1234.\nNote the "
    "following message, which will help our support "
    "staff\nfind the cause of this error.\n\n")
        RERAISE;
    END_TRY;
    return EXIT_SUCCESS;
}
```

When an uncaught exception occurs, this handler precedes the cryptic diagnostic with instructions for reporting the bug. For an assertion failure, it prints

```
An internal error has occurred from which there is no recovery.
Please report this error to Technical Support at 800-777-1234.
Note the following message, which will help our support staff
find the cause of this error.

Uncaught exception Assertion failed raised at stmt.c:201
aborting...
```

Further Reading

Several languages have built-in exception mechanisms; examples include ADA, Modula-3 (Nelson 1991), Eiffel (Meyer 1992), and C++ (Ellis and Stroustrup 1990). Except's TRY-EXCEPT statement is modeled after Modula-3's TRY-EXCEPT statement.

Several exception mechanisms have been proposed for C; they all provide facilities similar to the TRY-EXCEPT statement, sometimes with variations in syntax and semantics. Roberts (1989) describes an interface for an exception facility that is equivalent to the one provided by Except. His implementation is similar, but it's more efficient when an exception is raised. Except_raise calls longjmp to transfer to a handler. If that handler doesn't handle the exception, Except_raise is called again, and so is longjmp. If the handler for the exception is N exception frames down the exception stack, Except_raise and longjmp are called N times. Roberts's implementation makes one call to the appropriate handler or to the first FINALLY clause. To do this, it must place an upper bound on the number of exception handlers in a TRY-EXCEPT statement. Some C compilers, like Microsoft's, provide structured exception facilities as language extensions.

Some languages have built-in assertion mechanisms; Eiffel is an example. Most languages use facilities similar to C's `assert` macro or other compiler directives to specify assertions. For example, Digital's Modula-3 compiler recognizes comments of the form <*ASSERT *expression*> as compiler pragmas that specify assertions. Maguire (1993) devotes an entire chapter to using assertions in C programs.

Exercises

4.1 What's the effect of a statement that has both EXCEPT and FINALLY clauses? These are statements of the form

```
TRY
     S
EXCEPT(e₁)
     S₁
...
EXCEPT(eₙ)
     Sₙ
FINALLY
     S₀
END_TRY
```

4.2 Change the `Except` interface and implementation so that `Except_raise` makes only one call to `longjmp` to reach the appropriate handler or FINALLY clause, as described above and implemented by Roberts (1989).

4.3 UNIX systems use *signals* to announce some exceptional conditions, such as floating overflow and when a user strikes an interrupt key. Study the UNIX signal repertoire and design and implement an interface for a signal handler that turns signals into exceptions.

4.4 Some systems print a *stack trace* when a program aborts. This shows the state of the procedure-call stack when the program aborted, and it may include procedure names and arguments.

Change `Except_raise` to print a stack trace when it announces an uncaught exception. Depending on the calling conventions on your computer, you may be able to print the procedure names and the line numbers of the calls. For example, the trace might look like this:

```
Uncaught exception Assertion failed
raised in whilestmt() at stmt.c:201
called from statement() at stmt.c:63
called from compound() at decl.c:122
called from funcdefn() at decl.c:890
called from decl() at decl.c:95
called from program() at decl.c:788
called from main() at main.c:34
aborting...
```

4.5 On some systems, a program can invoke a debugger on itself when it has detected an error. This facility is particularly useful during development, when assertion failures may be common. If your system supports this facility, change `Except_raise` to start the debugger instead of calling `abort` after it announces an uncaught exception. Try to make your implementation work in production programs; that is, make it figure out at runtime whether or not to invoke the debugger.

4.6 If you have access to a C compiler, like `lcc` (Fraser and Hanson 1995), modify it to support exceptions, TRY statements, and RAISE and RERAISE expressions with the syntax and semantics described in this chapter, without using `setjmp` and `longjmp`. You will need to implement a mechanism similar to `setjmp` and `longjmp`, but it can be specialized for exception handling. For example, it's usually possible to instantiate the handlers with only a few instructions. Warning: This exercise is a large project.

5

MEMORY MANAGEMENT

All nontrivial C programs allocate memory at runtime. The standard C library provides four memory-management routines: malloc, calloc, realloc, and free. The Mem interface repackages these routines as a set of macros and routines that are less prone to error and that provide a few additional capabilities.

Unfortunately, memory-management bugs are common in C programs, and they are often difficult to diagnose and fix. For example, the fragment

```
p = malloc(nbytes);
...
free(p);
```

calls malloc to allocate a block of nbytes of memory, assigns the address of the first byte of that block to p, uses p and the block it points to, and frees the block. After the call to free, p holds a dangling pointer — a pointer that refers to memory that logically does not exist. Subsequently dereferencing p is an error, although if the block hasn't been reallocated for another purpose, the error might go undetected. This behavior is what makes these kinds of access errors hard to diagnose: when the error is detected, it may manifest itself at a place and time far away from the origin of the error.

The fragment

```
p = malloc(nbytes);
...
free(p);
```

```
    ...
    free(p);
```

illustrates another error: deallocating free memory. This error usually corrupts the data structures used by the memory-management functions, but it may go undetected until a subsequent call to one of those functions.

Another error is deallocating memory that wasn't allocated by `malloc`, `calloc`, or `realloc`. For example, the intent of

```
char buf[20], *p;
if (n >= sizeof buf)
    p = malloc(n);
else
    p = buf;
...
free(p);
```

is to avoid allocation when n is less than the size of `buf`; but the code erroneously calls `free` even when p points to `buf`. Again, this error usually corrupts the memory-management data structures and isn't detected until later.

Finally, the function

```
void itoa(int n, char *buf, int size) {
    char *p = malloc(43);

    sprintf(p, "%d", n);
    if (strlen(p) >= size - 1) {
        while (--size > 0)
            *buf++ = '*';
        *buf = '\0';
    } else
        strcpy(buf, p);
}
```

fills `buf[0..size-1]` with the decimal representation of the integer n or with asterisks if that representation takes more than `size-1` characters. This code looks robust, but it contains at least two errors. First, `malloc` returns the null pointer if the allocation fails, and the code fails to test for this condition. Second, the code creates a *memory leak*: it doesn't deallocate the memory it allocates. The program will slowly consume memory each time itoa is called. If itoa is called often, the program will eventually run out memory and fail. Also, itoa works correctly when size is less than two, but it does so by setting buf[0] to the null character. Perhaps a better design would be to insist that size exceed two and to enforce that constraint with a checked runtime error.

The macros and routines in the Mem interface offer some protection from these kinds of memory-management errors. They don't eliminate all such errors, however. For example, they can't guard against dereferencing corrupt pointers or using pointers to local variables that have gone out of scope. C novices often commit the latter error; this apparently simpler version of itoa is an example:

```
char *itoa(int n) {
    char buf[43];

    sprintf(buf, "%d", n);
    return buf;
}
```

itoa returns the address of its local array buf, but once itoa returns, buf no longer exists.

5.1 Interface

The Mem interface exports exceptions, routines, and macros:

⟨*mem.h*⟩≡
```
#ifndef MEM_INCLUDED
#define MEM_INCLUDED
#include "except.h"

⟨exported exceptions 70⟩
⟨exported functions 70⟩
⟨exported macros 70⟩

#endif
```

Mem's allocation functions are similar to those in the standard C library, but they don't accept zero sizes and never return null pointers:

⟨*exported exceptions* 70⟩≡
```
extern const Except_T Mem_Failed;
```

⟨*exported functions* 70⟩≡
```
extern void *Mem_alloc (long nbytes,
    const char *file, int line);
extern void *Mem_calloc(long count, long nbytes,
    const char *file, int line);
```

Mem_alloc allocates a block of at least nbytes and returns a pointer to the first byte. The block is aligned on an addressing boundary that is suitable for the data with the strictest alignment requirement. The contents of the block are uninitialized. It is a checked runtime error for nbytes to be nonpositive.

Mem_calloc allocates a block large enough to hold an array of count elements each of size nbytes, and returns a pointer to the first element. The block is aligned as for Mem_alloc, and is initialized to zeros. The null pointer and 0.0 are not necessarily represented by zeros, so Mem_calloc may not initialize them correctly. It is a checked runtime error for count or nbytes to be nonpositive.

The last two arguments to Mem_alloc and Mem_calloc are the file name and line number of the location of the call. These are supplied by the following macros, which are the usual way to invoke these functions.

⟨*exported macros* 70⟩≡
```
#define ALLOC(nbytes) \
    Mem_alloc((nbytes), __FILE__, __LINE__)
#define CALLOC(count, nbytes) \
    Mem_calloc((count), (nbytes), __FILE__, __LINE__)
```

If Mem_alloc or Mem_calloc cannot allocate the memory requested, they raise Mem_Failed and pass file and line to Except_raise so that the exception reports the location of the call. If file is the null pointer, Mem_alloc and Mem_calloc supply the locations within their implementations that raise Mem_Failed.

Many allocations have the form

```
struct T *p;
p = Mem_alloc(sizeof (struct T));
```

which allocates a block for an instance of the structure T and returns a pointer to that block. A better version of this idiom is

```
p = Mem_alloc(sizeof *p);
```

Using `sizeof *p` instead of `sizeof (struct T)` works for *any* pointer type, except void pointers, and `sizeof *p` is independent of the pointer's referent type. If the type of `p` is changed, this allocation remains correct, but the one with `sizeof (struct T)` must be changed to reflect the change in p's type. That is,

```
p = Mem_alloc(sizeof (struct T));
```

is correct only if `p` is really a pointer to a `struct T`. If `p` is changed to a pointer to another structure and the call isn't updated, the call may allocate too much memory, which wastes space, or too little memory, which is disastrous, because the client may scribble on unallocated storage.

This allocation idiom is so common that `Mem` provides macros that encapsulate both the allocation and the assignment:

⟨*exported macros* 70⟩+≡
```
#define  NEW(p) ((p) = ALLOC((long)sizeof *(p)))
#define NEW0(p) ((p) = CALLOC(1, (long)sizeof *(p)))
```

`NEW(p)` allocates an uninitialized block to hold `*p` and sets `p` to the address of that block. `NEW0(p)` does the same, but also clears the block. `NEW` is provided on the assumption that most clients initialize a block immediately after allocating it. The argument to the compile-time operator `sizeof` is used only for its type; it is not evaluated at runtime. So `NEW` and `NEW0` evaluate `p` exactly once, and it's safe to use an expression that has side effects as an actual argument to either macro, such as `NEW(a[i++])`, for example.

`malloc` and `calloc` take arguments of type `size_t`; `sizeof` yields a constant of type `size_t`. The type `size_t` is an unsigned integral type capable of representing the size of the largest object that can be declared, and it's used in the standard library wherever object sizes are specified. In practice, `size_t` is either unsigned int or unsigned long. `Mem_alloc` and `Mem_calloc` take integer arguments to avoid errors when negative numbers are passed to unsigned arguments. For example,

```
int n = -1;
...
p = malloc(n);
```

is clearly an error, but many implementations of malloc won't catch the error because when –1 is converted to a size_t, it usually winds up as a very large unsigned value.

Memory is deallocated by Mem_free:

⟨*exported functions* 70⟩+≡
```
extern void Mem_free(void *ptr,
    const char *file, int line);
```

⟨*exported macros* 70⟩+≡
```
#define FREE(ptr) ((void)(Mem_free((ptr), \
    __FILE__, __LINE__), (ptr) = 0))
```

Mem_free takes a pointer to the block to be deallocated. If ptr is non-null, Mem_free deallocates that block; if ptr is null, Mem_free has no effect. The FREE macro also takes a pointer to a block, calls Mem_free to deallocate the block, and sets ptr to the null pointer, which, as mentioned in Section 2.4, helps avoid dangling pointers. Since ptr is null after its referent has been deallocated by FREE, a subsequent dereference will usually cause the program to crash with some kind of addressing error. This definite error is better than the unpredictable behavior that dereferencing a dangling pointer can cause. Note that FREE evaluates ptr more than once.

As detailed in the sections that follow, there are two implementations that export the Mem interface. The *checking* implementation implements checked runtime errors to help catch access errors like those described in the previous section. In that implementation, it is a checked runtime error to pass Mem_free a nonnull ptr that was not returned by a previous call to Mem_alloc, Mem_calloc, or Mem_resize, or a ptr that has already been passed to Mem_free or Mem_resize. The values of Mem_free's file and line arguments are used to report these checked runtime errors.

In the *production* implementation, however, these access errors are unchecked runtime errors.

The function

⟨*exported functions* 70⟩+≡
```
extern void *Mem_resize(void *ptr, long nbytes,
    const char *file, int line);
```

⟨*exported macros* 70⟩+≡
```
#define RESIZE(ptr, nbytes) ((ptr) = Mem_resize((ptr), \
    (nbytes), __FILE__, __LINE__))
```

changes the size of the block allocated by a previous call to `Mem_alloc`, `Mem_calloc`, or `Mem_resize`. Like `Mem_free`, the first argument to `Mem_resize` is the pointer that holds the address of the block whose size is to be changed. `Mem_resize` expands or contracts the block so that it holds at least `nbytes` of memory, suitably aligned, and returns a pointer to the resized block. `Mem_resize` may move the block in order to change its size, so `Mem_resize` is logically equivalent to allocating a new block, copying some or all of the data from `ptr` to the new block, and deallocating `ptr`. If `Mem_resize` cannot allocate the new block, it raises `Mem_Failed`, with `file` and `line` as the exception coordinates. The macro `RESIZE` changes `ptr` to point at the new block — a common use of `Mem_resize`. Note that `RESIZE` evaluates `ptr` more than once.

If `nbytes` exceeds the size of the block pointed to by `ptr`, the excess bytes are uninitialized. Otherwise, `nbytes` beginning at `ptr` are copied to the new block.

It is a checked runtime error to pass `Mem_resize` a null `ptr`, and for `nbytes` to be nonpositive. In the checking implementation, it is a checked runtime error to pass `Mem_resize` a `ptr` that was not returned by a previous call to `Mem_alloc`, `Mem_calloc`, or `Mem_resize`, and to pass it one that has already been passed to `Mem_free` or `Mem_resize`. In the production implementation, these access errors are unchecked runtime errors.

The functions in the `Mem` interface can be used in addition to the standard C library functions `malloc`, `calloc`, `realloc`, and `free`. That is, a program can use both sets of allocation functions. The access errors reported as checked runtime errors by the checking implementation apply only to memory managed by that implementation. Only one implementation of the `Mem` interface may be used in any given program.

5.2 Production Implementation

In the production implementation, the routines encapsulate calls to the memory-management functions in the standard library in the safer package specified by the `Mem` interface:

⟨*mem.c*⟩≡
```
#include <stdlib.h>
#include <stddef.h>
#include "assert.h"
#include "except.h"
#include "mem.h"
```

⟨*data* 74⟩
⟨*functions* 74⟩

For example, Mem_alloc calls malloc and raises Mem_Failed when malloc returns the null pointer:

⟨*functions* 74⟩≡
```
void *Mem_alloc(long nbytes, const char *file, int line){
    void *ptr;

    assert(nbytes > 0);
    ptr = malloc(nbytes);
    if (ptr == NULL)
        ⟨raise Mem_Failed 74⟩
    return ptr;
}
```

⟨*raise* Mem_Failed 74⟩≡
```
{
    if (file == NULL)
        RAISE(Mem_Failed);
    else
        Except_raise(&Mem_Failed, file, line);
}
```

⟨*data* 74⟩≡
```
const Except_T Mem_Failed = { "Allocation Failed" };
```

If a client doesn't handle Mem_Failed, Except_raise will give the
caller's coordinates, which are passed to Mem_alloc when it reports the
unhandled exception. For example:

```
Uncaught exception Allocation Failed raised @parse.c:431
aborting...
```

Similarly, Mem_calloc encapsulates a call to calloc:

⟨*functions* 74⟩+≡
```
void *Mem_calloc(long count, long nbytes,
    const char *file, int line) {
    void *ptr;

    assert(count > 0);
    assert(nbytes > 0);
    ptr = calloc(count, nbytes);
    if (ptr == NULL)
        ⟨raise Mem_Failed 74⟩
    return ptr;
}
```

When either count or nbytes is zero, calloc's behavior is implementation defined. The Mem interface specifies what happens in these cases, which is one of its advantages and helps avoid bugs.

Mem_free just calls free:

⟨*functions* 74⟩+≡
```
void Mem_free(void *ptr, const char *file, int line) {
    if (ptr)
        free(ptr);
}
```

The standard permits null pointers to be passed to free, but Mem_free doesn't pass them, because old implementations of free may not accept null pointers.

Mem_resize has a much simpler specification than does realloc, which is reflected in its simpler implementation:

⟨*functions* 74⟩+≡
```
void *Mem_resize(void *ptr, long nbytes,
    const char *file, int line) {

    assert(ptr);
    assert(nbytes > 0);
    ptr = realloc(ptr, nbytes);
    if (ptr == NULL)
        ⟨raise Mem_Failed 74⟩
```

```
        return ptr;
    }
```

`Mem_resize`'s only purpose is to change the size of an existing block. `realloc` does this, too, but it also frees a block when `nbytes` is zero and allocates a block when `ptr` is the null pointer. These additional capabilities, which are only loosely related to changing the size of an existing block, invite bugs.

5.3 Checking Implementation

The functions exported by the checking implementation of the `Mem` interface catch the kinds of access errors described at the beginning of this chapter and report them as checked runtime errors.

⟨*memchk.c*⟩≡
```
    #include <stdlib.h>
    #include <string.h>
    #include "assert.h"
    #include "except.h"
    #include "mem.h"

    ⟨checking types 80⟩
    ⟨checking macros 79⟩
    ⟨data 74⟩
    ⟨checking data 77⟩
    ⟨checking functions 79⟩
```

`Mem_free` and `Mem_resize` can detect access errors if `Mem_alloc`, `Mem_calloc`, and `Mem_resize` never return the same address twice and if they remember all of the addresses they do return and which ones refer to allocated memory. Abstractly, these functions maintain a set S whose elements are the pairs (α, *free*) or (α, *allocated*), where α is the address returned by an allocation. The value *free* indicates that the address α does not refer to allocated memory; that is, it has been deallocated explicitly, and the value *allocated* indicates that α points to allocated memory.

`Mem_alloc` and `Mem_calloc` add the pair (*ptr*, *allocated*) to S, where *ptr* is their return value, and they guarantee that neither (*ptr*, *allocated*) nor (*ptr*, *free*) was in S before the addition. `Mem_free(ptr)` is legal if `ptr` is null or if (ptr, *allocated*) is in *S*. If ptr is nonnull and (ptr, *allocated*) is in *S*, Mem_free deallocates the block at ptr and changes the entry in *S* to (ptr, *free*). Similarly, Mem_resize(ptr, nbytes, ...) is legal only if (ptr, *allocated*) is in *S*. If so, Mem_resize calls Mem_alloc to allocate a new block, copies the contents of the old one to the new one, and calls Mem_free to deallocate the old one; these calls make the appropriate changes to *S*.

The condition that the allocation functions never return the same address twice can be implemented by never deallocating anything. This approach wastes space, and it's easy to do better: never deallocate the *byte* at an address previously returned by an allocation function. *S* can be implemented by keeping a table of the addresses of these bytes.

This scheme can be implemented by writing a memory allocator that sits on top of the standard library functions. This allocator maintains a hash table of block *descriptors*:

⟨checking data 77⟩≡

```
static struct descriptor {
    struct descriptor *free;
    struct descriptor *link;
    const void *ptr;
    long size;
    const char *file;
    int line;
} *htab[2048];
```

ptr is the address of the block, which is allocated elsewhere as described below, and size is the size of the block. file and line are the block's allocation coordinates — the source coordinates passed to the function that allocated the block. These values aren't used, but they're stored in descriptors so that debuggers can print them during a debugging session.

The link fields form a list of descriptors for blocks that hash to the same index in htab, which is an array of pointers to descriptors. These descriptors also form a list of free blocks; the head of this list is the dummy descriptor

⟨checking data 77⟩+≡

```
static struct descriptor freelist = { &freelist };
```

and the list is threaded through the `free` fields of the descriptors. This list is circular: `freelist` is the *last* descriptor on the list and its `free` field points to the first descriptor. At any given time, `htab` holds descriptors for all of the blocks, both free and allocated, and the free blocks are on `freelist`. Thus, the descriptor's `free` field is null if the block is *allocated* and nonnull if it's *free*, and `htab` implements S. Figure 5.1 shows these data structures at one point in time. The space associated with each descriptor structure appears behind it. Shaded spaces are allocated; clear spaces are free, solid lines emanate from `link` fields, and the dotted lines show the free list.

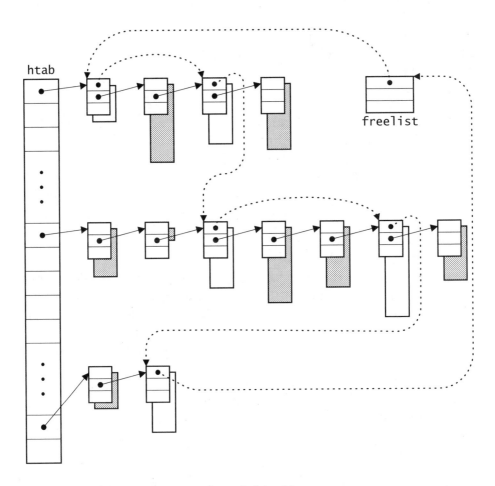

Figure 5.1 `htab` and `freelist` structures

Given an address, find searches for its descriptor. It returns either a pointer to the descriptor or the null pointer:

⟨*checking functions* 79⟩≡

```
static struct descriptor *find(const void *ptr) {
    struct descriptor *bp = htab[hash(ptr, htab)];

    while (bp && bp->ptr != ptr)
        bp = bp->link;
    return bp;
}
```

⟨*checking macros* 79⟩≡

```
#define hash(p, t) (((unsigned long)(p)>>3) & \
    (sizeof (t)/sizeof ((t)[0])-1))
```

The hash macro treats the address as a bit pattern, shifts it right three bits, and reduces it modulo the size of htab. find is enough to write a version of Mem_free in which access errors are checked runtime errors:

⟨*checking functions* 79⟩+≡

```
void Mem_free(void *ptr, const char *file, int line) {
    if (ptr) {
        struct descriptor *bp;
        ⟨set bp if ptr is valid 79⟩
        bp->free = freelist.free;
        freelist.free = bp;
    }
}
```

If ptr is nonnull and is a valid address, the block is deallocated by appending it to the free list for possible reuse by a subsequent call to Mem_alloc. A pointer is valid if it points to an allocated block:

⟨*set* bp *if* ptr *is valid* 79⟩≡

```
if (((unsigned long)ptr)%(sizeof (union align)) != 0
|| (bp = find(ptr)) == NULL || bp->free)
    Except_raise(&Assert_Failed, file, line);
```

The test `((unsigned long)ptr)%(sizeof (union align)) != 0` avoids calls to `find` for those addresses that aren't multiples of the strictest alignment and thus cannot possibly be valid block pointers.

As shown below, `Mem_alloc` always returns pointers that are aligned on an address that is a multiple of the size of the following union.

⟨*checking types* 80⟩≡
```
union align {
    int i;
    long l;
    long *lp;
    void *p;
    void (*fp)(void);
    float f;
    double d;
    long double ld;
};
```

This alignment ensures that any type of data can be stored in the blocks returned by `Mem_alloc`. If the `ptr` passed to `Mem_free` isn't so aligned, it can't possibly be in `htab` and is thus invalid.

`Mem_resize` catches access errors by making the same check, and then calls `Mem_free`, `Mem_alloc`, and the library function `memcpy`:

⟨*checking functions* 79⟩+≡
```
void *Mem_resize(void *ptr, long nbytes,
    const char *file, int line) {
    struct descriptor *bp;
    void *newptr;

    assert(ptr);
    assert(nbytes > 0);
    ⟨set bp if ptr is valid 79⟩
    newptr = Mem_alloc(nbytes, file, line);
    memcpy(newptr, ptr,
        nbytes < bp->size ? nbytes : bp->size);
    Mem_free(ptr, file, line);
    return newptr;
}
```

Likewise, Mem_calloc can be implemented by calling Mem_alloc and the library function memset:

⟨*checking functions* 79⟩+≡
```
void *Mem_calloc(long count, long nbytes,
    const char *file, int line) {
    void *ptr;

    assert(count > 0);
    assert(nbytes > 0);
    ptr = Mem_alloc(count*nbytes, file, line);
    memset(ptr, '\0', count*nbytes);
    return ptr;
}
```

All that remains is to allocate the descriptors themselves and the code for Mem_alloc. One way to do both tasks with one allocation is to allocate a block large enough to hold a descriptor and the storage requested by a call to Mem_alloc. This approach has two drawbacks. First, it complicates carving up a block of free storage to satisfy several smaller requests, because each request needs its own descriptor. Second, it makes the descriptors vulnerable to corruption by writes through pointers or indices that stray just outside of allocated blocks.

Allocating descriptors separately decouples their allocations from those done by Mem_alloc and reduces — but does not eliminate — the chances that they will be corrupted. dalloc allocates, initializes, and returns one descriptor, doling it out of the 512-descriptor chunks obtained from malloc:

⟨*checking functions* 79⟩+≡
```
static struct descriptor *dalloc(void *ptr, long size,
    const char *file, int line) {
    static struct descriptor *avail;
    static int nleft;

    if (nleft <= 0) {
        ⟨allocate descriptors 82⟩
        nleft = NDESCRIPTORS;
    }
    avail->ptr  = ptr;
    avail->size = size;
```

```
            avail->file = file;
            avail->line = line;
            avail->free = avail->link = NULL;
            nleft--;
            return avail++;
        }
```

⟨*checking macros* 79⟩+≡
```
    #define NDESCRIPTORS 512
```

The call to `malloc` might return the null pointer, which `dalloc` passes back to its caller.

⟨*allocate descriptors* 82⟩≡
```
    avail = malloc(NDESCRIPTORS*sizeof (*avail));
    if (avail == NULL)
        return NULL;
```

As shown below, `Mem_alloc` raises `Mem_Failed` when `dalloc` returns the null pointer.

`Mem_alloc` allocates a block of memory using the first-fit algorithm, one of many memory-allocation algorithms. It searches `freelist` for the first free block that is large enough to satisfy the request and divides that block to fill the request. If `freelist` doesn't contain a suitable block, `Mem_alloc` calls `malloc` to allocate a chunk of memory that's larger than `nbytes`, adds this chunk onto the free list, and tries again. Since the new chunk is larger than `nbytes`, it is used to fill the request the second time around. Here's the code:

⟨*checking functions* 79⟩+≡
```
    void *Mem_alloc(long nbytes, const char *file, int line){
        struct descriptor *bp;
        void *ptr;

        assert(nbytes > 0);
        ⟨round nbytes up to an alignment boundary 83⟩
        for (bp = freelist.free; bp; bp = bp->free) {
            if (bp->size > nbytes) {
                ⟨use the end of the block at bp->ptr 83⟩
            }
            if (bp == &freelist) {
```

```
                struct descriptor *newptr;
                ⟨newptr ← a block of size NALLOC + nbytes 84⟩
                newptr->free = freelist.free;
                freelist.free = newptr;
            }
        }
        assert(0);
        return NULL;
    }
```

Mem_alloc starts by rounding nbytes up so that every pointer it returns is a multiple of the size of the union align:

⟨round nbytes *up to an alignment boundary* 83⟩≡
```
    nbytes = ((nbytes + sizeof (union align) - 1)/
        (sizeof (union align)))*(sizeof (union align));
```

freelist.free points to the beginning of the free list, which is where the for loop starts. The first free block whose size exceeds nbytes is used to fill the request. The nbytes at the *end* of this free block are carved off, and the address of that block is returned after its descriptor is created, initialized, and added to htab:

⟨*use the end of the block at* bp->ptr 83⟩≡
```
    bp->size -= nbytes;
    ptr = (char *)bp->ptr + bp->size;
    if ((bp = dalloc(ptr, nbytes, file, line)) != NULL) {
        unsigned h = hash(ptr, htab);
        bp->link = htab[h];
        htab[h] = bp;
        return ptr;
    } else
        ⟨raise Mem_Failed 74⟩
```

Figure 5.2 shows the effect of this chunk: on the left is a descriptor that points to some free space before it's carved up. On the right, the allocated space is shaded and a new descriptor points to it. Notice that the new descriptor's free list link is null.

The test bp->size > nbytes guarantees that the value of bp->ptr is never reused. Large free blocks are divided to fill smaller requests until they're reduced to sizeof (union align) bytes, after which bp->size

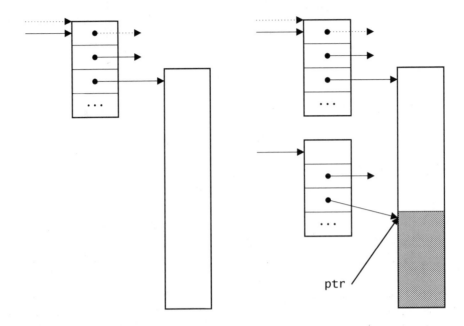

Figure 5.2 Allocating the tail of a free block

never exceeds nbytes. The first sizeof (union align) bytes of each chunk are never allocated.

If bp reaches freelist, the list does not hold a block whose size exceeds nbytes. In that case, a new chunk of size

⟨*checking macros* 79⟩+≡
```
#define NALLOC 4096
```

plus nbytes is added to the beginning of the free list; it will be visited on the *next* iteration of the for loop and will be used to fill the request. This new chunk has a descriptor just as if it had been previously allocated and freed:

⟨newptr ← *a block of size* NALLOC + nbytes 84⟩≡
```
if ((ptr = malloc(nbytes + NALLOC)) == NULL
|| (newptr = dalloc(ptr, nbytes + NALLOC,
        __FILE__, __LINE__)) == NULL)
    ⟨raise Mem_Failed 74⟩
```

Further Reading

One of the purposes of Mem is to improve the interface to the standard C allocation functions. Maguire (1993) gives a critique of these functions and describes a similar repackaging.

Memory-allocation bugs so pervade C programs that entire companies are devoted to building and selling tools that help diagnose and fix such bugs. One of the best is Purify (Hastings and Joyce 1992), which detects almost all kinds of access errors, including those described in Section 5.3. Purify checks every load and store instruction; since it does so by editing object code, it can be used even when source code is unavailable, such as for proprietary libraries. Instrumenting source code to catch access errors is at the other end of the implementation spectrum; for example, Austin, Breach, and Sohi (1994) describe a system in which "safe" pointers carry enough information to catch a wide range of access errors. LCLint (Evans 1996) has many of the features of tools like PC-Lint and can detect many potential memory-allocation errors at compile time.

Knuth (1973a) surveys all of the important memory-allocation algorithms, and explains why first fit is usually better than, for example, best fit, which looks for the free block whose size is closest to the request. The first-fit algorithm used in Mem_alloc is similar to the one described in Section 8.7 of Kernighan and Ritchie (1988).

There are endless variations on most memory-mangement algorithms, usually designed to improve performance for specific applications or allocation patterns. Quick fit (Weinstock and Wulf 1988) is one of the most widely used. It capitalizes on the observation that many applications allocate blocks of only few different sizes. Quick fit keeps N free lists, one for each of the N most frequently requested sizes. Allocating a block of one of these sizes simply removes the first block from the appropriate list, and freeing a block adds it to the appropriate list. When the lists are empty or the request is for an odd size, an alternate algorithm, such as first fit, is used.

Grunwald and Zorn (1993) describe a system that *generates* implementations of malloc and free tuned for a specific application. They first run the application with versions of malloc and free that collect statistics about block sizes, frequency of allocation versus deallocation, and so forth. They then feed these data to a program that generates source code for versions of malloc and free customized for the application. These versions often use quick fit with a small, application-specific set of block sizes.

Exercises

5.1 Maguire (1993) advocates initializing uninitialized memory to some distinctive bit pattern to help diagnose bugs that are caused by accessing uninitialized memory. What are the properties of a good bit pattern? Propose a suitable bit pattern and change the checking implementation of Mem_alloc to use it. Try to find an application where this change catches a bug.

5.2 Once a free block is whittled down to sizeof (union align) bytes in the chunk ⟨*use the end of the block at* bp->ptr 83⟩, it can never satisfy a request yet remains in the free list. Change this code to remove such blocks. Can you find an application for which measurements can detect the effect of this improvement?

5.3 Most implementations of first fit, such as the one in Section 8.7 of Kernighan and Ritchie (1988), combine adjacent free blocks to form larger free blocks. The checking implementation of Mem_alloc doesn't combine adjacent free blocks because it may not return the same address twice. Devise an algorithm for Mem_alloc that can combine adjacent free blocks without returning the same address twice.

5.4 Some programmers might argue that raising Assert_Failure in Mem_free is a draconian reaction to an access error because execution can continue if the erroneous call is simply logged and then ignored. Implement

```
extern void Mem_log(FILE *log);
```

If Mem_log is passed a nonnull file pointer, it announces access errors by writing messages to log instead of by raising Assert_Failure. These messages can record the coordinates of the erroneous call and of the allocation coordinates. For example, when Mem_free is called with a pointer to a block that has already been freed, it might write

```
** freeing free memory
Mem_free(0x6418) called from parse.c:461
This block is 48 bytes long and was allocated from sym.c:123
```

Similarly, when `Mem_resize` is called with a bad pointer, it might report

```
** resizing unallocated memory
Mem_resize(0xf7fff930,640) called from types.c:1101
```

Permit `Mem_log(NULL)` to turn off logging and reinstate assertion failure for access errors.

5.5 The checking implementation has all of the information it needs to report potential memory leaks. As described on page 68, a memory leak is an allocated block that is not referenced by any pointer and thus cannot be deallocated. Leaks cause programs to run out of memory eventually. They aren't a problem for programs that run for only a short time, but they're a serious problem for long-running programs, such as user interfaces and servers. Implement

```
extern void Mem_leak(apply(void *ptr, long size,
    const char *file, int line, void *cl), void *cl);
```

which calls the function pointed to by `apply` for every allocated block; `ptr` is the location of the block, `size` is its allocated size, and `file` and `line` are its allocation coordinates. Clients can pass an application-specific pointer, `cl`, to `Mem_leak`, and this pointer is passed along to `apply` as its last argument. `Mem_leak` doesn't know what `cl` is for, but presumably `apply` does. Together, `apply` and `cl` are called a *closure*: They specify an operation and some context-specific data for that operation. For example,

```
void inuse(void *ptr, long size,
    const char  *file, int line, void *cl) {
    FILE *log = cl;

    fprintf(log, "** memory in use at %p\n", ptr);
    fprintf(log, "This block is %ld bytes long "
        "and was allocated from %s:%d\n", size,
        file, line);
}
```

writes messages like

```
** memory in use at 0x13428
This block is 32 bytes long and was allocated from gen.c:23
```

to the log file described in the previous exercise. `inuse` is called by passing it and the file pointer for the log file to `Mem_leak`:

```
Mem_leak(inuse, log);
```

6

MORE MEMORY MANAGEMENT

Most implementations of `malloc` and `free` use memory-management algorithms that are necessarily based on the *sizes* of objects. The first-fit algorithm used in the previous chapter is an example. In some applications, deallocations are grouped and occur at the same time. Graphical user interfaces are an example. Space for scroll bars, buttons, and so forth, is allocated when a window is created, and deallocated when the window is destroyed. A compiler is another example. `lcc`, for example, allocates memory as it compiles a function and deallocates all of that memory at once when it finishes compiling the function.

Memory-management algorithms based on the *lifetimes* of objects are often better for these kinds of applications. Stack-based allocation is an example of this class of allocation algorithms, but it can be used only if object lifetimes are nested, which often is not the case.

This chapter describes a memory-management interface and an implementation that uses arena-based algorithms, which allocate memory from an arena and deallocate entire arenas at once. Calling `malloc` requires a subsequent call to `free`. As discussed in the previous chapter, it's easy to forget to call `free` or, worse, to deallocate an object that has already been deallocated, or one that shouldn't be deallocated.

With the arena-based allocator, there's no obligation to call `free` for every call to `malloc`; there's only a single call that deallocates all the memory allocated in a arena since the last deallocation. Both allocation and deallocation are more efficient, and there are no storage leaks. But the most important benefit of this scheme is that it simplifies code. *Applicative* algorithms allocate new data structures instead of changing existing ones. The arena-based allocator encourages simple applicative algorithms in place of algorithms that might be more space-efficient but are always more complex because they must remember when to call free.

There are two disadvantages of the arena-based scheme: It can use more memory, and it can create dangling pointers. If an object is allocated in the wrong arena and that arena is deallocated before the program is done with the object, the program will reference either unallocated memory or memory that has been reused for another, perhaps unrelated, arena. It's also possible to allocate objects in an arena that isn't deallocated as early as expected, which creates a storage leak. In practice, however, arena management is so easy that these problems rarely occur.

6.1 Interface

The Arena interface specifies two exceptions and functions that manage arenas and allocate memory from them:

⟨*arena.h*⟩≡
```
#ifndef ARENA_INCLUDED
#define ARENA_INCLUDED
#include "except.h"

#define T Arena_T
typedef struct T *T;

extern const Except_T Arena_NewFailed;
extern const Except_T Arena_Failed;
```
⟨*exported functions* 91⟩
```
#undef T
#endif
```

Arenas are created and destroyed by

⟨*exported functions* 91⟩≡
```
extern T    Arena_new    (void);
extern void Arena_dispose(T *ap);
```

Arena_new creates a new arena and returns an opaque pointer to the newly created arena. These pointers are passed to the other functions to specify an arena. If Arena_new cannot allocate the arena, it raises the exception Arena_NewFailed. Arena_dispose frees the memory associated with the arena *ap, disposes of the arena itself, and clears *ap. It is a checked runtime error to pass a null ap or *ap to Arena_dispose.

The allocation functions Arena_alloc and Arena_calloc are like the functions with similar names in the Mem interface, except they allocate memory from an arena.

⟨*exported functions* 91⟩+≡
```
extern void *Arena_alloc (T arena, long nbytes,
    const char *file, int line);
extern void *Arena_calloc(T arena, long count,
    long nbytes, const char *file, int line);
extern void  Arena_free  (T arena);
```

Arena_alloc allocates a block of at least nbytes in arena and returns a pointer to the first byte. The block is aligned on an addressing boundary that is suitable for the data with the strictest alignment requirement. The contents of the block are uninitialized. Arena_calloc allocates a block large enough to hold an array of count elements, each of size nbytes, in arena, and returns a pointer to the first byte. The block is aligned as for Arena_alloc, and is initialized to zeros. It is a checked runtime error for count or nbytes to be nonpositive.

The last two arguments to Arena_alloc and Arena_calloc are the file name and the line number of the location of the call. If Arena_alloc and Arena_calloc cannot allocate the memory requested, they raise Arena_Failed and pass file and line to Except_raise so that the exception reports the location of the call. If file is the null pointer, they supply the source locations within their implementations that raise Arena_Failed.

Arena_free deallocates *all* the storage in arena, which amounts to deallocating everything that has been allocated in arena since arena was created or since the last call to Arena_free for that arena.

It is a checked runtime error to pass a null T to any routine in this interface. The routines in this interface can be used with those in the Mem interface and with other allocators based on malloc and free.

6.2 Implementation

⟨*arena.c*⟩≡
```
#include <stdlib.h>
#include <string.h>
#include "assert.h"
#include "except.h"
#include "arena.h"
#define T Arena_T

const Except_T Arena_NewFailed =
    { "Arena Creation Failed" };
const Except_T Arena_Failed    =
    { "Arena Allocation Failed" };
```

⟨*macros* 98⟩
⟨*types* 92⟩
⟨*data* 96⟩
⟨*functions* 93⟩

An arena describes a chunk of memory:

⟨*types* 92⟩≡
```
struct T {
    T prev;
    char *avail;
    char *limit;
};
```

The prev field points to the head of the chunk, which begins with an arena structure as described below, and the limit field points just past the end of the chunk. The avail field points to the chunk's first free location; the space beginning at avail and up to limit is available for allocation.

To allocate N bytes when N does not exceed limit-avail, avail is incremented by N and its previous value is returned. If N exceeds limit-avail, a new chunk is allocated by calling malloc; the current value of *arena is "pushed" by storing it at the beginning of the new chunk, the fields of arena are initialized so they describe the new chunk, and allocation proceeds.

The arena structure thus heads a linked list of chunks in which the links are the prev fields in copies of the arena structures that begin each chunk. Figure 6.1 shows the state of an arena after three chunks have been allocated. The shading denotes allocated space; chunks can vary in size and may end with unallocated space if allocations don't exactly fill the chunks.

Arena_new allocates and returns an arena structure with its fields set to null pointers, which denotes an empty arena:

⟨*functions* 93⟩≡
```
T Arena_new(void) {
    T arena = malloc(sizeof (*arena));
```

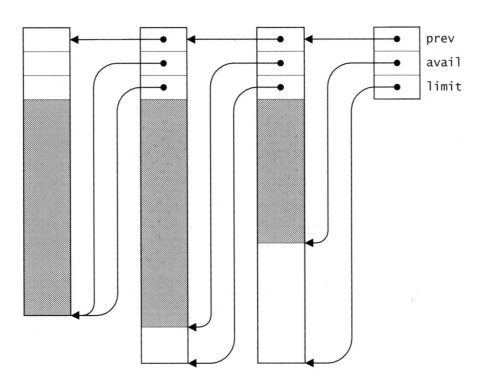

Figure 6.1 An arena with three chunks

```
        if (arena == NULL)
            RAISE(Arena_NewFailed);
        arena->prev = NULL;
        arena->limit = arena->avail = NULL;
        return arena;
    }
```

Arena_dispose calls Arena_free to deallocate the chunks in the arena; it then frees the arena structure itself and clears the pointer to the arena:

⟨*functions* 93⟩+≡
```
    void Arena_dispose(T *ap) {
        assert(ap && *ap);
        Arena_free(*ap);
        free(*ap);
        *ap = NULL;
    }
```

Arena uses malloc and free instead of, say, Mem_alloc and Mem_free, so that it's independent of other allocators.

Most allocations are trivial: They round the request amount up to the proper alignment boundary, increment the avail pointer by the amount of the rounded request, and return the previous value.

⟨*functions* 93⟩+≡
```
    void *Arena_alloc(T arena, long nbytes,
        const char *file, int line) {
        assert(arena);
        assert(nbytes > 0);
        ⟨round nbytes up to an alignment boundary 95⟩
        while (arena->avail + nbytes > arena->limit) {
            ⟨get a new chunk 95⟩
        }
        arena->avail += nbytes;
        return arena->avail - nbytes;
    }
```

As in the checking implementation of the Mem interface, the size of the union

⟨*types* 92⟩+≡
```
union align {
    int i;
    long l;
    long *lp;
    void *p;
    void (*fp)(void);
    float f;
    double d;
    long double ld;
};
```

gives the minimum alignment on the host machine. Its fields are those that are most likely to have the strictest alignment requirements, and it is used to round up nbytes:

⟨*round* nbytes *up to an alignment boundary* 95⟩≡
```
nbytes = ((nbytes + sizeof (union align) - 1)/
    (sizeof (union align)))*(sizeof (union align));
```

For most calls, nbytes is less than arena->limit - arena->avail; that is, the chunk has at least nbytes of free space, so the body of the while loop in Arena_alloc above is not executed. If the request cannot be satisfied from the current chunk, a new chunk must be allocated. This wastes the free space at the end of current chunk, which is illustrated in the second chunk on the list shown in Figure 6.1.

After a new chunk is allocated, the current value of *arena is saved at the beginning of the new chunk, and arena's fields are initialized so that allocation can continue:

⟨*get a new chunk* 95⟩≡
```
T ptr;
char *limit;
⟨ptr ← a new chunk 96⟩
*ptr = *arena;
arena->avail = (char *)((union header *)ptr + 1);
arena->limit = limit;
arena->prev  = ptr;
```

⟨*types* 92⟩+≡
```
union header {
```

```
        struct T b;
        union align a;
    };
```

The structure assignment *ptr = *arena pushes *arena by saving it at the beginning of the new chunk. The union header ensures that arena->avail is set to a properly aligned address for the first allocation in this new chunk.

As shown below, Arena_free keeps a few free chunks on a free list emanating from freechunks to reduce the number of times it must call malloc. This list is threaded through the prev fields of the chunks' initial arena structures, and the limit fields of those structures point just past the ends of their chunks. nfree is the number of chunks on the list. Arena_alloc gets a free chunk from this list or by calling malloc, and it sets the local variable limit for use in ⟨*get a new chunk* 95⟩ above:

⟨*data* 96⟩+≡
```
    static T freechunks;
    static int nfree;
```

⟨*ptr ← a new chunk* 96⟩≡
```
    if ((ptr = freechunks) != NULL) {
        freechunks = freechunks->prev;
        nfree--;
        limit = ptr->limit;
    } else {
        long m = sizeof (union header) + nbytes + 10*1024;
        ptr = malloc(m);
        if (ptr == NULL)
            ⟨raise Arena_Failed 96⟩
        limit = (char *)ptr + m;
    }
```

If a new chunk must be allocated, one is requested that is large enough to hold an arena structure plus nbytes, and have 10K bytes of available space left over. If malloc returns null, allocation fails and Arena_alloc raises Arena_Failed:

⟨*raise* Arena_Failed 96⟩≡
```
    {
        if (file == NULL)
```

```
                RAISE(Arena_Failed);
            else
                Except_raise(&Arena_Failed, file, line);
    }
```

Once arena points to the new chunk, the while loop in Arena_alloc
tries the allocation again. It still might fail: If the new chunk came from
freechunks, it might be too small to fill the request, which is why
there's a while loop instead of an if statement.

Arena_calloc simply calls Arena_alloc:

⟨*functions* 93⟩+≡
```
    void *Arena_calloc(T arena, long count, long nbytes,
        const char *file, int line) {
        void *ptr;

        assert(count > 0);
        ptr = Arena_alloc(arena, count*nbytes, file, line);
        memset(ptr, '\0', count*nbytes);
        return ptr;
    }
```

An arena is deallocated by adding its chunks to the list of free chunks,
which also restores *arena to its initial state as the list is traversed.

⟨*functions* 93⟩+≡
```
    void Arena_free(T arena) {
        assert(arena);
        while (arena->prev) {
            struct T tmp = *arena->prev;
            ⟨free the chunk described by arena 98⟩
            *arena = tmp;
        }
        assert(arena->limit == NULL);
        assert(arena->avail == NULL);
    }
```

The structure assignment to tmp copies to tmp all of the fields of the
arena structure pointed to by arena->prev. This assignment and the
assignment *arena = tmp thus "pops" the stack of arena structures

formed by the list of chunks. Once the entire list is traversed, all of the fields of `arena` should be null.

`freechunks` accumulates free chunks from all arenas and thus could get large. The length of the list isn't a problem, but the free storage it holds might be. Chunks on `freechunks` look like allocated memory to other allocators and thus might make calls to `malloc` fail, for example. To avoid tying up too much storage, `Arena_free` keeps no more than

⟨*macros* 98⟩≡
```
#define THRESHOLD 10
```

free chunks on `freechunks`. Once `nfree` reaches THRESHOLD, subsequent chunks are deallocated by calling `free`:

⟨*free the chunk described by* arena 98⟩≡
```
if (nfree < THRESHOLD) {
    arena->prev->prev = freechunks;
    freechunks = arena->prev;
    nfree++;
    freechunks->limit = arena->limit;
} else
    free(arena->prev);
```

In Figure 6.2, the chunk on the left is to be deallocated. When `nfree` is less than THRESHOLD, the chunk is added to `freechunks`. The deallocated chunk is shown on the right, and the dotted lines depict the pointers planted by the three assignments in the code above.

Further Reading

Arena-based allocators are also known as *pool allocators*, and have been described several times. `Arena`'s allocator (Hanson 1990) was originally developed for use in `lcc` (Fraser and Hanson 1995). `lcc`'s allocator is slightly simpler than `Arena`'s: Its arenas are allocated statically, and its deallocator doesn't call `free`. In its initial versions, allocation was done by macros that manipulated arena structures directly and called a function only when a new chunk was needed.

Barrett and Zorn (1993) describe how to choose the appropriate arena automatically. Their experiments suggest that the execution path to an allocation site is a good predictor of the lifetime of the block allocated at

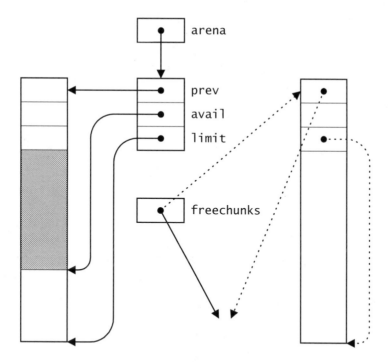

Figure 6.2 Deallocating a chunk when `nfree` < THRESHOLD

that site. This information includes the call chain and the address of the allocation site, and it is used to choose one of several application-specific arenas.

Vmalloc (Vo 1996) is a more general allocator that can be used to implement both the `Mem` and `Arena` interfaces. Vmalloc permits clients to organize memory into regions and to provide functions that manage the memory in each region. The Vmalloc library includes an implementation of the `malloc` interface that provides memory checks similar to those done by `Mem`'s checking implementation, and these checks can be controlled by setting environment variables.

Arena-based allocation collapses many explicit deallocations into one. *Garbage collectors* go one step further: They avoid *all* explicit deallocations. In languages with garbage collectors, programmers can almost ignore storage allocation, and storage allocation bugs can't occur. The advantages of this property are hard to overstate.

With a garbage collector, space is reclaimed automatically as necessary, usually when an allocation request can't be filled. A garbage collector finds all blocks that are referenced by program variables, and all blocks that are referenced by fields in these blocks, and so on. These are the *accessible* blocks; the rest are *inaccessible* and can be reused. There is a large body of literature on garbage collection: Appel (1991) is a brief survey that emphasizes recent algorithms, and Knuth (1973a) and Cohen (1981) cover the older algorithms in more depth.

To find accessible blocks, most collectors must know which variables point to blocks and which fields in blocks point to other blocks. Collectors are usually used in languages that have enough compile-time or runtime data to supply the necessary information. Examples include LISP, Icon, SmallTalk, ML, and Modula-3. *Conservative collectors* (Boehm and Weiser 1988) can deal with languages that don't provide enough type information, such as C and C++. They assume that *any* properly aligned bit pattern that looks like a pointer is one and that the block it points to is accessible. A conservative collector thus identifies some inaccessible blocks as accessible and therefore busy, but has no choice but to overestimate the set of accessible blocks. Despite this apparent handicap, conservative collectors work surprising well in some programs (Zorn 1993).

Exercises

6.1 Arena_alloc looks only in the chunk described by arena. If there's not enough free space in that chunk, it allocates a new chunk even if there is enough space in some other chunk further down the list. Change Arena_alloc so that it allocates space in an existing chunk if there's one that has enough space, and measure the resulting benefits. Can you find an application whose memory use is reduced significantly by this change?

6.2 When Arena_alloc needs a new chunk, it takes the first one on the free list, if there is one. A better choice would be to find the *largest* free chunk that satisfies the request, allocating a new one only if freechunks doesn't hold a suitable chunk. Keeping track of the largest chunk in freechunks would avoid fruitless traversals in this scheme. With this change, the while loop in Arena_alloc could be replaced with an if statement. Implement this scheme and measure its benefits. Does it make Arena_alloc noticeably slower? Does it use memory more efficiently?

6.3 Setting THRESHOLD to 10 means that free list will never hold more than about 100K bytes of memory, since Arena_alloc allocates chunks of at least 10K bytes. Devise a way for Arena_alloc and Arena_free to monitor allocation and deallocation patterns and to compute THRESHOLD dynamically based on these patterns. The goal is to keep the free list as small as possible and to minimize the number of calls to malloc.

6.4 Explain why the Arena interface doesn't support the function

```
void *Arena_resize(void **ptr, long nbytes,
    const char *file, int line)
```

which, like Mem_resize, would change the size of the block pointed to by ptr to nbytes and return a pointer to the resized block, which would reside in the same arena (but not necessarily the same chunk) as the block given by ptr. How would you change the implementation to support this function? What checked run-time errors would you support?

6.5 In a stack allocator, an allocation pushes the new space onto the top of a specified stack and returns the address of its first byte. *Marking* a stack returns a value that encodes the current height of that stack, and deallocation pops a stack back to a previously marked height. Design and implement an interface for a stack allocator. What checked runtime errors can you provide that will catch deallocation errors? Examples of such errors are deallocating at a point higher than the current the top of a stack, or deallocating at a point that has already been deallocated and subsequently reallocated.

6.6 One problem with having more than one memory-allocation interface is that other interfaces must choose between them without knowing the best one for a particular application. Design and implement a *single* interface that supports both kinds of allocators. This interface might, for example, provide an allocation function that is like Mem_alloc but that operates in an "allocation environment," which can be changed by other functions. This environment would specify memory-management details, such as which allocator and which arena to use, if it specified arena-based allocation. Other functions might, for example, push the current environment on an internal stack and establish a new environment, and pop the stack to reestablish a previous environment. Investigate these and other variations in your design.

7
LISTS

A *list* is a sequence of zero or more pointers. A list with zero pointers is an *empty list*. The number of pointers in a list is its *length*. Almost every nontrival application uses lists in some form. Lists so pervade programs that some languages provide them as built-in types; LISP, Scheme, and ML are the best known examples.

Lists are easy to implement, so programmers usually reimplement them for each application at hand, and there's no widely accepted standard interface for lists, although most application-specific interfaces have many similarities. The List abstract data type described below provides many of the facilities found in most of these application-specific interfaces. Sequences, described in Chapter 11, are another way to represent lists.

7.1 Interface

The complete List interface is

⟨*list.h*⟩≡
```
#ifndef LIST_INCLUDED
#define LIST_INCLUDED

#define T List_T
typedef struct T *T;

struct T {
    T rest;
```

```
        void *first;
};

extern T        List_append (T list, T tail);
extern T        List_copy   (T list);
extern T        List_list   (void *x, ...);
extern T        List_pop    (T list, void **x);
extern T        List_push   (T list, void *x);
extern T        List_reverse(T list);
extern int      List_length (T list);
extern void     List_free   (T *list);
extern void     List_map    (T list,
        void apply(void **x, void *cl), void *cl);
extern void **List_toArray(T list, void *end);

#undef T
#endif
```

A List_T is a pointer to a struct List_T. Most ADTs hide the representation details of their types. List reveals these details because for this particular ADT, the complications induced by the alternatives outweigh the benefits of doing so.

List_Ts have a trivial representation; it's hard to imagine many other representations whose implementations would offer advantages significant enough to justify hiding the fact that list elements are structures with two fields. The exercises explore some of the few alternatives.

Revealing List_T's representation simplifies the interface and its use in several ways. For example, variables of type struct List_T can be defined and initialized statically, which is useful for building lists at compile time, and avoids allocations. Likewise, other structures can have struct List_Ts embedded in them. A null List_T is an empty list, which is its natural representation, and functions aren't needed to access the first and rest fields.

All routines in this interface accept a null T for any list argument and interpret it as the empty list.

List_list creates and returns a list. It's called with N nonnull pointers followed by one null pointer, and it creates a list with N nodes whose first fields hold the N nonnull pointers and whose Nth rest field is null. For example, the assignments

```
List_T p1, p2;
p1 = List_list(NULL);
p2 = List_list("Atom", "Mem", "Arena", "List", NULL);
```

return the empty list and a list with four nodes holding the pointers to the strings Atom, Mem, Arena, and List. List_list can raise Mem_Failed.

List_list assumes the pointers passed in the variable part of its argument list are void. There's no prototype to provide the necessary implicit conversions, so programmers must provide casts when passing other than char pointers and void pointers as the second and subsequent arguments. For example, to build a list of four one-element lists that hold the strings Atom, Mem, Arena, and List, the correct call is

```
p = List_list(List_list("Atom",  NULL),
      (void *)List_list("Mem",   NULL),
      (void *)List_list("Arena", NULL),
      (void *)List_list("List",  NULL), NULL);
```

It is an unchecked runtime error to omit the casts shown in this example. Such casts are one of the pitfalls of variable length argument lists.

List_push(T list, void *x) adds a new node that holds x to the beginning of list, and returns the new list. List_push can raise Mem_Failed. List_push is another way to create a new list; for example,

```
p2 = List_push(NULL, "List");
p2 = List_push(p2,   "Arena");
p2 = List_push(p2,   "Mem");
p2 = List_push(p2,   "Atom");
```

creates the same list as the assignment to p2 above.

Given a nonempty list, List_pop(T list, void **x) assigns the first field of the first node to *x, if x is nonnull, removes and deallocates the first node, and returns the resulting list. Given an empty list, List_pop simply returns it and does not change *x.

List_append(T list, T tail) appends one list to another: It assigns tail to the last rest field in list. If list is null, it returns tail. Thus,

```
p2 = List_append(p2, List_list("Except", NULL));
```

sets p2 to the five-element list formed by appending the one-element list holding Except to the four-element list created above.

List_reverse reverses the order of the nodes in its list argument and returns the resulting list. For example,

```
p2 = List_reverse(p2);
```

returns a list that holds Except, List, Arena, Mem, and Atom.

All the routines described so far are *destructive*, or *nonapplicative* — they may change the lists passed to them and return the resulting lists. List_copy is an *applicative* function: It makes and returns a copy of its argument. Thus, after executing

```
List_T p3 = List_reverse(List_copy(p2));
```

p3 is the list Atom, Mem, Arena, and List, and Except; p2 remains unchanged. List_copy can raise Mem_Failed.

List_length returns the number of nodes in its argument.

List_free takes a pointer to a T. If *list is nonnull, List_free deallocates all of the nodes on *list and sets it to the null pointer. If *list is null, List_free has no effect. It is a checked runtime error to pass a null pointer to List_free.

List_map calls the function pointed to by apply for every node in list. Clients can pass an application-specific pointer, cl, to List_map, and this pointer is passed along to *apply as its second argument. For each node in list, *apply is called with a *pointer* to its first field and with cl. Since *apply is called with pointers to the first fields, it can change them. Taken together, apply and cl are called a *closure* or *callback*: They specify an operation and some context-specific data for that operation. For example, given

```
void mkatom(void **x, void *cl) {
    char **str = (char **)x;
    FILE *fp = cl;

    *str = Atom_string(*str);
    fprintf(fp, "%s\n", *str);
}
```

the call List_map(p3, mkatom, stderr) replaces the strings in p3 with equivalent atoms and prints

```
Atom
Mem
Arena
List
Except
```

on the error output. Another example is

```
void applyFree(void **ptr, void *cl) {
    FREE(*ptr);
}
```

which can be used to deallocate the space pointed to by the first fields of a list before the list itself is deallocated. For example:

```
List_T names;
...
List_map(names, applyFree, NULL);
List_free(&names);
```

frees the data in the list names and then frees the nodes themselves. It is an unchecked runtime error for apply to change list.

Given a list with N values, List_toArray(T list, void *end) creates an array in which elements zero through N-1 hold the N values from the first fields of the list and the Nth element holds the value of end, which is often the null pointer. List_toArray returns a pointer to the first element of this array. For example, the elements of p3 can be printed in sorted order by

```
int i;
char **array = (char **)List_toArray(p3, NULL);
qsort((void **)array, List_length(p3), sizeof (*array),
    (int (*)(const void *, const void *))compare);
for (i = 0; array[i]; i++)
    printf("%s\n", array[i]);
FREE(array);
```

As suggested by this example, clients must deallocate the array returned by List_toArray. If the list is empty, List_toArray returns a one-element array. List_toArray can raise Mem_Failed. compare and its use with the standard library function qsort are described on page 123.

7.2 Implementation

⟨*list.c*⟩≡
```
#include <stdarg.h>
#include <stddef.h>
#include "assert.h"
#include "mem.h"
#include "list.h"

#define T List_T

⟨functions 108⟩
```

List_push is the simplest of the List functions. It allocates one node, initializes it, and returns a pointer to it:

⟨*functions* 108⟩≡
```
T List_push(T list, void *x) {
    T p;

    NEW(p);
    p->first = x;
    p->rest  = list;
    return p;
}
```

The other list-creation function, List_list, is more complicated because it must cope with a variable number of arguments and must append a new node to the evolving list for each nonnull pointer argument. To do so, it uses a pointer to the pointer to which the new node should be assigned:

⟨*functions* 108⟩+≡
```
T List_list(void *x, ...) {
    va_list ap;
    T list, *p = &list;

    va_start(ap, x);
    for ( ; x; x = va_arg(ap, void *)) {
        NEW(*p);
```

```
        (*p)->first = x;
        p = &(*p)->rest;
    }
    *p = NULL;
    va_end(ap);
    return list;
}
```

p starts by pointing to list, so a pointer to the first node is assigned to list. Thereafter, p points to the rest field of the last node on the list, so an assignment to *p appends a node to the list. The following figure shows the effect of the initialization of p and of the statements in the body of the for loop as List_list builds a three-node list.

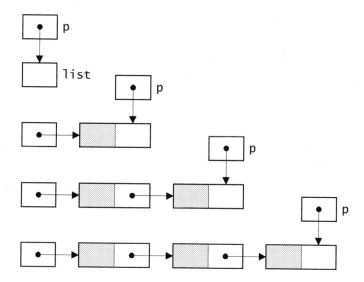

Each trip through the loop assigns the next pointer argument to x and breaks when it hits the first null-pointer argument, which might be the initial value of x. This idiom ensures that List_list(NULL) returns the empty list — a null pointer.

List_list's use of pointers to pointers — List_T *s — is typical of many list-manipulation algorithms. It uses one succinct mechanism to deal with two conditions: the initial node in a possibly empty list, and the interior nodes of a nonempty list. List_append illustrates another use of this idiom:

⟨*functions* 108⟩+≡
```
T List_append(T list, T tail) {
    T *p = &list;

    while (*p)
        p = &(*p)->rest;
    *p = tail;
    return list;
}
```

List_append walks p down list until it points to the null pointer at the end of the list to which tail should be assigned. If list itself is the null pointer, p ends up pointing to list, which has the desired effect of appending tail to the empty list.

List_copy is the last of the List functions that uses the pointer-to-pointer idiom:

⟨*functions* 108⟩+≡
```
T List_copy(T list) {
    T head, *p = &head;

    for ( ; list; list = list->rest) {
        NEW(*p);
        (*p)->first = list->first;
        p = &(*p)->rest;
    }
    *p = NULL;
    return head;
}
```

Pointers to pointers don't simplify List_pop or List_reverse, so the perhaps more obvious implementations suffice. List_pop removes the first node in a nonempty list and returns the new list, or simply returns an empty list:

⟨*functions* 108⟩+≡
```
T List_pop(T list, void **x) {
    if (list) {
        T head = list->rest;
        if (x)
            *x = list->first;
```

```
            FREE(list);
            return head;
        } else
            return list;
    }
```

If x is nonnull, *x is assigned the contents of the first field of the first node before that node is discarded. Notice that List_pop must save list->rest before deallocating the node pointed to by list.

List_reverse walks two pointers, list and next, down the list once and uses them to reverse the list in place as it goes; new always points to the first node of the reversed list:

⟨*functions* 108⟩+≡
```
  T List_reverse(T list) {
      T head = NULL, next;

      for ( ; list; list = next) {
          next = list->rest;
          list->rest = head;
          head = list;
      }
      return head;
  }
```

The following figure depicts the situation at each loop iteration just after the first statement in the loop body, the assignment to next, is executed for the third element in the list.

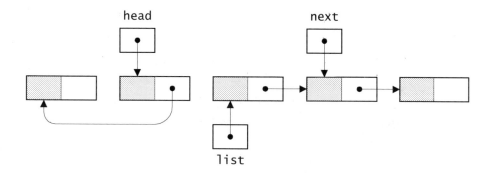

next points to the successor of list or is null if list points to the last
node, and head points to the reversed list, which begins with the predecessor of list or is null if list points to the first node. The second and
third statements in the loop body push the node pointed to by list onto
the front of head, and the increment expression list = next advances
list to its successor, at which point the list is:

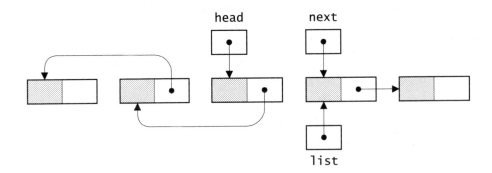

next is advanced again the next time through the loop body.

List_length walks down list counting its nodes, and List_free
walks down list deallocating each node:

⟨*functions* 108⟩+≡
```
int List_length(T list) {
    int n;

    for (n = 0; list; list = list->rest)
        n++;
    return n;
}

void List_free(T *list) {
    T next;

    assert(list);
    for ( ; *list; *list = next) {
        next = (*list)->rest;
        FREE(*list);
    }
}
```

List_map sounds complicated, but it's trivial, because the closure function does all the work. List_map simply walks down list calling the closure function with a pointer to each node's first field and with the client-specific pointer cl:

⟨*functions* 108⟩+≡
```
void List_map(T list,
    void apply(void **x, void *cl), void *cl) {
    assert(apply);
    for ( ; list; list = list->rest)
        apply(&list->first, cl);
}
```

List_toArray allocates an *N*+1-element array to hold the pointers in an *N*-element list, and copies the pointers into the array:

⟨*functions* 108⟩+≡
```
void **List_toArray(T list, void *end) {
    int i, n = List_length(list);
    void **array = ALLOC((n + 1)*sizeof (*array));

    for (i = 0; i < n; i++) {
        array[i] = list->first;
        list = list->rest;
    }
    array[i] = end;
    return array;
}
```

Allocating a one-element array for an empty list may seem a waste, but doing so means that List_toArray *always* returns a nonnull pointer to an array, so clients never need to check for null pointers.

Further Reading

Knuth (1973a) describes all of the important algorithms for manipulating singly linked lists, like those provided by List, and for manipulating doubly linked lists, which are provided by Ring (described in Chapter 12).

Lists are used for everything in list-manipulation languages like LISP and Scheme, and in functional languages like ML (Ullman 1994). Abelson and Sussman (1985) is one of the many textbooks that show how lists can be used to conquer almost any problem; it uses Scheme.

Exercises

7.1 Design a list ADT that hides the representation of lists and does not use null pointers for empty lists. Design the interface first, then do an implementation. One approach is to make `List_T` an opaque pointer that points to a list head, which holds a pointer to the list itself or to both the first and last node of the list. The list head could also hold the length of the list.

7.2 Rewrite `List_list`, `List_append`, and `List_copy` without using pointers to pointers.

7.3 Rewrite `List_reverse` using pointers to pointers.

7.4 `List_append`, which is one of the most frequently used list operations in many applications, must walk down to the end of the list, so it takes $O(N)$ time for N-element lists. Circularly linked lists are another representation for singly linked lists. The free list in the checking implementation of the `Mem` interface is an example of a circularly linked list. The `rest` field of the last node in a circularly linked list points to the first node, and the list itself is represented by a pointer to the last node. Thus, both the first and last node can be reached in constant time, and appending to a circularly linked list can be done in constant time. Design an interface for a list ADT that uses circularly linked lists. Experiment with interfaces that both hide and reveal this representation.

8

TABLES

An *associative table* is a set of key-value pairs. It's like an array except that the indices can be values of any type. Many applications use tables. Compilers, for example, maintain symbol tables, which map names to sets of attributes for those names. Some window systems maintain tables that map window titles into some kind of window-related data structures. Document-preparation systems use tables to represent indices: For example, the index might be a table in which the keys are one-character strings — one for each section of the index — and the values are other tables in which the keys are the strings for the index entries themselves and the values are lists of page numbers.

Tables have many uses, and the examples alone could fill a chapter. The Table interface is designed so that it can be used for many of these uses. It maintains key-value pairs, but it never inspects keys themselves; only clients inspect keys via functions passed to routines in Table. Section 8.2 describes a typical Table client, a program that prints the number of occurrences of words in its input. This program, wf, also uses the Atom and Mem interfaces.

8.1 Interface

Table represents an associative table with an opaque pointer type:

⟨table.h⟩≡
```
#ifndef TABLE_INCLUDED
#define TABLE_INCLUDED
```

```
#define T Table_T
typedef struct T *T;
```

⟨*exported functions* 116⟩

```
#undef T
#endif
```

The exported functions allocate and deallocate Table_Ts, add and remove key-value pairs from those tables, and visit the key-value pairs in them. It is a checked runtime error to pass a null Table_T or null key to any function in this interface.

Table_Ts are allocated and deallocated by

⟨*exported functions* 116⟩≡
```
    extern T    Table_new (int hint,
        int cmp(const void *x, const void *y),
        unsigned hash(const void *key));
    extern void Table_free(T *table);
```

Table_new's first argument, hint, is an estimate of the number of entries that the new table is expected to hold. All tables can hold an arbitrary number of entries regardless of the value of hint, but accurate values of hint may improve performance. It is a checked runtime error for hint to be negative. The functions cmp and hash manipulate client-specific keys. Given two keys, x and y, cmp(x,y) must return an integer less than zero, equal to zero, or greater than zero, if, respectively, x is less than y, x equals y, or x is greater than y. The standard library function strcmp is an example of a comparison function suitable for keys that are strings. hash must return a hash number for key; if cmp(x,y) returns zero, then hash(x) must be equal to hash(y). Each table can have its own hash and cmp functions.

Atoms are often used as keys, so if hash is the null function pointer, the keys in the new table are assumed to be atoms and the implementation of Table provides a suitable hash function. Similarly, if cmp is the null function pointer, keys are assumed to be atoms, and two keys x and y are equal if x = y.

Table_new can raise Mem_Failed.

Table_new's arguments — a size hint, a hash function, and a comparison function — provide more information than most implementations need. For example, the hash table implementation described in Section

8.3 needs a comparison function that tests only for equality, and implementations that use trees don't need the hint or the hash function. This complexity is the price of a design that permits multiple implementations, and this feature is one of the reasons designing good interfaces is difficult.

Table_free deallocates *table and sets it to the null pointer. It is a checked runtime error for table or *table to be null. Table_free does not deallocate the keys or values; see Table_map.

The functions

⟨*exported functions* 116⟩+≡
```
extern int   Table_length(T table);
extern void *Table_put   (T table, const void *key,
    void *value);
extern void *Table_get   (T table, const void *key);
extern void *Table_remove(T table, const void *key);
```

return the number of keys in a table, add a new key-value pair or change the value of an existing pair, fetch the value associated with a key, and remove a key-value pair.

Table_length returns the number of key-value pairs in table.

Table_put adds the key-value pair given by key and value to table. If table already holds key, value overwrites the previous value, and Table_put returns the *previous* value. Otherwise, key and value are added to table, which grows by one entry, and Table_put returns the null pointer. Table_put can raise Mem_Failed.

Table_get searches table for key and, if it's found, returns its associated value. If table doesn't hold key, Table_get returns the null pointer. Notice that returning the null pointer is ambiguous if table holds null pointer values.

Table_remove searches table for key and, if it's found, removes the key-value pair from table, which thus shrinks by one entry, and returns the removed value. If table doesn't hold key, Table_remove has no effect on table and returns the null pointer.

The functions

⟨*exported functions* 116⟩+≡
```
extern void   Table_map   (T table,
    void apply(const void *key, void **value, void *cl),
    void *cl);
extern void **Table_toArray(T table, void *end);
```

visit the key-value pairs and collect them into an array. `Table_map` calls the function pointed to by `apply` for every key-value pair in `table` in an unspecified order. `apply` and `cl` specify a closure: Clients can pass an application-specific pointer, `cl`, to `Table_map` and this pointer is passed along to `apply` at each call. For each pair in `table`, `apply` is called with its key, a *pointer* to its value, and `cl`. Since `apply` is called with pointers to the values, it can change them. `Table_map` can also be used to deallocate keys or values before deallocating the table. For example, assuming the keys are atoms,

```
static void vfree(const void *key, void **value,
    void *cl) {
    FREE(*value);
}
```

deallocates just the values, so

```
Table_map(table, vfree, NULL);
Table_free(&table);
```

deallocates the values in `table` and then `table` itself.

It is a checked runtime error for `apply` to change the contents of `table` by calling `Table_put` or `Table_remove`.

Given a table with N key-value pairs, `Table_toArray` builds an array with $2N+1$ elements and returns a pointer to the first element. The keys and values alternate, with keys appearing in the even-numbered elements and their associated values in the following odd-numbered elements. The last even-numbered element, at index $2N$, is assigned `end`, which is often the null pointer. The order of the key-value pairs in the array is unspecified. The program described in Section 8.2 illustrates the use of `Table_toArray`.

`Table_toArray` can raise `Mem_Failed`, and clients must deallocate the array it returns.

8.2   Example: Word Frequencies

`wf` lists the number of times each word appears in a list of named files or in the standard input if no files are specified. For example:

```
% wf table.c mem.c
table.c:
3    apply
7    array
13   assert
9    binding
18   book
2    break
10   buckets
...
4    y
mem.c:
1    allocation
7    assert
12   book
1    stdlib
9    void
...
```

As this output shows, the words in each file are listed in alphabetical order and are preceded by the number of times they appear in the file. For wf, a word is a letter followed by zero more letters or underscores, and case doesn't matter.

More generally, a word begins with a character in a *first* set followed by zero or more characters in a *rest* set. Words of this form are recognized by getword, which is a generalization of double's getword described in Section 1.1. It's used enough in this book to be packaged separately in its own interface:

⟨*getword.h*⟩≡
```
#include <stdio.h>

extern int getword(FILE *fp, char *buf, int size,
    int first(int c), int rest(int c));
```

getword consumes the next word in the file opened on fp, stores it as a null-terminated string in buf[0..size-1], and returns one. When it reaches the end of file without consuming a word, it returns zero. The functions first and rest test a character for membership in *first* and *rest*. A word is a contiguous sequence of characters; it starts with a character for which first returns a nonzero value followed by characters for which rest returns nonzero values. If a word is longer than size-2 characters, the excess characters are discarded. size must exceed one, and fp, buf, first, and rest must be nonnull.

⟨getword.c⟩≡
```
#include <ctype.h>
#include <string.h>
#include <stdio.h>
#include "assert.h"
#include "getword.h"

int getword(FILE *fp, char *buf, int size,
    int first(int c), int rest(int c)) {
    int i = 0, c;

    assert(fp && buf && size > 1 && first && rest);
    c = getc(fp);
    for ( ; c != EOF; c = getc(fp))
        if (first(c)) {
            ⟨store c in buf if it fits 120⟩
            c = getc(fp);
            break;
        }
    for ( ; c != EOF && rest(c); c = getc(fp))
        ⟨store c in buf if it fits 120⟩
    if (i < size)
        buf[i] = 0;
    else
        buf[size-1] = 0;
    if (c != EOF)
        ungetc(c, fp);
    return i > 0;
}
```

⟨store c in buf if it fits 120⟩≡
```
{
    if (i < size - 1)
        buf[i++] = c;
}
```

This version of getword is a bit more complex than the version in dou-ble because this one must work when a character is in *first* but not in *rest*. When first returns nonzero, that character is stored in buf and only subsequent characters are passed to rest.

wf's main function processes its arguments, which name files. main opens each file and calls wf with the file pointer and file name:

⟨*wf functions* 121⟩≡
```
int main(int argc, char *argv[]) {
    int i;

    for (i = 1; i < argc; i++) {
        FILE *fp = fopen(argv[i], "r");
        if (fp == NULL) {
            fprintf(stderr, "%s: can't open '%s' (%s)\n",
                argv[0], argv[i], strerror(errno));
            return EXIT_FAILURE;
        } else {
            wf(argv[i], fp);
            fclose(fp);
        }
    }
    if (argc == 1) wf(NULL, stdin);
    return EXIT_SUCCESS;
}
```

⟨*wf includes* 121⟩≡
```
#include <stdio.h>
#include <stdlib.h>
#include <errno.h>
```

If there are no arguments, main calls wf with a null file name and the file pointer for the standard input. The null file name tells wf not to print the name of the file.

wf uses a table to store the words and their counts. Each word is folded to lowercase, converted to an atom, and used as a key. Using atoms lets wf use the defaults for the table's hash and comparison func-tions. Values are pointers, but wf needs to associate an integer count with each key. It thus allocates space for a counter and stores a pointer to this space in the table.

⟨*wf functions* 121⟩+≡
```
void wf(char *name, FILE *fp) {
    Table_T table = Table_new(0, NULL, NULL);
    char buf[128];

    while (getword(fp, buf, sizeof buf, first, rest)) {
        const char *word;
        int i, *count;
        for (i = 0; buf[i] != '\0'; i++)
            buf[i] = tolower(buf[i]);
        word = Atom_string(buf);
        count = Table_get(table, word);
        if (count)
            (*count)++;
        else {
            NEW(count);
            *count = 1;
            Table_put(table, word, count);
        }
    }
    if (name)
        printf("%s:\n", name);
    { ⟨print the words 123⟩ }
    ⟨deallocate the entries and table 124⟩
}
```

⟨*wf includes* 121⟩+≡
```
#include <ctype.h>
#include "atom.h"
#include "table.h"
#include "mem.h"
#include "getword.h"
```

⟨*wf prototypes* 122⟩≡
```
void wf(char *, FILE *);
```

count is a pointer to an integer. If Table_get returns null, the word isn't in table, so wf allocates space for the counter, initializes it to one to account for this first occurrence of the word, and adds it to the table. When Table_get returns a nonnull pointer, the expression (*count)++ increments the integer pointed to by that pointer. This expression is much different than *count++, which would increment count instead of the integer it points to.

Membership in *first* and *rest* is tested by functions of the same names that use the predicates defined in the standard header ctype.h:

⟨*wf functions* 121⟩+≡
```
int first(int c) {
    return isalpha(c);
}

int rest(int c) {
    return isalpha(c) || c == '_';
}
```

⟨*wf prototypes* 122⟩+≡
```
int first(int c);
int rest (int c);
```

Once wf has read all of the words, it must sort and print them. qsort, the standard C library sorting function, sorts an array, so wf can sort the array returned by Table_toArray if it tells qsort that key-value pairs in the array should be treated as single elements. It can then print the words and their counts by walking down the array:

⟨*print the words* 123⟩≡
```
int i;
void **array = Table_toArray(table, NULL);
qsort(array, Table_length(table), 2*sizeof (*array),
    compare);
for (i = 0; array[i]; i += 2)
    printf("%d\t%s\n", *(int *)array[i+1],
        (char *)array[i]);
FREE(array);
```

qsort takes four arguments: the array, the number of elements, the size of each element in bytes, and a function that's called to compare two elements. To treat each of the *N* key-value pairs as a single element, wf tells qsort that there are *N* elements and that each takes the space occupied by two pointers.

qsort calls the comparison function with pointers to the elements. Each element is itself two pointers — one to the word and one to the count — so the comparision function is called with two pointers to pointers to characters. For instance, when `assert` from `mem.c` is compared with `book`, the arguments x and y are

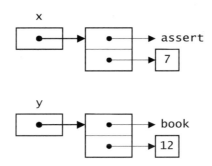

The comparison function can compare the words by calling `strcmp`:

⟨*wf functions* 121⟩+≡
```
int compare(const void *x, const void *y) {
    return strcmp(*(char **)x, *(char **)y);
}
```

⟨*wf includes* 121⟩+≡
```
#include <string.h>
```

⟨*wf prototypes* 122⟩+≡
```
int compare(const void *x, const void *y);
```

The wf function is called for each file-name argument, so, to save space, it should deallocate the table and the counts before it returns. A call to `Table_map` deallocates the counts, and `Table_free` deallocates the table itself.

⟨*deallocate the entries and* table 124⟩≡
```
Table_map(table, vfree, NULL);
Table_free(&table);
```

⟨*wf functions* 121⟩+≡
```
void vfree(const void *key, void **count, void *cl) {
```

```
        FREE(*count);
    }
```

⟨*wf prototypes* 122⟩+≡
```
    void vfree(const void *, void **, void *);
```

The keys aren't deallocated because they're atoms, and so must not be. Besides, some of them are likely to appear in subsequent files.

Collecting the various *wf.c* fragments forms the program wf:

⟨*wf.c*⟩≡
```
    ⟨wf includes 121⟩
    ⟨wf prototypes 122⟩
    ⟨wf functions 121⟩
```

8.3 Implementation

⟨*table.c*⟩≡
```
    #include <limits.h>
    #include <stddef.h>
    #include "mem.h"
    #include "assert.h"
    #include "table.h"

    #define T Table_T

    ⟨types 125⟩
    ⟨static functions 127⟩
    ⟨functions 126⟩
```

Hash tables are one of the obvious data structures for representing associative tables (trees are the other one; see Exercise 8.2). Each Table_T is thus a pointer to a structure that holds a hash table of *bindings*, which carry the key-value pairs:

⟨*types* 125⟩≡
```
    struct T {
        ⟨fields 126⟩
        struct binding {
            struct binding *link;
```

```
            const void *key;
            void *value;
        } **buckets;
    };
```

buckets points to an array with the appropriate number of elements. The cmp and hash functions are associated with a particular table, so they are also stored in the structure along with the number of elements in buckets:

⟨*fields* 126⟩≡
```
    int size;
    int (*cmp)(const void *x, const void *y);
    unsigned (*hash)(const void *key);
```

Table_new uses its hint argument to choose a prime for the size of buckets, and it saves either cmp and hash or pointers to static functions for comparing and hashing atoms:

⟨*functions* 126⟩≡
```
    T Table_new(int hint,
        int cmp(const void *x, const void *y),
        unsigned hash(const void *key)) {
        T table;
        int i;
        static int primes[] = { 509, 509, 1021, 2053, 4093,
            8191, 16381, 32771, 65521, INT_MAX };

        assert(hint >= 0);
        for (i = 1; primes[i] < hint; i++)
            ;
        table = ALLOC(sizeof (*table) +
            primes[i-1]*sizeof (table->buckets[0]));
        table->size = primes[i-1];
        table->cmp  = cmp  ?  cmp : cmpatom;
        table->hash = hash ? hash : hashatom;
        table->buckets = (struct binding **)(table + 1);
        for (i = 0; i < table->size; i++)
            table->buckets[i] = NULL;
        table->length = 0;
        table->timestamp = 0;
```

```
        return table;
    }
```

The for loop sets i to the index of the first element in primes that is equal to or exceeds hint, and primes[i-1] gives the number of elements in buckets. Notice that the loop starts at index 1. Mem's ALLOC allocates the structure and space for buckets. Table uses a prime for the size of its hash table because it has no control over how hash numbers for keys are computed. The values in primes are the primes nearest 2^n for n from 9 to 16, which yield a wide range of hash-table sizes. Atom uses a simpler algorithm because it also computes the hash numbers.

If cmp or hash is the null function pointer, the functions

⟨*static functions* 127⟩≡
```
    static int cmpatom(const void *x, const void *y) {
        return x != y;
    }

    static unsigned hashatom(const void *key) {
        return (unsigned long)key>>2;
    }
```

are used instead. Since atoms x and y are equal if x = y, cmpatom returns zero when x = y and one otherwise. This particular implementation of Table tests keys for equality only, so cmpatom doesn't need to test the relative order of x and y. An atom is an address and this address itself can be used as a hash number; it is shifted right two bits because it's likely that each atom starts on a word boundary, so the rightmost two bits are probably zero.

Each element in buckets heads a linked list of binding structures that hold a key, its associated value, and a pointer to the next binding structure on the list. Figure 8.1 gives an example. All of the keys in each list have the same hash number.

Table_get finds a binding by hashing its key, taking it modulo the number of elements in buckets, and searching the list for a key equal to key. It calls the table's hash and cmp functions.

⟨*functions* 126⟩+≡
```
    void *Table_get(T table, const void *key) {
        int i;
        struct binding *p;
```

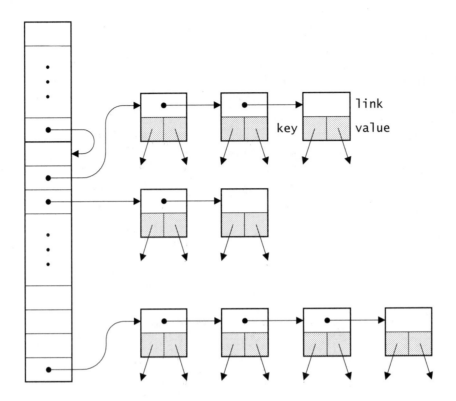

Figure 8.1 Table layout

```
        assert(table);
        assert(key);
        ⟨search table for key 128⟩
        return p ? p->value : NULL;
    }
```

⟨*search* table *for* key 128⟩≡
```
    i = (*table->hash)(key)%table->size;
    for (p = table->buckets[i]; p; p = p->link)
        if ((*table->cmp)(key, p->key) == 0)
            break;
```

This for loop terminates when it finds the key, and it thus leaves p pointing to the binding of interest. Otherwise, p ends up null.

Table_put is similar; it searches for a key and, if it finds it, changes the associated value. If Table_put doesn't find the key, it allocates and initializes a new binding, and adds that binding to the front of the appropriate list hanging off of buckets. It could link the new binding in anywhere on the list, but adding to the front of the list is the easiest and most efficient alternative.

⟨*functions*⟩+≡
```
void *Table_put(T table, const void *key, void *value) {
    int i;
    struct binding *p;
    void *prev;

    assert(table);
    assert(key);
    ⟨search table for key 128⟩
    if (p == NULL) {
        NEW(p);
        p->key = key;
        p->link = table->buckets[i];
        table->buckets[i] = p;
        table->length++;
        prev = NULL;
    } else
        prev = p->value;
    p->value = value;
    table->timestamp++;
    return prev;
}
```

Table_put increments two per-table counters:

⟨*fields* 126⟩+≡
```
int length;
unsigned timestamp;
```

length is the number of bindings in the table; it's returned by Table_length:

⟨*functions* 126⟩+≡
```
int Table_length(T table) {
```

```
        assert(table);
        return table->length;
    }
```

A table's `timestamp` is incremented every time the table is changed by
`Table_put` or `Table_remove`. `timestamp` is used to implement the
checked runtime error that `Table_map` must enforce: the table can't be
changed while `Table_map` is visiting its bindings. `Table_map` saves the
value of `timestamp` upon entry. After each call to `apply`, it asserts that
the table's `timestamp` is still equal to this saved value.

⟨*functions* 126⟩+≡
```
    void Table_map(T table,
        void apply(const void *key, void **value, void *cl),
        void *cl) {
        int i;
        unsigned stamp;
        struct binding *p;

        assert(table);
        assert(apply);
        stamp = table->timestamp;
        for (i = 0; i < table->size; i++)
            for (p = table->buckets[i]; p; p = p->link) {
                apply(p->key, &p->value, cl);
                assert(table->timestamp == stamp);
            }
    }
```

`Table_remove` also searches for a key, but does so by using a pointer
to a pointer to a `binding` so that it can remove the binding for the key if
it finds it:

⟨*functions* 126⟩+≡
```
    void *Table_remove(T table, const void *key) {
        int i;
        struct binding **pp;

        assert(table);
        assert(key);
        table->timestamp++;
```

```
i = (*table->hash)(key)%table->size;
for (pp = &table->buckets[i]; *pp; pp = &(*pp)->link)
    if ((*table->cmp)(key, (*pp)->key) == 0) {
        struct binding *p = *pp;
        void *value = p->value;
        *pp = p->link;
        FREE(p);
        table->length--;
        return value;
    }
return NULL;
}
```

The for loop is functionally equivalent to the one in ⟨*search* table *for key* 128⟩, except that pp points to the *pointer* to the binding for each key. pp starts by pointing to table->buckets[i] and follows along the list, pointing to the link field of the *k*th binding in the list when the *k*+1st binding is examined, as depicted below.

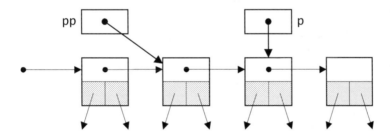

If *pp holds key, the binding can be unlinked from the list by setting *pp to (*pp)->link; p holds the value of *pp. If Table_remove finds the key, it also decrements the table's length.

Table_toArray is similar to List_toArray. It allocates an array to hold the key-value pairs followed by a terminating end pointer, and fills in the array by visiting each binding in table:

⟨*functions* 126⟩+≡
```
void **Table_toArray(T table, void *end) {
    int i, j = 0;
    void **array;
    struct binding *p;
```

```
        assert(table);
        array = ALLOC((2*table->length + 1)*sizeof (*array));
        for (i = 0; i < table->size; i++)
            for (p = table->buckets[i]; p; p = p->link) {
                array[j++] = (void *)p->key;
                array[j++] = p->value;
            }
        array[j] = end;
        return array;
    }
```

p->key must be cast from const void * to void * because the array is not declared const. The order of the key-value pairs in the array is arbitrary.

Table_free must deallocate the binding structures and the Table_T structure itself. The former step is needed only if the table isn't empty:

⟨*functions* 126⟩+≡
```
    void Table_free(T *table) {
        assert(table && *table);
        if ((*table)->length > 0) {
            int i;
            struct binding *p, *q;
            for (i = 0; i < (*table)->size; i++)
                for (p = (*table)->buckets[i]; p; p = q) {
                    q = p->link;
                    FREE(p);
                }
        }
        FREE(*table);
    }
```

Further Reading

Tables are so useful that many programming languages use them as built-in data types. AWK (Aho, Kernighan, and Weinberger 1988) is a recent example, but tables appeared in SNOBOL4 (Griswold 1972), which predates AWK, and in SNOBOL4's successor, Icon (Griswold and Griswold 1990). Tables in SNOBOL4 and Icon can be indexed by and can hold values of any type, but AWK tables (which are called arrays) can be indexed by and hold only strings and numbers. Table's implementation uses some of the same techniques used to implement tables in Icon (Griswold and Griswold 1986).

PostScript (Adobe Systems 1990), a page-description language, also has tables, which it calls dictionaries. PostScript tables can be indexed only by "names," which are PostScript's rendition of atoms, but can hold values of any type, including dictionaries.

Tables also appear in object-oriented languages, either as built-in types or in libraries. The foundation libraries in both SmallTalk and Objective-C include dictionaries, which are much like the tables exported by `Table`. These kinds of objects are often called *container* objects because they hold collections of other objects.

`Table`'s implementation uses fixed-size hash tables. As long as the *load factor*, which is the number of table entries divided by the number of elements in the hash table, is reasonably small, keys can be found by looking at only a few entries. Performance suffers, however, when the load factor gets too high. The load factor can be kept within reasonable bounds by expanding the hash table whenever the load factor exceeds, say, five. Exercise 8.5 explores an effective but naive implementation of *dynamic hash tables*, which expands the hash table and rehashes all the existing entries. Larson (1988) describes, in great detail, a more sophisticated approach in which the hash table is expanded (or contracted) incrementally, one hash chain at a time. Larson's approach eliminates the need for `hint`, and it can save storage because all tables can start small.

Exercises

8.1 There are many viable alternatives for associative-table ADTs. For example, in earlier versions of `Table`, `Table_get` returned pointers to the values instead of returning the values themselves, so clients could change them. In one design, `Table_put` always added a new binding to the table even if the key was already present, effectively "hiding" a previous binding with the same key, and `Table_remove` removed only the most recent binding. `Table_map`, however, visited all bindings in the table. Discuss the pros and cons of these and other alternatives. Design and implement a different table ADT.

8.2 The `Table` interface is designed so that other data structures can be used to implement tables. The comparison function reveals the relative order of two keys to admit implementations that use trees, for example. Reimplement `Table` using binary search trees or red-black trees. See Sedgewick (1990) for details about these data structures.

8.3 The order in which `Table_map` and `Table_toArray` visit the bindings in a table is unspecified. Suppose the interface were amended so that `Table_map` visited the bindings in the order they were added to the table and `Table_array` returned an array with the bindings in the same order. Implement this amendment. What are the practical advantages of this behavior?

8.4 Suppose the interface stipulated that `Table_map` and `Table_array` visited the bindings in *sorted* order. This stipulation would complicate the implementation of `Table`, but would simplify clients like `wf` that sort the table's bindings anyway. Discuss the merits of this proposal and implement it. Hint: In the current implementation, the average-case running time of `Table_put` is constant and that of `Table_get` is nearly so. What are the average-case running times of `Table_put` and `Table_get` in your revised implementation?

8.5 Once `buckets` is allocated, it's never expanded or contracted. Revise the `Table` implementation so that it uses a heuristic to adjust the size of buckets periodically as pairs are added and removed. Devise a test program that tests the effectiveness of your heuristics, and measure its benefit.

8.6 Implement the linear dynamic-hashing algorithm described in Larson (1988), and compare its performance with your solution to the previous exercise.

8.7 Revise *wf.c* to measure how much space is lost because atoms are never deallocated.

8.8 Change *wf.c*'s `compare` function so that it sorts the array in decreasing order of count values.

8.9 Change *wf.c* so that it prints the output for each file argument in alphabetical order of file names. With this change, the counts for `mem.c` would appear before those for `table.c` in the example shown at the beginning of Section 8.2.

9
SETS

A set is an *unordered* collection of *distinct* members. The basic operations on a set are testing for membership, adding members, and removing members. Other operations include set union, intersection, difference, and symmetric difference. Given two sets s and t, the union s + t is a set that contains everything in s and everything in t; the intersection s * t is the set whose members appear in both s and t, the difference s – t is the set whose members appear in s but not in t, and the symmetric difference, often written as s / t, is the set whose members appear in only one of s or t.

Sets are usually described in terms of a *universe* — the set of all possible members. For example, sets of characters are usually associated with the universe consisting of the 256 eight-bit character codes. When a universe U is specified, it's possible to form the complement of a set s, which is $U – s$.

The sets provided by the Set interface do not rely on universes. The interface exports functions that manipulate set members, but never inspect them directly. Like the Table interface, the Set interface is designed so that clients provide functions to inspect the properties of the members in specific sets.

Applications use sets much the way they use tables. Indeed, the sets provided by Set are like tables: set members are the keys and the values associated with the keys are ignored.

9.1 Interface

⟨*set.h*⟩≡
```
#ifndef SET_INCLUDED
#define SET_INCLUDED

#define T Set_T
typedef struct T *T;
```

⟨*exported functions* 138⟩

```
#undef T
#endif
```

The functions exported by Set fall into four groups: allocation and deallocation, basic set operations, set traversal, and operations that accept set operands and return new sets, such as set union. The functions in the first three groups are similar to those in the Table interface.

Set_Ts are allocated and deallocated by

⟨*exported functions* 138⟩≡
```
extern T    Set_new (int hint,
    int cmp(const void *x, const void *y),
    unsigned hash(const void *x));
extern void Set_free(T *set);
```

Set_new allocates, initializes, and returns a new T. hint is an estimate of the number of members the set is expected to contain; accurate values of hint may improve performance, but any nonnegative value is acceptable. cmp and hash are used to compare two members and to map members onto unsigned integers. Given two members x and y, cmp(x,y) must return an integer less than zero, equal to zero, or greater than zero, if, respectively, x is less than y, x equals y, or x is greater than y. If cmp(x,y) is zero, then only one of x or y will appear in a set, and hash(x) must be equal to hash(y). Set_new can raise Mem_Failed.

If cmp is the null function pointer, the members are assumed to be atoms; two members x and y are assumed identical if x = y. Likewise, if hash is the null function pointer, Set_new provides a hash function suitable for atoms.

Set_free deallocates *set and assigns it the null pointer. Set_free does not deallocate the members; Set_map can be used for that. It is a checked runtime error to pass a null set or *set to Set_free.

The basic operations are provided by the functions

⟨*exported functions* 138⟩+≡
```
extern int   Set_length(T set);
extern int   Set_member(T set, const void *member);
extern void  Set_put   (T set, const void *member);
extern void *Set_remove(T set, const void *member);
```

Set_length returns set's *cardinality,* or the number of members it contains. Set_member returns one if member is in set and zero if it is not. Set_put adds member to set, unless it is already there; Set_put can raise Mem_Failed. Set_remove removes member from set if set contains member, and returns the member removed (which might be a different pointer than member). Otherwise, Set_remove does nothing and returns null. It is a checked runtime error to pass a null set or member to any of these routines.

The following functions visit all the members in a set.

⟨*exported functions* 138⟩+≡
```
extern void   Set_map    (T set,
    void apply(const void *member, void *cl), void *cl);
extern void **Set_toArray(T set, void *end);
```

Set_map calls apply for each member of set. It passes the member and the client-specific pointer cl to apply. It does not otherwise inspect cl. Notice that unlike in Table_map, apply cannot change the members stored in set. It is a checked runtime error to pass a null apply or set to Set_map, and for apply to change set by calling Set_put or Set_remove.

Set_toArray returns a pointer to an $N+1$-element array that holds the N elements of set in an arbitrary order. The value of end, which is often the null pointer, is assigned to the $N+1$st element of the array. Set_toArray can raise Mem_Failed. Clients must arrange to deallocate the returned array. It is a checked runtime error to pass a null set to Set_toArray.

The functions

⟨*exported functions* 138⟩+≡
```
extern T Set_union(T s, T t);
extern T Set_inter(T s, T t);
extern T Set_minus(T s, T t);
extern T Set_diff (T s, T t);
```

perform the four set operations described at the beginning of this chapter. Set_union returns s + t, Set_inter returns s * t, Set_minus returns s − t, and Set_diff return s / t. All four create and return new Ts and can raise Mem_Failed. These functions interpret a null s or t as the empty set, but they always return a new, nonnull T. Thus, Set_union(s, NULL) returns a copy of s. For each of these functions, it is a checked runtime error for both s and t to be null and, when both s and t are nonnull, for them to have different comparison and hash functions. That is, s and t must have been created by calls to Set_new that specified the same comparison and hash functions.

9.2   Example: Cross-Reference Listings

xref prints cross-reference lists of the identifiers in its input files, which helps, for example, to find all of the uses of specific identifiers in a program's source files. For example,

```
% xref xref.c getword.c
...
FILE    getword.c: 6
        xref.c: 18 43 72

...
c       getword.c: 7 8 9 10 11 16 19 22 27 34 35
        xref.c: 141 142 144 147 148

...
```

says that FILE is used on line 6 in getword.c and on lines 18, 43, and 72 in xref.c. Similarly, c appears on 11 different lines in getword.c and on 5 lines in xref.c. A line number is listed only once, even if the identifier appears more than once on that line. The output lists the files and line numbers in sorted order.

If there are no program arguments, xref emits a cross-reference list of the identifiers in the standard input, omitting the file names shown in the sample output above:

```
% cat xref.c getword.c | xref
...
FILE 18 43 72 157
...
c 141 142 144 147 148 158 159 160 161 162 167 170 173 178
185 186 ...
```

xref's implementation shows how sets and tables can be used together. It builds a table indexed by identifiers in which each associated value is another table indexed by file name. The values in this table are sets of pointers to integers, which hold the line numbers. Figure 9.1 depicts this structure and shows the details for the identifier FILE as described after the first display above. The value associated with FILE in the single top-level table (which is the value of identifiers in the code below) is a second-level Table_T with two keys: atoms for getword.c and xref.c. The values associated with these keys are Set_Ts that hold pointers to the line numbers on which FILE appears. There is a second-level table for each identifier in the top-level table, and a set for each key-value pair in each second-level table.

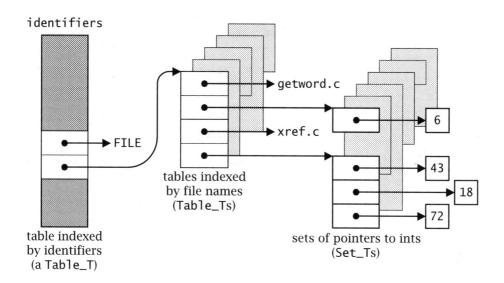

Figure 9.1 Cross-reference list data structures

⟨*xref.c*⟩≡
  ⟨*xref includes* 142⟩
  ⟨*xref prototypes* 143⟩
  ⟨*xref data* 146⟩
  ⟨*xref functions* 142⟩

xref's main function is much like wf's: It creates the table of identifiers, then processes its file-name arguments. It opens each file and calls the function xref with the file pointer, the file name, and the identifier table. If there are no arguments, it calls xref with a null file pointer, the file pointer for the standard input, and the identifier table:

⟨*xref functions* 142⟩≡
```
int main(int argc, char *argv[]) {
    int i;
    Table_T identifiers = Table_new(0, NULL, NULL);

    for (i = 1; i < argc; i++) {
        FILE *fp = fopen(argv[i], "r");
        if (fp == NULL) {
            fprintf(stderr, "%s: can't open '%s' (%s)\n",
                argv[0], argv[i], strerror(errno));
            return EXIT_FAILURE;
        } else {
            xref(argv[i], fp, identifiers);
            fclose(fp);
        }
    }
    if (argc == 1) xref(NULL, stdin, identifiers);
    ⟨print the identifiers 143⟩
    return EXIT_SUCCESS;
}
```

⟨*xref includes* 142⟩≡
```
#include <stdio.h>
#include <stdlib.h>
#include <errno.h>
#include "table.h"
```

xref builds a complicated data structure, and it's easier to understand how it is built if you first examine how its contents are printed, which you can do by navigating the components in the data structure. Writing separate chunks or functions for each component helps you to understand the details of this voyage.

The first step builds an array of the identifiers and their values, sorts the array on the identifiers, and then walks down the array calling another function, print, to deal with the values. This step is much like wf's chunk ⟨*print the words* 123⟩.

⟨*print the identifiers* 143⟩≡
```
{
    int i;
    void **array = Table_toArray(identifiers, NULL);
    qsort(array, Table_length(identifiers),
        2*sizeof (*array), compare);
    for (i = 0; array[i]; i += 2) {
        printf("%s", (char *)array[i]);
        print(array[i+1]);
    }
    FREE(array);
}
```

The keys in identifiers are atoms, so compare, the comparison function passed to the standard library function qsort, is identical to the compare used in wf and uses strcmp to compare pairs of identifiers (page 123 explains qsort's arguments):

⟨*xref functions* 142⟩+≡
```
int compare(const void *x, const void *y) {
    return strcmp(*(char **)x, *(char **)y);
}
```

⟨*xref includes* 142⟩+≡
```
#include <string.h>
```

⟨*xref prototypes* 142⟩≡
```
int compare(const void *x, const void *y);
```

Each value in identifiers is another table, which is passed to print. The keys in this table are atoms for the file names, so they can be captured in an array, sorted, and traversed by code similar to that used above.

⟨*xref functions* 142⟩+≡
```
void print(Table_T files) {
    int i;
    void **array = Table_toArray(files, NULL);

    qsort(array, Table_length(files), 2*sizeof (*array),
        compare);
    for (i = 0; array[i]; i += 2) {
        if (*(char *)array[i] != '\0')
            printf("\t%s:", (char *)array[i]);
        ⟨print the line numbers in the set array[i+1] 144⟩
        printf("\n");
    }
    FREE(array);
}
```

⟨*xref prototypes* 143⟩+≡
```
void print(Table_T);
```

print can use compare because the keys are just strings. If there are no
file name arguments, each of the tables passed to print has only one
entry, and the key is a zero-length atom. print uses this convention to
avoid printing the file name before emitting the list of line numbers.

Each value in the tables passed to print is a set of line numbers.
Because Set implements sets of pointers, xref represents line numbers
by pointers to integers and adds these pointers to the sets. To print
them, it calls Set_toArray to build and return a null-terminated array of
pointers to integers; it then sorts the array and prints the integers:

⟨*print the line numbers in the set* array[i+1] 144⟩≡
```
{
    int j;
    void **lines = Set_toArray(array[i+1], NULL);
    qsort(lines, Set_length(array[i+1]), sizeof (*lines),
        cmpint);
    for (j = 0; lines[j]; j++)
        printf(" %d", *(int *)lines[j]);
    FREE(lines);
}
```

cmpint is like compare, but it takes two pointers to pointers to integers and compares the integers:

⟨*xref functions* 142⟩+≡
```
int cmpint(const void *x, const void *y) {
    if (**(int **)x < **(int **)y)
        return -1;
    else if (**(int **)x > **(int **)y)
        return +1;
    else
        return 0;
}
```

⟨*xref prototypes* 143⟩+≡
```
int cmpint(const void *x, const void *y);
```

xref builds the data structure printed by the code just discussed. It uses getword to read the identifiers in its input. For each identifier, it walks down the data structure to the appropriate set and adds the current line number to the set:

⟨*xref functions* 142⟩+≡
```
void xref(const char *name, FILE *fp,
        Table_T identifiers){
    char buf[128];

    if (name == NULL)
        name = "";
    name = Atom_string(name);
    linenum = 1;
    while (getword(fp, buf, sizeof buf, first, rest)) {
        Set_T set;
        Table_T files;
        const char *id = Atom_string(buf);
        ⟨files ← file table in identifiers associated with id 147⟩
        ⟨set ← set in files associated with name 147⟩
        ⟨add linenum to set, if necessary 148⟩
    }
}
```

⟨*xref includes* 142⟩+≡
```
#include "atom.h"
#include "set.h"
#include "mem.h"
#include "getword.h"
```

⟨*xref prototypes* 143⟩+≡
```
void xref(const char *, FILE *, Table_T);
```

linenum is a global variable that is incremented whenever first trips over a new-line character; first is the function passed to getword to identify the initial character in an identifier:

⟨*xref data* 146⟩≡
```
int linenum;
```

⟨*xref functions* 142⟩+≡
```
int first(int c) {
    if (c == '\n')
        linenum++;
    return isalpha(c) || c == '_';
}

int rest(int c) {
    return isalpha(c) || c == '_' || isdigit(c);
}
```

⟨*xref includes* 142⟩+≡
```
#include <ctype.h>
```

getword and the first and rest functions passed to it are described starting on page 119.

⟨*xref prototypes* 143⟩+≡
```
int first(int c);
int rest (int c);
```

The code that navigates through the tables to the appropriate set must cope with missing components. For example, an identifier won't have an entry in identifiers when it is encountered for the first time, so the code creates the file table and adds the identifier–file table pair to iden-tifiers on the fly:

⟨files ← *file table in* identifiers *associated with* id 147⟩≡
```
   files = Table_get(identifiers, id);
   if (files == NULL) {
       files = Table_new(0, NULL, NULL);
       Table_put(identifiers, id, files);
   }
```

Likewise, there's no set of line numbers on the first occurrence of an identifier in a new file, so a new set is created and added to the files table when it is first needed:

⟨set ← *set in* files *associated with* name 147⟩≡
```
   set = Table_get(files, name);
   if (set == NULL) {
       set = Set_new(0, intcmp, inthash);
       Table_put(files, name, set);
   }
```

The sets are sets of pointers to integers; intcmp and inthash compare and hash the integers. intcmp is like cmpint, above, but its arguments are the pointers in the set, so it can call cmpint. The integer itself can be used as its own hash number:

⟨*xref functions* 142⟩+≡
```
   int intcmp(const void *x, const void *y) {
       return cmpint(&x, &y);
   }

   unsigned inthash(const void *x) {
       return *(int *)x;
   }
```

⟨*xref prototypes* 143⟩+≡
```
   int      intcmp (const void *x, const void *y);
   unsigned inthash(const void *x);
```

By the time control reaches ⟨*add* linenum *to* set, *if necessary* 148⟩, set is the set into which the current line number should be inserted. This could be done with the code:

```
int *p;
NEW(p);
*p = linenum;
Set_put(set, p);
```

But if set already holds linenum, this code creates a memory leak, because the pointer to the newly allocated space won't be added to the table. This leak can be avoided by allocating the space only when linenum isn't in set:

⟨*add* linenum *to* set, *if necessary* 148⟩≡
```
    {
        int *p = &linenum;
        if (!Set_member(set, p)) {
            NEW(p);
            *p = linenum;
            Set_put(set, p);
        }
    }
```

9.3 Implementation

The implementation of Set is much like the implementation of Table. It represents sets with hash tables and uses the comparison and hash functions to locate members in these tables. The exercises explore some of the viable alternatives to this implementation and to the Table implementation.

⟨*set.c*⟩≡
```
    #include <limits.h>
    #include <stddef.h>
    #include "mem.h"
    #include "assert.h"
    #include "arith.h"
    #include "set.h"
    #define T Set_T
```

⟨*types* 149⟩
⟨*static functions* 150⟩
⟨*functions* 149⟩

A Set_T is a hash table in which the chains hold the members:

⟨*types* 149⟩≡
```
struct T {
    int length;
    unsigned timestamp;
    int (*cmp)(const void *x, const void *y);
    unsigned (*hash)(const void *x);
    int size;
    struct member {
        struct member *link;
        const void *member;
    } **buckets;
};
```

length is the number of members in the set; timestamp is used to implement the checked runtime error in Set_map that forbids apply from changing the set, and cmp and hash hold the comparison and hash functions.

Like Table_new, Set_new computes the appropriate number of elements for the buckets array, stores that number in the size field, and allocates the space for a struct T and the buckets array:

⟨*functions* 149⟩≡
```
T Set_new(int hint,
    int cmp(const void *x, const void *y),
    unsigned hash(const void *x)) {
    T set;
    int i;
    static int primes[] = { 509, 509, 1021, 2053, 4093,
        8191, 16381, 32771, 65521, INT_MAX };

    assert(hint >= 0);
    for (i = 1; primes[i] < hint; i++)
        ;
    set = ALLOC(sizeof (*set) +
        primes[i-1]*sizeof (set->buckets[0]));
```

```
        set->size = primes[i-1];
        set->cmp  = cmp  ?  cmp : cmpatom;
        set->hash = hash ? hash : hashatom;
        set->buckets = (struct member **)(set + 1);
        for (i = 0; i < set->size; i++)
            set->buckets[i] = NULL;
        set->length = 0;
        set->timestamp = 0;
        return set;
    }
```

Set_new uses hint to choose one of the values in primes for the number of elements in buckets (see page 127). If the members are atoms, which is indicated by null function pointers for either cmp or hash, Set_new uses the following comparison and hash functions, which are the same ones used by Table_new.

⟨*static functions* 150⟩≡

```
    static int cmpatom(const void *x, const void *y) {
        return x != y;
    }

    static unsigned hashatom(const void *x) {
        return (unsigned long)x>>2;
    }
```

9.3.1 Member Operations

Testing for membership is like looking up a key in a table: hash the potential member and search the appropriate list emanating from buckets:

⟨*functions* 149⟩+≡

```
    int Set_member(T set, const void *member) {
        int i;
        struct member *p;

        assert(set);
        assert(member);
        ⟨search set for member 151⟩
```

```
        return p != NULL;
    }
```

⟨*search* set *for* member 151⟩≡
```
    i = (*set->hash)(member)%set->size;
    for (p = set->buckets[i]; p; p = p->link)
        if ((*set->cmp)(member, p->member) == 0)
            break;
```

p is nonnull if the search succeeds and null otherwise, so testing p determines Set_member's outcome.

Adding a new member is similar: search the set for the member, and add it if the search fails.

⟨*functions* 149⟩+≡
```
    void Set_put(T set, const void *member) {
        int i;
        struct member *p;

        assert(set);
        assert(member);
        ⟨search set for member 151⟩
        if (p == NULL) {
            ⟨add member to set 151⟩
        } else
            p->member = member;
        set->timestamp++;
    }
```

⟨*add* member *to* set 151⟩≡
```
    NEW(p);
    p->member = member;
    p->link = set->buckets[i];
    set->buckets[i] = p;
    set->length++;
```

timestamp is used in Set_map to enforce its checked runtime error.

Set_remove deletes a member by walking a pointer to a pointer to a member structure, pp, down the appropriate hash chain until *pp is null or (*pp)->member is the member of interest, in which case the assignment *pp = (*pp)->link below removes the structure from the chain.

⟨functions 149⟩+≡
```
void *Set_remove(T set, const void *member) {
    int i;
    struct member **pp;

    assert(set);
    assert(member);
    set->timestamp++;
    i = (*set->hash)(member)%set->size;
    for (pp = &set->buckets[i]; *pp; pp = &(*pp)->link)
        if ((*set->cmp)(member, (*pp)->member) == 0) {
            struct member *p = *pp;
            *pp = p->link;
            member = p->member;
            FREE(p);
            set->length--;
            return (void *)member;
        }
    return NULL;
}
```

Walking pp down the hash chain is the same idiom used in Table_remove; see page 130.

Set_remove and Set_put keep track of the number of members in the set by decrementing and incrementing its length field, which Set_length returns:

⟨functions 149⟩+≡
```
int Set_length(T set) {
    assert(set);
    return set->length;
}
```

If the set is nonempty, Set_free must first walk the hash chains deallocating the member structures before it can deallocate the set itself and clear *set.

⟨functions 149⟩+≡
```
void Set_free(T *set) {
    assert(set && *set);
    if ((*set)->length > 0) {
```

```
        int i;
        struct member *p, *q;
        for (i = 0; i < (*set)->size; i++)
            for (p = (*set)->buckets[i]; p; p = q) {
                q = p->link;
                FREE(p);
            }
    }
    FREE(*set);
}
```

Set_map is almost identical to Table_map: It traverses the hash chains calling apply for each member.

⟨*functions* 149⟩+≡
```
  void Set_map(T set,
      void apply(const void *member, void *cl), void *cl) {
      int i;
      unsigned stamp;
      struct member *p;

      assert(set);
      assert(apply);
      stamp = set->timestamp;
      for (i = 0; i < set->size; i++)
          for (p = set->buckets[i]; p; p = p->link) {
              apply(p->member, cl);
              assert(set->timestamp == stamp);
          }
  }
```

One difference is that Set_map passes each member — not a pointer to each member — to apply, so apply can't change the pointers in the set. It can, however, use a cast to change the values these members point to, which could modify the set's semantics.

Set_toArray is simpler than Table_toArray; like List_toArray, it allocates an array and just copies the members into it:

⟨*functions* 149⟩+≡
```
  void **Set_toArray(T set, void *end) {
      int i, j = 0;
```

```
        void **array;
        struct member *p;

        assert(set);
        array = ALLOC((set->length + 1)*sizeof (*array));
        for (i = 0; i < set->size; i++)
            for (p = set->buckets[i]; p; p = p->link)
                array[j++] = (void *)p->member;
        array[j] = end;
        return array;
    }
```

p->member must be cast from const void * to void * because the array is not declared const.

9.3.2 Set Operations

All four set operations have similar implementations. s + t, for example, is implemented by adding each element of s and t to a new set, which can be done by making a copy of s then adding each member of t to the copy, if it's not already in that set:

⟨*functions* 149⟩+≡
```
    T Set_union(T s, T t) {
        if (s == NULL) {
            assert(t);
            return copy(t, t->size);
        } else if (t == NULL)
            return copy(s, s->size);
        else {
            T set = copy(s, Arith_max(s->size, t->size));
            assert(s->cmp == t->cmp && s->hash == t->hash);
            { ⟨for each member q in t 154⟩
                Set_put(set, q->member);
            }
            return set;
        }
    }
```

⟨*for each member* q *in* t 154⟩≡
```
    int i;
```

```
        struct member *q;
        for (i = 0; i < t->size; i++)
            for (q = t->buckets[i]; q; q = q->link)
```

The internal function copy returns a copy of its argument, which must be nonnull.

⟨*static functions* 150⟩+≡
```
    static T copy(T t, int hint) {
        T set;

        assert(t);
        set = Set_new(hint, t->cmp, t->hash);
        { ⟨for each member q in t 154⟩
            ⟨add q->member to set 155⟩
        }
        return set;
    }
```

⟨*add* q->member *to* set 155⟩≡
```
    {
        struct member *p;
        const void *member = q->member;
        int i = (*set->hash)(member)%set->size;
        ⟨add member to set 151⟩
    }
```

Set_union and copy both have access to privileged information: they know the representation for sets and can thus specify the size of the hash table for a new set by passing the appropriate hint to Set_new. Set_union supplies a hint when it makes a copy of s; it uses the size of the larger hash table in s or t because the resulting set will have at least as many members as Set_union's largest argument. copy could call Set_put to add each member to the copy, but it uses ⟨*add* q->member *to* set 155⟩, which does the addition directly, to avoid Set_put's fruitless search.

Intersection, s * t, creates a new set with the hash table from s or t, whichever is smaller, and adds members to the new set only if they appear in both s and t:

```
⟨functions 149⟩+≡
  T Set_inter(T s, T t) {
     if (s == NULL) {
         assert(t);
         return Set_new(t->size, t->cmp, t->hash);
     } else if (t == NULL)
         return Set_new(s->size, s->cmp, s->hash);
     else if (s->length < t->length)
         return Set_inter(t, s);
     else {
         T set = Set_new(Arith_min(s->size, t->size),
             s->cmp, s->hash);
         assert(s->cmp == t->cmp && s->hash == t->hash);
         { ⟨for each member q in t 154⟩
             if (Set_member(s, q->member))
                 ⟨add q->member to set 155⟩
         }
         return set;
     }
  }
```

If s has fewer members than t, Set_inter calls itself with s and t
swapped. This causes the for loop in the last else clause to walk through
the smaller set.

Difference, s – t, creates a new set and adds to it the members from s
that do *not* appear in t. The code below *switches* the names of the arguments so that it can use the chunk ⟨*for each member* q *in* t 154⟩ to
sequence through s:

```
⟨functions 149⟩+≡
  T Set_minus(T t, T s) {
     if (t == NULL){
         assert(s);
         return Set_new(s->size, s->cmp, s->hash);
     } else if (s == NULL)
         return copy(t, t->size);
     else {
         T set = Set_new(Arith_min(s->size, t->size),
             s->cmp, s->hash);
         assert(s->cmp == t->cmp && s->hash == t->hash);
         { ⟨for each member q in t 154⟩
```

```
            if (!Set_member(s, q->member))
                ⟨add q->member to set 155⟩
        }
        return set;
    }
}
```

Symmetric difference, s / t, is the set whose elements appear in either
s or t but not both. If s or t is the empty set, then s / t is t or s. Otherwise, s / t is equivalent to (s − t) + (t − s), which can be done by making a pass over s, adding to the new set each member that's not in t,
then a pass over t, adding to the new set each member that's not in s.
The chunk ⟨*for each member* q *in* t 154⟩ can be used for both passes by
swapping the values of s and t between passes:

⟨*functions* 149⟩+≡
```
    T Set_diff(T s, T t) {
        if (s == NULL) {
            assert(t);
            return copy(t, t->size);
        } else if (t == NULL)
            return copy(s, s->size);
        else {
            T set = Set_new(Arith_min(s->size, t->size),
                s->cmp, s->hash);
            assert(s->cmp == t->cmp && s->hash == t->hash);
            { ⟨for each member q in t 154⟩
                if (!Set_member(s, q->member))
                    ⟨add q->member to set 155⟩
            }
            { T u = t; t = s; s = u; }
            { ⟨for each member q in t 154⟩
                if (!Set_member(s, q->member))
                    ⟨add q->member to set 155⟩
            }
            return set;
        }
    }
```

More efficient implementations of these four operations are possible;
some of them are explored in the exercises. A special case, which might

be important for some applications, is when the hash tables in s and t are the same size; see Exercise 9.7.

Further Reading

The sets exported by Set are modeled on the sets in Icon (Griswold and Griswold 1990), and the implementation is similar to Icon's (Griswold and Griswold 1986). Bit vectors are often used to represent sets with fixed, small universes; Chapter 13 describes an interface that uses this approach.

Icon is one of the few languages that have sets as a built-in data type. Sets are the central data type in SETL, and most of its operators and control structures are designed to manipulate sets.

Exercises

9.1 Implement Set using Table.

9.2 Implement Table using Set.

9.3 The implementations of Set and Table have much in common. Design and implement a third interface that distills their common properties. The purpose of this interface is to support the implementations of ADTs like sets and tables. Reimplement Set and Table using your new interface.

9.4 Design an interface for *bags*. A bag is like a set but members can appear more than once; for example, { 1 2 3 } is a set of integers, and { 1 1 2 2 3 } is a bag of integers. Implement your interface using the support interface designed in the previous exercise.

9.5 copy makes a copy of its set argument one member at a time. Since it knows the number of members in the copy, it could allocate all of the member structures at once and then dole them out to the appropriate hash chains as it fills in the copy. Implement this scheme and measure its benefits.

9.6 Some of the set operations might be made more efficient by storing the hash numbers in the member structures so that hash is called only once for each member, and the comparison functions are called only when the hash numbers are equal. Analyze the expected savings of this improvement and, if it looks worthwhile, implement it and measure the results.

9.7 When s and t have the same number of buckets, s + t is equal to the union of the subsets whose members are those on the same hash chain. That is, each hash chain in s + t is the union of the elements in the corresponding hash chains of s and t. This occurs frequently because many applications specify the same hint whenever they call Set_new. Change the implementations of s + t, s * t, s − t, and s / t to detect this case and use the appropriate simpler, more efficient implementation.

9.8 If an identifier appears on several consecutive lines, xref emits each line number. For example:

```
c        getword.c: 7 8 9 10 11 16 19 22 27 34 35
```

Modify xref.c so that it replaces two or more consecutive line numbers by a line range:

```
c        getword.c: 7-11 16 19 22 27 34-35
```

9.9 xref allocates a lot of memory, but deallocates only the arrays created by Table_toArray. Change xref so that it eventually deallocates everything it allocates (except the atoms, of course). It's easiest to do so incrementally as the data structure is being printed. Use the solution to Exercise 5.5 to check that you've deallocated everything.

9.10 Explain why cmpint and intcmp use explicit comparisons to compare integers instead of returning the result of subtracting them. That is, what's wrong with the following — apparently much simpler — version of cmpint?

```
int cmpint(const void *x, const void *y) {
    return **(int **)x - **(int **)y;
}
```

10

DYNAMIC ARRAYS

An *array* is a homogenous sequence of values in which the elements in the sequence are associated one-to-one with indices in a contiguous range. Arrays in some form appear as built-in data types in virtually all programming languages. In some languages, like C, all array indices have the same lower bounds, and in other languages, like Modula-3, each array can have its own bounds. In C, all arrays have indices that start at zero.

Array sizes are specified at either compile time or runtime. The sizes of *static* arrays are known at compile time. In C, for example, declared arrays must have sizes known at compile time; that is, in the declaration int a[n], n must be constant expression. A static array may be allocated at runtime; for example, local arrays are allocated at runtime when the function in which they appear is called, but their sizes are known at compile time.

The arrays returned by functions like Table_toArray are *dynamic* arrays because space for them is allocated by calling malloc or an equivalent allocation function. So, their sizes can be determined at runtime. Some languages, such as Modula-3, have linquistic support for dynamic arrays. In C, however, they must be constructed explicitly as illustrated by functions like Table_toArray.

The various toArray functions show just how useful dynamic arrays are; the Array ADT described in this chapter provides a similar but more general facility. It exports functions that allocate and deallocate dynamic arrays, access them with bounds checks, and expand or contract them to hold more or fewer elements.

This chapter also describes the ArrayRep interface. It reveals the representation for dynamic arrays for those few clients that need more efficient access to the array elements. Together, Array and ArrayRep illustrate a *two-level interface* or a *layered interface*. Array specifies a high-level view of an array ADT, and ArrayRep specifies another, more detailed view of the ADT at a lower level. The advantage of this organization is that importing ArrayRep clearly identifies those clients that depend on the representation of dynamic arrays. Changes to the representation thus affect only them, not the presumably much larger population of clients that import Array.

10.1 Interfaces

The Array ADT

⟨*array.h*⟩≡
```
#ifndef ARRAY_INCLUDED
#define ARRAY_INCLUDED

#define T Array_T
typedef struct T *T;
```
⟨*exported functions* 162⟩
```
#undef T
#endif
```

exports functions that operate on an array of N elements accessed by indices zero through $N-1$. Each element in a particular array is a fixed size, but different arrays can have elements of different sizes. Array_Ts are allocated and deallocated by

⟨*exported functions* 162⟩≡
```
extern T    Array_new (int length, int size);
extern void Array_free(T *array);
```

Array_new allocates, initializes, and returns a new array of length elements with bounds zero through length–1, unless length is zero, in which case the array has no elements. Each element occupies size bytes. The bytes in each element are initialized to zero. size must include any padding that may be required for alignment, so that the actual array can be created by allocating length·size bytes when length is positive. It is a checked runtime error for `length` to be negative or for `size` to be nonpositive, and `Array_new` can raise `Mem_Failed`.

    `Array_free` deallocates and clears `*array`. It is a checked runtime error for `array` or `*array` to be null.

    Unlike most of the other ADTs in this book, which build structures of void pointers, the `Array` interface places no restrictions on the values of the elements; each element is just a sequence of `size` bytes. The rationale for this design is that `Array_Ts` are used most often to build other ADTs; the sequences described in Chapter 11 are an example.

    The functions

⟨*exported functions* 162⟩+≡
```
extern int Array_length(T array);
extern int Array_size  (T array);
```

return the number of elements in `array` and their size.

    Array elements are accessed by

⟨*exported functions* 162⟩+≡
```
extern void *Array_get(T array, int i);
extern void *Array_put(T array, int i, void *elem);
```

`Array_get` returns a pointer to element number `i`; it's analogous to `&a[i]` when `a` is a declared C array. Clients access the value of the element by dereferencing the pointer returned by `Array_get`. `Array_put` overwrites the value of element `i` with the new element pointed to by `elem`. Unlike `Table_put`, `Array_put` returns `elem`. It can't return the previous value of element `i` because the elements are not necessarily pointers, and they can be any number of bytes long.

    It is a checked runtime error for `i` to be greater than or equal to the length of `array`, or for `elem` to be null. It is an unchecked runtime error to call `Array_get` and then change the size of `array` via `Array_resize` *before* dereferencing the pointer returned by `Array_get`. It is also an unchecked runtime error for the storage beginning at `elem` to overlap in any way with the storage of `array`'s `i`th element.

⟨*exported functions* 162⟩+≡
```
extern void Array_resize(T array, int length);
extern T    Array_copy  (T array, int length);
```

Array_resize changes the size of array so that it holds length elements, expanding or contracting it as necessary. If length exceeds the current length of the array, the new elements are initialized to zero. Calling Array_resize invalidates any values returned by previous calls to Array_get. Array_copy is similar, but returns a copy of array that holds its first length elements. If length exceeds the number of elements in array, the excess elements in the copy are initialized to zero. Array_resize and Array_copy can raise Mem_Failed.

Array has no functions like Table_map and Table_toArray because Array_get provides the machinery necessary to perform the equivalent operations.

It is a checked runtime error to pass a null T to any function in this interface.

The ArrayRep interface reveals that an Array_T is represented by a pointer to a *descriptor* — a structure whose fields give the number of elements in the array, the size of the elements, and a pointer to the storage for the array.

⟨*arrayrep.h*⟩≡
```
#ifndef ARRAYREP_INCLUDED
#define ARRAYREP_INCLUDED

#define T Array_T

struct T {
    int length;
    int size;
    char *array;
};

extern void ArrayRep_init(T array, int length,
    int size, void *ary);

#undef T
#endif
```

Figure 10.1 shows the descriptor for an array of 100 integers returned by Array_new(100, sizeof int) on a machine with four-byte integers. If the array has no elements, the array field is null. Array descriptors are sometimes called *dope vectors*.

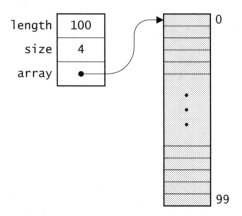

Figure 10.1 The `Array_T` created by `Array_new(100, sizeof int)`

Clients of `ArrayRep` may read the fields of a descriptor but may not write them; writing them is an unchecked runtime error. `ArrayRep` guarantees that if `array` is a T and `i` is nonnegative and less than `array->length`,

```
array->array + i*array->size
```

is the address of element `i`.

`ArrayRep` also exports `ArrayRep_init`, which initializes the fields in the `Array_T` structure pointed to by `array` to the values of the arguments `length`, `size`, and `ary`. This function is provided so that clients can initialize `Array_T`s they've embedded in other structures. It is a checked runtime error for `array` to be null, `size` to be nonpositive, `length` to be nonzero, and `ary` to be null; also for `length` to be nonpositive and `ary` to be nonnull. It is an unchecked runtime error to initialize a T structure by means other than calling `ArrayRep_init`.

10.2 Implementation

A single implementation exports both the `Array` and `ArrayRep` interfaces:

⟨*array.c*⟩≡
```
#include <stdlib.h>
#include <string.h>
#include "assert.h"
#include "array.h"
#include "arrayrep.h"
#include "mem.h"

#define T Array_T

⟨functions 166⟩
```

Array_new allocates space for a descriptor and for the array itself if length is positive, and calls ArrayRep_init to initialize the descriptor's fields:

⟨*functions* 166⟩≡
```
T Array_new(int length, int size) {
    T array;

    NEW(array);
    if (length > 0)
        ArrayRep_init(array, length, size,
            CALLOC(length, size));
    else
        ArrayRep_init(array, length, size, NULL);
    return array;
}
```

ArrayRep_init is the only valid way to initialize the fields of descriptors; clients that allocate descriptors by other means must call ArrayRep_init to initialize them.

⟨*functions* 166⟩+≡
```
void ArrayRep_init(T array, int length, int size,
    void *ary) {
    assert(array);
    assert(ary && length>0 || length==0 && ary==NULL);
    assert(size > 0);
    array->length = length;
    array->size   = size;
```

```
        if (length > 0)
            array->array = ary;
        else
            array->array = NULL;
    }
```

Calling `ArrayRep_init` to initialize a T structure helps reduce coupling:
These calls clearly identify clients that allocate descriptors themselves
and thus depend on the representation. It's possible to add fields without affecting these clients as long as `ArrayRep_init` doesn't change.
This scenario would occur, for example, if a field for an identifying serial
number were added to the T structure, and this field were initialized
automatically by `ArrayRep_init`.

   `Array_free` deallocates the array itself and the T structure, and clears
its argument:

⟨*functions* 166⟩+≡
```
    void Array_free(T *array) {
        assert(array && *array);
        FREE((*array)->array);
        FREE(*array);
    }
```

`Array_free` doesn't have to check if `(*array)->array` is null because
FREE accepts null pointers.

   `Array_get` and `Array_put` fetch and store elements in an Array_T:

⟨*functions* 166⟩+≡
```
    void *Array_get(T array, int i) {
        assert(array);
        assert(i >= 0 && i < array->length);
        return array->array + i*array->size;
    }

    void *Array_put(T array, int i, void *elem) {
        assert(array);
        assert(i >= 0 && i < array->length);
        assert(elem);
        memcpy(array->array + i*array->size, elem,
            array->size);
```

```
        return elem;
    }
```

Notice that `Array_put` returns its third argument, *not* the address of the array element into which those bytes were just stored.

Array_length and Array_size return the similarly named descriptor fields:

⟨*functions* 166⟩+≡
```
   int Array_length(T array) {
       assert(array);
       return array->length;
   }

   int Array_size(T array) {
       assert(array);
       return array->size;
   }
```

Clients of `ArrayRep` may access these fields directly from the descriptor.

Array_resize calls Mem's RESIZE to change the number of elements in the array, and changes the array's length field accordingly.

⟨*functions* 166⟩+≡
```
   void Array_resize(T array, int length) {
       assert(array);
       assert(length >= 0);
       if (length > 0)
           RESIZE(array->array, length*array->size);
       else
           FREE(array->array);
       array->length = length;
   }
```

Unlike with Mem's RESIZE, a new length of zero is legal, in which case the array is deallocated, and henceforth the descriptor describes an empty dynamic array.

Array_copy is much like Array_resize, except that it copies array's descriptor and part or all of its array:

⟨*functions* 166⟩+≡
```
  T Array_copy(T array, int length) {
      T copy;

      assert(array);
      assert(length >= 0);
      copy = Array_new(length, array->size);
      if (copy->length > array->length
      && array->length > 0)
          memcpy(copy->array, array->array, array->length);
      else if (array->length > copy->length
      && copy->length > 0)
          memcpy(copy->array, array->array, copy->length);
      return copy;
  }
```

Further Reading

Some languages support variants of dynamic arrays. Modula-3 (Nelson 1991), for example, permits arrays with arbitrary bounds to be created during execution, but they can't be expanded or contracted. Lists in Icon (Griswold and Griswold 1990) are like dynamic arrays that can be expanded or contracted by adding or deleting elements from either end; these are much like the sequences described in the next chapter. Icon also supports fetching sublists from a list and replacing a sublist with a list of a different size.

Exercises

10.1 Design and implement an ADT that provides dynamic arrays of pointers. It should provide "safe" access to the elements of these arrays via functions similar in spirit to the functions provided by Table. Use Array or Array_Rep in your implementation.

10.2 Design an ADT for dynamic matrices — arrays with two dimensions — and implement it using Array. Can you generalize your design to arrays of N dimensions?

10.3 Design an implement and ADT for *sparse* dynamic arrays — arrays in which most of the elements are zero. Your design should accept an array-specific value for zero and the implementation should store only those elements that are not equal to zero.

10.4 Add the function

```
extern void Array_reshape(T array, int length,
    int size);
```

to the `Array` interface and its implementation. `Array_reshape` changes the number of elements in `array` and the size of each element to `length` and `size`, respectively. Like `Array_resize`, the reshaped array retains the first `length` elements of the original array; if `length` exceeds the original length, the excess elements are set to zero. The *i*th element in `array` becomes the *i*th element in the reshaped array. If `size` is less than the original size, each element is truncated; if `size` exceeds the original size, the excess bytes are set to zero.

11

SEQUENCES

A *sequence* holds N values associated with the integer indices zero through $N{-}1$ when N is positive. An empty sequence holds no values. Like arrays, values in a sequence may be accessed by indexing; they can also be added to or removed from either end of a sequence. Sequences expand automatically as necessary to accommodate their contents. Values are pointers.

Sequences are one of the most useful ADTs in this book. Despite their relatively simple specification, they can be used as arrays, lists, stacks, queues, and deques, and they often subsume the facilities of separate ADTs for these data structures. A sequence can be viewed as a more abstract version of the dynamic array described in the previous chapter. A sequence hides bookkeeping and resizing details in its implementation.

11.1 Interface

A sequence is an instance of the opaque pointer type defined in the Seq interface:

⟨*seq.h*⟩≡
```
#ifndef SEQ_INCLUDED
#define SEQ_INCLUDED

#define T Seq_T
typedef struct T *T;
```

171

⟨*exported functions* 172⟩

```
#undef T
#endif
```

It is a checked runtime error to pass a null T to any routine in this interface.

Sequences are created by the functions

⟨*exported functions* 172⟩≡
```
extern T Seq_new(int hint);
extern T Seq_seq(void *x, ...);
```

Seq_new creates and returns an empty sequence. hint is an estimate of the maximum number of values the new sequence will hold. If that number is unknown, a hint of zero creates a small sequence. Sequences expand as necessary to hold their contents regardless of the value of hint. It is a checked runtime error for hint to be negative.

Seq_seq creates and returns a sequence whose values are initialized to its nonnull pointer arguments. The argument list is terminated by the first null pointer. Thus

```
Seq_T names;
...
names = Seq_seq("C", "ML", "C++", "Icon", "AWK", NULL);
```

creates a sequence with five values and assigns it to names. The values in the argument list are associated with the indices zero through four. The pointers passed in the variable part of Seq_seq's argument list are assumed to be void pointers, so programmers must provide casts when passing other than char or void pointers; see page 105. Seq_new and Seq_seq can raise Mem_Failed.

⟨*exported functions* 172⟩+≡
```
extern void Seq_free(T *seq);
```

deallocates the sequence *seq and clears *seq. It is a checked runtime error for seq or *seq to be null pointers.

⟨*exported functions* 172⟩+≡
```
extern int Seq_length(T seq);
```

returns the number of values in the sequence seq.

The values in an *N*-value sequence are associated with the integer indices zero through *N*–1. These values are accessed by the functions

⟨*exported functions* 172⟩+≡
```
extern void *Seq_get(T seq, int i);
extern void *Seq_put(T seq, int i, void *x);
```

Seq_get returns the ith value in seq. Seq_put changes the ith value to x and returns the previous value. It is a checked runtime error for i to be equal to or greater than *N*. Seq_get and Seq_put access the ith value in constant time.

A sequence is expanded by adding values to either end:

⟨*exported functions* 172⟩+≡
```
extern void *Seq_addlo(T seq, void *x);
extern void *Seq_addhi(T seq, void *x);
```

Seq_addlo adds x to the low end of seq and returns x. Adding a value to the beginning of a sequence increments both the indices of the existing values and the length of the sequence by one. Seq_addhi adds x to the high end of seq and returns x. Adding a value to the end of a sequence increments the length of the sequence by one. Seq_addlo and Seq_addhi can raise Mem_Failed.

Similarly, a sequence is contracted by removing values from either end:

⟨*exported functions* 172⟩+≡
```
extern void *Seq_remlo(T seq);
extern void *Seq_remhi(T seq);
```

Seq_remlo removes and returns the value at the low end of seq. Removing the value at the beginning of a sequence decrements both the indices of the remaining values and the length of the sequence by one. Seq_remhi removes and returns the value at the high end of seq. Removing the value at the end of a sequence decrements the length of the sequence by one. It is a checked runtime error to pass an empty sequence to Seq_remlo or Seq_remhi.

11.2 Implementation

As suggested at the beginning of this chapter, a sequence is a high-level abstraction of a dynamic array. Its representation thus includes a dynamic array — not a pointer to an Array_T, but an Array_T structure itself — and its implementation imports both Array and ArrayRep:

⟨*seq.c*⟩≡
```
#include <stdlib.h>
#include <stdarg.h>
#include <string.h>
#include "assert.h"
#include "seq.h"
#include "array.h"
#include "arrayrep.h"
#include "mem.h"

#define T Seq_T

struct T {
    struct Array_T array;
    int length;
    int head;
};
```

⟨*static functions* 179⟩
⟨*functions* 175⟩

The length field holds the number of values in the sequence and the array field holds the array in which the values are stored. This array always has at least length elements, but some of them are unused when length is less than array.length. The array is used as a circular buffer to hold the sequence values. The zeroth value of the sequence is stored in element number head of the array, and successive values are stored in successive elements modulo the array size. That is, if the ith value in the sequence is stored in element number array.length−1, the i+1st value is stored in element zero of the array. Figure 11.1 shows one way in which a seven-value sequence can be stored in a 16-element array. The box on the left is the Seq_T with its embedded Array_T, shown lightly

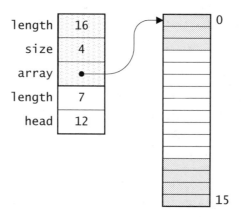

Figure 11.1 A 16-element sequence

shaded. The box on the right is the array; its shading shows the elements occupied by values in the sequence.

As detailed below, values are added to the beginning of the sequence by decrementing head modulo the array size, and they are removed from the beginning by incrementing head modulo the array size. A sequence always has an array even when it's empty.

A new sequence is created by allocating a dynamic array that can hold hint pointers, or 16 pointers if hint is zero:

⟨*functions* 175⟩≡
```
T Seq_new(int hint) {
    T seq;

    assert(hint >= 0);
    NEW0(seq);
    if (hint == 0)
        hint = 16;
    ArrayRep_init(&seq->array, hint, sizeof (void *),
        ALLOC(hint*sizeof (void *)));
    return seq;
}
```

Using NEW0 initializes the length and head fields to zero. Seq_seq calls Seq_new to create an empty sequence, then crawls through its arguments calling Seq_addhi to append each one to the new sequence:

⟨*functions* 175⟩+≡
```
T Seq_seq(void *x, ...) {
    va_list ap;
    T seq = Seq_new(0);

    va_start(ap, x);
    for ( ; x; x = va_arg(ap, void *))
        Seq_addhi(seq, x);
    va_end(ap);
    return seq;
}
```

Seq_seq uses the macros for handling variable length argument lists much as List_list does; see page 108.

Deallocating a sequence can be done by Array_free, which deallocates the array and its descriptor:

⟨*functions* 175⟩+≡
```
void Seq_free(T *seq) {
    assert(seq && *seq);
    assert((void *)*seq == (void *)&(*seq)->array);
    Array_free((Array_T *)seq);
}
```

The call to Array_free works only because the address of *seq is equal to &(*seq)->array as asserted in the code. That is, the Array_T structure must be the *first* field of the Seq_T structure so that the pointer returned by NEW0 in Seq_new is a pointer both to a Seq_T and to an Array_T.

Seq_length simply returns the sequence's length field:

⟨*functions* 175⟩+≡
```
int Seq_length(T seq) {
    assert(seq);
    return seq->length;
}
```

The ith value in a sequence is stored in the (head + i) mod array.length element of its array. A type cast makes it possible to index the array directly:

⟨seq[i] 177⟩≡
```
((void **)seq->array.array)[
    (seq->head + i)%seq->array.length]
```

Seq_get simply returns this array element, and Seq_put sets it to x:

⟨*functions* 175⟩+≡
```
void *Seq_get(T seq, int i) {
    assert(seq);
    assert(i >= 0 && i < seq->length);
    return ⟨seq[i] 177⟩;
}

void *Seq_put(T seq, int i, void *x) {
    void *prev;

    assert(seq);
    assert(i >= 0 && i < seq->length);
    prev = ⟨seq[i] 177⟩;
    ⟨seq[i] 177⟩ = x;
    return prev;
}
```

Seq_remlo and Seq_remhi remove values from a sequence.
Seq_remhi is the simpler of the two because it just decrements the
length field and returns the value indexed by the new value of length:

⟨*functions* 175⟩+≡
```
void *Seq_remhi(T seq) {
    int i;

    assert(seq);
    assert(seq->length > 0);
    i = --seq->length;
    return ⟨seq[i] 177⟩;
}
```

Seq_remlo is slightly more complicated because it must return the value
indexed by head (which is the value at index zero in the sequence), increment head modulo the array size, and decrement length:

⟨*functions* 175⟩+≡
```
void *Seq_remlo(T seq) {
    int i = 0;
    void *x;

    assert(seq);
    assert(seq->length > 0);
    x = ⟨seq[i] 177⟩;
    seq->head = (seq->head + 1)%seq->array.length;
    --seq->length;
    return x;
}
```

Seq_addlo and Seq_addhi add values to a sequence and thus must cope with the possibility that its array is full, which occurs when length is equal to array.length. When this condition occurs, both functions call expand to enlarge the array; it does this by calling Array_resize. Seq_addhi is again the simpler of the two functions because, after checking for expansion, it stores the new value at the index given by length and increments length:

⟨*functions* 175⟩+≡
```
void *Seq_addhi(T seq, void *x) {
    int i;

    assert(seq);
    if (seq->length == seq->array.length)
        expand(seq);
    i = seq->length++;
    return ⟨seq[i] 177⟩ = x;
}
```

Seq_addlo also checks for expansion, but then decrements head modulo the array size and stores x in the array element indexed by the new value of head, which is the value at index zero in the sequence:

⟨*functions* 175⟩+≡
```
void *Seq_addlo(T seq, void *x) {
    int i = 0;
```

```
        assert(seq);
        if (seq->length == seq->array.length)
            expand(seq);
        if (--seq->head < 0)
            seq->head = seq->array.length - 1;
        seq->length++;
        return ⟨seq[i] 177⟩ = x;
    }
```

Alternatively, Seq_addlo could decrement seq->head with

```
    seq->head = Arith_mod(seq->head - 1, seq->array.length);
```

expand encapsulates a call to Array_resize that doubles the size of a
sequence's array:

⟨*static functions* 179⟩≡
```
    static void expand(T seq) {
        int n = seq->array.length;

        Array_resize(&seq->array, 2*n);
        if (seq->head > 0)
            ⟨slide tail down 179⟩
    }
```

As this code suggests, expand must also cope with the use of the array
as a circular buffer. Unless head just happens to be zero, the elements at
the tail end of the original array — from head down — must be moved to
the end of enlarged array to open up the middle, as illustrated in Figure
11.2, and head must be adjusted accordingly:

⟨*slide tail down* 179⟩≡
```
    {
        void **old = &((void **)seq->array.array)[seq->head];
        memcpy(old+n, old, (n - seq->head)*sizeof (void *));
        seq->head += n;
    }
```

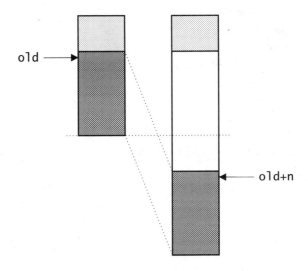

Figure 11.2 Expanding a sequence

Further Reading

Sequences are nearly identical to lists in Icon (Griswold and Griswold 1990), but the names of the operations are taken from the `Sequence` interface in the library that accompanies the DEC implementation of Modula-3 (Horning, et al. 1993). The implementation described in this chapter is also similar to the DEC implementation. Exercise 11.1 explores the Icon implementation.

Exercises

11.1 Icon implements lists — its version of sequences — with a doubly linked list of chunks where each chunk holds, say, M values. This representation avoids the use of `Array_resize` because new chunks can be added to either end of the list as necessary to satisfy calls to `Seq_addlo` and `Seq_addhi`. The disadvantage of this representation is that the chunks must be traversed to access the ith value, which takes time proportional to i/M. Use this representation to build a new implementation for `Seq` and develop some test programs to measure its performance. Suppose that an access to value i is almost always followed by an access to value i−1 or i+1; can you modify your implementation to make this case run in constant time?

11.2 Devise an implementation for Seq that doesn't use Array_resize. For example, when the original array of N elements fills up, it could be converted to an array of pointers to arrays, each of which holds, say, $2N$ elements, so the converted sequence can hold $2N^2$ values. If N is 1,024, the converted sequence can hold over two million elements, each of which can be accessed in constant time. Each of the $2N$-element arrays in this "edge-vector" representation can be allocated lazily, that is, only after a value is stored in it.

11.3 Suppose you forbid Seq_addlo and Seq_remlo; devise an implementation that allocates space incrementally but can access any element in logarithmic time. Hint: Skip lists (Pugh 1990).

11.4 Sequences are expanded but never contracted. Modify Seq->remlo and Seq->remhi so that they contract a sequence whenever more than half of its array is unused; that is, when seq->length becomes less than seq->array.length/2. When is this modification a *bad* idea? Hint: thrashing.

11.5 Implement xref again using sequences instead of sets to hold the line numbers. Since the files are read sequentially, you won't have to sort the line numbers because they will appear in the sequences in increasing order.

11.6 Rewrite Seq_free so that the assertion it now uses is unnecessary. Be careful — you cannot use Array_free.

12

RINGS

A *ring* is much like a sequence: It holds N values associated with the integer indices zero through $N-1$ when N is positive. An empty ring holds no values. Values are pointers. Like the values in a sequence, values in a ring may be accessed by indexing.

Unlike to a sequence, however, values can be added to a ring *any-where*, and *any* value in a ring can be removed. In addition, the values can be renumbered: "rotating" a ring left decrements the index of each value by one modulo the length of the ring; rotating it right increments the indices by one modulo the ring length. The price for the flexibility of adding values to and removing values from arbitrary locations in a ring is that accessing the ith value is not guaranteed to take constant time.

12.1 Interface

As suggested by its name, a ring is an abstraction of a doubly linked list, but the Ring ADT reveals only that a ring is an instance of an opaque pointer type:

⟨*ring.h*⟩≡
```
#ifndef RING_INCLUDED
#define RING_INCLUDED

#define T Ring_T
typedef struct T *T;
```

⟨*exported functions* 184⟩

```
#undef T
#endif
```

It is a checked runtime error to pass a null T to any routine in this interface.

Rings are created by the functions that parallel similar functions in the Seq interface:

⟨*exported functions* 184⟩≡
```
extern T Ring_new (void);
extern T Ring_ring(void *x, ...);
```

Ring_new creates and returns an empty ring. Ring_ring creates and returns a ring whose values are initialized to its nonnull pointer arguments. The argument list is terminated by the first null pointer argument. Thus

```
Ring_T names;
...
names = Ring_seq("Lists", "Tables", "Sets", "Sequences",
    "Rings", NULL);
```

creates a ring with the five values shown, and assigns it to names. The values in the argument list are associated with the indices zero through four. The pointers passed in the variable part of the ring's argument list are assumed to be void pointers, so programmers must provide casts when passing other than char or void pointers; see page 105. Ring_new and Ring_ring can raise Mem_Failed.

⟨*exported functions* 184⟩+≡
```
extern void Ring_free  (T *ring);
extern int  Ring_length(T  ring);
```

Ring_free deallocates the ring in *ring and clears *ring. It is a checked runtime error for ring or *ring to be null pointers. Ring_length returns the number of values in ring.

The values in a ring of length N are associated with the integer indices zero through N–1. These values are accessed by the functions

⟨*exported functions* 184⟩+≡
```
extern void *Ring_get(T ring, int i);
extern void *Ring_put(T ring, int i, void *x);
```

Ring_get returns the ith value in ring. Ring_put changes the ith value in ring to x and returns the previous value. It is a checked runtime error for i to be equal to or greater than *N*.

Values may be added anywhere in a ring by

⟨*exported functions* 184⟩+≡
```
extern void *Ring_add(T ring, int pos, void *x);
```

Ring_add adds x to ring at position pos and returns x. The positions in a ring with *N* values specify locations *between* values as depicted in the following diagram, which shows a five-element ring holding the integers zero through four.

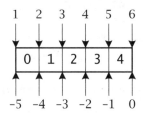

The middle row of numbers are the indices, the top row are the positive positions, and the bottom row are the nonpositive positions. The nonpositive positions specify locations from the end of the ring without knowing its length. The positions zero and one are also valid for empty rings. Ring_add accepts either form of position. It is a checked runtime error to specify a nonexistent position, which inlcudes the positive positions than exceed one plus the length of the ring and the negative positions whose absolute values exceed the length of the ring.

Adding a new value increments both the indices of the values to its right and the length of the ring by one. Ring_add can raise Mem_Failed.

The functions

⟨*exported functions* 184⟩+≡
```
extern void *Ring_addlo(T ring, void *x);
extern void *Ring_addhi(T ring, void *x);
```

are equivalent to their similarly named counterparts in the Seq interface. Ring_addlo is equivalent to Ring_add(ring, 1, x), and Ring_addhi is equivalent to Ring_add(ring, 0, x). Ring_addlo and Ring_addhi can raise Mem_Failed.

The function

⟨*exported functions* 184⟩+≡
```
extern void *Ring_remove(T ring, int i);
```

removes and returns the ith value in ring. Removing a value decrements the indices of the remaining values to its right by one and the length of the ring by one. It is a checked runtime error for i to be equal to or exceed the length of ring.

Like the Seq functions with similar names, the functions

⟨*exported functions* 184⟩+≡
```
extern void *Ring_remlo(T ring);
extern void *Ring_remhi(T ring);
```

remove and return the value at the low or high end of ring. Ring_remlo is equivalent to Ring_remove(ring, 0), and Ring_remhi is equivalent to Ring_remove(ring, Ring_length(ring) - 1). It is a checked runtime error to pass an empty ring to Ring_remlo or Ring_remhi.

The name "ring" comes from the function

⟨*exported functions* 184⟩+≡
```
extern void Ring_rotate(T ring, int n);
```

which renumbers the values in ring by "rotating" it left or right. If n is positive, ring is rotated to the right — clockwise — n values, and the indices of each value are incremented by n modulo the length of ring. Rotating an eight-value ring that holds the strings A through H three places to the right is illustrated by the following diagram; the arrows point to the first element.

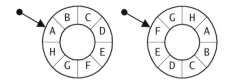

If n is negative, ring is rotated to the left — counterclockwise — n values and the indices of each value are decremented by n modulo the length of ring. If n modulo the length of the ring is zero, Ring_rotate has no effect. It is a checked runtime error for the absolute value of n to exceed the length of ring.

12.2 Implementation

The implementation represents a ring as a structure with two fields:

⟨*ring.c*⟩≡
```
#include <stdlib.h>
#include <stdarg.h>
#include <string.h>
#include "assert.h"
#include "ring.h"
#include "mem.h"

#define T Ring_T

struct T {
    struct node {
        struct node *llink, *rlink;
        void *value;
    } *head;
    int length;
};
```

⟨*functions* 188⟩

The head field points to a doubly linked list of node structures in which the value fields hold the values in the ring. head points to the value associated with index zero; successive values are in the nodes linked by the rlink fields, and each node's llink field points to its predecessor. Figure 12.1 shows the structures for a ring with six values. The dotted lines emanate from the llink fields and go counterclockwise, and the solid lines emanate from the rlink fields and go clockwise.

An empty ring has a zero length field and a null head field, which is what Ring_new returns:

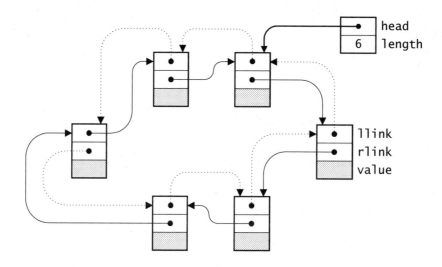

Figure 12.1 A six-element ring

⟨*functions* 188⟩≡
```
T Ring_new(void) {
    T ring;

    NEW0(ring);
    ring->head = NULL;
    return ring;
}
```

Ring_ring creates an empty ring, then calls Ring_addhi to append each of its pointer arguments up to but not including the first null pointer:

⟨*functions* 188⟩+≡
```
T Ring_ring(void *x, ...) {
    va_list ap;
    T ring = Ring_new();

    va_start(ap, x);
    for ( ; x; x = va_arg(ap, void *))
        Ring_addhi(ring, x);
    va_end(ap);
    return ring;
}
```

Deallocating a ring first deallocates the node structures, then deallocates the ring header. It doesn't matter in which order the nodes are deallocated, so Ring_free just follows the rlink pointers.

⟨*functions* 188⟩+≡
```
void Ring_free(T *ring) {
    struct node *p, *q;

    assert(ring && *ring);
    if ((p = (*ring)->head) != NULL) {
        int n = (*ring)->length;
        for ( ; n-- > 0; p = q) {
            q = p->rlink;
            FREE(p);
        }
    }
    FREE(*ring);
}
```

The function

⟨*functions* 188⟩+≡
```
int Ring_length(T ring) {
    assert(ring);
    return ring->length;
}
```

returns the number of values in a ring.

Ring_get and Ring_put must both find the ith value in a ring. Doing this amounts to traversing the list to the ith node structure, which is accomplished by the following chunk.

⟨q ← i*th node* 189⟩≡
```
{
    int n;
    q = ring->head;
    if (i <= ring->length/2)
        for (n = i; n-- > 0; )
            q = q->rlink;
    else
        for (n = ring->length - i; n-- > 0; )
```

```
        q = q->llink;
   }
```

This code takes the shortest route to the ith node: If i is does not exceed one-half the ring's length, the first for loop goes clockwise via the rlink pointers to the desired node. Otherwise, the second for loop goes counterclockwise via the llink pointers. In Figure 12.1, for example, values 0 through 3 are reached by going right, and values 4 and 5 are reached by going left.

Given this chunk, the two access functions are easy:

⟨*functions* 188⟩+≡
```
   void *Ring_get(T ring, int i) {
       struct node *q;

       assert(ring);
       assert(i >= 0 && i < ring->length);
       ⟨q ← ith node 189⟩
       return q->value;
   }

   void *Ring_put(T ring, int i, void *x) {
       struct node *q;
       void *prev;

       assert(ring);
       assert(i >= 0 && i < ring->length);
       ⟨q ← ith node 189⟩
       prev = q->value;
       q->value = x;
       return prev;
   }
```

The functions that add values to a ring must allocate a node, initialize it, and insert it into its proper place in the doubly linked list. They must also cope with adding a node to an empty ring. Ring_addhi is the easiest one of these functions: It adds a new node to the left of the node pointed to by head, as shown in Figure 12.2. Shading distinguishes the new node, and the heavier lines in the righthand figure indicate which links are changed. Here's the code:

⟨*functions* 188⟩+≡
```
  void *Ring_addhi(T ring, void *x) {
      struct node *p, *q;

      assert(ring);
      NEW(p);
      if ((q = ring->head) != NULL)
          ⟨insert p to the left of q 191⟩
      else
          ⟨make p ring's only value 191⟩
      ring->length++;
      return p->value = x;
  }
```

Adding a value to an empty ring is easy: `ring->head` points to the new node, and the node's links point to the node itself.

⟨*make* p *ring's only value* 191⟩≡
```
  ring->head = p->llink = p->rlink = p;
```

As suggested in Figure 12.2, `Ring_addhi` aims q at the first node in the ring and inserts the new node to its left. This insertion involves initializing the links of the new node and redirecting q's `llink` and q's predecessor's `rlink`:

⟨*insert* p *to the left of* q 191⟩≡
```
  {
      p->llink = q->llink;
      q->llink->rlink = p;
```

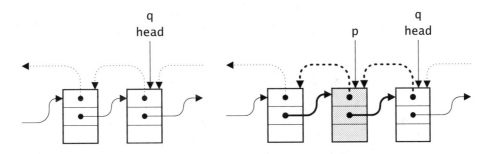

Figure 12.2 Inserting a new node to the left of head

```
        p->rlink = q;
        q->llink = p;
    }
```

The second through fifth diagrams in the Figure 12.3's sequence illustrate the individual effect of these four statements. At each step, heavy arcs show the new links. It's instructive to redraw this sequence when q points to the only node in the doubly linked list.

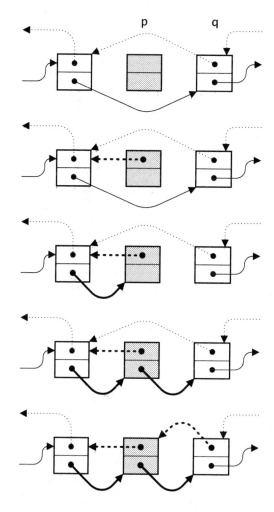

Figure 12.3 Inserting a new node to the left of q

Ring_addlo is almost as easy, but the new node becomes the *first* node in the ring. This transformation can be accomplished by calling Ring_addhi then rotating the ring one value to the right, which is done by setting head to its predecessor:

⟨*functions* 188⟩+≡
```
void *Ring_addlo(T ring, void *x) {
    assert(ring);
    Ring_addhi(ring, x);
    ring->head = ring->head->llink;
    return x;
}
```

Ring_add is the most complicated of the three functions that add values to a ring because it deals with the arbitrary positions described in the previous section, which include adding values to either end of the ring. These cases can be handled by letting Ring_addlo and Ring_addhi deal with additions at the ends, which incidently takes care of the empty ring case, and, for the other cases, converts a position to the index of the value to the *right* of the position and adds the new node to its left, as above.

⟨*functions* 188⟩+≡
```
void *Ring_add(T ring, int pos, void *x) {
    assert(ring);
    assert(pos >= -ring->length && pos<=ring->length+1);
    if (pos == 1 || pos == -ring->length)
        return Ring_addlo(ring, x);
    else if (pos == 0 || pos == ring->length + 1)
        return Ring_addhi(ring, x);
    else {
        struct node *p, *q;
        int i = pos < 0 ? pos + ring->length : pos - 1;
        ⟨q ← ith node 189⟩
        NEW(p);
        ⟨insert p to the left of q 191⟩
        ring->length++;
        return p->value = x;
    }
}
```

The first two if statements cover positions that specify the ends of the ring. The initialization of i handles the positions that correspond to the indices one through ring->length - 1.

The three functions that remove values are easier than those that add values because there are fewer boundary conditions; the only one is when the last value in a ring is removed. Ring_remove is the most general of the three functions: It finds the ith node and removes it from the doubly linked list:

⟨*functions* 188⟩+≡
```
void *Ring_remove(T ring, int i) {
    void *x;
    struct node *q;

    assert(ring);
    assert(ring->length > 0);
    assert(i >= 0 && i < ring->length);
    ⟨q ← ith node 189⟩
    if (i == 0)
        ring->head = ring->head->rlink;
    x = q->value;
    ⟨delete node q 194⟩
    return x;
}
```

If i is zero, Ring_remove deletes the first node and thus must redirect head to the new first node.

Adding a node involves four pointer assignments; deleting one requires only two:

⟨*delete node* q 194⟩≡
```
q->llink->rlink = q->rlink;
q->rlink->llink = q->llink;
FREE(q);
if (--ring->length == 0)
    ring->head = NULL;
```

The second and third diagrams in Figure 12.4 illustrate the individual effect of the two statements at the beginning of this chunk. The affected links are shown with heavy arcs. The third statement in ⟨*delete node* q 194⟩ frees the node, and the last two statements decrement ring's

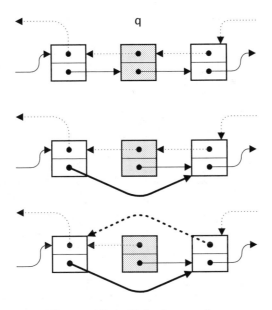

Figure 12.4 Deleting node q

length and clear its head pointer if its last node was just deleted. Again, it's instructive to draw the sequence for deleting a node from one- and two-node lists.

Ring_remhi is similar, but finding the doomed node is easier:

⟨*functions* 188⟩+≡
```
void *Ring_remhi(T ring) {
    void *x;
    struct node *q;

    assert(ring);
    assert(ring->length > 0);
    q = ring->head->llink;
    x = q->value;
    ⟨delete node q 194⟩
    return x;
}
```

As shown above, Ring_addlo is implemented by calling Ring_addhi and changing ring's head to point to its predecessor. The symmetric idiom implements `Ring_remlo`: Change `ring`'s `head` to point to its successor and call `Ring_remhi`.

⟨*functions* 188⟩+≡
```
void *Ring_remlo(T ring) {
    assert(ring);
    assert(ring->length > 0);
    ring->head = ring->head->rlink;
    return Ring_remhi(ring);
}
```

The last operation rotates a ring. If n is positive, an *N*-value ring is rotated clockwise, which means that the value with index n modulo *N* becomes its new `head`. If n is negative, the ring is rotated counterclockwise, which means its `head` moves to the value with index n + *N*.

⟨*functions* 188⟩+≡
```
void Ring_rotate(T ring, int n) {
    struct node *q;
    int i;

    assert(ring);
    assert(n >= -ring->length && n <= ring->length);
    if (n >= 0)
        i = n%ring->length;
    else
        i = n + ring->length;
    ⟨q ← ith node 189⟩
    ring->head = q;
}
```

Using ⟨q ← i*th node* 189⟩ here ensures that the rotation takes the shortest route.

Further Reading

Both Knuth (1973a) and Sedgewick (1990) cover the algorithms for manipulating doubly linked lists in detail.

Some of the operations provided in Icon for removing and adding values to a list are similar to those provided by `Ring`. Exercise 12.4 explores the Icon implementation. The scheme used in `Ring_add` for specifying positions is from Icon.

Exercises

12.1 Rewrite the loop in `Ring_free` to eliminate the variable n; use the list structure to determine when the loop ends.

12.2 Inspect the implementation of `Ring_rotate` carefully. Explain why the consequent of the second if statement must be written as `i = n + ring->length`.

12.3 The call `Ring_get(ring, i)` is often followed closely by another call, such as `Ring_get(ring, i + 1)`. Modify the implementation so that a ring remembers its most recently accessed index and the corresponding node, and use this information to avoid the loops in ⟨q ← *ith node* 189⟩ when possible. Don't forget to update this information when values are added or removed. Devise a test program for which measurements demonstrate the benefits of your improvement.

12.4 Icon implements lists, which are similar to rings, as doubly linked lists of arrays that each hold *N* values. These arrays are used as circular buffers, like the arrays in the `Seq` implementation. Finding the *i*th value walks down approximately *i/N* arrays in the ring's list and then computes the index into that array for the *i*th value. Adding a value either adds it to a vacant slot in an existing array or adds a new array. Removing a value vacates a slot in an array and, if it is the last one occupied in that array, removes the array from the list and deallocates it. This representation is more complicated than the one described in this chapter, but it performs better for large rings. Reimplement rings using this representation, and measure the performance of both implementations. How big must rings become before the improvement can be detected?

13

BIT VECTORS

The sets described in Chapter 9 can hold arbitrary elements because the elements are manipulated only by functions supplied by clients. Sets of integers are less flexible, but they're used often enough to warrant a separate ADT. The Bit interface exports functions that manipulate bit vectors, which can be used to represent sets of integers from zero to $N-1$. For example, 256-bit vectors can be used to represent sets of characters efficiently.

Bit provides most of the set-manipulation functions provided by Set, and also a few functions that are specific to bit vectors. Unlike the sets provided by Set, the sets represented by bit vectors have a well-defined universe, which is the set of integers in the range zero to $N-1$. Thus, Bit can provide functions that Set cannot, such as the complement of a set.

13.1 Interface

The name "bit vector" reveals that the representation for sets of integers is essentially a sequence of bits. Nevertheless, the Bit interface exports only an opaque type that represents a bit vector:

⟨*bit.h*⟩≡
```
#ifndef BIT_INCLUDED
#define BIT_INCLUDED

#define T Bit_T
typedef struct T *T;
```

⟨*exported functions* 200⟩

```
#undef T
#endif
```

The length of a bit vector is fixed when the vector is created by Bit_new:

⟨*exported functions* 200⟩≡
```
extern T   Bit_new   (int length);
extern int Bit_length(T set);
extern int Bit_count (T set);
```

Bit_new creates a new vector of length bits and sets all the bits to zero.
The vector represents the integers zero through length–1, inclusive. It is
a checked runtime error for length to be negative. Bit_new can raise
Mem_failed.
　　Bit_length returns the number of bits in set, and Bit_count
returns the number of ones in set.
　　It is a checked runtime error to pass a null T to any routine in this
interface, except for Bit_union, Bit_inter, Bit_minus, and Bit_diff.

⟨*exported functions* 200⟩+≡
```
extern void Bit_free(T *set);
```

frees *set and clears *set. It is a checked runtime error for set or *set
to be null.
　　Individual elements of a set — bits in its vector — are manipulated by
the functions

⟨*exported functions* 200⟩+≡
```
extern int Bit_get(T set, int n);
extern int Bit_put(T set, int n, int bit);
```

Bit_get returns bit n and thus tests whether n is in set; that is,
Bit_get returns one if bit n in set is one and zero otherwise. Bit_put
sets bit n to bit and returns the previous value of that bit. It is a checked
runtime error for n to be negative or to be equal to or greater than the
length of set, or for bit to be other than zero or one.
　　The functions above manipulate individual bits in a set; the functions

⟨*exported functions* 200⟩+≡
```
extern void Bit_clear(T set, int lo, int hi);
extern void Bit_set  (T set, int lo, int hi);
extern void Bit_not  (T set, int lo, int hi);
```

manipulate contiguous sequences of bits in a set — subsets of a set. `Bit_clear` clears bits `lo` through `hi` inclusive; `Bit_set` sets bits `lo` through `hi` inclusive, and `Bit_not` complements bits `lo` through `hi`. It is a checked runtime error for `lo` to exceed `hi`, and for `lo` or `hi` to be negative or to be equal to or greater than the length of `set`.

⟨*exported functions* 200⟩+≡
```
extern int Bit_lt (T s, T t);
extern int Bit_eq (T s, T t);
extern int Bit_leq(T s, T t);
```

`Bit_lt` returns one if s ⊂ t and zero otherwise. If s ⊂ t, s is a proper subset of t. `Bit_eq` returns one if s = t and zero otherwise. `Bit_leq` returns one if s ⊆ t and zero otherwise. For all three functions, it is a checked runtime error for s and t to have different lengths.

The function

⟨*exported functions* 200⟩+≡
```
extern void Bit_map(T set,
    void apply(int n, int bit, void *cl), void *cl);
```

calls `apply` for each bit in `set`, beginning at bit zero. n is the bit number, which is between zero and one less than the length of the set, `bit` is the value of bit n, and `cl` is supplied by the client. Unlike the function passed to `Table_map`, `apply` *may* change `set`. If the call to `apply` for bit n changes bit k where k > n, the change will be seen by a subsequent call to `apply`, because `Bit_map` must process the bits in place. To do otherwise would require `Bit_map` to make a copy of the vector before processing its bits.

The following functions implement the four standard set operations, which are described in Chapter 9. Each function returns a new set whose value is the result of the operation.

⟨*exported functions* 200⟩+≡
```
extern T Bit_union(T s, T t);
extern T Bit_inter(T s, T t);
```

```
extern T Bit_minus(T s, T t);
extern T Bit_diff (T s, T t);
```

Bit_union returns the union of s and t, denoted s + t, which is the inclusive OR of the two bit vectors. Bit_inter returns the intersection of s and t, s * t, which is the logical AND of the two bit vectors. Bit_minus returns the difference of s and t, s − t, which is the logical AND of s and the complement of t. Bit_diff returns the symmetric difference of s and t, s / t, which is the exclusive OR of the two bit vectors.

These four functions accept null pointers for either s or t, but not for both, and interpret them as empty sets. Bit_union(s, NULL) thus returns a copy of s. These functions always return a nonnull T. It is a checked runtime error for both s and t to be null, and for s and t to have different lengths. These functions can raise Mem_Failed.

13.2 Implementation

A Bit_T is a pointer to a structure that carries the length of the bit vector and the vector itself:

⟨*bit.c*⟩≡
```
#include <stdarg.h>
#include <string.h>
#include "assert.h"
#include "bit.h"
#include "mem.h"

#define T Bit_T

struct T {
    int length;
    unsigned char *bytes;
    unsigned long *words;
};
```

⟨*macros* 203⟩
⟨*static data* 207⟩
⟨*static functions* 212⟩
⟨*functions* 203⟩

The `length` field gives the number of bits in the vector, and `bytes` points to at least $\lceil length/8 \rceil$ bytes. The bits are accessed by indexing `bytes`; `bytes[i]` refers to the byte holding bits $8 \cdot i$ through $8 \cdot i + 7$, where $8 \cdot i$ is the least significant bit in the byte. Notice that this convention uses only eight bits of each character; on machines where characters have more than eight bits, the excess bits go unused.

It's possible to store the bits in an array of, say, unsigned longs, if all the operations that access individual bits, like `Bit_get`, use the same convention for accessing the bits. `Bit` uses an array of characters to permit table-driven implementations of `Bit_count`, `Bit_set`, `Bit_clear`, and `Bit_not`.

Some operations, like `Bit_union`, manipulate all the bits in parallel. For these operations, the vectors are accessed BPW bits at a time via `words`, where

⟨*macros* 203⟩≡
```
#define BPW (8*sizeof (unsigned long))
```

`words` must point to an integral number of unsigned longs; `nwords` computes the number of unsigned longs needed for a bit vector of `length` bits:

⟨*macros* 203⟩+≡
```
#define nwords(len) (((((len) + BPW - 1)&(~(BPW-1)))/BPW)
```

`Bit_new` uses `nwords` when it allocates a new T:

⟨*functions* 203⟩≡
```
  T Bit_new(int length) {
      T set;

      assert(length >= 0);
      NEW(set);
      if (length > 0)
          set->words = CALLOC(nwords(length),
              sizeof (unsigned long));
      else
          set->words = NULL;
      set->bytes = (unsigned char *)set->words;
      set->length = length;
```

```
        return set;
    }
```

Bit_new may allocate as many as sizeof (unsigned long) − 1 excess bytes. These excess bytes must be zero in order for the functions below to work properly.

Bit_free deallocates the set and clears its argument, and Bit_length returns the length field.

⟨*functions* 203⟩+≡
```
    void Bit_free(T *set) {
        assert(set && *set);
        FREE((*set)->words);
        FREE(*set);
    }

    int Bit_length(T set) {
        assert(set);
        return set->length;
    }
```

13.2.1 Member Operations

Bit_count returns the number of members in a set — that is, the number of one bits in the set. It could simply walk through the set and test every bit, but it's just as easy to use the two halves of a byte — its two four-bit "nibbles" — as indices into a table that gives the number of one bits for each of the 16 possible nibbles:

⟨*functions* 203⟩+≡
```
    int Bit_count(T set) {
        int length = 0, n;
        static char count[] = {
            0,1,1,2,1,2,2,3,1,2,2,3,2,3,3,4 };

        assert(set);
        for (n = nbytes(set->length); --n >= 0; ) {
            unsigned char c = set->bytes[n];
            length += count[c&0xF] + count[c>>4];
        }
```

```
        return length;
    }
```

⟨*macros* 203⟩+≡
```
    #define nbytes(len) ((((len) + 8 - 1)&(~(8-1)))/8)
```

nbytes computes ⌈*len/8*⌉, and it's used in operations that sequence through vectors one bit at a time. Each iteration of the loop counts the number of bits in byte n of the set by adding to length the sum of the number of bits in the byte's two four-bit nibbles. This loop may access some extraneous bits, but since Bit_new initializes them to zeros, they can't corrupt the result.

Bit n is bit number n%8 in byte n/8, where the bit numbers in a byte start at zero and increase from the right to the left; that is, the least significant bit is bit zero and the most significant bit is bit seven. Bit_get returns the value of bit n by shifting byte n/8 to the right n%8 bits and returning only the rightmost bit:

⟨*functions* 203⟩+≡
```
    int Bit_get(T set, int n) {
        assert(set);
        assert(0 <= n && n < set->length);
        return ⟨bit n in set 205⟩;
    }
```

⟨*bit* n *in* set 205⟩≡
```
    ((set->bytes[n/8]>>(n%8))&1)
```

Bit_put uses a similar idiom to set bit n: When bit is one, Bit_put shifts a one left by n%8 bits and ORs that result into byte n/8.

⟨*functions* 203⟩+≡
```
    int Bit_put(T set, int n, int bit) {
        int prev;

        assert(set);
        assert(bit == 0 || bit == 1);
        assert(0 <= n && n < set->length);
        prev = ⟨bit n in set 205⟩;
        if (bit == 1)
            set->bytes[n/8] |=   1<<(n%8);
```

```
        else
            set->bytes[n/8] &= ~(1<<(n%8));
        return prev;
    }
```

As shown, `Bit_put` clears bit n by forming a mask in which bit n%8 is zero and all the other bits are one; it then ANDs this mask into byte n/8.

`Bit_set`, `Bit_clear`, and `Bit_not` all use similar techniques to set, clear, and complement a range of bits in a set, but they're more complicated because they must cope with ranges that straddle byte boundaries. For example, if `set` has 60 bits,

```
    Bit_set(set, 3, 54)
```

sets bits three through seven in the first byte, all of the bits in bytes one through five, and bits zero through six in byte six, where byte numbers start at zero. These three regions appear, right to left, in the three shades in the following figure.

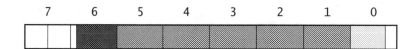

The four most significant bits of byte seven aren't used and thus are always zero. The code for `Bit_set` reflects these three regions:

⟨*functions* 203⟩+≡
```
    void Bit_set(T set, int lo, int hi) {
        ⟨check set, lo, and hi 206⟩
        if (lo/8 < hi/8) {
            ⟨set the most significant bits in byte lo/8 207⟩
            ⟨set all the bits in bytes lo/8+1..hi/8-1 207⟩
            ⟨set the least significant bits in byte hi/8 207⟩
        } else
            ⟨set bits lo%8..hi%8 in byte lo/8 208⟩
    }
```

⟨*check* set, lo, *and* hi 206⟩≡
```
        assert(set);
```

```
    assert(0 <= lo && hi < set->length);
    assert(lo <= hi);
```

When `lo` and `hi` refer to bits in different bytes, the number of bits that get set in byte `lo/8` depends on `lo%8`: If `lo%8` is zero, all of the bits get set; if it's seven, only the most significant bit is set. These and the other possibilities can be stored in a table of masks indexed by `lo%8`:

⟨*static data* 207⟩≡
```
    unsigned char msbmask[] = {
        0xFF, 0xFE, 0xFC, 0xF8,
        0xF0, 0xE0, 0xC0, 0x80
    };
```

ORing `msbmask[lo%8]` into byte `lo/8` sets the appropriate bits:

⟨*set the most significant bits in byte* `lo/8` 207⟩≡
```
    set->bytes[lo/8] |= msbmask[lo%8];
```

In the second region, all of the bits in each byte get set to one:

⟨*set all the bits in bytes* `lo/8+1..hi/8-1` 207⟩≡
```
    {
        int i;
        for (i = lo/8+1; i < hi/8; i++)
            set->bytes[i] = 0xFF;
    }
```

`hi%8` determines which bits in the byte `hi/8` get set: If `hi%8` is zero, only the least significant bit is set; if it's seven, all of the bits are set. Again, `hi%8` can be used as an index into a table to select the appropriate mask to OR into byte `hi/8`:

⟨*set the least significant bits in byte* `hi/8` 207⟩≡
```
    set->bytes[hi/8] |= lsbmask[hi%8];
```

⟨*static data* 207⟩+≡
```
    unsigned char lsbmask[] = {
        0x01, 0x03, 0x07, 0x0F,
        0x1F, 0x3F, 0x7F, 0xFF
    };
```

When `lo` and `hi` refer to bits in the same byte, the masks given by `msbmask[lo%8]` and `lsbmask[hi%8]` can be combined to set the appropriate bits. For example,

```
Bit_set(set, 9, 13)
```

sets bits one through five in the second byte of set; this can be done by ORing in the mask 0x3E, which is the AND of `msbmask[1]` and `lsbmask[5]`. In general, the two masks overlap in just those bits that should be set, so the code for this case is:

⟨*set bits* lo%8..hi%8 *in byte* lo/8 208⟩≡
```
set->bytes[lo/8] |= ⟨mask for bits lo%8..hi%8 208⟩;
```

⟨*mask for bits* lo%8..hi%8 208⟩≡
```
(msbmask[lo%8]&lsbmask[hi%8])
```

`Bit_clear` and `Bit_not` are similar to `Bit_set`, and use `msbmask` and `lsbmask` in similar ways. For `Bit_clear`, `msbmask` and `lsbmask` provide the *complements* of the masks that are ANDed with bytes `lo/8` and `hi/8`, respectively:

⟨*functions* 203⟩+≡
```
void Bit_clear(T set, int lo, int hi) {
    ⟨check set, lo, and hi 206⟩
    if (lo/8 < hi/8) {
        int i;
        set->bytes[lo/8] &= ~msbmask[lo%8];
        for (i = lo/8+1; i < hi/8; i++)
            set->bytes[i] = 0;
        set->bytes[hi/8] &= ~lsbmask[hi%8];
    } else
        set->bytes[lo/8] &= ~⟨mask for bits lo%8..hi%8 208⟩;
}
```

`Bit_not` must flip bits `lo` through `hi`, which it does by using an exclusive OR with masks to cover the appropriate bits:

⟨*functions* 203⟩+≡
```
void Bit_not(T set, int lo, int hi) {
    ⟨check set, lo, and hi 206⟩
```

```
if (lo/8 < hi/8) {
    int i;
    set->bytes[lo/8] ^= msbmask[lo%8];
    for (i = lo/8+1; i < hi/8; i++)
        set->bytes[i] ^= 0xFF;
    set->bytes[hi/8] ^= lsbmask[hi%8];
} else
    set->bytes[lo/8] ^= ⟨mask for bits lo%8..hi%8 208⟩;
}
```

Bit_map calls apply for every bit in a set. It passes the bit number, its value, and a client-supplied pointer.

⟨*functions* 203⟩+≡

```
void Bit_map(T set,
    void apply(int n, int bit, void *cl), void *cl) {
    int n;

    assert(set);
    for (n = 0; n < set->length; n++)
        apply(n, ⟨bit n in set 205⟩, cl);
}
```

As shown, Bit_map delivers the bits using the same numbering that is implicit in Bit_get and the other Bit functions that take bit numbers as arguments. The value of n/8 changes only every eight bytes, so it's tempting to copy each byte from set->bytes[n/8] to a temporary variable, then dole out each bit by shifting it and masking. But this improvement violates the interface, which stipulates that if apply changes a bit that it hasn't yet seen, it will see the new value in a subsequent call.

13.2.2 Comparisons

Bit_eq compares sets s and t and returns one if they're equal and zero if they're not. This can be done by comparing the corresponding unsigned longs in s and t, and the loop can quit as soon as it's known that s ≠ t:

⟨*functions* 203⟩+≡

```
int Bit_eq(T s, T t) {
    int i;
```

```
        assert(s && t);
        assert(s->length == t->length);
        for (i = nwords(s->length); --i >= 0; )
            if (s->words[i] != t->words[i])
                return 0;
        return 1;
    }
```

Bit_leq compares sets s and t and determines whether s is equal to t or a proper subset of t. $s \subseteq t$ if, for every bit in s, the corresponding bit in t is one. In terms of sets, $s \subseteq t$ if the intersection of s and the complement of t is empty. Thus, $s \subseteq t$ if s&~t is equal to zero; this relationship holds for each unsigned long in s and t, too. If, for all i, s->u.words[i] $\subseteq$ t->u.words[i], then $s \subseteq t$. Bit_leq uses this property to stop comparing as soon as the outcome is known:

⟨*functions* 203⟩+≡
```
    int Bit_leq(T s, T t) {
        int i;

        assert(s && t);
        assert(s->length == t->length);
        for (i = nwords(s->length); --i >= 0; )
            if ((s->words[i]&~t->words[i]) != 0)
                return 0;
        return 1;
    }
```

Bit_lt returns one if s is a *proper* subset of t; $s \subset t$ if $s \subseteq t$ and $s \neq t$, which can be done by ensuring that s->u.words[i]&~t->u.words[i] is equal to zero and that at least one of s->u.words[i] is not equal to the corresponding t->u.words[i]:

⟨*functions* 203⟩+≡
```
    int Bit_lt(T s, T t) {
        int i, lt = 0;

        assert(s && t);
        assert(s->length == t->length);
        for (i = nwords(s->length); --i >= 0; )
            if ((s->words[i]&~t->words[i]) != 0)
```

```
                    return 0;
              else if (s->words[i] != t->words[i])
                    lt |= 1;
          return lt;
     }
```

13.2.3 Set Operations

The functions that implement the set operations s + t, s * t, s – t, and s / t can manipulate their operands one long integer at a time, because their functions are independent of bit numbers. These functions also interpret a null T as an empty set, but one of s or t must be nonnull in order to determine the length of the result. These functions have similar implementations, but three differences: in the result when s and t refer to the same set, in they handle null arguments, and in how they form the result for two nonempty sets. The similarities are captured by the setop macro:

⟨*macros* 203⟩+≡

```
  #define setop(sequal, snull, tnull, op) \
      if (s == t) { assert(s); return sequal; } \
      else if (s == NULL) { assert(t); return snull; } \
      else if (t == NULL) return tnull; \
      else { \
          int i; T set; \
          assert(s->length == t->length); \
          set = Bit_new(s->length); \
          for (i = nwords(s->length); --i >= 0; ) \
              set->words[i] = s->words[i] op t->words[i]; \
          return set; }
```

Bit_union typifies these functions:

⟨*functions* 203⟩+≡

```
  T Bit_union(T s, T t) {
      setop(copy(t), copy(t), copy(s), |)
  }
```

If s and t refer to the same set, the result is a copy of the set. If either s or t is null, the result is a copy of the other set, which must be nonnull.

Otherwise, the result is a set whose unsigned longs are the bitwise OR of the unsigned longs in s and t.

The private function copy duplicates its argument set by allocating a new set of the same length and copying the bits from its argument:

⟨*static functions* 212⟩≡
```
static T copy(T t) {
    T set;

    assert(t);
    set = Bit_new(t->length);
    if (t->length > 0)
        memcpy(set->bytes, t->bytes, nbytes(t->length));
    return set;
}
```

Bit_inter returns an empty set if either of its arguments is null; otherwise, it returns a set that is the bitwise AND of its operands:

⟨*functions* 203⟩+≡
```
T Bit_inter(T s, T t) {
    setop(copy(t),
        Bit_new(t->length), Bit_new(s->length), &)
}
```

If s is null, s – t is the empty set, but if t is null, s – t is equal to s. If both s and t are nonnull, s – t is the bitwise AND of s and the *complement* of t. When s and t are the same Bit_T, s – t is the empty set.

⟨*functions* 203⟩+≡
```
T Bit_minus(T s, T t) {
    setop(Bit_new(s->length),
        Bit_new(t->length), copy(s), & ~)
}
```

setop's third argument, & ~, causes the body of the loop to be

```
set->words[i] = s->words[i] & ~t->words[i];
```

Bit_diff implements symmetric difference, s / t, which is the bitwise exclusive OR of s and t. When s is null, s / t is equal to t and vice versa.

⟨*functions* 203⟩+≡
```
T Bit_diff(T s, T t) {
    setop(Bit_new(s->length), copy(t), copy(s), ^)
}
```

As shown, s / t is the empty set when s and t refer to the same Bit_T.

Further Reading

Briggs and Torczon (1993) describe a set representation that's designed specifically for large, sparse sets and that can initialize those sets in constant time. Gimpel (1974) introduced the spatially multiplexed sets described in Exercise 13.5.

Exercises

13.1 In sparse sets, most of the bits are zero. Revise the implementation of Bit so that it saves space for sparse sets by, for example, not storing long runs of zeros.

13.2 Design an interface that supports the sparse sets described by Briggs and Torczon (1993), and implement your interface.

13.3 Bit_set uses the loop

```
for (i = lo/8+1; i < hi/8; i++)
    set->bytes[i] = 0xFF;
```

to set all of the bits from bytes lo/8+1 to hi/8. Bit_clear and Bit_not have similar loops. Revise these loops to clear, set, and complement unsigned longs instead of bytes, when possible. Be careful about alignment constraints. Can you find an application where this change yields a measurable improvement in execution time?

13.4 Suppose the Bit functions kept track of the number of one bits in a set. What Bit functions could be simplified or improved? Implement this scheme and devise a test program that quantifies the possible speed-up. Characterize under what conditions the benefit is worth the cost.

13.5 In a *spatially multiplexed set*, the bits are stored one word apart. On a computer with 32-bit ints, an array of N unsigned ints can hold 32 N-bit sets. Each one-bit column of the array is one set. A 32-bit mask with only bit i set identifies the set in column i. An advantage of this representation is that some operations can be done in constant time by manipulating only these masks. The union of two sets, for example, is a set whose mask is the union of the operands' masks. Many N-bit sets can share an N-word array; allocating a new set allocates one of the free columns in the array, or allocates a new array if there are no free columns. This property can save space, but it complicates storage management considerably, because the implementation must keep track of the N-word arrays that have free columns for any value of N. Reimplement Bit using this representation; if you're forced to change the interface, design a new one.

14

FORMATTING

The standard C library functions printf, fprintf, and vprintf format data for output, and sprintf and vsprintf format data into strings. These functions are called with a format string and a list of arguments whose values are to be formatted. Formatting is controlled by conversion specifiers of the form %c embedded in the format string; the ith occurrence of %c describes how to format the ith argument in the list of arguments that follow the format string. The other characters are copied verbatim. For example, if name is the string Array and count is 8,

```
sprintf(buf, "The %s interface has %d functions\n",
    name, count)
```

fills buf with the string "The Array interface has 8 functions\n", where \n denotes a new-line character, as usual. The conversion specifiers can also include width, precision, and padding specifications. For example, using %06d instead of %d in the format string above would fill buf with "The Array interface has 000008 functions\n".

While undoubtedly useful, these functions have at least four shortcomings. First, the set of conversion specifiers is fixed; there's no way to provide client-specific codes. Second, the formatted result can be printed or stored only in a string; there's no way to specify a client-specific output routine. The third and most dangerous shortcoming is that sprintf and vsprintf can attempt to store more characters in the output string than it can hold; there's no way to specify the size of the output string. Finally, there is no type-checking for the arguments passed in the vari-

215

able part of the argument list. The Fmt interface fixes the first three of these shortcomings.

14.1 Interface

The Fmt interface exports 11 functions, one type, one variable, and one exception:

⟨*fmt.h*⟩≡
```
#ifndef FMT_INCLUDED
#define FMT_INCLUDED
#include <stdarg.h>
#include <stdio.h>
#include "except.h"

#define T Fmt_T
typedef void (*T)(int code, va_list *app,
    int put(int c, void *cl), void *cl,
    unsigned char flags[256], int width, int precision);

extern char *Fmt_flags;
extern const Except_T Fmt_Overflow;

⟨exported functions 216⟩

#undef T
#endif
```

Technically, Fmt isn't an abstract data type, but it does export a type, Fmt_T, that defines the type of the format conversion functions associated with each formatting code, as detailed below.

14.1.1 Formatting Functions

The two primary formatting functions are:

⟨*exported functions* 216⟩≡
```
extern void Fmt_fmt (int put(int c, void *cl), void *cl,
    const char *fmt, ...);
```

```
extern void Fmt_vfmt(int put(int c, void *cl), void *cl,
    const char *fmt, va_list ap);
```

Fmt_fmt formats its fourth and subsequent arguments according to the format string given by its third argument, fmt, and calls put(c, cl) to emit each formatted character c; c is treated as an unsigned char, so the value passed to put is always positive. Fmt_vfmt formats the arguments pointed to by ap according to the format string given by fmt just as it does for Fmt_fmt, described below.

The argument cl may point to client-supplied data, and is simply passed along uninterpreted to the client's put function. The put function returns an integer, usually its argument. The Fmt functions don't use this capability, but this design permits the standard I/O function fputc to be used as a put function on some machines when a FILE* is passed as cl. For example,

```
Fmt_fmt((int (*)(int, void *))fputc, stdout,
    "The %s interface has %d functions\n", name, count)
```

prints

```
The Array interface has 8 functions
```

on the standard output when name is Array and count is 8. The cast is necessary because fputc has type int (*)(int, FILE*) and put has type int (*)(int, void *). This usage is correct only where a FILE pointer has the same representation as a void pointer.

The syntax diagram shown in Figure 14.1 defines the syntax of conversion specifiers. The characters in a conversion specifier define a path through this diagram, and valid specifiers traverse a path from start to finish. A specifier begins with a % and is followed by optional flag characters, whose interpretation depends on the format code; an optional field width, period, and precision; and concludes with a single-character format code, denoted by C in Figure 14.1. The valid flag characters are those that appear in the string pointed to by Fmt_flags; they usually specify justification, padding, and truncation. It is a checked runtime error for a flag character to appear more than 255 times in one specifier. If an asterisk appears for the field width or precision, the next argument is assumed to be an integer and is used for the width or precision. Thus, one specifier can consume zero or more arguments, depending on the appearance of asterisks and on the specific conversion function associ-

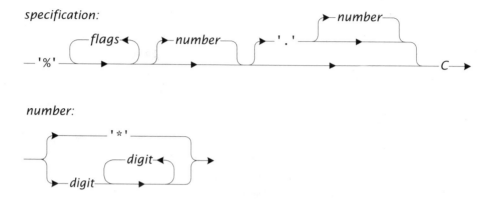

specification:

number:

Figure 14.1 Conversion-specifier syntax

ated with the format code. It is a checked runtime error for a width or precision to specify a value equal to INT_MIN, the most negative integer.

The precise interpretations of the flags, width, and precision depend on the conversion functions associated with the conversion specifiers. The functions calls are those registered at the time of the call to Fmt_fmt.

The default conversion specifiers and their associated conversion functions are a subset of those for printf and related functions in the standard I/O library. The initial value of Fmt_flags points to the string "-+ 0", whose characters are thus the valid flag characters. A - causes the converted string to be left-justified in the given field width; otherwise, it's right-justified. A + causes the result of a signed conversion to start with a - or + sign. A space causes the result of a signed conversion to begin with a space if it's positive. A 0 causes a numeric conversion to be padded to the field width with leading zeros; otherwise blanks are used. A negative width is treated as a - flag plus the corresponding positive width. A negative precision is treated as if no precision were given.

The default conversion specifiers are summarized in Table 14.1. These are a subset of those defined in the standard C library.

The functions

⟨*exported functions* 216⟩+≡
```
extern void Fmt_print (const char *fmt, ...);
extern void Fmt_fprint(FILE *stream,
    const char *fmt, ...);
```

```
extern int Fmt_sfmt   (char *buf, int size,
    const char *fmt, ...);
extern int Fmt_vsfmt(char *buf, int size,
    const char *fmt, va_list ap);
```

are similar to the C library functions printf, fprintf, sprintf, and vsprintf.

Fmt_fprint formats its third and subsequent arguments according to the format string given by fmt and writes the formatted output to the indicated stream. Fmt_print writes its formatted output to the standard output.

Fmt_sfmt formats its fourth and subsequent arguments according to the format string given by fmt, and stores the formatted output as a null-terminated string in buf[0..size-1]. Fmt_vsfmt is similar, but takes its arguments from the variable length argument-list pointer ap. Both functions return the number of characters stored into buf, not counting the terminating null character. Fmt_sfmt and Fmt_vsfmt raise Fmt_Overflow if they emit more than size characters, including the terminating null character. It is a checked runtime error for size to be nonpositive.

The two functions

⟨*exported functions* 216⟩+≡
```
extern char *Fmt_string (const char *fmt, ...);
extern char *Fmt_vstring(const char *fmt, va_list ap);
```

are like Fmt_sfmt and Fmt_vsfmt, except that they allocate strings large enough to hold the formatted results and return these strings. Clients are responsible for deallocating them. Fmt_string and Fmt_vstring can raise Mem_Failed.

It is a checked runtime error to pass a null put, buf, or fmt to any of the formatting functions described above.

14.1.2 Conversion Functions

Each format character *C* is associated with a conversion function. These associations can be changed by calling

⟨*exported functions* 216⟩+≡
```
extern T Fmt_register(int code, T cvt);
```

Table 14.1 Default conversion specifiers

conversion specifier argument type	description
c int	The argument is interpreted as an unsigned character and is emitted.
d int	The argument is converted to its signed decimal representation. The precision, if given, specifies the minimum number of digits; leading zeros are added, if necessary. The default precision is one. If both the – and 0 flags appear, or if a precision is given, the 0 flag is ignored. If both the + and space flags appear, the space flag is ignored. If the argument and the precision are zero, there are no characters in the converted result.
o u x unsigned	The argument is converted to its unsigned representation in octal (o), decimal (u), or hexadecimal (x). For x, the letters abcdef are used for the digits whose values exceed 9. The flags and precision are interpreted as for d.
f double	The argument is converted to its decimal representation with the form $x.y$. The precision gives the number of digits to the right of the decimal point; the default is 6. If the precision is given explicitly as 0, the decimal point is omitted. When a decimal point appears, x has at least one digit. It is a checked runtime error for the precision to exceed 99. The flags are interpreted as for d.
e double	The argument is converted to its decimal representation with the form $x.ye\pm p$. x is always one digit and p is always two digits. The flags and precision are interpreted as for d.
g double	The argument is converted to its decimal representation as for f or e depending on its value. The precision gives the number of significant digits; the default is one. The result has the form $x.ye\pm p$ if p is less than –4 or p is greater than or equal to the precision; otherwise, the result has the form $x.y$. There are no trailing zeros in y, and the decimal point is omitted when y is zero. It is a checked runtime error for the precision to exceed 99.
p void *	The argument is converted to the hexadecimal representation of its value as for u. The flags and precision are interpreted as for d.
s char *	Successive characters from the argument are emitted until a null character is encountered or the number of characters given by an explicit precision have been emitted. All flags except – are ignored.

Fmt_register installs cvt as the conversion function for the format character given by code, and returns a pointer to the previous function. Clients may thus override conversion functions temporarily, and then restore the previous function. It is a checked runtime error for code to be less than one or more than 255. It is also a checked runtime error for a format string to use a conversion specifier that has no associated conversion function.

Many conversion functions are variations on the functions used for the %d and %s conversion specifiers. Fmt exports two utility functions used by its internal conversion functions for numerics and strings.

⟨*exported functions* 216⟩+≡
```
    extern void Fmt_putd(const char *str, int len,
        int put(int c, void *cl), void *cl,
        unsigned char flags[256], int width, int precision);
    extern void Fmt_puts(const char *str, int len,
        int put(int c, void *cl), void *cl,
        unsigned char flags[256], int width, int precision);
```

Fmt_putd assumes that str[0..len−1] holds the string representation of a signed number, and emits the string according to the conversions specified by flags, width, and precision as described for %d in Table 14.1. Similarly, Fmt_puts emits str[0..len−1] according to the conversions specified by flags, width, and precision as described for %s. It is a checked runtime error to pass a null str, a negative len, a null flags, or a null put to Fmt_putd or Fmt_puts.

Fmt_putd and Fmt_puts are not themselves conversion functions, but they can be called by conversion functions. They are most useful when writing client-specific conversion functions, as illustrated below.

The type Fmt_T defines the signature of a conversion function — the types of its arguments and its return type. A conversion function is called with seven arguments. The first two are the format code and a pointer to the variable-length argument-list pointer that must be used to access the data to be formatted. The third and fourth arguments are the client's output function and associated data. The last three arguments are the flags, field width, and precision. The flags are given by a character array of 256 elements; the ith element is equal to number of times the flag character i appears in the conversion specifier. width and precision are equal to INT_MIN when they are not given explicitly.

A conversion function must use expressions like

```
va_arg(*app, type)
```

to fetch the arguments that are to be formatted according to the code
with which the conversion function is associated. *type* is the expected
type of argument. This expression fetches the argument's value, then
increments *app so that it points to the next argument. It is an
unchecked runtime error for a conversion function to increment *app
incorrectly.

Fmt's private conversion function for the code %s illustrates how to
write conversion functions, and how to use Fmt_puts. The specifier %s is
like printf's %s: Its function emits characters from the string until it
encounters a null character, or until it has emitted the number of characters given using an optional precision. The – flag or a negative width
specify left-justification. The conversion function uses va_arg to fetch
the argument from the variable length argument list and calls Fmt_puts:

⟨*conversion functions* 222⟩≡
```
    static void cvt_s(int code, va_list *app,
        int put(int c, void *cl), void *cl,
        unsigned char flags[], int width, int precision) {
        char *str = va_arg(*app, char *);

        assert(str);
        Fmt_puts(str, strlen(str), put, cl, flags,
            width, precision);
    }
```

Fmt_puts interprets flags, width, and precision and emits the string
accordingly:

⟨*functions* 222⟩≡
```
    void Fmt_puts(const char *str, int len,
        int put(int c, void *cl), void *cl,
        unsigned char flags[], int width, int precision) {

        assert(str);
        assert(len >= 0);
        assert(flags);
        ⟨normalize width and flags 223⟩
        if (precision >= 0 && precision < len)
            len = precision;
```

```
        if (!flags['-'])
            pad(width - len, ' ');
        ⟨emit str[0..len-1] 223⟩
        if ( flags['-'])
            pad(width - len, ' ');
    }
```

```
⟨emit str[0..len-1] 223⟩≡
    {
        int i;
        for (i = 0; i < len; i++)
            put((unsigned char)*str++, cl);
    }
```

The cast to unsigned char ensures that the values passed to put are always small, positive integers as stipulated in Fmt's specification.

width and precision are equal to INT_MIN when the width or precision are omitted. This interface provides the flexibility needed for client-specific conversion functions to use all combinations of explicit and omitted widths and precisions, as well as repeated flags. But the default conversions don't need this generality; they all treat an omitted width as an explicit width of zero, a negative width as the – flag along with the corresponding positive width, a negative precision as an omitted precision, and repeated occurrences of a flag as one occurrence. If there is an explicit precision, the 0 flag is ignored, and, as shown above, at most precision characters from str are emitted.

```
⟨normalize width and flags 223⟩≡
    ⟨normalize width 223⟩
    ⟨normalize flags 224⟩
```

```
⟨normalize width 223⟩≡
    if (width == INT_MIN)
        width = 0;
    if (width < 0) {
        flags['-'] = 1;
        width = -width;
    }
```

⟨*normalize* flags 224⟩≡
```
if (precision >= 0)
    flags['0'] = 0;
```

As the calls to pad suggest, width - len spaces must be emitted to justify the output correctly:

⟨*macros* 224⟩≡
```
#define pad(n,c) do { int nn = (n); \
    while (nn-- > 0) \
        put((c), cl); } while (0)
```

pad is a macro because it needs access to put and cl.

The next section describes the implementation of the other default conversion functions.

14.2 Implementation

The implementation of Fmt consists of the functions defined in the interface, the conversion functions associated with the default conversion specifiers, and the table that maps conversion specifiers to conversion functions.

⟨*fmt.c*⟩≡
```
#include <stdarg.h>
#include <stdlib.h>
#include <stdio.h>
#include <string.h>
#include <limits.h>
#include <float.h>
#include <ctype.h>
#include <math.h>
#include "assert.h"
#include "except.h"
#include "fmt.h"
#include "mem.h"
#define T Fmt_T

⟨types 226⟩
⟨macros 224⟩
```

⟨*conversion functions* 222⟩
⟨*data* 225⟩
⟨*static functions* 225⟩
⟨*functions* 222⟩

⟨*data* 225⟩≡
```
const Except_T Fmt_Overflow = { "Formatting Overflow" };
```

14.2.1 Formatting Functions

Fmt_vfmt is the heart of the implementation, because all of the other
interface functions call it to do the actual formatting. Fmt_fmt is the
simplest example; it initializes a va_list pointer to the variable part of
its argument list and calls Fmt_vfmt:

⟨*functions* 222⟩+≡
```
void Fmt_fmt(int put(int c, void *), void *cl,
    const char *fmt, ...) {
    va_list ap;

    va_start(ap, fmt);
    Fmt_vfmt(put, cl, fmt, ap);
    va_end(ap);
}
```

Fmt_print and Fmt_fprint call Fmt_vfmt with outc as the put function and with the stream for the standard output or the given stream as
the associated data:

⟨*static functions* 225⟩≡
```
static int outc(int c, void *cl) {
    FILE *f = cl;

    return putc(c, f);
}
```

⟨*functions* 222⟩+≡
```
void Fmt_print(const char *fmt, ...) {
    va_list ap;
```

```
        va_start(ap, fmt);
        Fmt_vfmt(outc, stdout, fmt, ap);
        va_end(ap);
    }

    void Fmt_fprint(FILE *stream, const char *fmt, ...) {
        va_list ap;

        va_start(ap, fmt);
        Fmt_vfmt(outc, stream, fmt, ap);
        va_end(ap);
    }
```

Fmt_sfmt calls Fmt_vsfmt:

⟨*functions* 222⟩+≡
```
    int Fmt_sfmt(char *buf, int size, const char *fmt, ...) {
        va_list ap;
        int len;

        va_start(ap, fmt);
        len = Fmt_vsfmt(buf, size, fmt, ap);
        va_end(ap);
        return len;
    }
```

Fmt_vsfmt calls Fmt_vfmt with a put function and with a pointer to a structure that keeps track of the string being formatted into buf and of how many characters it can hold:

⟨*types* 226⟩≡
```
    struct buf {
        char *buf;
        char *bp;
        int size;
    };
```

buf and size are copies of Fmt_vsfmt's similarly named parameters, and bp points to the location in buf where the next formatted character is to be stored. Fmt_vsfmt initializes a local instance of this structure and passes a pointer to it to Fmt_vfmt:

⟨*functions* 222⟩+≡
```
int Fmt_vsfmt(char *buf, int size, const char *fmt,
    va_list ap) {
    struct buf cl;

    assert(buf);
    assert(size > 0);
    assert(fmt);
    cl.buf = cl.bp = buf;
    cl.size = size;
    Fmt_vfmt(insert, &cl, fmt, ap);
    insert(0, &cl);
    return cl.bp - cl.buf - 1;
}
```

The call to Fmt_vfmt above calls the private function insert with each character to be emitted and also the pointer Fmt_vsfmt's local buf structure. insert checks that there's room for the character, deposits it at location given by the bp field, and increments the bp field:

⟨*static functions* 225⟩+≡
```
static int insert(int c, void *cl) {
    struct buf *p = cl;

    if (p->bp >= p->buf + p->size)
        RAISE(Fmt_Overflow);
    *p->bp++ = c;
    return c;
}
```

Fmt_string and Fmt_vstring work the same way, except that they use a different put function. Fmt_string calls Fmt_vstring:

⟨*functions* 222⟩+≡
```
char *Fmt_string(const char *fmt, ...) {
    char *str;
    va_list ap;

    assert(fmt);
    va_start(ap, fmt);
    str = Fmt_vstring(fmt, ap);
```

```
            va_end(ap);
            return str;
    }
```

Fmt_vstring initializes a buf structure to a string that can hold 256 characters, and passes a pointer to this structure to Fmt_vfmt:

⟨*functions* 222⟩+≡
```
    char *Fmt_vstring(const char *fmt, va_list ap) {
        struct buf cl;

        assert(fmt);
        cl.size = 256;
        cl.buf = cl.bp = ALLOC(cl.size);
        Fmt_vfmt(append, &cl, fmt, ap);
        append(0, &cl);
        return RESIZE(cl.buf, cl.bp - cl.buf);
    }
```

append is like Fmt_vsfmt's put, except that it doubles the size of the string on the fly, when necessary, to hold the formatted characters.

⟨*static functions* 225⟩+≡
```
    static int append(int c, void *cl) {
        struct buf *p = cl;

        if (p->bp >= p->buf + p->size) {
            RESIZE(p->buf, 2*p->size);
            p->bp = p->buf + p->size;
            p->size *= 2;
        }
        *p->bp++ = c;
        return c;
    }
```

When Fmt_vstring is finished, the string pointed to by the buf field might be too long, which is why Fmt_vstring calls RESIZE to deallocate the excess characters.

The buck stops at Fmt_vfmt. It interprets the format string and, for each formatting specifier, calls the appropriate conversion function. For the other characters in the format string, it calls the put function:

⟨*functions* 222⟩+≡
```
void Fmt_vfmt(int put(int c, void *cl), void *cl,
    const char *fmt, va_list ap) {
    assert(put);
    assert(fmt);
    while (*fmt)
        if (*fmt != '%' || *++fmt == '%')
            put((unsigned char)*fmt++, cl);
        else
            ⟨format an argument 229⟩
}
```

Most of the work in ⟨*format an argument* 229⟩ goes into consuming the flags, field width, and precision, and into dealing with the possibility that the conversion specifier doesn't have a corresponding conversion function. In the chunk below, `width` gives the field width, and `precision` gives the precision.

⟨*format an argument* 229⟩≡
```
{
    unsigned char c, flags[256];
    int width = INT_MIN, precision = INT_MIN;
    memset(flags, '\0', sizeof flags);
    ⟨get optional flags 230⟩
    ⟨get optional field width 231⟩
    ⟨get optional precision 232⟩
    c = *fmt++;
    assert(cvt[c]);
    (*cvt[c])(c, &ap, put, cl, flags, width, precision);
}
```

`cvt` is an array of pointers to conversion functions, and it's indexed by a format character. Declaring `c` to be an unsigned char in the chunk above is necessary to ensure that `*fmt` is interpreted as an integer in the range 0 to 255.

`cvt` is initialized to the conversion functions for the default conversion specifiers, assuming the ASCII collating sequence:

⟨*data* 225⟩+≡
```
static T cvt[256] = {
/*   0- 7 */ 0,      0, 0,       0,      0,      0,      0,      0,
```

```
/*   8- 15 */ 0,      0, 0,     0,     0,     0,     0,     0,
/*  16- 23 */ 0,      0, 0,     0,     0,     0,     0,     0,
/*  24- 31 */ 0,      0, 0,     0,     0,     0,     0,     0,
/*  32- 39 */ 0,      0, 0,     0,     0,     0,     0,     0,
/*  40- 47 */ 0,      0, 0,     0,     0,     0,     0,     0,
/*  48- 55 */ 0,      0, 0,     0,     0,     0,     0,     0,
/*  56- 63 */ 0,      0, 0,     0,     0,     0,     0,     0,
/*  64- 71 */ 0,      0, 0,     0,     0,     0,     0,     0,
/*  72- 79 */ 0,      0, 0,     0,     0,     0,     0,     0,
/*  80- 87 */ 0,      0, 0,     0,     0,     0,     0,     0,
/*  88- 95 */ 0,      0, 0,     0,     0,     0,     0,     0,
/*  96-103 */ 0,      0, 0, cvt_c, cvt_d, cvt_f, cvt_f, cvt_f,
/* 104-111 */ 0,      0, 0,     0,     0,     0,     0, cvt_o,
/* 112-119 */ cvt_p,  0, 0, cvt_s,     0, cvt_u,     0,     0,
/* 120-127 */ cvt_x,  0, 0,     0,     0,     0,     0,     0
};
```

Fmt_register installs a new conversion function by storing a pointer to it in the appropriate element of cvt. It returns the previous value of that element:

⟨functions 222⟩+≡
```
T Fmt_register(int code, T newcvt) {
    T old;

    assert(0 < code
        && code < (int)(sizeof (cvt)/sizeof (cvt[0])));
    old = cvt[code];
    cvt[code] = newcvt;
    return old;
}
```

The chunks that scan the conversion specifier follow the syntax shown in Figure 14.1, incrementing fmt as they go. The first one consumes the flags:

⟨data 225⟩+≡
```
char *Fmt_flags = "-+ 0";
```

⟨get optional flags 230⟩≡
```
if (Fmt_flags) {
```

```
        unsigned char c = *fmt;
        for ( ; c && strchr(Fmt_flags, c); c = *++fmt) {
            assert(flags[c] < 255);
            flags[c]++;
        }
    }
```

Next comes the field width:

⟨*get optional field width* 231⟩≡
```
    if (*fmt == '*' || isdigit(*fmt)) {
        int n;
        ⟨n ← next argument or scan digits 231⟩
        width = n;
    }
```

An asterisk can appear for the width or precision, in which case the next integer argument provides their values.

⟨n ← *next argument or scan digits* 231⟩≡
```
    if (*fmt == '*') {
        n = va_arg(ap, int);
        assert(n != INT_MIN);
        fmt++;
    } else
        for (n = 0; isdigit(*fmt); fmt++) {
            int d = *fmt - '0';
            assert(n <= (INT_MAX - d)/10);
            n = 10*n + d;
        }
```

As this code suggests, when an argument specifies a width or precision, it must not specify INT_MIN, which is reserved as the default value. When a width or precision is given explicitly, it must not exceed INT_MAX, which is equivalent to the constraint $10 \cdot n + d \leq \text{INT\_MAX}$ — that is, $10 \cdot n + d$ doesn't overflow. This test must be made without actually causing overflow, which is why the constraint is rearranged in the assertion above.

A period announces an approaching optional precision:

⟨*get optional precision* 232⟩≡
```
if (*fmt == '.' && (*++fmt == '*' || isdigit(*fmt))) {
    int n;
    ⟨n ← next argument or scan digits 231⟩
    precision = n;
}
```

Notice that a period *not* followed by an asterisk or a digit is consumed and is interpreted as an explicitly omitted precision.

14.2.2 Conversion Functions

cvt_s, the conversion function for %s, is shown on page 222. cvt_d is the conversion function for %d, and it is typical of the functions that format numbers. It fetches the integer argument, converts it to an unsigned integer, and generates the appropriate string in a local buffer, most significant digit first. It then calls Fmt_putd to emit the string.

⟨*conversion functions* 222⟩+≡
```
static void cvt_d(int code, va_list *app,
    int put(int c, void *cl), void *cl,
    unsigned char flags[], int width, int precision) {
    int val = va_arg(*app, int);
    unsigned m;
    ⟨declare buf and p, initialize p 233⟩

    if (val == INT_MIN)
        m = INT_MAX + 1U;
    else if (val < 0)
        m = -val;
    else
        m = val;
    do
        *--p = m%10 + '0';
    while ((m /= 10) > 0);
    if (val < 0)
        *--p = '-';
    Fmt_putd(p, (buf + sizeof buf) - p, put, cl, flags,
        width, precision);
}
```

⟨*declare* buf *and* p, *initialize* p 233⟩≡
```
char buf[43];
char *p = buf + sizeof buf;
```

cvt_d does unsigned arithmetic for the same reasons that Atom_int does; see Section 3.2, which also explains why buf has 43 characters.

⟨*functions* 222⟩+≡
```
void Fmt_putd(const char *str, int len,
    int put(int c, void *cl), void *cl,
    unsigned char flags[], int width, int precision) {
    int sign;

    assert(str);
    assert(len >= 0);
    assert(flags);
```
⟨*normalize* width *and* flags 223⟩
⟨*compute the sign* 233⟩
```
    { ⟨emit str justified in width 234⟩ }
}
```

Fmt_putd must emit the string in str as specified by flags, width, and precision. If a precision is given, it specifies the minimum number of digits that must appear. That many digits must be emitted, which may require adding leading zeros. Fmt_putd first determines whether or not a sign or leading space is needed, then sets sign to that character:

⟨*compute the sign* 233⟩≡
```
    if (len > 0 && (*str == '-' || *str == '+')) {
        sign = *str++;
        len--;
    } else if (flags['+'])
        sign = '+';
    else if (flags[' '])
        sign = ' ';
    else
        sign = 0;
```

The order of the if statements in ⟨*compute the sign* 233⟩ implements the rule that a + flag takes precedence over a space flag. The length of the converted result, n, depends on the precision, the value converted, and the sign:

⟨*emit* str *justified in* width 234⟩≡
```
    int n;
    if (precision < 0)
        precision = 1;
    if (len < precision)
        n = precision;
    else if (precision == 0 && len == 1 && str[0] == '0')
        n = 0;
    else
        n = len;
    if (sign)
        n++;
```

n is assigned the number of characters that will be emitted, and this code handles the special case when a value of zero is converted with a precision of zero, in which case, no characters from the converted result are emitted.

Fmt_putd can now emit the sign, if the output is to be left-justified; or it can emit the sign and the padding, if the output is to be right-justified with leading zeros; or it can emit the padding and the sign, if the output is to be right-justified with spaces.

⟨*emit* str *justified in* width 234⟩+≡
```
    if (flags['-']) {
        ⟨emit the sign 234⟩
    } else if (flags['0']) {
        ⟨emit the sign 234⟩
        pad(width - n, '0');
    } else {
        pad(width - n, ' ');
        ⟨emit the sign 234⟩
    }
```

⟨*emit the sign* 234⟩≡
```
    if (sign)
        put(sign, cl);
```

Fmt_putd can finally emit the converted result, including the leading zeros, if dictated by the precision, and the padding, if the output is left-justified:

⟨*emit* str *justified in* width 234⟩+≡
```
   pad(precision - len, '0');
   ⟨emit str[0..len-1] 223⟩
   if (flags['-'])
      pad(width - n, ' ');
```

cvt_u is simpler than cvt_d, but it can use all of Fmt_putd's machinery for emitting the converted result. It emits the decimal representation for the next unsigned integer:

⟨*conversion functions* 222⟩+≡
```
   static void cvt_u(int code, va_list *app,
      int put(int c, void *cl), void *cl,
      unsigned char flags[], int width, int precision) {
      unsigned m = va_arg(*app, unsigned);
      ⟨declare buf and p, initialize p 233⟩

      do
         *--p = m%10 + '0';
      while ((m /= 10) > 0);
      Fmt_putd(p, (buf + sizeof buf) - p, put, cl, flags,
         width, precision);
   }
```

The octal and hexadecimal conversions are like the unsigned decimal conversions, except that the output bases are different, which simplifies the conversions themselves.

⟨*conversion functions* 222⟩+≡
```
   static void cvt_o(int code, va_list *app,
      int put(int c, void *cl), void *cl,
      unsigned char flags[], int width, int precision) {
      unsigned m = va_arg(*app, unsigned);
      ⟨declare buf and p, initialize p 233⟩

      do
         *--p = (m&0x7) + '0';
```

```
        while ((m >>= 3) != 0);
        Fmt_putd(p, (buf + sizeof buf) - p, put, cl, flags,
            width, precision);
    }

static void cvt_x(int code, va_list *app,
        int put(int c, void *cl), void *cl,
        unsigned char flags[], int width, int precision) {
        unsigned m = va_arg(*app, unsigned);
        ⟨declare buf and p, initialize p 233⟩

        ⟨emit m in hexadecimal 236⟩
    }
```

⟨emit m in hexadecimal 236⟩≡
```
    do
        *--p = "0123456789abcdef"[m&0xf];
    while ((m >>= 4) != 0);
    Fmt_putd(p, (buf + sizeof buf) - p, put, cl, flags,
        width, precision);
```

cvt_p emits a pointer as a hexadecimal number. The precision and all
flags except - are ignored. The argument is interpreted as a pointer, and
it's converted to an unsigned long in which to do the conversion, because
an unsigned might not be big enough to hold a pointer.

⟨conversion functions 222⟩+≡
```
    static void cvt_p(int code, va_list *app,
        int put(int c, void *cl), void *cl,
        unsigned char flags[], int width, int precision) {
        unsigned long m = (unsigned long)va_arg(*app, void*);
        ⟨declare buf and p, initialize p 233⟩

        precision = INT_MIN;
        ⟨emit m in hexadecimal 236⟩
    }
```

cvt_c is the conversion function associated with %c; it formats a single character, left- or right-justified in width characters. It ignores the
precision and the other flags.

⟨*conversion functions* 222⟩+≡
```
    static void cvt_c(int code, va_list *app,
        int put(int c, void *cl), void *cl,
        unsigned char flags[], int width, int precision) {
        ⟨normalize width 223⟩
        if (!flags['-'])
            pad(width - 1, ' ');
        put((unsigned char)va_arg(*app, int), cl);
        if ( flags['-'])
            pad(width - 1, ' ');
    }
```

cvt_c fetches an integer instead of a character because character arguments passed in the variable part of an argument list suffer the default
argument promotions, and are thus converted to and passed as integers.
cvt_c converts the resulting integer to an unsigned char so that signed,
unsigned, and plain characters are all emitted the same way.

Converting a floating-point value to its decimal representation accurately is surprisingly difficult to do in a machine-independent way.
Machine-dependent algorithms are faster and more accurate, so the conversion function associated with the e, f, and g conversion specifiers
uses

⟨*format a* double *argument into* buf 237⟩≡
```
    {
        static char fmt[] = "%.dd?";
        assert(precision <= 99);
        fmt[4] = code;
        fmt[3] =        precision%10 + '0';
        fmt[2] = (precision/10)%10 + '0';
        sprintf(buf, fmt, va_arg(*app, double));
    }
```

to convert the absolute value of val into buf; it then emits buf.

The difference between the floating-point conversion specifiers is in
how they format the various parts of a floating-point value. The longest
output comes from the specifier %.99f, which may require
DBL_MAX_10_EXP+1+1+99+1 characters. DBL_MAX_10_EXP and DBL_MAX
are defined in the standard header file float.h. DBL_MAX is the largest
value that can be represented as a double, and DBL_MAX_10_EXP is
$\log_{10}$DBL_MAX; that is, it's the largest decimal exponent that can be rep-

resented by a double. For 64-bit doubles in IEEE 754 format, DBL_MAX is 1.797693×10^{308} and DBL_MAX_10_EXP is 308. The assignments to fmt[2] and fmt[3] assume the ASCII collating sequence.

Thus, if DBL_MAX is converted with the conversion specifier %.99f, the result may have DBL_MAX_10_EXP+1 digits before the decimal point, a decimal point, 99 digits after the decimal point, and a terminating null character. Limiting the precision to 99 limits the size of the buffer needed to hold the converted result, and makes the buffer's maximum size known at compile time. The converted results from the other conversion specifiers, %e and %g, take fewer characters than the result for %f. cvt_f handles all three codes:

⟨conversion functions 222⟩+≡
```
static void cvt_f(int code, va_list *app,
    int put(int c, void *cl), void *cl,
    unsigned char flags[], int width, int precision) {
    char buf[DBL_MAX_10_EXP+1+1+99+1];

    if (precision < 0)
        precision = 6;
    if (code == 'g' && precision == 0)
        precision = 1;
    ⟨format a double argument into buf 237⟩
    Fmt_putd(buf, strlen(buf), put, cl, flags,
        width, precision);
}
```

Further Reading

Plauger (1992) describes the implementation of the C library's printf family of output functions, including low-level code for converting strings to floating-point values and vice versa. His code also shows how to implement the other printf-style formatting flags and codes.

Section 4.8 in Hennessy and Patterson (1994) describes the IEEE 754 floating-point standard and the implementation of floating-point addition and multiplication. Goldberg (1991) surveys the properties of floating-point arithmetic that most concern programmers.

Floating-point conversions have been implemented many times, but it's easy to botch these conversions by making them inaccurate or too slow. The litmus test for these conversions is if, given a floating-point value x, the output conversion produces a string from which the input conversion recreates a y that is bitwise identical to x. Clinger (1990) describes how to do the input conversion accurately, and shows that, for some x, this conversion requires arithmetic of arbitrary precision. Steele and White (1990) describe how to do an accurate output conversion.

Exercises

14.1 Fmt_vstring uses RESIZE to deallocate the unused portion of the string that it returns. Devise a way to do this deallocation only when it pays; that is, when the space deallocated is worth the effort it takes to deallocate it.

14.2 Use the algorithms described in Steele and White (1990) to implement the e, f, and g conversions.

14.3 Write a conversion function that takes the conversion specifier from the next integer argument and associates it with the character @. For example,

```
Fmt_string("The offending value is %@\n",
    x.format, x.value);
```

would format x.value according to the format code carried along in x.format.

14.4 Write a conversion function for emitting the elements in a Bit_T as a sequence of integers in which a run of ones is emitted as a range; for example, 1 32-45 68 70-71.

15

LOW-LEVEL STRINGS

C is not a string-processing language per se, but it does include facilities for manipulating arrays of characters, which are commonly called strings. By convention, an *N*-character string is an array of *N*+1 characters in which the last character is the null character; that is, it has the value zero.

The language itself has only two features that help process strings. Pointers to characters can be used to traverse character arrays, and string literals can be used to initialize arrays of characters. For example,

```
char msg[] = "File not found";
```

is shorthand for

```
char msg[] = { 'F', 'i', 'l', 'e', ' ', 'n', 'o', 't',
       ' ', 'f', 'o', 'u', 'n', 'd', '\0' };
```

Incidently, character constants, like 'F', are ints, not chars, which explains why sizeof 'F' is equal to sizeof (int).

String literals can also stand for arrays initialized to the given characters. For example,

```
char *msg = "File not found";
```

is equivalent to

```
static char t376[] = "File not found";
char *msg = t376;
```

where t376 is an internal name generated by the compiler.

A string literal can be used anywhere the name of a read-only array can be used. For example, Fmt's cvt_x uses a string literal in an expression:

```
do
     *--p = "0123456789abcdef"[m&0xf];
while ((m >>= 4) != 0);
```

The assignment is equivalent to the more verbose

```
{
    static char digits[] = "0123456789abcdef";
    *p++ = digits[m&0xf];
}
```

digits is a compiler-generated name.

The C library includes a suite of functions that manipulate null-terminated strings. These functions, defined in the standard header string.h, copy, search, scan, compare, and transform strings. strcat is typical:

```
char *strcat(char *dst, const char *src)
```

It appends src to the end of dst; that is, it copies characters up to and including the null character from src to successive elements in dst beginning at the element in dst that holds the null character.

strcat illustrates the two drawbacks of the functions defined in string.h. First, a client must allocate the space for the result, such as dst in strcat. Second, and most important, all of the functions are unsafe — none of them can check to see whether the result string is large enough. If dst isn't big enough to hold the additional characters from src, strcat will scribble on unallocated storage or storage used for something else. Some of the functions, like strncat, take additional arguments that limit the number of characters copied to their results, which helps, but allocation errors can still occur.

The functions in the Str interface described in this chapter avoid these drawbacks and provide a convenient way to manipulate substrings of their string arguments. These functions are safer than those in string.h because most of the Str functions allocate the space for their results. The cost associated with these allocations is the price for safety.

These allocations are often needed anyway, because clients of the string.h functions must allocate the results when their sizes depend on the outcomes of computations. As for the string.h functions, clients of the Str functions must still deallocate the results. The Text interface described in the next chapter exports another set of string-manipulation functions that avoid some of the allocation overhead of the Str functions.

15.1 Interface

⟨*str.h*⟩≡
```
#ifndef STR_INCLUDED
#define STR_INCLUDED
#include <stdarg.h>

⟨exported functions 244⟩

#undef T
#endif
```

All of the string arguments to the functions in the Str interface are given by a pointer to a null-terminated array of characters and *positions*. Like Ring positions, string positions identify locations *between* characters including the position after the last nonnull character. Positive positions specify the location from the left end of a string; position one is the location to the left of the first character. Nonpositive positions specify positions from the right end of the string; position zero is the location to the right of the last character. For example, the following diagram shows the positions in the string Interface.

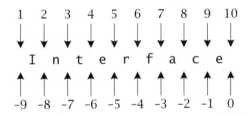

Two positions i and j in the string s specify the substring between them, denoted by s[i:j]. If s points to the string Interface, s[-4:0] is the substring face. These positions can be given in either order: s[0:-4] also specifies face. Substrings can be null; s[3:3] and s[3:-7] both specify the null substring between the n and t in Interface. s[i:i+1] is always the character to the right of i for any valid position i, except the rightmost position.

Character indices are another way to specify substrings and may seem more natural, but they have disadvantages. Order is important when specifying substrings with indices. For example, the indices in the string Interface run from zero to nine inclusive. If substrings are specified with two indices where the substring starts *after* the first index and ends *before* the second one, s[1..6] specifies the substring terf. But this convention must permit the index of the null character in order to specify the substring face with s[4..9], and it cannot specify the leading null substring. Changing this convention so that a substring ends *after* the second index makes it impossible to specify a null substring. Other conventions that use negative indices could be used, but they're more cumbersome than positions.

Positions are better than character indices because they avoid these confusing boundary cases. And nonpositive positions can be used to access the tail of a string without knowing its length.

Str exports functions that create and return null-terminated strings, and that return information about strings and positions in them. The functions that create strings are:

⟨*exported functions* 244⟩≡
```
extern char *Str_sub(const char *s, int i, int j);
extern char *Str_dup(const char *s, int i, int j, int n);
extern char *Str_cat(const char *s1, int i1, int j1,
    const char *s2, int i2, int j2);
extern char *Str_catv  (const char *s, ...);
extern char *Str_reverse(const char *s, int i, int j);
extern char *Str_map   (const char *s, int i, int j,
    const char *from, const char *to);
```

All of these functions allocate the space for their results, and they all can raise Mem_Failed. It is a checked runtime error to pass a null string pointer to any function in this interface, except as detailed below for Str_catv and Str_map.

Str_sub returns s[i:j], the substring of s between the positions i and j. For example, the calls

```
Str_sub("Interface",  6, 10)
Str_sub("Interface",  6,  0)
Str_sub("Interface", -4, 10)
Str_sub("Interface", -4,  0)
```

all return face. The positions can be given in either order. It is a checked runtime error to pass an i and j that do not specify a substring in s to any function in this interface.

Str_dup returns a string with n copies of s[i:j]. It is a checked runtime error for n to be negative. Str_dup is often used to copy a string; for example, Str_dup("Interface", 1, 0, 1) returns a copy of Interface. Note the use of the positions 1 and 0 to specify all of Interface.

Str_cat returns the concatentation of s1[i1:j1] and s2[i2:j2]; that is, a string consisting of the characters from s1[i1:j1] followed by the characters from s2[i2:j2]. Str_catv is similar; it takes zero more triples that each specify a string and two positions, and returns the concatenation of these substrings. The argument list is terminated by a null pointer. For example,

```
Str_catv("Interface", -4, 0, " plant", 1, 0, NULL)
```

returns the string face plant.

Str_reverse returns the string consisting of the characters from s[i:j] in the opposite order in which they appear in s.

Str_map returns a string consisting of the characters from s[i:j] mapped according to the values given by from and to. Each character from s[i:j] that appears in from is mapped to the corresponding character in to. Characters that do not appear in from are mapped to themselves. For example,

```
Str_map(s, 1, 0, "ABCDEFGHIJKLMNOPQRSTUVWXYZ",
                 "abcdefghijklmnopqrstuvwxyz")
```

returns a copy of s in which uppercase characters are replaced by their lowercase equivalents.

If both from and to are null, the mapping specified by the most recent call to Str_map is used. If s is null, i and j are ignored, from and to are used only to establish the default mapping, and Str_map returns null.

The following are checked runtime errors: for only one of the from or to pointers to be null; for nonnull from and to strings to specify strings of different lengths; for all of s, from, and to to be null; and for both from and to be null on the first call to Str_map.

The remaining functions in the Str interface return information about strings or positions in strings; none allocate space.

⟨*exported functions* 244⟩+≡
```
extern int Str_pos(const char *s, int i);
extern int Str_len(const char *s, int i, int j);
extern int Str_cmp(const char *s1, int i1, int j1,
    const char *s2, int i2, int j2);
```

Str_pos returns the positive position corresponding to s[i:i]. A positive position can always be converted to an index by subtracting one, so Str_pos is often used when an index is needed. For example, if s points to the string Interface,

```
printf("%s\n", &s[Str_pos(s, -4)-1])
```

prints face.

Str_len returns the number of characters in s[i:j].

Str_cmp returns a value that is less than zero, equal to zero, or greater than zero if s1[i1:j1] is lexically less than, equal to, or greater than s2[i2:j2].

The following functions search strings for characters and other strings. When the search succeeds, these functions return positive positions that reflect the result of the search; when the search fails, they return zero. Functions with names that include _r search from the right ends of their argument strings; the others search from the left ends.

⟨*exported functions* 244⟩+≡
```
extern int Str_chr  (const char *s, int i, int j, int c);
extern int Str_rchr (const char *s, int i, int j, int c);
extern int Str_upto (const char *s, int i, int j,
    const char *set);
extern int Str_rupto(const char *s, int i, int j,
    const char *set);
extern int Str_find (const char *s, int i, int j,
    const char *str);
```

```
extern int Str_rfind(const char *s, int i, int j,
    const char *str);
```

Str_chr and Str_rchr return the position in s before the leftmost or rightmost occurrence of the character c in s[i:j], or zero if c doesn't appear in s[i:j].

Str_upto and Str_rupto return the position in s before the leftmost or rightmost occurrence in s[i:j] of any character in set, or zero if none of the characters in set appear in s[i:j]. It is a checked runtime error to pass a null set to these functions.

Str_find and Str_rfind return the position in s before the leftmost or rightmost occurrence of str in s[i:j], or zero if str doesn't appear in s[i:j]. It is a checked runtime error to pass a null str to these functions.

The functions

⟨*exported functions* 244⟩+≡
```
    extern int Str_any   (const char *s, int i,
        const char *set);
    extern int Str_many  (const char *s, int i, int j,
        const char *set);
    extern int Str_rmany (const char *s, int i, int j,
        const char *set);
    extern int Str_match (const char *s, int i, int j,
        const char *str);
    extern int Str_rmatch(const char *s, int i, int j,
        const char *str);
```

step over substrings; they return the positive positions that follow or precede the matched substrings.

Str_any returns the positive position in s after the character s[i:i+1] if that character appears in set, or zero if s[i:i+1] doesn't appear in set.

Str_many returns the positive position in s after a contiguous sequence of one or more characters from set at the beginning of s[i:j], or zero if s[i:j] doesn't begin with a character from set. Str_rmany returns the positive position in s *before* a contiguous sequence of one of more characters from set at the end of s[i:j], or zero if s[i:j] doesn't end with a character from set. It is checked runtime error to pass a null set to Str_any, Str_many, or Str_rmany.

Str_match returns the positive position in s after the occurrence of str at the beginning of s[i:j], or zero if s[i:j] doesn't begin with str. Str_rmatch returns the positive position in s *before* the occurrence of str at the end of s[i:j], or zero if s[i:j] doesn't end with str. It is checked runtime error to pass a null str to Str_match or Str_rmatch.

Str_rchr, Str_rupto, and Str_rfind search from the right ends of their argument strings, but return positions to the *left* of the characters or strings they seek. For example, the calls

```
Str_find ("The rain in Spain", 1, 0, "rain")
Str_rfind("The rain in Spain", 1, 0, "rain")
```

both return 5, because rain appears only once in their first arguments. The calls

```
Str_find ("The rain in Spain", 1, 0, "in")
Str_rfind("The rain in Spain", 1, 0, "in")
```

return 7 and 16, respectively, because in appears three times.

Str_many and Str_match step right and return the positions after the characters they step over. Str_rmany and Str_rmatch step left; they return the positions *before* the characters. For example,

```
Str_sub(name, 1, Str_rmany(name, 1, 0, " \t"))
```

returns a copy of name without its trailing blanks and tabs, if there are any. The function basename shows another typical use of these conventions. basename accepts a UNIX-style path name and returns the file name without its leading directories or a specific trailing suffix, as illustrated by the following examples.

```
basename("/usr/jenny/main.c", 1, 0, ".c")         main
basename("../src/main.c",     1, 0, "")           main.c
basename("main.c",            1, 0, "c")          main.
basename("main.c",            1, 0, ".obj")       main.c
basename("examples/wfmain.c", 1, 0, "main.c")     wf
```

basename uses Str_rchr to find the rightmost slash and Str_rmatch to isolate the suffix.

```
char *basename(char *path, int i, int j, char *suffix) {
    i = Str_rchr(path, i, j, '/');
    j = Str_rmatch(path, i + 1, 0, suffix);
    return Str_dup(path, i + 1, j, 1);
}
```

The value returned by Str_rchr, which is assigned to i, is the position before the rightmost slash, if there is one, or zero. In either case, the file name starts at position i + 1. Str_match examines the file name and returns the position before the suffix or after the file name. Again, in either case, j is set to the position after the file name. Str_dup returns the substring in path between i + 1 and j.

The function

⟨*exported functions* 244⟩+≡
```
    extern void Str_fmt(int code, va_list *app,
        int put(int c, void *cl), void *cl,
        unsigned char flags[], int width, int precision);
```

is a conversion function that can be used with the formatting functions in the Fmt interface to format substrings. It consumes *three* arguments — a string pointer and two positions — and it formats the substring in the style specified by the Fmt's %s format. It is a checked runtime error for the string pointer, app, or flags to be null.

For example, if Str_fmt is associated with the format code S by

```
    Fmt_register('S', Str_fmt)
```

then

```
    Fmt_print("%10S\n", "Interface", -4, 0)
```

prints the line _____face, where _ denotes a space.

15.2 Example: Printing Identifiers

A program that prints the C keywords and identifiers in its input illustrates the use of the use of Str_fmt, as well as the use of the functions that examine strings for characters or other strings.

⟨*ids.c*⟩≡

```
#include <stdlib.h>
#include <stdio.h>
#include "fmt.h"
#include "str.h"

int main(int argc, char *argv[]) {
    char line[512];
    static char set[] = "0123456789_"
        "abcdefghijklmnopqrstuvwxyz"
        "ABCDEFGHIJKLMNOPQRSTUVWXYZ";

    Fmt_register('S', Str_fmt);
    while (fgets(line, sizeof line, stdin) != NULL) {
        int i = 1, j;
        while ((i = Str_upto(line, i, 0, &set[10])) > 0){
            j = Str_many(line, i, 0, set);
            Fmt_print("%S\n", line, i, j);
            i = j;
        }
    }
    return EXIT_SUCCESS;
}
```

The inner while loop scans `line[i:0]` for the next identifier, beginning with i equal to one. `Str_upto` returns the position in `line` of the next underscore or letter in `line[i:0]`, and that position is assigned to i. `Str_many` returns the position after a run of digits, underscores, and letters. Thus, i and j identify the next identifier, and `Fmt_print` prints it with `Str_fmt`, which is associated with the format code S. Assigning j to i causes the next iteration of the while loop to look for the next identifier. When `line` holds the declaration for `main` above, the values of i and j passed to `Fmt_print` are as shown below.

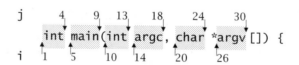

There are no allocations in this program. Using positions often avoids allocations in these kinds of applications.

15.3 Implementation

⟨*str.c*⟩≡
```
#include <string.h>
#include <limits.h>
#include "assert.h"
#include "fmt.h"
#include "str.h"
#include "mem.h"

⟨macros 251⟩
⟨functions 252⟩
```

The implementation must deal with converting positions to indices and vice versa, because the functions use indices to access the actual characters. The index of the character to the right of the positive position i is $i - 1$. The index of the character to the right of a negative position i is $i + len$, where `len` is the number of characters in the string. The macro

⟨*macros* 251⟩≡
```
#define idx(i, len) ((i) <= 0 ? (i) + (len) : (i) - 1)
```

encapsulates these definitions; given a position i in a string of length `len`, `idx(i, len)` is the index of the character to the right of i.

The `Str` functions convert their position arguments to indices, and then use these indices to access the string. The `convert` macro encapsulates the steps in this conversion:

⟨*macros* 251⟩+≡
```
#define convert(s, i, j) do { int len; \
    assert(s); len = strlen(s); \
    i = idx(i, len); j = idx(j, len); \
    if (i > j) { int t = i; i = j; j = t; } \
    assert(i >= 0 && j <= len); } while (0)
```

The positions i and j are converted to indices in the range zero to the length of s, and they're swapped, if necessary, so that i never exceeds j. The concluding assertion enforces the checked runtime error that i and j specify valid positions in s. Once converted, j − i is the length of the specified substring.

Str_sub illustrates the typical use of convert.

⟨functions 252⟩≡
```
char *Str_sub(const char *s, int i, int j) {
    char *str, *p;

    convert(s, i, j);
    p = str = ALLOC(j - i + 1);
    while (i < j)
        *p++ = s[i++];
    *p = '\0';
    return str;
}
```

The position that specifies the end of the substring is converted to the index of the character that follows the substring, which might be the terminating null character. Thus, j − i is the length of the desired substring, which, counting the null character, needs j − i + 1 bytes of storage.

Str_sub and some of the other Str functions can be written using the string routines in the standard C library, like strncpy; see Exercise 15.2.

15.3.1 String Operations

Str_dup allocates space for n copies of s[i:j] plus a terminating null character, and then copies s[i:j] n times, provided s[i:j] is nonempty.

⟨functions 252⟩+≡
```
char *Str_dup(const char *s, int i, int j, int n) {
    int k;
    char *str, *p;

    assert(n >= 0);
    convert(s, i, j);
    p = str = ALLOC(n*(j - i) + 1);
```

```
         if (j - i > 0)
             while (n-- > 0)
                 for (k = i; k < j; k++)
                     *p++ = s[k];
         *p = '\0';
         return str;
     }
```

Str_reverse is like Str_sub, except that it copies the characters backward:

⟨*functions* 252⟩+≡
```
    char *Str_reverse(const char *s, int i, int j) {
        char *str, *p;

        convert(s, i, j);
        p = str = ALLOC(j - i + 1);
        while (j > i)
            *p++ = s[--j];
        *p = '\0';
        return str;
    }
```

Str_cat could just call Str_catv, but it's used enough to warrant its own tailor-made implementation:

⟨*functions* 252⟩+≡
```
    char *Str_cat(const char *s1, int i1, int j1,
                  const char *s2, int i2, int j2) {
        char *str, *p;

        convert(s1, i1, j1);
        convert(s2, i2, j2);
        p = str = ALLOC(j1 - i1 + j2 - i2 + 1);
        while (i1 < j1)
            *p++ = s1[i1++];
        while (i2 < j2)
            *p++ = s2[i2++];
        *p = '\0';
        return str;
    }
```

Str_catv is a bit more complicated, because it must make two passes over its variable number of arguments:

⟨*functions* 252⟩+≡
```
char *Str_catv(const char *s, ...) {
    char *str, *p;
    const char *save = s;
    int i, j, len = 0;
    va_list ap;

    va_start(ap, s);
    ⟨len ← the length of the result 254⟩
    va_end(ap);
    p = str = ALLOC(len + 1);
    s = save;
    va_start(ap, s);
    ⟨copy each s[i:j] to p, increment p 255⟩
    va_end(ap);
    *p = '\0';
    return str;
}
```

The first pass computes the length of the result by summing the lengths of the argument substrings. After the space for the result is allocated, the second pass appends the substring given by each triple to the result. The first pass computes the length of each substring by converting the positions to indices, which give the length:

⟨len ← *the length of the result* 254⟩≡
```
while (s) {
    i = va_arg(ap, int);
    j = va_arg(ap, int);
    convert(s, i, j);
    len += j - i;
    s = va_arg(ap, const char *);
}
```

The second pass is almost identical: The only difference is that the assignment to len is replaced with a loop that copies the substring:

⟨*copy each* s[i:j] *to* p, *increment* p 255⟩≡
```
while (s) {
    i = va_arg(ap, int);
    j = va_arg(ap, int);
    convert(s, i, j);
    while (i < j)
        *p++ = s[i++];
    s = va_arg(ap, const char *);
}
```

Str_map builds an array map in which map[c] is the mapping for c as specified by from and to. The characters in s[i:j] are mapped and copied into a new string by using them as indices into map:

⟨*map* s[i:j] *into a new string* 255⟩≡
```
char *str, *p;
convert(s, i, j);
p = str = ALLOC(j - i + 1);
while (i < j)
    *p++ = map[(unsigned char)s[i++]];
*p = '\0';
```

The cast prevents characters whose values exceed 127 from being sign-extended to negative indices.

map is built by initializing it so that map[c] is equal to c; that is, each character is mapped to itself. Then the characters in from are used to index the elements in map to which the corresponding characters in to are assigned:

⟨*rebuild* map 255⟩≡
```
unsigned c;
for (c = 0; c < sizeof map; c++)
    map[c] = c;
while (*from && *to)
    map[(unsigned char)*from++] = *to++;
assert(*from == 0 && *to == 0);
```

The assertion above implements the checked runtime error that the lengths of from and to must be equal.

Str_map uses this chunk when both from and to are nonnull, and it uses ⟨*map* s[i:j] *into a new string* 255⟩ when s is nonnull:

⟨*functions* 252⟩+≡
```
char *Str_map(const char *s, int i, int j,
    const char *from, const char *to) {
    static char map[256] = { 0 };

    if (from && to) {
        ⟨rebuild map 255⟩
    } else {
        assert(from == NULL && to == NULL && s);
        assert(map['a']);
    }
    if (s) {
        ⟨map s[i:j] into a new string 255⟩
        return str;
    } else
        return NULL;
}
```

Initially, all of the elements of map are zero. There's no way to specify a null character in to, so the assertion that map['a'] is nonzero implements the checked runtime error that the first call to Str_map must not have null from and to pointers.

The positive position to the left of the character with index i is i + 1. Str_pos uses this property to return the positive position corresponding to the arbitrary position i in s. It converts i to an index, validates it, and converts it back to a positive position, which it returns.

⟨*functions* 252⟩+≡
```
int Str_pos(const char *s, int i) {
    int len;

    assert(s);
    len = strlen(s);
    i = idx(i, len);
    assert(i >= 0 && i <= len);
    return i + 1;
}
```

Str_len returns the length of the substring s[i:j] by converting i and j to indices and returning the number of characters between them:

```
⟨functions 252⟩+≡
  int Str_len(const char *s, int i, int j) {
      convert(s, i, j);
      return j - i;
  }
```

The implementation of Str_cmp is straightforward but tedious, because it involves some bookkeeping:

```
⟨functions 252⟩+≡
  int Str_cmp(const char *s1, int i1, int j1,
      const char *s2, int i2, int j2) {
      ⟨string compare 257⟩
  }
```

Str_cmp starts by converting i1 and j1 to indices in s1, and i2 and j2 to indices in s2:

```
⟨string compare 257⟩≡
  convert(s1, i1, j1);
  convert(s2, i2, j2);
```

Next, s1 and s2 are adjusted so that each points directly to its first character.

```
⟨string compare 257⟩+≡
  s1 += i1;
  s2 += i2;
```

The shorter of s1[i1:j1] and s2[i2:j2] determines the how many characters will be compared, which is done by calling strncmp.

```
⟨string compare 257⟩+≡
  if (j1 - i1 < j2 - i2) {
      int cond = strncmp(s1, s2, j1 - i1);
      return cond == 0 ? -1 : cond;
  } else if (j1 - i1 > j2 - i2) {
      int cond = strncmp(s1, s2, j2 - i2);
      return cond == 0 ? +1 : cond;
  } else
      return strncmp(s1, s2, j1 - i1);
```

When s1[i1:j1] is shorter than s2[i2:j2] and memcmp returns zero, s1[i1:j1] is equal to a prefix of s2[i2:j2] and is thus less than s2[i2:j2]. The second if statement handles the opposite case, and the else clause applies when the lengths of the arguments are equal.

The standard stipulates that strncmp (and memcmp) must treat the characters in s1 and s2 as unsigned characters, which gives a well-defined result when character values greater than 127 appear in s1 or s2. For example, strncmp("\344", "\127", 1) must return a positive value, but some implementations of strncmp incorrectly compare "plain" characters, which may be signed or unsigned. For these implementations, strncmp("\344", "\127", 1) may return a negative value. Some implementations of memcmp produce the same error.

15.3.2 Analyzing Strings

The remaining functions inspect substrings from the left to the right or vice versa for occurrences of characters or other strings. They all return a positive position if the search succeeds, and zero otherwise. Str_chr is typical:

⟨*functions* 252⟩+≡
```
int Str_chr(const char *s, int i, int j, int c) {
    convert(s, i, j);
    for ( ; i < j; i++)
        if (s[i] == c)
            return i + 1;
    return 0;
}
```

Str_rchr is similar, but starts its search from the right end of s[i:j]:

⟨*functions* 252⟩+≡
```
int Str_rchr(const char *s, int i, int j, int c) {
    convert(s, i, j);
    while (j > i)
        if (s[--j] == c)
            return j + 1;
    return 0;
}
```

Both functions return the positive position to the left of the occurrence of c, when c appears in s[i:j].

Str_upto and Str_rupto are similar to Str_chr and Str_rchr, except that they look for an occurrence in s[i:j] of any one of the characters in a set:

⟨*functions* 252⟩+≡
```
int Str_upto(const char *s, int i, int j,
    const char *set) {
    assert(set);
    convert(s, i, j);
    for ( ; i < j; i++)
        if (strchr(set, s[i]))
            return i + 1;
    return 0;
}

int Str_rupto(const char *s, int i, int j,
    const char *set) {
    assert(set);
    convert(s, i, j);
    while (j > i)
        if (strchr(set, s[--j]))
            return j + 1;
    return 0;
}
```

Str_find searches for the occurrence of a string in s[i:j]. Its implementation treats search strings of length zero or one as special cases.

⟨*functions* 252⟩+≡
```
int Str_find(const char *s, int i, int j,
    const char *str) {
    int len;

    convert(s, i, j);
    assert(str);
    len = strlen(str);
    if (len == 0)
        return i + 1;
    else if (len == 1) {
```

```
          for ( ; i < j; i++)
              if (s[i] == *str)
                  return i + 1;
      } else
          for ( ; i + len <= j; i++)
              if (⟨s[i...] ≡ str[0..len-1] 260⟩)
                  return i + 1;
      return 0;
  }
```

If str has no characters, the search always succeeds. If str has only one
character, Str_find is equivalent to Str_chr. In the general case,
Str_find looks for str in s[i:j], but it must be careful not to accept a
match that extends past the end of the substring:

⟨s[i...] ≡ str[0..len-1] 260⟩≡
  (strncmp(&s[i], str, len) == 0)

Str_rfind has the same three cases, but must cope with comparing
strings backward.

⟨functions 252⟩+≡
```
  int Str_rfind(const char *s, int i, int j,
      const char *str) {
      int len;

      convert(s, i, j);
      assert(str);
      len = strlen(str);
      if (len == 0)
          return j + 1;
      else if (len == 1) {
          while (j > i)
              if (s[--j] == *str)
                  return j + 1;
      } else
          for ( ; j - len >= i; j--)
              if (strncmp(&s[j-len], str, len) == 0)
                  return j - len + 1;
      return 0;
  }
```

`Str_rfind` must be careful not to accept a match that extends past the *beginning* of the substring.

`Str_any` and its cousins don't search for characters or strings; they simply step over them if they appear at the beginning or end of the substring in question. `Str_any` returns `Str_pos(s,i) + 1` if `s[i:i+1]` is a character in `set`:

⟨*functions* 252⟩+≡
```
    int Str_any(const char *s, int i, const char *set) {
        int len;

        assert(s);
        assert(set);
        len = strlen(s);
        i = idx(i, len);
        assert(i >= 0 && i <= len);
        if (i < len && strchr(set, s[i]))
            return i + 2;
        return 0;
    }
```

If the test succeeds, the index $i + 1$ is converted to a positive position by adding one, which explains why `Str_any` returns $i + 2$.

`Str_many` steps over a run of one or more characters in `set` that occur at the beginning of `s[i:j]`:

⟨*functions* 252⟩+≡
```
    int Str_many(const char *s, int i, int j,
        const char *set) {
        assert(set);
        convert(s, i, j);
        if (i < j && strchr(set, s[i])) {
            do
                    i++;
            while (i < j && strchr(set, s[i]));
            return i + 1;
        }
        return 0;
    }
```

Str_rmany backs up over a run of one or more characters in set that occur at the end of s[i:j]:

⟨*functions* 252⟩+≡
```
int Str_rmany(const char *s, int i, int j,
    const char *set) {
    assert(set);
    convert(s, i, j);
    if (j > i && strchr(set, s[j-1])) {
        do
            --j;
        while (j >= i && strchr(set, s[j]));
        return j + 2;
    }
    return 0;
}
```

When the do-while loop terminates, j is equal to i − 1 or is the index of a character that is *not* in set. In the first case, Set_rmany must return i + 1; in the second case, it must return the position to the *right* of the character s[j]. The value j + 2 is the correct one in both cases.

Str_match returns Str_pos(s,i) + strlen(str) if str occurs at the beginning of s[i:j]. Like Str_find, search strings with lengths zero or one get special treatment:

⟨*functions* 252⟩+≡
```
int Str_match(const char *s, int i, int j,
    const char *str) {
    int len;

    convert(s, i, j);
    assert(str);
    len = strlen(str);
    if (len == 0)
        return i + 1;
    else if (len == 1) {
        if (i < j && s[i] == *str)
            return i + 2;
    } else if (i + len <= j && ⟨s[i...] ≡ str[0..len−1] 260⟩)
        return i + len + 1;
```

```
        return 0;
    }
```

The general case must be careful not to consider a match that extends past the end of s[i:j].

Similar situations occur in Str_rmatch, which must avoid a match that extends past the beginning of s[i:j], and which can treat search strings with lengths zero or one as special cases.

⟨*functions* 252⟩+≡

```
    int Str_rmatch(const char *s, int i, int j,
        const char *str) {
        int len;

        convert(s, i, j);
        assert(str);
        len = strlen(str);
        if (len == 0)
            return j + 1;
        else if (len == 1) {
            if (j > i && s[j-1] == *str)
                return j;
        } else if (j - len >= i
        && strncmp(&s[j-len], str, len) == 0)
            return j - len + 1;
        return 0;
    }
```

15.3.3 Conversion Functions

The last function is Str_fmt, which is a conversion function as specified in the Fmt interface. The calling sequence for conversion functions is described on page 221. The flags, width, and precision arguments dictate how the string is to be formatted.

The important feature of Str_fmt is that it consumes *three* arguments from the variable part of the argument list passed to one of the Fmt functions. These three arguments specify the string and two positions within that string. These positions give the length of the substring, which, along with flags, width, and precision, determine how the substring is emitted. Str_fmt lets Fmt_puts interpret these values and emit the string:

⟨*functions* 252⟩+≡
```
    void Str_fmt(int code, va_list *app,
        int put(int c, void *cl), void *cl,
        unsigned char flags[], int width, int precision) {
        char *s;
        int i, j;

        assert(app && flags);
        s = va_arg(*app, char *);
        i = va_arg(*app, int);
        j = va_arg(*app, int);
        convert(s, i, j);
        Fmt_puts(s + i, j - i, put, cl, flags,
            width, precision);
    }
```

Further Reading

Plauger (1992) gives a brief critique of the functions defined in string.h, and shows how to implement them. Roberts (1995) describes a simple string interface that is similar to Str and based on string.h.

The design of the Str interface is lifted almost verbatim from the string-manipulation facilities in the Icon programming language (Griswold and Griswold 1990). Using positions instead of indices and using nonpositive positions to specify locations relative to the ends of strings originated with Icon.

Str's functions are modeled after Icon's similarly named string functions. The Icon functions are more powerful because they use Icon's goal-directed evaluation mechanism. For example, Icon's find function can return the positions of *all* the occurrences of one string in another as dictated by the context in which it is called. Icon also has a string-scanning facility that, with goal-directed evaluation, is a powerful pattern matching capability.

Str_map can be used to implement a surprisingly varied number of string transformations. For example, if s is a seven-character string,

```
    Str_map("abcdefg", 1, 0, "gfedcba", s)
```

returns the reverse of s. Griswold (1980) explores such uses of mappings.

Exercises

15.1 Extend `ids.c` so that it recognizes and ignores C comments, string literals, and keywords. Generalize your extended version to accept command-line arguments to specify additional identifiers that are to be ignored.

15.2 The `Str` implementation could use the string and memory functions in the standard C library, like `strncpy` and `memcpy`, to copy strings. For example, `Str_sub` could be written as follows.

```
char *Str_sub(const char *s, int i, int j) {
    char *str;

    convert(s, i, j);
    str = strncpy(ALLOC(j - i + 1), s + i, j - i);
    str[j - i] = '\0';
    return str;
}
```

Some C compilers recognize calls to the `string.h` functions and generate in-line code that may be much faster than the corresponding loops in C. Highly optimized assembly-language implementations are also usually faster. Reimplement `Str` using the `string.h` functions where possible; measure the results using a specific C compiler on a specific machine, then characterize the improvements for each function in terms of the lengths of their string arguments.

15.3 Design and implement a function that searches a substring for a pattern specified by a *regular expression*, like those supported in AWK and described in Aho, Kernighan, and Weinberger (1988). This function needs to return two values: the position at which match begins and its length.

15.4 Icon has an extensive string scanning facility. Its ? operator establishes a scanning environment that supplies a string and a position in this string. String functions like `find` can be invoked with only one argument, in which case they operate on the string and the position in the current scanning environment. Study Icon's string-scanning facility, described in Griswold and Griswold (1990), and design and implement an interface that provides similar functionality.

15.5 `string.h` defines the function

```
char *strtok(char *s, const char *set);
```

which splits s into tokens separated by characters in set. The string s is split into tokens by calling strtok repeatedly. s is passed only on the first call, and strtok searches for the first character that is *not* in set, overwrites that character with a null character, and returns s. Subsequent calls, which have the form strtok(NULL, set), cause strtok to continue from where it left off and search for the first character that *is* in set, overwrite that character with a null character, and return a pointer to the beginning of the token. set can be different on each call. When a search fails, strtok returns null. Extend the Str interface with a function that provides similar capabilities but does not modify its argument. Can you improve on strtok's design?

15.6 The Str functions always allocate space for their results, and these allocations might be unnecessary in some applications. Suppose the functions accepted an optional destination, and allocated space only if the destination was the null pointer. For example,

```
char *Str_dup(char *dst, int size,
    const char *s, int i, int j, int n);
```

would store its result in dst[0..size-1] and return dst, if dst were nonnull; otherwise, it would allocate space for its result, as the current version does. Design an interface based on this approach. Be sure to specify what happens when size is too small. Compare your design with the Str interface. Which is simpler? Which is less prone to error?

15.7 Here's another proposal for avoiding allocations in the Str functions. Suppose the function

```
void Str_result(char *dst, int size);
```

posts dst as the "result string" for the next call to a Str function. If the result string is nonnull, the Str functions store their results in dst[0..size-1] and clear the result string pointer. If the result string is null, they allocate space for their results, as usual. Discuss the pros and cons of this proposal.

16

HIGH-LEVEL STRINGS

The functions exported by the Str interface described in the previous chapter augment the conventions for handling strings in C. By convention, strings are arrays of characters in which the last character is null. While this representation is adequate for many applications, it does have two significant disadvantages. First, finding the length of a string requires searching the string for its terminating null character, so computing the length takes time proportional to the length of the string. Second, the functions in the Str interface and some of those in the standard library assume that strings can be changed, so either they or their callers must allocate space for string results; in applications that do not modify strings, many of these allocations are unnecessary.

The Text interface described in this chapter uses a slightly different representation for strings that addresses both of these disadvantages. Lengths are computed in constant time, because they're carried along with the string, and allocations occur only when necessary. The strings provided by Text are immutable — that is, they cannot be changed in place — and they can contain embedded null characters. Text provides functions for converting between its string representation and C-style strings; these conversions are the price for Text's improvements.

16.1 Interface

The Text interface represents a string by a two-element *descriptor*, which gives the length of the string and points to its first character:

⟨*exported types* 270⟩≡
```
typedef struct T {
    int len;
    const char *str;
} T;
```

⟨*text.h*⟩≡
```
#ifndef TEXT_INCLUDED
#define TEXT_INCLUDED
#include <stdarg.h>

#define T Text_T
```

⟨*exported types* 270⟩
⟨*exported data* 274⟩
⟨*exported functions* 271⟩

```
#undef T
#endif
```

The string pointed to by the str field is *not* terminated with a null character. Strings pointed to by Text_Ts may contain any character, including the null character. Text reveals the representation of descriptors so that clients may access the fields directly. Given a Text_T s, s.len gives the length of the string, and the actual characters are accessed by s.str[0..s.len-1].

Clients can read the fields of a Text_T and the characters in the string it points to, but they must not change the fields or the characters in the string, except via functions in this interface, or in Text_Ts they initialize, or in those returned by Text_box. It is an unchecked runtime error to change the string described by a Text_T. It is also a checked runtime error to pass a Text_T with a negative len field or a null str field to any function in this interface.

Text exports functions that pass and return descriptors by *value*; that is, descriptors themselves are passed to and returned by functions, instead of passing pointers to descriptors. As a result, none of the Text functions allocate descriptors.

When necessary, some Text functions do allocate space for the strings themselves. This string space is managed completely by Text; clients must never deallocate strings, except as described below. Deallocating strings by external means, such as calling free or Mem_free, is an unchecked runtime error.

The functions

⟨*exported functions* 271⟩≡

```
extern T    Text_put(const char *str);
extern char *Text_get(char *str, int size, T s);
extern T    Text_box(const char *str, int len);
```

convert between descriptors and C-style strings. Text_put copies the null-terminated string str into the string space and returns a descriptor for the new string. Text_put can raise Mem_Failed. It is checked runtime error for str to be null.

Text_get copies the string described by s into str[0..size-2], appends a null character, and returns str. It is a checked runtime error for size to be less than s.len+1. If str is null, Text_get ignores size, calls Mem_alloc to allocate s.len+1 bytes, copies s.str into that space, and returns a pointer to the beginning of the allocated space. When str is null, Text_get can raise Mem_Failed.

Clients call Text_box to build descriptors for constant strings or for strings that they allocate. It "boxes" str and len in a descriptor and returns the descriptor. For example,

```
static char editmsg[] = "Last edited by: ";
...
Text_T msg = Text_box(editmsg, sizeof (editmsg) - 1);
```

assigns to msg a Text_T for "Last edited by: ". Note that the second argument to Text_box omits the null character at the end of editmsg. If this character is not omitted, it will be treated as part of the string described by msg. It is a checked runtime error for str to be null or for len to be negative.

Many of the Text functions accept string positions, which are defined as in Str. Positions identify locations *between* characters, including before the first character and after the last one. Positive positions identify positions from the left of the string beginning with the first character, and nonpositive positions identify positions from the right of the string. For example, the following figure from Chapter 15 shows the positions in the string `Interface`.

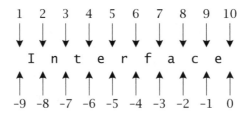

The function

⟨*exported functions* 271⟩+≡
```
extern T Text_sub(T s, int i, int j);
```

returns a descriptor for the substring of s between positions i and j. The positions i and j can be given in either order. For example, if

```
Text_T s = Text_put("Interface");
```

the expressions

```
Text_sub(s,  6, 10)
Text_sub(s,  0, -4)
Text_sub(s, 10, -4)
Text_sub(s,  6,  0)
```

all return descriptors for the substring `face`.

Since clients don't change the characters in a string, and strings don't need to be terminated with a null character, Text_sub simply returns a Text_T in which the str field points to the first character of the substring of s and the len field is the length of the substring. s and the value returned may thus *share* the characters in the actual string, and Text_sub does *no* allocation. Clients must not count on s and the return value sharing the same string, however, because Text may give empty strings and one-character strings special treatment. Most of the functions exported by Text are similar to those exported by Str, but many of them don't accept position arguments because Text_sub provides the same capability at little cost.

The function

⟨*exported functions* 271⟩+≡
```
extern int Text_pos(T s, int i);
```

returns the positive position in s corresponding to the arbitrary position
i. For example, if s is assigned Interface as shown above,

```
Text_pos(s, -4)
```

returns 6.

It is a checked runtime error for i in Text_pos or for i or j in
Text_sub to specify a nonexistent position in s.

The functions

⟨*exported functions* 271⟩+≡
```
extern T Text_cat     (T s1, T s2);
extern T Text_dup     (T s, int n);
extern T Text_reverse(T s);
```

concatenate, duplicate, and reverse strings; all can raise Mem_Failed.
Text_cat returns a descriptor for the string that's the result of concatenating s1 and s2; if either s1 or s2 describes the empty string, the other
argument is returned. Also, Text_cat makes a new copy of s1 and s2
only when necessary.

Text_dup returns a descriptor for the string that's the result of concatenating n copies of s; it is a checked runtime error for n to be negative. Text_reverse returns a string that holds the characters from s in
the opposite order.

⟨*exported functions* 271⟩+≡
```
extern T Text_map(T s, const T *from, const T *to);
```

returns the outcome of mapping s according to the strings pointed to by
from and to as follows. For each character in s that appears in from, the
corresponding character in to appears in the result string. If a character
in s doesn't appear in from, that character itself appears unchanged in
the output. For example,

```
Text_map(s, &Text_ucase, &Text_lcase)
```

returns a copy of s in which uppercase letters have been folded to their lowercase counterparts. Text_ucase and Text_lcase are examples of the predefined descriptors exported by Text. The complete list is:

⟨*exported data* 274⟩≡
```
extern const T Text_cset;
extern const T Text_ascii;
extern const T Text_ucase;
extern const T Text_lcase;
extern const T Text_digits;
extern const T Text_null;
```

Text_cset is a string consisting of all 256 eight-bit characters, Text_ascii holds the 127 ASCII characters, Text_ucase is the string ABCDEFGHIJKLMNOPQRSTUVWXYZ, Text_lcase is the string abcdefghijklmnopqrstuvwxyz, Text_digits is 0123456789, and Text_null is the empty string. Clients can form other common strings by taking substrings of these.

Text_map remembers the most recent nonnull from and to values, and uses these values if from and to are *both* null. It is a checked run-time error for only one of from or to to be null, or for from->len to be different than to->len when from and to are both nonnull. Text_map can raise Mem_Failed.

Strings are compared by

⟨*exported functions* 271⟩+≡
```
extern int Text_cmp(T s1, T s2);
```

which returns a value that's less than zero, equal to zero, or greater than zero if, respectively, s1 is lexically less than s2, s1 is equal to s2, or s1 is greater than s2.

Text exports a set of string-analysis functions that are nearly identical to those exported by Str. These functions, described below, *do* accept positions in the string to be examined, because these positions usually encode the state of the analysis. In the descriptions that follow, s[i:j] denotes the substring of s between positions i and j, and s[i] denotes the character to the right of position i.

The following functions look for occurrences of single characters or sets of characters; in all cases, it is a checked runtime error for i or j to specify nonexistent positions.

⟨*exported functions* 271⟩+≡
```
    extern int Text_chr  (T s, int i, int j, int c);
    extern int Text_rchr (T s, int i, int j, int c);
    extern int Text_upto (T s, int i, int j, T set);
    extern int Text_rupto(T s, int i, int j, T set);
    extern int Text_any  (T s, int i, T set);
    extern int Text_many (T s, int i, int j, T set);
    extern int Text_rmany(T s, int i, int j, T set);
```

Text_chr returns the positive position to the left of the leftmost occurrence of c in s[i:j], and Text_rchr returns the positive position to the left of the rightmost occurrence of c in s[i:j]. Both functions return zero if c doesn't appear in s[i:j]. Text_upto returns the positive position to the left of the leftmost occurrence of any character from set in s[i:j], and Text_rupto returns the positive position to the left of the rightmost occurrence of any character from set in s[i:j]. Both functions return zero if none of the characters from set appear in s[i:j].

Text_any returns Text_pos(s, i) + 1 if s[i] is equal to c, and zero otherwise. If s[i:j] begins with a character from set, Text_many returns the positive position following a contiguous nonempty sequence of characters from set; otherwise, it returns zero. If s[i:j] ends with a character from set, Text_rmany returns the positive position *before* a nonempty sequence of characters from set; otherwise Text_rmany returns zero.

The remaining analysis functions look for occurrences of strings.

⟨*exported functions* 271⟩+≡
```
    extern int Text_find  (T s, int i, int j, T str);
    extern int Text_rfind (T s, int i, int j, T str);
    extern int Text_match (T s, int i, int j, T str);
    extern int Text_rmatch(T s, int i, int j, T str);
```

Text_find returns the positive position to the left of the leftmost occurrence of str in s[i:j], and Text_rfind returns the positive position to the left of the rightmost occurrence of str in s[i:j]. If str doesn't appear in s[i:j], both functions return zero.

Text_match returns Text_pos(s, i) + str.len if s[i:j] begins with str, and zero otherwise. Text_rmatch returns Text_pos(s, j) − str.len if s[i:j] ends with str, and zero otherwise.

The function

⟨*exported functions* 271⟩+≡
```
    extern void Text_fmt(int code, va_list *app,
        int put(int c, void *cl), void *cl,
        unsigned char flags[], int width, int precision);
```

can be used with the Fmt interface as a conversion function. It consumes
a pointer to a Text_T and formats its string according to the optional
flags, width, and precision arguments in the same way that the
printf code %s formats its string argument. A pointer to a Text_T is
used because, in Standard C, passing small structures in the variable part
of a variable length argument list may not be portable. It is a checked
runtime error for the pointer to the Text_T to be null, or for app or
flags to be null.

Text gives clients some limited control over its allocation of the string
space, which is where it stores the actual strings for the results of the
functions described above that return descriptors. Specifically, the following functions manage that space as a stack.

⟨*exported types* 270⟩+≡
```
    typedef struct Text_save_T *Text_save_T;
```

⟨*exported functions* 271⟩+≡
```
    extern Text_save_T Text_save(void);
    extern void        Text_restore(Text_save_T *save);
```

Text_save returns a value of the opaque pointer type Text_save_T that
encodes the "top" of the string space. This value can later be passed to
Text_restore to deallocate that portion of the string space that was
allocated since the Text_save_T value was created. If h is a value of type
Text_save_T, calling Text_restore(h) invalidates all descriptors and
all Text_save_T values that were created after h. It is a checked runtime
error to pass a null Text_save_T to Text_restore. It is an unchecked
runtime error to use these values. Text_save can raise Mem_Failed.

16.2 Implementation

The implementation of Text is much like the implementation of Str, but
the Text functions can take advantage of several important special
cases, as detailed below.

⟨*text.c*⟩≡
```
#include <string.h>
#include <limits.h>
#include "assert.h"
#include "fmt.h"
#include "text.h"
#include "mem.h"

#define T Text_T
```

⟨*macros* 278⟩
⟨*types* 287⟩
⟨*data* 277⟩
⟨*static functions* 286⟩
⟨*functions* 278⟩

The constant descriptors all point to one string consisting of all 256 characters:

⟨*data* 277⟩≡
```
static char cset[] =
    "\000\001\002\003\004\005\006\007\010\011\012\013\014\015\016\017"
    "\020\021\022\023\024\025\026\027\030\031\032\033\034\035\036\037"
    "\040\041\042\043\044\045\046\047\050\051\052\053\054\055\056\057"
    "\060\061\062\063\064\065\066\067\070\071\072\073\074\075\076\077"
    "\100\101\102\103\104\105\106\107\110\111\112\113\114\115\116\117"
    "\120\121\122\123\124\125\126\127\130\131\132\133\134\135\136\137"
    "\140\141\142\143\144\145\146\147\150\151\152\153\154\155\156\157"
    "\160\161\162\163\164\165\166\167\170\171\172\173\174\175\176\177"
    "\200\201\202\203\204\205\206\207\210\211\212\213\214\215\216\217"
    "\220\221\222\223\224\225\226\227\230\231\232\233\234\235\236\237"
    "\240\241\242\243\244\245\246\247\250\251\252\253\254\255\256\257"
    "\260\261\262\263\264\265\266\267\270\271\272\273\274\275\276\277"
    "\300\301\302\303\304\305\306\307\310\311\312\313\314\315\316\317"
    "\320\321\322\323\324\325\326\327\330\331\332\333\334\335\336\337"
    "\340\341\342\343\344\345\346\347\350\351\352\353\354\355\356\357"
    "\360\361\362\363\364\365\366\367\370\371\372\373\374\375\376\377"
    ;
const T Text_cset   = { 256, cset };
const T Text_ascii  = { 127, cset };
const T Text_ucase  = {  26, cset + 'A' };
```

```
const T Text_lcase  = {  26, cset + 'a' };
const T Text_digits = {  10, cset + '0' };
const T Text_null   = {   0, cset };
```

The Text functions accept positions, but convert them to indices of the character to the right of the position in order to access the characters in the string. A positive position is converted to an index by subtracting one, and a nonpositive position is converted to an index by adding the length of the string:

⟨*macros* 278⟩≡

```
#define idx(i, len) ((i) <= 0 ? (i) + (len) : (i) - 1)
```

An index is converted to a positive position by adding one, as illustrated by the implementation of Text_pos, which converts its position argument to an index, then converts the index back to a positive position.

⟨*functions* 278⟩≡

```
int Text_pos(T s, int i) {
    assert(s.len >= 0 && s.str);
    i = idx(i, s.len);
    assert(i >= 0 && i <= s.len);
    return i + 1;
}
```

The first assertion in Text_pos implements the checked runtime error that all Text_Ts must have nonnegative len fields and nonnull str fields. The second assertion is the checked runtime error that the position i — now an index — corresponds to a valid position in s. If s has N characters, the valid indices are zero through $N–1$, but the valid positions are one through $N+1$, which is why the second assertion accepts indices as large as N.

Text_box and Text_sub both build and return new descriptors.

⟨*functions* 278⟩+≡

```
T Text_box(const char *str, int len) {
    T text;

    assert(str);
    assert(len >= 0);
    text.str = str;
```

```
        text.len = len;
        return text;
}
```

Text_sub is similar, but it must convert its position arguments to indices so that it can compute the length of the result:

⟨*functions* 278⟩+≡
```
    T Text_sub(T s, int i, int j) {
        T text;

        ⟨convert i and j to indices in 0..s.len 279⟩
        text.len = j - i;
        text.str = s.str + i;
        return text;
    }
```

As shown, there are j – i characters between i and j, after they've been converted from positions to indices. The code for that conversion also swaps i and j so that i always specifies the index of the leftmost character.

⟨*convert* i *and* j *to indices in* 0..s.len 279⟩≡
```
    assert(s.len >= 0 && s.str);
    i = idx(i, s.len);
    j = idx(j, s.len);
    if (i > j) { int t = i; i = j; j = t; }
    assert(i >= 0 && j <= s.len);
```

The position to the right of the last character is converted to the index of a nonexistent character, and the assertions accept such positions. ⟨*convert* i *and* j *to indices in* 0..s.len 279⟩ is used only when these indices are not used to fetch or store a character. Text_sub, for example, uses them only to compute a starting position and length. Other Text functions use the resulting values of i and j only after they've checked that i and j are valid indices.

Text_put and Text_get copy strings in and out of the string space. Text implements its own allocation function, *alloc(int len), to allocate len bytes of string space for several reasons. First, alloc avoids the block headers used in general-purpose allocators, so that it can arrange for strings to be adjacent. This leads to several important optmizations for `Text_dup` and `Text_cat`. Second, `alloc` can ignore alignment, because there are no alignment restrictions for characters. Finally, `alloc` must cooperate with `Text_save` and `Text_restore`. `alloc` is described starting on page 286, along with `Text_save` and `Text_restore`.

`Text_put` is typical of the few `Text` functions that allocate string space. It calls `alloc` to allocate the space required, copies its argument string into that space, and returns the appropriate descriptor:

⟨*functions* 278⟩+≡
```
T Text_put(const char *str) {
    T text;

    assert(str);
    text.len = strlen(str);
    text.str = memcpy(alloc(text.len), str, text.len);
    return text;
}
```

`Text_put` calls `memcpy` instead of `strcpy` because it must *not* append a null character to `text.str`.

`Text_get` does just the reverse: It copies a string from the string space to a C-style string. If the pointer to the C-style string is null, `Text_get` calls Mem's general-purpose allocator to allocate space for the string and its terminating null character:

⟨*functions* 278⟩+≡
```
char *Text_get(char *str, int size, T s) {
    assert(s.len >= 0 && s.str);
    if (str == NULL)
        str = ALLOC(s.len + 1);
    else
        assert(size >= s.len + 1);
    memcpy(str, s.str, s.len);
    str[s.len] = '\0';
    return str;
}
```

`Text_get` calls `memcpy` instead of `strncpy` because it must copy null characters that appear in s.

16.2.1 String Operations

Text_dup makes n copies of its Text_T argument s.

⟨*functions* 278⟩+≡
```
T Text_dup(T s, int n) {
    assert(s.len >= 0 && s.str);
    assert(n >= 0);
    ⟨Text_dup 281⟩
}
```

There are several important special cases in which allocation of n copies of s can be avoided. For example, if s is the null string or n is zero, Text_dup returns the null string; if n is one, Text_dup can just return s:

⟨*Text_dup* 281⟩≡
```
if (n == 0 || s.len == 0)
    return Text_null;
if (n == 1)
    return s;
```

If s has been created recently, s.str might lie at the end of the string space; that is, s.str + s.len might be equal to the address of the next free byte. If so, only n − 1 copies of s are needed, because the original s can serve as the first duplicate. The macro isatend(s, n), defined on page 286, checks whether s.str is at the end of the string space, and whether there's space for at least n characters.

⟨*Text_dup* 281⟩+≡
```
{
    T text;
    char *p;
    text.len = n*s.len;
    if (isatend(s, text.len - s.len)) {
        text.str = s.str;
        p = alloc(text.len - s.len);
        n--;
    } else
        text.str = p = alloc(text.len);
    for ( ; n-- > 0; p += s.len)
        memcpy(p, s.str, s.len);
```

```
        return text;
    }
```

Text_cat returns the concatentation of two strings, s1 and s2.

⟨*functions* 278⟩+≡
```
    T Text_cat(T s1, T s2) {
        assert(s1.len >= 0 && s1.str);
        assert(s2.len >= 0 && s2.str);
        ⟨Text_cat 282⟩
    }
```

As for Text_dup, there are several important special cases that avoid allocations. First, if either s1 or s2 is the null string, Text_cat can simply return the other descriptor:

⟨*Text_cat* 282⟩≡
```
    if (s1.len == 0)
        return s2;
    if (s2.len == 0)
        return s1;
```

s1 and s2 might already be adjacent, in which case Text_cat can return a descriptor for the combined result:

⟨*Text_cat* 282⟩+≡
```
    if (s1.str + s1.len == s2.str) {
        s1.len += s2.len;
        return s1;
    }
```

If s1 lies at the end of the string space, then only s2 needs to be copied; otherwise, both strings must be copied:

⟨*Text_cat* 282⟩+≡
```
    {
        T text;
        text.len = s1.len + s2.len;
        if (isatend(s1, s2.len)) {
            text.str = s1.str;
            memcpy(alloc(s2.len), s2.str, s2.len);
```

```
    } else {
        char *p;
        text.str = p = alloc(s1.len + s2.len);
        memcpy(p,            s1.str, s1.len);
        memcpy(p + s1.len, s2.str, s2.len);
    }
    return text;
}
```

Text_reverse, which returns a copy of its argument s with its characters in the opposite order, has only two important special cases: when s
is the null string and when it has only one character:

⟨*functions* 278⟩+≡
```
    T Text_reverse(T s) {
        assert(s.len >= 0 && s.str);
        if (s.len == 0)
            return Text_null;
        else if (s.len == 1)
            return s;
        else {
            T text;
            char *p;
            int i = s.len;
            text.len = s.len;
            text.str = p = alloc(s.len);
            while (--i >= 0)
                *p++ = s.str[i];
            return text;
        }
    }
```

The implementation of Text_map is similar to the implementation of
Str_map. First, it uses the from and to strings to build an array that
maps characters; given an input character c, map[c] is the character that
appears in the output string. map is initialized so that map[k] is equal to
k, then the characters in from are used to index the elements in map that
are to be mapped to the corresponding characters in to:

⟨*rebuild* map 283⟩≡
```
    int k;
```

```
for (k = 0; k < (int)sizeof map; k++)
    map[k] = k;
assert(from->len == to->len);
for (k = 0; k < from->len; k++)
    map[from->str[k]] = to->str[k];
inited = 1;
```

The `inited` flag is set to one after `map` has been initialized, and `inited` is used to implement the checked runtime error that the first call to `Text_map` must specify nonnull `from` and `to` strings:

⟨*functions* 278⟩+≡
```
T Text_map(T s, const T *from, const T *to) {
    static char map[256];
    static int inited = 0;

    assert(s.len >= 0 && s.str);
    if (from && to) {
        ⟨rebuild map 283⟩
    } else {
        assert(from == NULL && to == NULL);
        assert(inited);
    }
    if (s.len == 0)
        return Text_null;
    else {
        T text;
        int i;
        char *p;
        text.len = s.len;
        text.str = p = alloc(s.len);
        for (i = 0; i < s.len; i++)
            *p++ = map[s.str[i]];
        return text;
    }
}
```

`Str_map` doesn't need the `inited` flag because it's impossible to map a character to the null character with `Str_map`; asserting that `map['a']` is nonzero was enough to implement the checked runtime error (see page 256). `Text_map`, however, permits all possible mappings, and thus cannot use a value in `map` to implement the check.

`Text_cmp` compares two strings `s1` and `s2` and returns a value that's less than zero, equal to zero, or greater than zero when `s1` is less than, equal to, or greater than `s2`, respectively. The important special case is when `s1` and `s2` point to the same string, in which case the shorter string is less than the longer one. Likewise, when one of the strings is a prefix of the other, the shorter one is less.

⟨*functions* 278⟩+≡
```
int Text_cmp(T s1, T s2) {
    assert(s1.len >= 0 && s1.str);
    assert(s2.len >= 0 && s2.str);
    if (s1.str == s2.str)
        return s1.len - s2.len;
    else if (s1.len < s2.len) {
        int cond = memcmp(s1.str, s2.str, s1.len);
        return cond == 0 ? -1 : cond;
    } else if (s1.len > s2.len) {
        int cond = memcmp(s1.str, s2.str, s2.len);
        return cond == 0 ? +1 : cond;
    } else
        return memcmp(s1.str, s2.str, s1.len);
}
```

16.2.2 Memory Management

`Text` implements its own memory allocator so that it can take advantage of adjacent strings in `Text_dup` and `Text_cat`. Since the string space holds only characters, `Text`'s allocator can also avoid block headers and alignment issues, which saves space. The allocator is a simple variant of the arena allocator described in Chapter 6. The string space is like a single arena in which the allocated chunks appear in the list emanating from `head`:

⟨*data* 277⟩+≡
```
static struct chunk {
    struct chunk *link;
    char *avail;
    char *limit;
} head = { NULL, NULL, NULL }, *current = &head;
```

The limit field points to the byte one past the end of the chunk, avail points to the first free byte, and link points to the next chunk, all of which is free. current points to the "current" chunk, which is the one in which allocations are made. The definition above initializes current to point to a zero-length chunk; the first allocation appends a new chunk to head.

alloc allocates len bytes from the current chunk, or allocates a new chunk of at least 10K bytes:

⟨*static functions* 286⟩≡
```
static char *alloc(int len) {
    assert(len >= 0);
    if (current->avail + len > current->limit) {
        current = current->link =
            ALLOC(sizeof (*current) + 10*1024 + len);
        current->avail = (char *)(current + 1);
        current->limit = current->avail + 10*1024 + len;
        current->link = NULL;
    }
    current->avail += len;
    return current->avail - len;
}
```

current->avail is the address of the free byte at the end of the string space. A Text_T s appears at the end of the string space if s.str + s.len is equal to current->avail. The macro isatend is thus

⟨*macros* 278⟩+≡
```
#define isatend(s, n) ((s).str+(s).len == current->avail\
    && current->avail + (n) <= current->limit)
```

Text_dup and Text_cat can take advantage of strings that appear at the end of the string space only when there's enough free space in that chunk to satisfy the request, which explains isatend's second parameter.

Text_save and Text_restore give clients a way to save and restore the location of the end of the string space, which is given by the values of current and current->avail. Text_save returns an opaque pointer to an instance of

⟨*types* 287⟩≡
```
struct Text_save_T {
    struct chunk *current;
    char *avail;
};
```

which carries the values of current and current->avail.

⟨*functions* 278⟩+≡
```
Text_save_T Text_save(void) {
    Text_save_T save;

    NEW(save);
    save->current = current;
    save->avail = current->avail;
    alloc(1);
    return save;
}
```

Text_save calls alloc(1) to create a "hole" in the string space so that isatend will fail for any string allocated before the hole. Thus, it's impossible for a string to straddle the end of the string space that's returned to the client.

Text_restore restores the values of current and current->avail, deallocates the Text_save_T structure and clears *save, and deallocates all of the chunks that follow the current one.

⟨*functions* 278⟩+≡
```
void Text_restore(Text_save_T *save) {
    struct chunk *p, *q;

    assert(save && *save);
    current = (*save)->current;
    current->avail = (*save)->avail;
    FREE(*save);
    for (p = current->link; p; p = q) {
        q = p->link;
        FREE(p);
    }
    current->link = NULL;
}
```

16.2.3 Analyzing Strings

The remaining functions exported by Text inspect strings; none of them allocate new ones.

Text_chr looks for the leftmost occurrence of a character in s[i:j]:

⟨*functions* 278⟩+≡
```
int Text_chr(T s, int i, int j, int c) {
    ⟨convert i and j to indices in 0..s.len 279⟩
    for ( ; i < j; i++)
        if (s.str[i] == c)
            return i + 1;
    return 0;
}
```

If s.str[i] is equal to c, i + 1 is the position to the left of that character in s. Text_rchr is similar, but looks for the rightmost occurrence of c:

⟨*functions* 278⟩+≡
```
int Text_rchr(T s, int i, int j, int c) {
    ⟨convert i and j to indices in 0..s.len 279⟩
    while (j > i)
        if (s.str[--j] == c)
            return j + 1;
    return 0;
}
```

Text_upto and Text_rupto are like Text_chr and Text_rchr, except that they search for occurrences of any character in a set of characters, which is specified with a Text_T:

⟨*functions* 278⟩+≡
```
int Text_upto(T s, int i, int j, T set) {
    assert(set.len >= 0 && set.str);
    ⟨convert i and j to indices in 0..s.len 279⟩
    for ( ; i < j; i++)
        if (memchr(set.str, s.str[i], set.len))
            return i + 1;
    return 0;
}
```

```
int Text_rupto(T s, int i, int j, T set) {
    assert(set.len >= 0 && set.str);
    ⟨convert i and j to indices in 0..s.len 279⟩
    while (j > i)
        if (memchr(set.str, s.str[--j], set.len))
            return j + 1;
    return 0;
}
```

Str_upto and Str_rupto use the C library function strchr to check whether a character in s appears in set. The Text functions can't use strchr because both s and set might contain null characters, so they use memchr, which doesn't interpret null characters as string terminators.

Text_find and Text_rfind, which find occurrences of strings in s[i:j], have a similar problem: The Str variants of these functions use strncmp to compare substrings, but the Text functions must use memcmp, which copes with null characters. Text_find uses memcmp as it searches for the leftmost occurrence in s[i:j] of the string given by str. The cases that merit special attention are when str is the null string or when it has only one character.

⟨functions 278⟩+≡
```
    int Text_find(T s, int i, int j, T str) {
        assert(str.len >= 0 && str.str);
        ⟨convert i and j to indices in 0..s.len 279⟩
        if (str.len == 0)
            return i + 1;
        else if (str.len == 1) {
            for ( ; i < j; i++)
                if (s.str[i] == *str.str)
                    return i + 1;
        } else
            for ( ; i + str.len <= j; i++)
                if (equal(s, i, str))
                    return i + 1;
        return 0;
    }
```

⟨*macros* 278⟩+≡
```
#define equal(s, i, t) \
    (memcmp(&(s).str[i], (t).str, (t).len) == 0)
```

In the general case, `Text_find` must not inspect characters beyond the substring `s[i:j]`, which is the reason for the termination condition in the for loop.

`Text_rfind` is like `Text_find`, but it searches for the rightmost occurrence of `str`, and it avoids inspecting characters that appear before `s[i:j]`.

⟨*functions* 278⟩+≡
```
int Text_rfind(T s, int i, int j, T str) {
    assert(str.len >= 0 && str.str);
    ⟨convert i and j to indices in 0..s.len 279⟩
    if (str.len == 0)
        return j + 1;
    else if (str.len == 1) {
        while (j > i)
            if (s.str[--j] == *str.str)
                return j + 1;
    } else
        for ( ; j - str.len >= i; j--)
            if (equal(s, j - str.len, str))
                return j - str.len + 1;
    return 0;
}
```

`Text_any` steps over the character to the right of position `i` in `s`, if that character appears in `set`, and returns `Text_pos(s, i) + 1`.

⟨*functions* 278⟩+≡
```
int Text_any(T s, int i, T set) {
    assert(s.len >= 0 && s.str);
    assert(set.len >= 0 && set.str);
    i = idx(i, s.len);
    assert(i >= 0 && i <= s.len);
    if (i < s.len && memchr(set.str, s.str[i], set.len))
        return i + 2;
    return 0;
}
```

When s[i] is in set, Text_any returns i + 2 because i + 1 is the position of s[i], so i + 2 is the position *after* s[i].

Text_many and Text_rmany are often called after Text_upto and Text_rupto. They step over a run of one or more characters given by a set and return the position to the left of the first character that's not in the set. Text_many steps over the run that appears at the beginning of s[i:j]:

⟨*functions* 278⟩+≡
```
    int Text_many(T s, int i, int j, T set) {
        assert(set.len >= 0 && set.str);
        ⟨convert i and j to indices in 0..s.len 279⟩
        if (i < j && memchr(set.str, s.str[i], set.len)) {
            do
                i++;
            while (i < j
            && memchr(set.str, s.str[i], set.len));
            return i + 1;
        }
        return 0;
    }
```

Text_rmany steps left over the run of one or more characters from set that appear at the end of s[i:j]:

⟨*functions* 278⟩+≡
```
    int Text_rmany(T s, int i, int j, T set) {
        assert(set.len >= 0 && set.str);
        ⟨convert i and j to indices in 0..s.len 279⟩
        if (j > i && memchr(set.str, s.str[j-1], set.len)) {
            do
                --j;
            while (j >= i
            && memchr(set.str, s.str[j], set.len));
            return j + 2;
        }
        return 0;
    }
```

The do-while loop ends when j is the index of a character that's *not* in set or when j is equal to i − 1. In the first case, j + 2 is the position to the right of the offending character and thus to the left of the run of characters in set. In the second case, j + 2 is to the left of s[i:j], which consists entirely of characters in set.

Text_match steps over an occurrence of a string given by str, if s[i:j] begins with that string. As with Text_find, Text_match's important special cases are when str is the null string and when str has only one character. Text_match must not inspect characters outside of s[i:j]; the condition in the third if statement below ensures that only characters in s[i:j] are examined.

⟨*functions* 278⟩+≡
```
int Text_match(T s, int i, int j, T str) {
    assert(str.len >= 0 && str.str);
    ⟨convert i and j to indices in 0..s.len 279⟩
    if (str.len == 0)
        return i + 1;
    else if (str.len == 1) {
        if (i < j && s.str[i] == *str.str)
            return i + 2;
    } else if (i + str.len <= j && equal(s, i, str))
        return i + str.len + 1;
    return 0;
}
```

Text_rmatch is like Text_match, but it returns the position before the string in str if s[i:j] ends with that string, and it's careful not to examine characters before s[i:j].

⟨*functions* 278⟩+≡
```
int Text_rmatch(T s, int i, int j, T str) {
    assert(str.len >= 0 && str.str);
    ⟨convert i and j to indices in 0..s.len 279⟩
    if (str.len == 0)
        return j + 1;
    else if (str.len == 1) {
        if (j > i && s.str[j-1] == *str.str)
            return j;
    } else if (j - str.len >= i
    && equal(s, j - str.len, str))
        return j - str.len + 1;
```

```
        return 0;
    }
```

16.2.4 Conversion Functions

The last function is `Text_fmt`, which is a format-conversion function for use with the functions exported by the Fmt interface. `Text_fmt` is used to print `Text_T`s in the same style as `printf`'s `%s` format. It just calls `Fmt_puts`, which interprets the `flags`, `width`, and `precision` specifications for `Text_T`s in the same way as `printf` does for C strings.

⟨*functions* 278⟩+≡
```
    void Text_fmt(int code, va_list *app,
        int put(int c, void *cl), void *cl,
        unsigned char flags[], int width, int precision) {
        T *s;

        assert(app && flags);
        s = va_arg(*app, T*);
        assert(s && s->len >= 0 && s->str);
        Fmt_puts(s->str, s->len, put, cl, flags,
            width, precision);
    }
```

Unlike all the other functions in the Text interface, `Text_fmt` consumes a *pointer* to a `Text_T`, not a `Text_T`. `Text_T`s are small, typically two words, and it's impossible to distinguish two-word structures from doubles in variable length argument lists in a portable way. So, some C implementations cannot reliably pass two-word structures by value in a variable length argument list. Passing a pointer to a `Text_T` avoids these problems in all implementations.

Further Reading

`Text_T`s are similar in both their semantics and implementation to strings in SNOBOL4 (Griswold 1972) and Icon (Griswold and Griswold 1990). Both of these languages are general-purpose, string-processing languages, and have built-in features that are similar to the functions exported by Text.

Similar techniques for representing and manipulating strings have long been used in compilers and other applications that analyze strings; the XPL compiler generator (McKeeman, Horning, and Wortman 1970) is an early example. In systems in which all the Text_Ts are known, garbage collection can be used to manage the string space. Icon uses XPL's garbage-collection algorithm to reclaim string space that's not referenced by any of the known Text_Ts (Hanson 1980). It compacts the strings for the known Text_Ts by copying them to the beginning of the string space.

Hansen (1992) describes a completely different representation for strings in which a substring descriptor carries enough information to retrieve the larger string of which it is a part. This representation makes it possible, among other things, to extend a string to either the left or the right.

"Ropes" are another representation in which a string is represented by a tree of substrings (Boehm, Atkinson, and Plass 1995). The characters in a rope can be traversed in linear time, just like those in a Text_T or in a C string, but the substring operation takes logarithmic time. Concatenation, however, is much faster: Concatenating two ropes takes constant time. Another useful feature is that a rope can be described by a function for generating the ith character.

Exercises

16.1 Rewrite `ids.c`, described in Section 15.2, using the Text functions.

16.2 `Text_save` and `Text_restore` aren't very robust. For example, the following sequence is erroneous, but the error is not detected.

```
Text_save_T x, y;
x = Text_save();
...
y = Text_save();
...
Text_restore(&x);
...
Text_restore(&y);
```

After the call to `Text_restore(&x)`, `y` is invalid, because it describes a string-space location after `x`. Revise the implementation of `Text` so that this error is a checked runtime error.

16.3 `Text_save` and `Text_restore` permit only stacklike allocation. Garbage collection would be better, but requires that all accessible `Text_Ts` be known. Design an extended version of the `Text` interface that includes a function to "register" a `Text_T`, and a function `Text_compact` that uses the scheme described in Hanson (1980) to compact the strings referenced by all the registered `Text_Ts` into the beginning of the string space, thereby reclaiming the space occupied by unregistered `Text_Ts`.

16.4 Extend the functions that search for strings, like `Text_find` and `Text_match`, to accept `Text_Ts` that specify *regular expressions* instead of just strings. Kernighan and Plauger (1976) describe regular expressions and the implementation of an automaton that matches them.

16.5 Design an interface and an implementation based on the substring model described in Hansen (1992).

17

EXTENDED-PRECISION ARITHMETIC

A computer with 32-bit integers can represent the signed integers from $-2{,}147{,}483{,}648$ to $+2{,}147{,}483{,}647$ (using a two's-complement representation) and the unsigned integers from zero to $4{,}294{,}967{,}295$. These ranges are large enough for many — perhaps most — applications, but some applications need larger ranges. Integers represent every integral value in a relatively compact range. Floating-point numbers represent relatively few values in a huge range. Floating-point numbers can be used when approximations to the exact values are acceptable, such as in many scientific applications, but floating-point numbers cannot be used when all of the integer values in a large range are required.

This chapter describes a low-level interface, XP, that exports functions for arithmetic operations on extended integers of fixed precision. The values that can be represented are limited only by the available memory. This interface is designed to serve higher-level interfaces like those in the next two chapters. These higher-level interfaces are designed for use in applications that need integer values in a potentially huge range.

17.1 Interface

An n-digit unsigned integer x is represented by the polynomial

$$x = x_{n-1}b^{n-1} + x_{n-2}b^{n-2} + \ldots + x_1b^1 + x_0$$

where b is the base and $0 \le x_i < b$. On a computer with 32-bit unsigned integers, n is 32, b is 2, and each coefficient x_i is represented by one of the 32 bits. This representation can be generalized to represent an unsigned integer in any base. If, for example, b is 10, then each x_i is a number between zero and nine inclusive, and x can be represented by an array. The number 2,147,483,647 could be represented by the array

```
unsigned char x[] = { 7, 4, 6, 3, 8, 4, 7, 4, 1, 2 };
```

where x[i] holds x_i. The digits x_i appear in x, least significant digit first, which is the most convenient order for implementing the arithmetic operations.

Choosing a larger base may save memory, because the larger the base, the larger the digits. For example, if b is $2^{16} = 65,536$, each digit is a number between zero and 65,535 inclusive, and it takes only two digits (four bytes) to represent 2,147,483,647:

```
unsigned short x[] = { 65535, 32767 };
```

and the 64-digit number

34905295108476594914784961990389813341776463849338784399082 0577

is represented by the 14-element (28-byte) array

```
{ 38625,  9033, 28867,  3500, 30620, 54807, 4503,
  60627, 34909, 43799, 33017, 28372, 31785,    8 }.
```

If b is 2^k and k is the size in bits of one of the predefined unsigned integer types in C, then a smaller base can be used without wasting space. Perhaps more important, large bases complicate the implementation of some of the arithmetic operations. As detailed below, these complications can be avoided if an unsigned long integer can hold $b^3 - 1$. XP uses $b = 2^8$ and stores each digit in an unsigned character, because Standard C guarantees that an unsigned long has at least 32 bits, which holds at least three bytes, so an unsigned long can hold $b^3 - 1 = 2^{24} - 1$. With $b = 2^8$, it takes four bytes to represent the value 2,147,483,647:

```
unsigned char x[] = { 255, 255, 255, 127 };
```

and 27 bytes to represent the 64-digit number shown above:

{ 225, 150, 73, 35, 195, 112, 172,   13, 156, 119, 23, 214, 151, 17,
  211, 236, 93, 136, 23, 171, 249, 128, 212, 110, 41, 124,   8 }.

The XP interface reveals these representation details:

⟨*xp.h*⟩≡
```
#ifndef XP_INCLUDED
#define XP_INCLUDED

#define T XP_T
typedef unsigned char *T;

⟨exported functions 299⟩

#undef T
#endif
```

That is, an XP_T is an array of unsigned characters that holds the digits of an n-digit number in base 2^8, least significant digit first.

The XP functions described below take n as an input argument and XP_Ts as input and output arguments, and these arrays must be large enough to accommodate n digits. It is a unchecked runtime error to pass to any function in this interface a null XP_T, an XP_T that is too small, or a nonpositive length. XP is a dangerous interface, because it omits most checked runtime errors. There are two reasons for this design. XP's intended clients are higher-level interfaces that presumably specify and implement the checked runtime errors necessary to avoid errors. Second, XP's interface is as simple as possible so that some of the functions can be implemented in assembly language, if performance considerations necessitate. This latter consideration is why none of the XP functions do allocations.

The functions

⟨*exported functions* 299⟩≡
```
extern int XP_add(int n, T z, T x, T y, int carry);
extern int XP_sub(int n, T z, T x, T y, int borrow);
```

implement $z = x + y + $ carry and $z = x - y - $ borrow. Here and below, x, y, and z denote the integer values represented by the arrays x, y, and z, which are assumed to have n digits. carry and borrow must be zero or one. XP_add sets z[0..n-1] to the n-digit sum $x + y + $ carry, and returns the carry-out of the most significant digit. XP_sub sets z[0..n-1] to the n-digit difference $x - y - \text{borrow}$ and returns the borrow-out of the most significant digit. Thus, if XP_add returns one, $x + y + \text{carry}$ doesn't fit in n digits, and if XP_sub returns one, $y > x$. For just these two functions, it is *not* an error for any of x, y, or z to be the same XP_T.

⟨*exported functions* 299⟩+≡
```
extern int XP_mul(T z, int n, T x, int m, T y);
```

implements $z = z + x \cdot y$, where x has n digits and y has m digits. z must be large enough to hold n+m digits: XP_mul *adds* the n+m-digit product $x \cdot y$ to z. When z is initialized to zero, XP_mul sets z[0..n+m-1] to $x \cdot y$. XP_mul returns the carry-out of the most significant digit of the augmented n+m-digit product. It is an unchecked runtime error for z to be the same XP_T as x or y.

XP_mul illustrates where the const qualifier might help identify input and output parameters and document these kinds of runtime errors. The declaration

```
extern int XP_mul(T z, int n, const unsigned char *x,
                  int m, const unsigned char *y);
```

makes it explicit that XP_mul reads x and y and writes z, and thus implies that z should not be the same as x or y. const T cannot be used for x and y, because it means "constant pointer to an unsigned char" instead of the intended "pointer to a constant unsigned char" (see page 29). Exercise 19.5 explores some other definitions of T that work correctly with const.

The const qualifier does not prevent the same XP_T from being passed as x and z (or y and z), however, because an unsigned char * can be passed to a const unsigned char *. But this use of const does permit a const unsigned char * to be passed as x and y; in XP's declaration for XP_mul above, type casts must be used to pass these values. The meager benefits of const don't outweigh its verbosity in XP.

The function

⟨*exported functions* 299⟩+≡
```
extern int XP_div(int n, T q, T x, int m, T y, T r,T tmp);
```

implements division: It computes $q = x/y$ and $r = x \bmod y$; q and x have n digits, and r and y have m digits. If y is zero, XP_div returns zero and leaves q and r unchanged; otherwise, it returns one. tmp must be able to hold at least n+m+2 digits. It is an unchecked runtime error for q or r to be one of x or y, for q and r to be the same XP_T, or for tmp to be too small.

The functions

⟨*exported functions* 299⟩+≡
```
extern int XP_sum      (int n, T z, T x, int y);
extern int XP_diff     (int n, T z, T x, int y);
extern int XP_product (int n, T z, T x, int y);
extern int XP_quotient(int n, T z, T x, int y);
```

implement addition, subtraction, multiplication, and division of an n-digit XP_T by a single base 2^8 digit y. XP_sum sets z[0..n-1] to $x + y$ and returns the carry-out of the most significant digit. XP_diff sets z[0..n-1] to $x - y$ and returns the borrow-out of the most significant digit. For XP_sum and XP_diff, y must be positive and must not exceed the base, 2^8.

XP_product sets z[0..n-1] to $x \cdot y$ and returns the carry-out of the most significant digit; the carry can be as large as $2^8 - 1$. XP_quotient sets z[0..n-1] to x/y and returns the remainder, $x \bmod y$; the remainder can be as large as $y - 1$. For XP_product and XP_quotient, y must not exceed $2^8 - 1$.

⟨*exported functions* 299⟩+≡
```
extern int XP_neg(int n, T z, T x, int carry);
```

sets z[0..n-1] to $\sim x + $ carry and returns the carry-out of the most significant digit. When carry is zero, XP_neg implements one's-complement negation; when carry is one, XP_neg implements a two's-complement negation.

XP_Ts are compared by

⟨*exported functions*⟩+≡
```
extern int XP_cmp(int n, T x, T y);
```

which returns a value less than zero, equal to zero, or greater than zero if, respectively, $x < y$, $x = y$, or $x > y$.

XP_Ts can be shifted with the functions

⟨*exported functions* 299⟩+≡
```
extern void XP_lshift(int n, T z, int m, T x,
    int s, int fill);
extern void XP_rshift(int n, T z, int m, T x,
    int s, int fill);
```

which assign to z the value of x shifted left or right s bits, where z has n digits and x has m digits. When n exceeds m, the bits in the missing digits at the most significant end of x are treated as if they were equal to zero for a left shift and equal to fill for a right shift. The vacated bits are filled with fill, which must be equal to zero or one. When fill is zero, XP_rshift implements a logical right shift; when fill is one, XP_rshift can be used to implement an arithmetic right shift.

⟨*exported functions* 299⟩+≡
```
extern int           XP_length (int n, T x);
extern unsigned long XP_fromint(int n, T z,
    unsigned long u);
extern unsigned long XP_toint  (int n, T x);
```

XP_length returns the number of digits in x; that is, it returns the index plus one of the most significant nonzero digit in x[0..n-1]. XP_fromint sets z[0..n-1] to $u \bmod 2^{8n}$ and returns $u/2^{8n}$; that is, the bits in u that don't fit in z. XP_toint returns $x \bmod (\text{ULONG\_MAX}+1)$; that is, the least significant $8 \cdot$ sizeof (unsigned long) bits of x.

The remaining XP functions convert between strings and XP_Ts.

⟨*exported functions* 299⟩+≡
```
extern int   XP_fromstr(int n, T z, const char *str,
    int base, char **end);
extern char *XP_tostr  (char *str, int size, int base,
    int n, T x);
```

XP_fromstr is like strtoul in the C library; it interprets the string in str as an unsigned integer in base. It ignores leading white space, and accepts one or more digits in base. For bases between 11 and 36, XP_fromstr interprets either lowercase or uppercase letters as digits greater than nine. It is a checked runtime error for base to be less than two or more than 36.

The n-digit XP_T z *accumulates* the integer specified in str using the usual multiplicative algorithm:

```
for (p = str; *p is a digit; p++)
    z ← base·z + *p's value
```

z is *not* initialized to zero; clients must initialize z properly. XP_fromstr returns the first nonzero carry-out of the multiplication base·*z*, or zero otherwise. Thus, XP_fromstr returns nonzero if the number does not fit in z.

If end is nonnull, *end is assigned the pointer to the character that terminated XP_fromstr's interpretation because either the multiplication overflowed or a nondigit was scanned. If the characters in str do not specify an integer in base, XP_fromstr returns zero and sets *end to str, if end is nonnull. It is a checked runtime error for str to be null.

XP_tostr fills str with a null-terminated string that is the character representation of x in base, and returns str. x is set to zero. Uppercase letters are used for digits that exceed nine when base exceeds 10. It is a checked runtime error for base to be less than two or more than 36. It is also a checked runtime error for str to be null or for size to be too small; that is, for the character representation of x plus a null character to require more than size characters.

17.2 Implementation

⟨*xp.c*⟩≡
```
#include <ctype.h>
#include <string.h>
#include "assert.h"
#include "xp.h"

#define T XP_T
#define BASE (1<<8)
```

⟨*data* 320⟩
⟨*functions* 304⟩

XP_fromint and XP_toint illustrate the kinds of arithmetic manipulations the XP functions must perform. XP_fromint initializes an XP_T so that it is equal to an unsigned long value:

⟨*functions* 304⟩≡
```
unsigned long XP_fromint(int n, T z, unsigned long u) {
    int i = 0;

    do
        z[i++] = u%BASE;
    while ((u /= BASE) > 0 && i < n);
    for ( ; i < n; i++)
        z[i] = 0;
    return u;
}
```

The u%BASE is not strictly necessary, because the assignment to z[i] does the modulus implicitly. All of the arithmetic XP functions do these kinds of explicit operations to help document the algorithms they use. Since the base is a constant power of two, most compilers will convert multiplication, division, or modulus by the base to the equivalent left shift, right shift, or logical and.

XP_toint is the inverse of XP_fromint: It returns the least significant $8 \cdot$ sizeof (unsigned long) bits of an XP_T as an unsigned long.

⟨*functions* 304⟩+≡
```
unsigned long XP_toint(int n, T x) {
    unsigned long u = 0;
    int i = (int)sizeof u;

    if (i > n)
        i = n;
    while (--i >= 0)
        u = BASE*u + x[i];
    return u;
}
```

A nonzero, n-digit XP_T has fewer than n significant digits when it has one or more leading zeros. XP_length returns the number of significant digits, not counting the leading zeros:

⟨*functions* 304⟩+≡
```
int XP_length(int n, T x) {
    while (n > 1 && x[n-1] == 0)
        n--;
```

```
        return n;
    }
```

17.2.1 Addition and Subtraction

The algorithms for implementing addition and subtraction are system-
atic renditions of the pencil-and-paper techniques from grade school. An
example in base 10 best illustrates the addition $z = x + y$:

$$
\begin{array}{rcccc}
  & 1 & 0 & 1 & 0 \\
  & 9 & 4 & 2 & 8 \\
+ &   & 7 & 3 & 2 \\
\hline
1 & 0 & 11 & 06 & 10
\end{array}
$$

Addition proceeds from the least significant to most significant digit,
and, in this example, the initial value of the carry is zero. Each step
forms the sum $S = \text{carry} + x_i + y_i$; z_i is S mod b, and the new carry is
S/b, where b is the base — 10 in this example. The small numbers in the
top row are the carry values, and the two-digit numbers in the bottom
row are the values of S. In this example, the carry-out is one, because the
sum doesn't fit in four digits. XP_add implements exactly this algorithm,
and returns the final value of the carry:

⟨*functions* 304⟩+≡
```
    int XP_add(int n, T z, T x, T y, int carry) {
        int i;

        for (i = 0; i < n; i++) {
            carry += x[i] + y[i];
            z[i] = carry%BASE;
            carry /= BASE;
        }
        return carry;
    }
```

At each iteration, carry holds the single-digit sum S momentarily; then
it holds just the carry. Each digit is a number between zero and $b-1$, and
the carry can be zero or one, so $(b-1) + (b-1) + 1 = 2b - 1 = 511$ is the
largest value of a single-digit sum, which easily fits in an int.

Subtraction, $z = x - y$, is similar to addition:

$$
\begin{array}{ccccc}
0 & 1 & 1 & 0 & 0 \\
  & 9 & 4 & 2 & 8 \\
- &   & 7 & 3 & 2 \\
\hline
  & 18 & 06 & 09 & 16
\end{array}
$$

Subtraction proceeds from the least significant to most significant digit, and, in this example, the initial value of the borrow is zero. Each step forms the difference $D = x_i + b - \text{borrow} - y_i$; z_i is $D \bmod b$, and the new borrow is $1 - D/b$. The small numbers in the top row are the borrow values, and the two-digit numbers in the bottom row are the values of D.

⟨*functions* 304⟩+≡
```
int XP_sub(int n, T z, T x, T y, int borrow) {
    int i;

    for (i = 0; i < n; i++) {
        int d = (x[i] + BASE) - borrow - y[i];
        z[i] = d%BASE;
        borrow = 1 - d/BASE;
    }
    return borrow;
}
```

D is at most $(b-1) + b - 0 - 0 = 2b - 1 = 511$, which fits in an int. If the final borrow is nonzero, then x is less than y.

Single-digit addition and subtraction are simpler than the more general functions, and they use the second operand as the carry or borrow:

⟨*functions* 304⟩+≡
```
int XP_sum(int n, T z, T x, int y) {
    int i;

    for (i = 0; i < n; i++) {
        y += x[i];
        z[i] = y%BASE;
        y /= BASE;
    }
    return y;
}
```

```
int XP_diff(int n, T z, T x, int y) {
    int i;

    for (i = 0; i < n; i++) {
        int d = (x[i] + BASE) - y;
        z[i] = d%BASE;
        y = 1 - d/BASE;
    }
    return y;
}
```

XP_neg is like single-digit addition, but x's digits are complemented before the addition:

⟨*functions* 304⟩+≡
```
    int XP_neg(int n, T z, T x, int carry) {
        int i;

        for (i = 0; i < n; i++) {
            carry += (unsigned char)~x[i];
            z[i] = carry%BASE;
            carry /= BASE;
        }
        return carry;
    }
```

The cast ensures that ~x[i] is less than b.

17.2.2 Multiplication

If x has n digits and y has m digits, $z = x \cdot y$ forms m partial products each with n digits, and the sum of these m partial products forms a result with $n+m$ digits. The following example illustrates this process for $n = 4$ and $m = 3$ when the initial value of z is zero:

```
                    7  3  2
             ×   9  4  2  8
             ─────────────
                 5  8  5  6
              1  4  6  4
           2  9  2  8
     +  6  5  8  8
     ─────────────────────
        6  9  0  1  2  9  6
```

The partial products do not have to be computed explicitly; each one can
be added to z as the digits in the product are computed. For example, the
digits in the first partial product, $8 \cdot 732$, are computed from the least
significant to most significant digit. The ith digit of this partial product
is added to the ith digit of z along with the normal carry computation
used in addition. The ith digit of the second partial product, $2 \cdot 732$, is
added to the $i+1$st digit of z. In general, when the partial product involving x_i is computed, the digits are added to z beginning at its ith digit.

⟨*functions* 304⟩+≡
```c
    int XP_mul(T z, int n, T x, int m, T y) {
        int i, j, carryout = 0;

        for (i = 0; i < n; i++) {
            unsigned carry = 0;
            for (j = 0; j < m; j++) {
                carry += x[i]*y[j] + z[i+j];
                z[i+j] = carry%BASE;
                carry /= BASE;
            }
            for ( ; j < n + m - i; j++) {
                carry += z[i+j];
                z[i+j] = carry%BASE;
                carry /= BASE;
            }
            carryout |= carry;
        }
        return carryout;
    }
```

As the digits from the partial products are added to z in the first nested for loop, the carry can be as large as $b - 1$, so the sum, stored in `carry`, can be as large as $(b-1)(b-1) + (b-1) = b^2 - b = 65{,}280$, which fits in an unsigned. After adding a partial product to z, the second nested for loop adds the carry to the remaining digits in z, and records the carry that spills out of the most significant end of z for *this* addition. If this carry is ever equal to one, the carry-out of $z + x \cdot y$ is one.

Single-digit multiplication is equivalent to calling XP_mul, with m equal to one and z initialized to zero:

⟨*functions* 304⟩+≡
```
int XP_product(int n, T z, T x, int y) {
    int i;
    unsigned carry = 0;

    for (i = 0; i < n; i++) {
        carry += x[i]*y;
        z[i] = carry%BASE;
        carry /= BASE;
    }
    return carry;
}
```

17.2.3 Division and Comparison

Division is the most complicated of the arithmetic functions. There are several algorithms that may be used, each with their pros and cons. Perhaps the easiest algorithm to understand is the one that is derived from the following mathematical rules to compute $q = x/y$ and $r = x \bmod y$.

if $x < y$ then $q \leftarrow 0, r \leftarrow x$
else
$\qquad q' \leftarrow x/2y, r' \leftarrow x \bmod 2y$
$\qquad$ if $r' < y$ then $q \leftarrow 2q', r \leftarrow r'$ else $q \leftarrow 2q' + 1, r \leftarrow r' - y$

The intermediate computations involving q' and r' must be done using XP_Ts, of course.

The problem with this recursive algorithm is the allocations for q' and r'. There can be as many as lg x (log base 2) of these allocations, because lg x is the maximum recursion depth. The XP interface forbids these implicit allocations.

XP_div uses an efficient iterative algorithm for the general case when $x \geq y$ and y has at least two significant digits; it uses much simpler algorithms for the easier cases when $x < y$ and when y has only one digit.

⟨*functions* 304⟩+≡
```
int XP_div(int n, T q, T x, int m, T y, T r, T tmp) {
    int nx = n, my = m;

    n = XP_length(n, x);
    m = XP_length(m, y);
    if (m == 1) {
        ⟨single-digit division 311⟩
    } else if (m > n) {
        memset(q, '\0', nx);
        memcpy(r, x, n);
        memset(r + n, '\0', my - n);
    } else {
        ⟨long division 312⟩
    }
    return 1;
}
```

XP_div checks for single-digit division first because that case handles division by zero.

Single-digit division is easy, because the quotient digits can be computed using ordinary unsigned integer division in C. Division proceeds from the most significant to the least significant digit, and the initial value of the carry is zero. Dividing 9,428 by 7 in base 10 illustrates the steps:

$$\begin{array}{r} 1 \ \ 3 \ \ 4 \ \ 6 \\ \hline 7 \ \big| \ 09 \ 24 \ 32 \ 48 \ \ \ 6 \end{array}$$

At each step, the partial dividend $R = \text{carry} \cdot b + x_i$; the quotient digit $q_i = R/y_0$ and the new carry is $R \bmod y_0$. The carry values are the small digits above. The final value of the carry is the remainder. This operation is exactly what is implemented by XP_quotient, which returns the remainder:

⟨*functions* 304⟩+≡
```
int XP_quotient(int n, T z, T x, int y) {
```

```
int i;
unsigned carry = 0;

for (i = n - 1; i >= 0; i--) {
    carry = carry*BASE + x[i];
    z[i] = carry/y;
    carry %= y;
}
return carry;
}
```

R — the value assigned to carry in XP_quotient — can be as large as $(b-1)b+(b-1) = b^2 - 1 = 65,535$, which fits in an unsigned.

In XP_div, the call to XP_quotient returns r's least significant digit, so the rest must be set to zero explicitly:

⟨*single-digit division* 311⟩≡
```
if (y[0] == 0)
    return 0;
r[0] = XP_quotient(nx, q, x, y[0]);
memset(r + 1, '\0', my - 1);
```

In the general case, an n-digit dividend is divided by an m-digit divisor, where $n \geq m$ and $m > 1$. Dividing $615,367$ by 296 in base 10 illustrates the process. The dividend is extended with a leading zero so that n exceeds m:

```
                    2   0   7   8
    2   9   6 | 0   6   1   5   3   6   7
                0   5   9   2
                0   2   3   3
                0   0   0   0
                    2   3   3   6
                    2   0   7   2
                        2   6   4   7
                        2   3   6   8
                            2   7   9
```

Computing each quotient digit, q_k, efficiently is the crux of the long division problem because that computation involves m-digit operands.

Assuming for the moment that we know how to compute the quotient digits, the following pseudocode outlines an implementation of long division.

```
rem ← x with a leading zero
for (k = n - m; k >= 0; k--) {
    compute qk
    dq ← y*qk
    q->digits[k] = qk;
    rem ← rem - dq · bᵏ
    }
r ← rem
```

rem starts equal to x with a leading zero. The loop computes the $n-m+1$ quotient digits, most significant digit first, by dividing the m-digit divisor into the $m+1$-digit prefix of rem. At the end of each iteration, rem is reduced by subtracting the product of qk and y, which shortens rem by one digit. For the example above, $n = 6$, $m = 3$, and the loop body is executed four times, for $k = 6-3 = 3$, 2, 1, and 0. The table below lists the values of k, rem, qk, and dq for each iteration. The underlining in the second column identifies the prefix of rem that is divided by y, which is 296.

k	rem	qk	dq
3	<u>0615</u>367	2	0592
2	<u>0233</u>67	0	0000
1	<u>2336</u>7	7	2072
0	<u>2647</u>	8	2368
	279		

XP_div needs space to hold the digits for the two temporaries rem and dq; it needs $n+1$ bytes for rem and $m+1$ bytes for dq, which is why tmp must be at least $n+m+2$ bytes long. Fleshing out the pseudocode above, the chunk for long division becomes

⟨*long division* 312⟩≡
```
int k;
unsigned char *rem = tmp, *dq = tmp + n + 1;
assert(2 <= m && m <= n);
```

```
memcpy(rem, x, n);
rem[n] = 0;
for (k = n - m; k >= 0; k--) {
    int qk;
    ⟨compute qk, dq ← y·qk 314⟩
    q[k] = qk;
    ⟨rem ← rem - dq·bᵏ 315⟩
}
memcpy(r, rem, m);
⟨fill out q and r with 0s 313⟩
```

tmp[0..n] holds the $n+1$ digits for rem, and tmp[n+1..n+1+m] holds dq's $m+1$ digits. rem always has $k+m+1$ digits in tmp[0..k+m]. This code computes an $n-m+1$-digit quotient and an m-digit remainder; the remaining digits in q and r must be set to zero:

⟨fill out q and r with 0s 313⟩≡

```
{
    int i;
    for (i = n-m+1; i < nx; i++)
        q[i] = 0;
    for (i = m; i < my; i++)
        r[i] = 0;
}
```

All that remains is computing the quotient digits. A simple — but unsuitable — approach starts with qk equal to $b-1$ and decrements it while y·qk exceeds the $m+1$-digit prefix of rem:

```
qk = BASE-1;
dq ← y·qk;
while (rem[k..k+m] < dq) {
    qk--;
    dq ← y·qk;
}
```

This approach is too slow: The loop might take $b-1$ iterations, and each iteration requires an m-digit multiplication and an $m+1$-digit comparison. A better approach is to *estimate* qk more accurately using normal integer arithmetic, and then adjust it when the estimate is wrong. It turns out that dividing the three-digit prefix of rem by the two-digit pre-

fix of y gives an estimate of qk that is either correct or just one too large.
Thus, the loop above is replaced by a single test:

⟨*compute* qk, dq ← y·qk 314⟩≡
```
    {
        int i;
        assert(2 <= m && m <= k+m && k+m <= n);
        ⟨qk ← y[m-2..m-1]/rem[k+m-2..k+m] 314⟩
        dq[m] = XP_product(m, dq, y, qk);
        for (i = m; i > 0; i--)
            if (rem[i+k] != dq[i])
                break;
        if (rem[i+k] < dq[i])
            dq[m] = XP_product(m, dq, y, --qk);
    }
```

XP_product, shown above, computes y[0..m-1]·qk, assigns the result to
dq, and returns the final carry, which is dq's final digit. The for loop compares rem[k..k+m] with dq one digit at a time. If dq exceeds the $m+1$-
digit prefix of rem, qk is one too large, so it is decremented and dq is
recomputed.

Estimating qk can be done with normal integer division:

⟨qk ← y[m-2..m-1]/rem[k+m-2..k+m] 314⟩≡
```
    {
        int km = k + m;
        unsigned long y2 = y[m-1]*BASE + y[m-2];
        unsigned long r3 = rem[km]*(BASE*BASE) +
            rem[km-1]*BASE + rem[km-2];
        qk = r3/y2;
        if (qk >= BASE)
            qk = BASE - 1;
    }
```

r3 can be as large as $(b-1)b^2 + (b-1)b + (b-1) = b^3 - 1 = 16,777,215$,
which fits in an unsigned long. This computation is what constrains the
choice of BASE. An unsigned long can hold values less than 2^{32}, which
dictates that $b^3 - 1 < 2^{32}$, so BASE must be less than $2^{10.6666}$ and thus
cannot exceed 1,625. 256 is the largest power of two that does not
exceed 1,625 and is also the size of a built-in type.

The final piece in the long-division puzzle is to subtract dq from the $m+1$-digit prefix of rem, which reduces rem and shortens it by one digit. This subtraction can be done by conceptually shifting dq left by k digits and subtracting that from rem. XP_sub, shown above, can be used to do this subtraction by passing it pointers to the appropriate digits in rem:

⟨rem ← rem − dq · b^k 315⟩≡
```
    {
        int borrow;
        assert(0 <= k && k <= k+m);
        borrow = XP_sub(m + 1, &rem[k], &rem[k], dq, 0);
        assert(borrow == 0);
    }
```

The code in ⟨*compute* qk, dq ← y·qk 314⟩ shows that two multidigit numbers are compared by comparing their digits, most significant digit first. XP_cmp does exactly this for its two XP_T arguments:

⟨*functions* 304⟩+≡
```
    int XP_cmp(int n, T x, T y) {
        int i = n - 1;

        while (i > 0 && x[i] == y[i])
            i--;
        return x[i] - y[i];
    }
```

17.2.4 Shifting

Two functions in XP's implementation shift XP_Ts left and right by a specified number of bits. A shift of s bits is done in two steps: The first step shifts $8 \cdot (s/8)$ bits by moving a byte at a time, and the second step shifts the remaining $s \bmod 8$ bits, $s \bmod 8$ bits at a time. fill is set to a byte of all ones or zeroes so that it can be used to fill a byte a time, as shown below.

⟨*functions* 304⟩+≡
```
    void XP_lshift(int n, T z, int m, T x, int s, int fill) {
        fill = fill ? 0xFF : 0;
        ⟨shift left by s/8 bytes 316⟩
        s %= 8;
```

```
        if (s > 0)
            ⟨shift z left by s bits 317⟩
    }
```

These steps are illustrated by the following figure, which shows what happens when a six-digit XP_T with 44 ones is shifted left by 13 bits into an eight-digit XP_T; the light shading on the right identifies the vacated bits, which are set to fill.

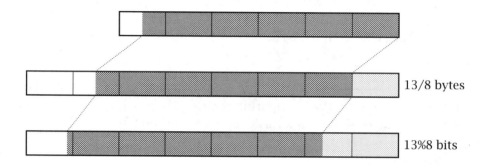

Shifting left $s/8$ bytes can be summarized by the following assignments.

```
    z[m+(s/8)..n-1] ← 0
    z[s/8..m+(s/8)-1] ← x[0..m-1]
    z[0..(s/8)-1] ← fill.
```

The first assignment clears the digits in z that don't appear in x shifted left by $s/8$ bytes. In the second assignment, x_i is copied to $z_{i+s/8}$, most significant byte first, and the third assignment sets z's $s/8$ least significant bytes to the fill. Each of these assignments involves a loop, and the initialization code handles the case when n is less than m:

⟨shift left by s/8 bytes 316⟩≡
```
    {
        int i, j = n - 1;
        if (n > m)
            i = m - 1;
        else
            i = n - s/8 - 1;
        for ( ; j >= m + s/8; j--)
```

```
            z[j] = 0;
        for ( ; i >= 0; i--, j--)
            z[j] = x[i];
        for ( ; j >= 0; j--)
            z[j] = fill;
    }
```

In the second step, s has been reduced to the number of bits to shift. This shift is equivalent to multiplying z by 2^s, then setting the s least significant bits of z to the fill:

⟨*shift z left by* s *bits* 317⟩≡
```
    {
        XP_product(n, z, z, 1<<s);
        z[0] |= fill>>(8-s);
    }
```

fill is either zero or 0xFF, so fill>>(8-s) forms s fill bits in the least significant bits of a byte.

A similar two-step process is used for shifting right: The first step shifts s/8 bytes to the right, and the second step shifts the remaining s mod 8 bits.

⟨*functions* 304⟩+≡
```
    void XP_rshift(int n, T z, int m, T x, int s, int fill) {
        fill = fill ? 0xFF : 0;
        ⟨shift right by s/8 bytes 318⟩
        s %= 8;
        if (s > 0)
            ⟨shift z right by s bits 318⟩
    }
```

Shifting a six-digit XP_T with 44 ones right by 13 bits into an eight-digit XP_T illustrates the steps in right shift in the following figure; again the light shading on the left identifies the vacated and excess bits, which are set to fill.

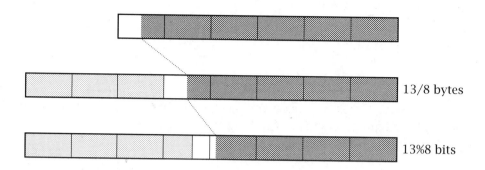

13/8 bytes

13%8 bits

The three assignments for right shift are

```
z[0..m-(s/8)-1] ← x[s/8..m-1]
z[m-(s/8)..m-1] ← fill
z[m..n-1] ← fill.
```

The first assignment copies x_i to $z_{i-s/8}$, least significant byte first, starting with byte s/8. The second assignment sets the vacated bytes to the fill, and the third sets the digits in z that don't appear in x to fill. The second and third assignments can, of course, be done in the same loop:

⟨*shift right by* s/8 *bytes* 318⟩≡
```
    {
        int i, j = 0;
        for (i = s/8; i < m && j < n; i++, j++)
            z[j] = x[i];
        for ( ; j < n; j++)
            z[j] = fill;
    }
```

The second step shifts z right by s bits, which is equivalent to dividing z by 2^s:

⟨*shift* z *right by* s *bits* 318⟩≡
```
    {
        XP_quotient(n, z, z, 1<<s);
        z[n-1] |= fill<<(8-s);
    }
```

The expression fill<<(8-s) forms s fill bits in the most significant bits of a byte, which is then OR'ed into z's most significant byte.

17.2.5 String Conversions

The last two XP functions convert XP_Ts to strings and vice versa. XP_fromstr converts a string to an XP_T; it accepts optional white space followed by one or more digits in the specified base, which must be from two to 36 inclusive. For bases that exceed 10, letters specify the digits that exceed nine. XP_fromstr stops scanning its string argument when it encounters an illegal character or the null character, or when the carry-out from the multiplication is nonzero.

⟨*functions* 304⟩+≡
```
   int XP_fromstr(int n, T z, const char *str,
       int base, char **end) {
       const char *p = str;

       assert(p);
       assert(base >= 2 && base <= 36);
       ⟨skip white space 320⟩
       if (⟨*p is a digit in base 320⟩) {
           int carry;
           for ( ; ⟨*p is a digit in base 320⟩; p++) {
               carry = XP_product(n, z, z, base);
               if (carry)
                   break;
               XP_sum(n, z, z, map[*p-'0']);
           }
           if (end)
               *end = (char *)p;
           return carry;
       } else {
           if (end)
               *end = (char *)str;
           return 0;
       }
   }
```

⟨*skip white space* 320⟩≡
```
while (*p && isspace(*p))
    p++;
```

If end is nonnull, XP_fromstr sets *end to the pointer to the character that terminated the scan.

If c is a digit character, map[c-'0'] is the corresponding digit value; for example, map['F'-'0'] is 15.

⟨*data* 320⟩≡
```
static char map[] = {
      0,  1,  2,  3,  4,  5,  6,  7,  8,  9,
     36, 36, 36, 36, 36, 36, 36,
     10, 11, 12, 13, 14, 15, 16, 17, 18, 19, 20, 21, 22,
     23, 24, 25, 26, 27, 28, 29, 30, 31, 32, 33, 34, 35,
     36, 36, 36, 36, 36, 36,
     10, 11, 12, 13, 14, 15, 16, 17, 18, 19, 20, 21, 22,
     23, 24, 25, 26, 27, 28, 29, 30, 31, 32, 33, 34, 35
};
```

map[c-'0'] is 36 for those few invalid digit characters that lie between 0 and z in the ASCII collating sequence. This value is chosen so that c is a digit in base if map[c-'0'] is less than base. Thus, XP_fromstr tests whether *p is a digit character with

⟨*p *is a digit in base* 320⟩≡
```
(*p && isalnum(*p) && map[*p-'0'] < base)
```

XP_tostr uses the usual algorithm for computing the string representation of x, which peels off the digits last one first, but XP_tostr uses the XP functions to do the arithmetic.

⟨*functions* 304⟩+≡
```
char *XP_tostr(char *str, int size, int base,
        int n, T x) {
    int i = 0;

    assert(str);
    assert(base >= 2 && base <= 36);
    do {
        int r = XP_quotient(n, x, x, base);
```

```
        assert(i < size);
        str[i++] =
            "0123456789ABCDEFGHIJKLMNOPQRSTUVWXYZ"[r];
        while (n > 1 && x[n-1] == 0)
            n--;
    } while (n > 1 || x[0] != 0);
    assert(i < size);
    str[i] = '\0';
    ⟨reverse str 321⟩
    return str;
}
```

The digits end up in `str` backward, so `XP_tostr` concludes by reversing them:

```
⟨reverse str 321⟩≡
    {
        int j;
        for (j = 0; j < --i; j++) {
            char c = str[j];
            str[j] = str[i];
            str[i] = c;
        }
    }
```

Further Reading

Most of the arithmetic functions in XP are straightforward implementations of the algorithms everyone learned in grade school. Chapter 4 in Hennessy and Patterson (1994) and Section 4.3 in Knuth (1981) describe the classical algorithms for implementing the arithmetic operations. Knuth (1981) nicely summarizes the long history of these algorithms.

Division is difficult because of the constraints imposed in computing the quotient digits. The algorithm used in `XP_div` is taken from Brinch-Hansen (1994), which includes the proof that the estimated quotient digit is off by at most one. Brinch-Hansen also shows how to avoid correcting qk most of time by scaling the operands. Scaling costs an extra single-digit multiplication and division, but can avoid most of the second calls to `product` when qk must be decremented.

Exercises

17.1 Implement the recursive division algorithm and compare its execution time and space performance with the Brinch-Hansen algorithm used in XP_div. Are there any conditions under which the recursive algorithm is preferable?

17.2 Implement the "shift and subtract" division algorithm described in Chapter 4 of Hennessy and Patterson (1994) and compare its performance with the Brinch-Hansen algorithm used in XP_div.

17.3 Most of the XP functions take time proportional to the number of digits in their operands. Representing XP_Ts in base 2^{16} would thus make these functions run twice as fast. Division, however, presents a problem, because

$$(2^{16})^3 - 1 = 28,147,497,610,655.$$

This exceeds ULONG_MAX on most 32-bit computers, and normal C integer arithmetic can't be used to estimate the quotient digits in a portable fashion. Devise a way around this problem, implement XP using base 2^{16}, and measure the benefits. Is the added complexity of division worth the benefits?

17.4 Do Exercise 17.3 for base 2^{32}.

17.5 Extended-precision arithmetic in larger bases, like 2^{32}, is often easier to implement in assembly language, because many machines have double-precision instructions and it's usually easy to capture carries and borrows. Assembly-language implementations are invariably faster, too. Reimplement XP in assembly language on your favorite computer and quantify its speed improvements.

17.6 Implement an XP function that generates random numbers, uniformly distributed in a specified range.

18

ARBITRARY-PRECISION ARITHMETIC

T his chapter describes the AP interface, which provides signed integers of *arbitrary* precision and arithmetic operations on them. That is, unlike XP_Ts, the integers provided by AP can be negative or positive, and they can have an arbitrary number of digits. The values that can be represented are limited only by the available memory. These integers can be used in applications that need integer values in a potentially huge range. For example, some mutual-fund companies track share prices to the nearest centicent — 1/10,000 of a dollar — and thus might do all computations in centicents. A 32-bit unsigned integer can represent only $429,496.7295, which is only a tiny fraction of the billions of dollars held by some funds.

AP uses XP, of course, but AP is a high-level interface: It reveals only an opaque type that represents arbitrary-precision signed integers. AP exports functions to allocate and deallocate these integers, and to perform the usual arithmetic operations on them. It also implements the checked runtime errors that XP omits. Most applications should use AP or the MP interface described in the next chapter.

18.1 Interface

The AP interface hides the representation of an arbitrary-precision signed integer behind an opaque pointer type:

⟨*ap.h*⟩≡
```
#ifndef AP_INCLUDED
#define AP_INCLUDED
#include <stdarg.h>

#define T AP_T
typedef struct T *T;
```

⟨*exported functions* 324⟩

```
#undef T
#endif
```

It is a checked runtime error to pass a null AP_T to any function in this interface, except where noted below.

AP_Ts are created by

⟨*exported functions* 324⟩≡
```
extern T AP_new    (long int n);
extern T AP_fromstr(const char *str, int base,
    char **end);
```

AP_new creates a new AP_T, initializes it to the value of n, and returns it. AP_fromstr creates a new AP_T, initializes it to the value specified by str and base, and returns it. AP_new and AP_fromstr can raise Mem_Failed.

AP_fromstr is like strtol in the C library; it interprets the string in str as an integer in base. It ignores leading white space, and accepts an optional sign followed by one or more digits in base. For bases between 11 and 36, AP_fromstr interprets either lowercase or uppercase letters as digits greater than nine. It is a checked runtime error for base to be less than two or more than 36.

If end is nonnull, *end is assigned the pointer to the character that terminated AP_fromstr's interpretation. If the characters in str do not specify an integer in base, AP_fromstr returns null and sets *end to str, if end is nonnull. It is a checked runtime error for str to be null.

The functions

⟨*exported functions* 324⟩+≡
```
extern long int AP_toint(T x);
extern char    *AP_tostr(char *str, int size,
```

```
        int base, T x);
    extern void     AP_fmt(int code, va_list *app,
        int put(int c, void *cl), void *cl,
        unsigned char flags[], int width, int precision);
```

extract and print the integers represented by AP_Ts. AP_toint returns a
long int with the same sign as x and a magnitude equal to |x| mod
(LONG_MAX+1), where LONG_MAX is the largest positive long int. If x is
LONG_MIN, which is -LONG_MAX-1 on two's-complement machines,
AP_toint returns -((LONG_MAX+1) mod (LONG_MAX+1)), which is zero.

AP_tostr fills str with a null-terminated string that is the character
representation of x in base, and returns str. Uppercase letters are used
for digits that exceed nine when base exceeds 10. It is a checked runtime
error for base to be less than two or more than 36.

If str is nonnull, AP_tostr fills str up to size characters. It is a
checked runtime error for size to be too small — that is, for the character representation of x plus a null character to require more than size
characters. If str is null, size is ignored; AP_tostr allocates a string
large enough to hold the representation of x, and returns that string. It is
the client's responsibility to deallocate the string. When str is null,
AP_tostr can raise Mem_Failed.

AP_fmt can be used with the functions in the Fmt interface as a conversion function to format AP_Ts. It consumes an AP_T and formats it
according to the optional flags, width, and precision in the same way
that the printf specifier %d formats its integer argument. AP_fmt can
raise Mem_Failed. It is a checked runtime error for app or flags to be
null.

AP_Ts are deallocated by

⟨*exported functions* 324⟩+≡
```
    extern void AP_free(T *z);
```

AP_free deallocates *z and sets *z to null. It is a checked runtime
error for z or *z to be null.

The following functions perform arithmetic operations on AP_Ts. Each
returns an AP_T for the result, and each can raise Mem_Failed.

⟨*exported functions* 324⟩+≡
```
    extern T AP_neg(T x);
    extern T AP_add(T x, T y);
    extern T AP_sub(T x, T y);
```

```
extern T AP_mul(T x, T y);
extern T AP_div(T x, T y);
extern T AP_mod(T x, T y);
extern T AP_pow(T x, T y, T p);
```

AP_neg returns $-x$, AP_add returns $x + y$, AP_sub returns $x - y$, and AP_mul returns $x \cdot y$. Here and below, x and y denote the integer values represented by x and y. AP_div returns x/y, and AP_mod returns x mod y. Division truncates to the left: toward minus infinity when one of x or y is negative and toward zero otherwise, so the remainder is always positive. More precisely, the quotient, q, is the maximum integer that does not exceed the real number w such that $w \cdot y = x$, and the remainder is defined to be $x - y \cdot q$. This definition is identical to the one implemented by the Arith interface described in Chapter 2. For AP_div and AP_mod, it is a checked runtime error for y to be zero.

AP_pow returns x^y when p is null. When p is nonnull, AP_pow returns (x^y) mod p. It is a checked runtime error for y to be negative, or for p to be nonnull and less than two.

The convenience functions

⟨*exported functions* 324⟩+≡
```
extern T    AP_addi(T x, long int y);
extern T    AP_subi(T x, long int y);
extern T    AP_muli(T x, long int y);
extern T    AP_divi(T x, long int y);
extern long AP_modi(T x, long int y);
```

are similar to the functions described above but take a long int for y. For example, AP_addi(x, y) is equivalent to AP_add(x, AP_new(y)). The rules regarding division and modulus are the same as for AP_div and AP_mod. Each of these functions can raise Mem_Failed.

AP_Ts can be shifted with the functions

⟨*exported functions* 324⟩+≡
```
extern T AP_lshift(T x, int s);
extern T AP_rshift(T x, int s);
```

AP_lshift returns an AP_T equal to x shifted left by s bits, which is equivalent to multiplying x by 2^s. AP_rshift returns an AP_T equal to x shifted right by s bits, which is equivalent to dividing x by 2^s. The values returned by both functions have the same sign as x, unless the shift values are zero, and the vacated bits are set to zero. It is a checked runtime error for s to be negative, and the shift functions can raise Mem_Failed.

AP_Ts are compared by

⟨*exported functions* 324⟩+≡
```
extern int AP_cmp (T x, T y);
extern int AP_cmpi(T x, long int y);
```

Both functions return an integer less than zero, equal to zero, or greater than zero, if, respectively, $x < y$, $x = y$, or $x > y$.

18.2 Example: A Calculator

A calculator that does arbitrary-precision computations illustrates the use of the AP interface. The implementation of the AP interface, described in the next section, illustrates the use of the XP interface.

The calculator, calc, uses Polish suffix notation: Values are pushed onto a stack, and operators pop their operands from the stack and push their results. A value is one or more consecutive decimal digits, and the operators are as follows.

~	negation
+	addition
–	subtraction
*	multiplication
/	division
%	remainder
^	exponentiation
d	duplicate the value at the top of the stack
p	print the value at the top of the stack
f	print all the values on the stack from the top down
q	quit

White-space characters separate values but are otherwise ignored; other characters are announced as unrecognized operators. The size of the stack is limited only by available memory, but a diagnostic announces stack underflow.

calc is a simple program that has three main tasks: interpreting the input, computing values, and managing a stack.

⟨*calc.c*⟩≡
```
#include <ctype.h>
#include <stdio.h>
#include <string.h>
#include <stdlib.h>
#include "stack.h"
#include "ap.h"
#include "fmt.h"

⟨calc data 328⟩
⟨calc functions 328⟩
```

As the inclusion of stack.h suggests, calc uses the stack interface described in Chapter 2 for its stack:

⟨*calc data* 328⟩≡
```
Stack_T sp;
```

⟨*initialization* 328⟩≡
```
sp = Stack_new();
```

calc must not call Stack_pop when sp is empty, so it wraps all pop operations in a function that checks for underflow:

⟨*calc functions* 328⟩≡
```
AP_T pop(void) {
    if (!Stack_empty(sp))
        return Stack_pop(sp);
    else {
        Fmt_fprint(stderr, "?stack underflow\n");
        return AP_new(0);
    }
}
```

Always returning an AP_T, even when the stack is empty, simplifies error-checking elsewhere in calc.

The main loop in calc reads the next "token" — value or operator — and switches on it:

⟨*calc functions* 328⟩+≡
```
   int main(int argc, char *argv[]) {
       int c;

       ⟨initialization 328⟩
       while ((c = getchar()) != EOF)
           switch (c) {
           ⟨cases 329⟩
           default:
               if (isprint(c))
                   Fmt_fprint(stderr, "?'%c'", c);
               else
                   Fmt_fprint(stderr, "?'\\%03o'", c);
               Fmt_fprint(stderr, " is unimplemented\n");
               break;
           }
       ⟨clean up and exit 329⟩
   }
```

⟨*clean up and exit* 329⟩≡
```
   ⟨clear the stack 333⟩
   Stack_free(&sp);
   return EXIT_SUCCESS;
```

An input character is either white space, the first digit of a value, an operator, or something else, which is an error as shown in the default case above. White space is simply ignored:

⟨*cases* 329⟩≡
```
   case ' ': case '\t': case '\n': case '\f': case '\r':
       break;
```

A digit is the beginning of a value; calc gathers up the digits that follow the first one into a buffer, and uses AP_fromstr to convert the run of digits to an AP_T:

⟨*cases* 329⟩+≡
```
   case '0': case '1': case '2': case '3': case '4':
   case '5': case '6': case '7': case '8': case '9': {
       char buf[512];
       ⟨gather up digits into buf 333⟩
```

```
    Stack_push(sp, AP_fromstr(buf, 10, NULL));
    break;
}
```

Each operator pops zero or more operands from the stack and pushes zero or more results. Addition is typical:

⟨*cases* 329⟩+≡
```
case '+': {
    ⟨pop x and y off the stack 330⟩
    Stack_push(sp, AP_add(x, y));
    ⟨free x and y 330⟩
    break;
}
```

⟨*pop* x *and* y *off the stack* 330⟩≡
```
    AP_T y = pop(), x = pop();
```

⟨*free* x *and* y 330⟩≡
```
    AP_free(&x);
    AP_free(&y);
```

It is easy to make the error of having two or more copies of one AP_T on the stack, which makes it impossible to know which AP_Ts should be freed. The code above shows the simple protocol that avoids this problem: The only "permanent" AP_Ts are those on the stack; all others are freed by calling AP_free.

Subtraction and multiplication are similar in form to addition:

⟨*cases* 329⟩+≡
```
case '-': {
    ⟨pop x and y off the stack 330⟩
    Stack_push(sp, AP_sub(x, y));
    ⟨free x and y 330⟩
    break;
}
case '*': {
    ⟨pop x and y off the stack 330⟩
    Stack_push(sp, AP_mul(x, y));
    ⟨free x and y 330⟩
```

```
        break;
    }
```

Division and remainder are also simple, but they must guard against a zero divisor.

⟨*cases* 329⟩+≡
```
    case '/': {
        ⟨pop x and y off the stack 330⟩
        if (AP_cmpi(y, 0) == 0) {
            Fmt_fprint(stderr, "?/ by 0\n");
            Stack_push(sp, AP_new(0));
        } else
            Stack_push(sp, AP_div(x, y));
        ⟨free x and y 330⟩
        break;
    }
    case '%': {
        ⟨pop x and y off the stack 330⟩
        if (AP_cmpi(y, 0) == 0) {
            Fmt_fprint(stderr, "?%% by 0\n");
            Stack_push(sp, AP_new(0));
        } else
            Stack_push(sp, AP_mod(x, y));
        ⟨free x and y 330⟩
        break;
    }
```

Exponentiation must guard against a nonpositive power:

⟨*cases* 329⟩+≡
```
    case '^': {
        ⟨pop x and y off the stack 330⟩
        if (AP_cmpi(y, 0) <= 0) {
            Fmt_fprint(stderr, "?nonpositive power\n");
            Stack_push(sp, AP_new(0));
        } else
            Stack_push(sp, AP_pow(x, y, NULL));
        ⟨free x and y 330⟩
        break;
    }
```

Duplicating the value at the top of the stack is accomplished by popping it off the stack, so that underflow is detected, and pushing the value and a copy of the value. The only way to copy an AP_T is to add zero to it.

⟨*cases* 329⟩+≡
```
case 'd': {
    AP_T x = pop();
    Stack_push(sp, x);
    Stack_push(sp, AP_addi(x, 0));
    break;
}
```

Printing an AP_T is accomplished by associating AP_cvt with a format code and using that code in a format string passed to Fmt_fmt; calc uses D.

⟨*initialization* 328⟩+≡
```
Fmt_register('D', AP_fmt);
```

⟨*cases* 329⟩+≡
```
case 'p': {
    AP_T x = pop();
    Fmt_print("%D\n", x);
    Stack_push(sp, x);
    break;
}
```

Printing all the values on the stack reveals a weakness in the Stack interface: There's no way to access the values under the top one, or to tell how many values are on the stack. A better stack interface might include functions like Table_length and Table_map; without them, calc must create a temporary stack, pour the contents of the main stack onto the temporary stack, printing the values as it goes, and then pour the values from the temporary stack back onto the main stack.

⟨*cases* 329⟩+≡
```
case 'f':
    if (!Stack_empty(sp)) {
        Stack_T tmp = Stack_new();
        while (!Stack_empty(sp)) {
```

```
                AP_T x = pop();
                Fmt_print("%D\n", x);
                Stack_push(tmp, x);
            }
        while (!Stack_empty(tmp))
                Stack_push(sp, Stack_pop(tmp));
            Stack_free(&tmp);
        }
        break;
```

The remaining cases negate values, clear the stack, and quit:

⟨*cases* 329⟩+≡
```
    case '~': {
        AP_T x = pop();
        Stack_push(sp, AP_neg(x));
        AP_free(&x);
        break;
    }
    case 'c': ⟨clear the stack 333⟩ break;
    case 'q': ⟨clean up and exit 329⟩
```

⟨*clear the stack* 333⟩≡
```
    while (!Stack_empty(sp)) {
        AP_T x = Stack_pop(sp);
        AP_free(&x);
    }
```

calc deallocates the stacked AP_Ts as it clears the stack to avoid creating objects that are unreachable and whose storage could never be deallocated.

The final chunk of calc reads a run of one or more digits into buf:

⟨*gather up digits into* buf 333⟩≡
```
    {
        int i = 0;
        for ( ; c != EOF && isdigit(c); c = getchar(), i++)
            if (i < (int)sizeof (buf) - 1)
                buf[i] = c;
        if (i > (int)sizeof (buf) - 1) {
            i = (int)sizeof (buf) - 1;
```

```
        Fmt_fprint(stderr,
            "?integer constant exceeds %d digits\n", i);
    }
    buf[i] = 0;
    if (c != EOF)
        ungetc(c, stdin);
}
```

As this code shows, calc announces excessively long numbers and truncates them.

18.3 Implementation

The implementation of the AP interface illustrates a typical use of the XP
interface. AP uses a sign-magnitude representation for signed numbers:
An AP_T points to a structure that carries the sign of the number and its
absolute value as an XP_T:

⟨*ap.c*⟩≡
```
#include <ctype.h>
#include <limits.h>
#include <stdlib.h>
#include <string.h>
#include "assert.h"
#include "ap.h"
#include "fmt.h"
#include "xp.h"
#include "mem.h"

#define T AP_T

struct T {
    int sign;
    int ndigits;
    int size;
    XP_T digits;
};
```

⟨*macros* 337⟩
⟨*prototypes* 336⟩

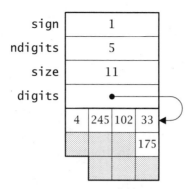

Figure 18.1 Little endian layout for an AP_T equal to 751,702,468,129

⟨*static functions* 335⟩
⟨*functions* 335⟩

sign is either 1 or –1. size is the number of digits allocated and pointed to by digits; it can exceed ndigits, which is the number of digits in use. That is, an AP_T represents the number given by the XP_T in digits[0..ndigits-1]. AP_Ts are always normalized: Their most significant digit is nonzero, unless the value is zero. Thus, ndigits is often less than size. Figure 18.1 shows the layout of an 11-digit AP_T that is equal to 751,702,468,129 on a little endian computer with 32-bit words and 8-bit characters. The unused elements of the digits array are shaded.

AP_Ts are allocated by

⟨*functions* 335⟩≡
```
T AP_new(long int n) {
    return set(mk(sizeof (long int)), n);
}
```

which calls the static function mk to do the actual allocation; mk allocates an AP_T capable of holding size digits and initializes it to zero.

⟨*static functions* 335⟩≡
```
static T mk(int size) {
    T z = CALLOC(1, sizeof (*z) + size);
```

```
        assert(size > 0);
        z->sign = 1;
        z->size = size;
        z->ndigits = 1;
        z->digits = (XP_T)(z + 1);
        return z;
    }
```

There are two representations for zero in a sign-magnitude representation; by convention, AP uses only the positive representation, as the code in mk suggests.

AP_new calls the static function set to initialize an AP_T to the value of a long int, and, as usual, set handles the most negative long int as a special case:

⟨*static functions* 335⟩+≡
```
    static T set(T z, long int n) {
        if (n == LONG_MIN)
            XP_fromint(z->size, z->digits, LONG_MAX + 1UL);
        else if (n < 0)
            XP_fromint(z->size, z->digits, -n);
        else
            XP_fromint(z->size, z->digits, n);
        z->sign = n < 0 ? -1 : 1;
        return normalize(z, z->size);
    }
```

The assignment to z->sign is the idiom that ensures that the sign value is either 1 or –1, and that the sign of zero is one. An XP_T is unnormalized, because its most significant digit can be zero. When an AP function forms an XP_T that might be unnormalized, it calls normalize to fix it by computing the correct ndigits field:

⟨*static functions* 335⟩+≡
```
    static T normalize(T z, int n) {
        z->ndigits = XP_length(n, z->digits);
        return z;
    }
```

⟨*prototypes* 336⟩≡
```
    static T normalize(T z, int n);
```

An AP_T is deallocated by

⟨*functions* 335⟩+≡
```
void AP_free(T *z) {
    assert(z && *z);
    FREE(*z);
}
```

AP_new is the only way to allocate an AP_T, so it is safe for AP_free to "know" that the space for the structure and the digit array were allocated with a single allocation.

18.3.1 Negation and Multiplication

Negation is the easiest arithmetic operation to implement, and it illustrates a recurring problem with a sign-magnitude representation:

⟨*functions* 335⟩+≡
```
T AP_neg(T x) {
    T z;

    assert(x);
    z = mk(x->ndigits);
    memcpy(z->digits, x->digits, x->ndigits);
    z->ndigits = x->ndigits;
    z->sign = iszero(z) ? 1 : -x->sign;
    return z;
}
```

⟨*macros* 337⟩≡
```
#define iszero(x) ((x)->ndigits==1 && (x)->digits[0]==0)
```

Negating x simply copies the value and flips the sign, except when the value is zero. The macro iszero takes advantage of the constraint that AP_Ts are normalized: The value zero has only one digit.

The magnitude of $x \cdot y$ is $|x| \cdot |y|$, and it might have as many digits as the sum of the number of digits in x and y. The result is positive when x and y have the same sign or when x or y is zero, and negative otherwise. A sign is –1 or 1, so the comparison

⟨x *and* y *have the same sign* 338⟩≡
  ((x->sign^y->sign) == 0)

is true when x and y have the same sign and false otherwise. AP_mul calls
XP_mul to compute $|x| \cdot |y|$ and computes the sign itself:

⟨*functions* 335⟩+≡
```
  T AP_mul(T x, T y) {
      T z;

      assert(x);
      assert(y);
      z = mk(x->ndigits + y->ndigits);
      XP_mul(z->digits, x->ndigits, x->digits, y->ndigits,
          y->digits);
      normalize(z, z->size);
      z->sign = iszero(z)
          || ⟨x and y have the same sign 338⟩ ? 1 : -1;
      return z;
  }
```

Recall that XP_mul computes $z = z + x \cdot y$, and that mk initializes z to both
a normalized and an unnormalized zero.

18.3.2 Addition and Subtraction

Addition is more complicated, because it may require subtraction,
depending on the signs and values of x and y. The following table summarizes the cases.

	$y < 0$	$y \geq 0$
$x < 0$	$-(\|x\| + \|y\|)$	$\begin{array}{ll} y - \|x\| & \text{if } y \geq \|x\| \\ -(\|x\| - y) & \text{if } y < \|x\| \end{array}$
$x \geq 0$	$\begin{array}{ll} x - \|y\| & \text{if } x > \|y\| \\ -(\|y\| - x) & \text{if } x \leq \|y\| \end{array}$	$x + y$

$|x| + |y|$ is equivalent to $x + y$, when x and y are nonnegative, so the cases
on the diagonal can both be handled by computing $|x| + |y|$ and setting

the sign to the sign of x. The result may have one more digit than the longest of x and y.

⟨*functions* 335⟩+≡
```
  T AP_add(T x, T y) {
      T z;

      assert(x);
      assert(y);
      if (⟨x and y have the same sign 338⟩) {
          z = add(mk(maxdigits(x,y) + 1), x, y);
          z->sign = iszero(z) ? 1 : x->sign;
      } else
          ⟨set z to x+y when x and y have different signs 340⟩
      return z;
  }
```

⟨*macros* 337⟩+≡
```
  #define maxdigits(x,y) ((x)->ndigits > (y)->ndigits ? \
      (x)->ndigits : (y)->ndigits)
```

add calls XP_add to do the actual addition:

⟨*static functions* 335⟩+≡
```
  static T add(T z, T x, T y) {
      int n = y->ndigits;

      if (x->ndigits < n)
          return add(z, y, x);
      else if (x->ndigits > n) {
          int carry = XP_add(n, z->digits, x->digits,
              y->digits, 0);
          z->digits[z->size-1] = XP_sum(x->ndigits - n,
              &z->digits[n], &x->digits[n], carry);
      } else
          z->digits[n] = XP_add(n, z->digits, x->digits,
              y->digits, 0);
      return normalize(z, z->size);
  }
```

The first test in add ensures that x is the longer operand. If x is longer than y, XP_add computes the n-digit sum in z->digits[0..n-1] and returns the carry. The sum of this carry and x->digits[n..x->ndigits-1] becomes z->digits[n..z->size-1]. If x and y have the same number of digits, XP_add computes the n-digit sum as in the previous case, and the carry is z's most significant digit.

The other addition cases can be simplified, too. When $x < 0$, $y \geq 0$, and $|x| > |y|$, the magnitude of $x + y$ is $|x| - |y|$, and the sign is negative. When $x \geq 0$, $y < 0$, and $|x| > |y|$, the magnitude of $x + y$ is also $|x| - |y|$, but the sign is positive. In both cases, the sign of the result is the same as the sign of x. sub, described below, does the subtraction, and cmp compares $|x|$ and $|y|$. The result may have as many digits as x.

⟨*set z to* x+y *when* x *and* y *have different signs* 340⟩≡
```
if (cmp(x, y) > 0) {
    z = sub(mk(x->ndigits), x, y);
    z->sign = iszero(z) ? 1 : x->sign;
}
```

When $x < 0$, $y \geq 0$, and $|x| \leq |y|$, the magnitude of $x + y$ is $|y| - |x|$, and the sign is positive. When $x \geq 0$, $y < 0$, and $|x| \leq |y|$, the magnitude of $x + y$ is also $|y| - |x|$, but the sign is negative. In both of these cases, the sign of the result is the opposite of the sign of x, and it may have as many digits as y.

⟨*set z to* x+y *when* x *and* y *have different signs* 340⟩+≡
```
else {
    z = sub(mk(y->ndigits), y, x);
    z->sign = iszero(z) ? 1 : -x->sign;
}
```

Subtraction benefits from a similar analysis. The following table lays out the cases.

	$y < 0$	$y \geq 0$
$x < 0$	$-(\lvert x\rvert - \lvert y\rvert)$ if $\lvert x\rvert > \lvert y\rvert$ $\lvert y\rvert - \lvert x\rvert$ if $\lvert x\rvert \leq \lvert y\rvert$	$-(\lvert x\rvert + y)$
$x \geq 0$	$x + \lvert y\rvert$	$x - y$ if $x > y$ $-(y - x)$ if $x \leq y$

Here, the off-diagonal cases are the easy ones, and both can be handled by computing $|x| + |y|$ and setting the sign of the result to the sign of x:

⟨*functions* 335⟩+≡
```
T AP_sub(T x, T y) {
    T z;

    assert(x);
    assert(y);
    if (!⟨x and y have the same sign 338⟩) {
        z = add(mk(maxdigits(x,y) + 1), x, y);
        z->sign = iszero(z) ? 1 : x->sign;
    } else
        ⟨set z to x–y when x and y have the same sign 341⟩
    return z;
}
```

The diagonal cases depend on the relative values of x and y. When $|x| > |y|$, the magnitude of $x - y$ is $|x| - |y|$ and the sign is the same as the sign of x; when $|x| \le |y|$, the magnitude of $x - y$ is $|y| - |x|$ and the sign is the opposite of the sign of x.

⟨*set z to x–y when x and y have the same sign* 341⟩≡
```
if (cmp(x, y) > 0) {
    z = sub(mk(x->ndigits), x, y);
    z->sign = iszero(z) ? 1 : x->sign;
} else {
    z = sub(mk(y->ndigits), y, x);
    z->sign = iszero(z) ? 1 : -x->sign;
}
```

Like add, sub calls the XP functions to implement subtraction; y never exceeds x.

⟨*static functions* 335⟩+≡
```
static T sub(T z, T x, T y) {
    int borrow, n = y->ndigits;

    borrow = XP_sub(n, z->digits, x->digits,
        y->digits, 0);
    if (x->ndigits > n)
```

```
            borrow = XP_diff(x->ndigits - n, &z->digits[n],
                &x->digits[n], borrow);
        assert(borrow == 0);
        return normalize(z, z->size);
    }
```

When x is longer than y, the call to XP_sub computes the n-digit difference in z->digits[0..n-1] and returns the borrow. The difference
between this borrow and x->digits[n..x->ndigits-1] becomes
z->digits[n..z->size-1], and the final borrow is zero because $|x| \geq |y|$
in all calls to sub. If x and y have the same number of digits, XP_sub
computes the n-digit difference as in the previous case, but there is no
borrow to propagate.

18.3.3 Division

Division is like multiplication, but is complicated by the truncation rules.
When x and y have the same sign, the quotient is $|x|/|y|$ and is positive,
and the remainder is $|x| \bmod |y|$. When x and y have different signs, the
quotient is negative; its magnitude is $|x|/|y|$ when $|x| \bmod |y|$ is zero and
$|x|/|y| + 1$ when $|x| \bmod |y|$ is nonzero. The remainder is $|x| \bmod |y|$ when
that value is zero and $|y| - (|x| \bmod |y|)$ when $|x| \bmod |y|$ is nonzero. The
remainder is thus always positive. The quotient and remainder might
have as many digits as x and y, respectively.

⟨*functions* 335⟩+≡
```
    T AP_div(T x, T y) {
        T q, r;

        ⟨q ← x/y, r ← x mod y 343⟩
        if (!⟨x and y have the same sign 338⟩ && !iszero(r)) {
            int carry = XP_sum(q->size, q->digits,
                q->digits, 1);
            assert(carry == 0);
            normalize(q, q->size);
        }
        AP_free(&r);
        return q;
    }
```

⟨*q ← x/y, r ← x mod y* 343⟩≡
```
  assert(x);
  assert(y);
  assert(!iszero(y));
  q = mk(x->ndigits);
  r = mk(y->ndigits);
  {
      XP_T tmp = ALLOC(x->ndigits + y->ndigits + 2);
      XP_div(x->ndigits, q->digits, x->digits,
          y->ndigits, y->digits, r->digits, tmp);
      FREE(tmp);
  }
  normalize(q, q->size);
  normalize(r, r->size);
  q->sign = iszero(q)
      || ⟨x and y have the same sign 338⟩ ? 1 : -1;
```

AP_div doesn't bother adjusting the remainder when *x* and *y* have different signs because it discards the remainder. AP_mod does just the opposite: It adjusts only the remainder and discards the quotient.

⟨*functions* 335⟩+≡
```
  T AP_mod(T x, T y) {
      T q, r;

      ⟨q ← x/y, r ← x mod y 343⟩
      if (!⟨x and y have the same sign 338⟩ && !iszero(r)) {
          int borrow = XP_sub(r->size, r->digits,
              y->digits, r->digits, 0);
          assert(borrow == 0);
          normalize(r, r->size);
      }
      AP_free(&q);
      return r;
  }
```

18.3.4 Exponentiation

AP_pow returns x^y when p, the third argument, is null. When p is non-null, AP_pow returns (x^y) mod *p*.

⟨*functions* 335⟩+≡
```
T AP_pow(T x, T y, T p) {
    T z;

    assert(x);
    assert(y);
    assert(y->sign == 1);
    assert(!p || p->sign==1 && !iszero(p) && !isone(p));
    ⟨special cases 344⟩
    if (p)
        ⟨z ← xʸ mod p 346⟩
    else
        ⟨z ← xʸ 345⟩
    return z;
}
```

⟨*macros* 337⟩+≡
```
#define isone(x) ((x)->ndigits==1 && (x)->digits[0]==1)
```

To compute $z = x^y$, it's tempting to set z to one and multiply it by x, y times. The problem is that if y is big, say, 200 decimal digits, this approach takes much longer than the age of the universe. Mathematical rules help simplify the computation:

$$z = \begin{cases} \left(x^{y/2}\right)^2 = (x^{y/2})(x^{y/2}) & \text{if } x \text{ is even} \\ x \cdot x^{y-1} = (x^{y/2})(x^{y/2})x & \text{otherwise} \end{cases}$$

These rules permit x^y to be computed by calling AP_pow recursively and multiplying and squaring the result. The depth of the recursion (and hence the number operations) is proportional to lg y. The recursion bottoms out when x or y is zero or one, because $0^y = 0$, $1^y = 1$, $x^0 = 1$, and $x^1 = x$. The first three of these special cases are handled by

⟨*special cases* 344⟩≡
```
if (iszero(x))
    return AP_new(0);
if (iszero(y))
    return AP_new(1);
if (isone(x))
    return AP_new(⟨y is even 345⟩ ? 1 : x->sign);
```

⟨*y is even* 345⟩≡
```
(((y)->digits[0]&1) == 0)
```

The recursive case implements the fourth special case as well as the two cases described by the equation above:

⟨$z \leftarrow x^y$ 345⟩≡
```
if (isone(y))
    z = AP_addi(x, 0);
else {
    T y2 = AP_rshift(y, 1), t = AP_pow(x, y2, NULL);
    z = AP_mul(t, t);
    AP_free(&y2);
    AP_free(&t);
    if (!⟨y is even 345⟩) {
        z = AP_mul(x, t = z);
        AP_free(&t);
    }
}
```

y is positive, so shifting it right one bit computes $y/2$. The intermediate results — $y/2$, $x^{y/2}$, and $(x^{y/2})(x^{y/2})$ — are deallocated to avoid creating unreachable storage.

When p is nonnull, AP_pow computes $x^y \bmod p$. When $p > 1$, we can't actually compute x^y because it might be too big; for example, if x is 10 decimal digits and y is 200, x^y has more digits than atoms in the universe; $x^y \bmod p$, however, is a much smaller number. The following mathematical rule about modular multiplication can be used to avoid numbers that are too big:

$$(x \cdot y) \bmod p = ((x \bmod p) \cdot (y \bmod p)) \bmod p.$$

AP_mod and the static function mulmod collaborate to implement this rule. mulmod uses AP_mod and AP_mul to implement $x \cdot y \bmod p$, taking care to deallocate the temporary product $x \cdot y$.

⟨*static functions* 335⟩+≡
```
static T mulmod(T x, T y, T p) {
    T z, xy = AP_mul(x, y);
```

```
        z = AP_mod(xy, p);
        AP_free(&xy);
        return z;
    }
```

The AP_pow code when p is nonnull is nearly identical to the easier case when p is null, except that mulmod is called for the multiplications, p is passed to the recursive call to AP_pow, and x is reduced mod p when y is odd.

⟨$z \leftarrow x^y \bmod p$ 346⟩≡
```
    if (isone(y))
        z = AP_mod(x, p);
    else {
        T y2 = AP_rshift(y, 1), t = AP_pow(x, y2, p);
        z = mulmod(t, t, p);
        AP_free(&y2);
        AP_free(&t);
        if (!⟨y is even 345⟩) {
            z = mulmod(y2 = AP_mod(x, p), t = z, p);
            AP_free(&y2);
            AP_free(&t);
        }
    }
```

18.3.5 Comparisons

The outcome of comparing x and y depends on their signs and magnitudes. AP_cmp returns a value less than zero, equal to zero, or greater than zero when $x < y$, $x = y$, or $x > y$. When x and y have different signs, AP_cmp can simply return the sign of x; otherwise, it must compare their magnitudes:

⟨*functions* 335⟩+≡
```
    int AP_cmp(T x, T y) {
        assert(x);
        assert(y);
        if (!⟨x and y have the same sign 338⟩)
            return x->sign;
        else if (x->sign == 1)
            return cmp(x, y);
```

```
        else
            return cmp(y, x);
    }
```

When x and y are positive, $x < y$ if $|x| < |y|$, and so on. When x and y are negative, however, $x < y$ if $|x| > |y|$, which is why the arguments are reversed in the second call to cmp. XP_cmp does the actual comparison, after cmp checks for operands of different lengths:

⟨*static functions* 335⟩+≡
```
    static int cmp(T x, T y) {
        if (x->ndigits != y->ndigits)
            return x->ndigits - y->ndigits;
        else
            return XP_cmp(x->ndigits, x->digits, y->digits);
    }
```

⟨*prototypes* 336⟩+≡
```
    static int cmp(T x, T y);
```

18.3.6 Convenience Functions

The six convenience functions take an AP_T as their first argument and a signed long as their second. Each initializes a temporary AP_T by passing the long to set, then calls the more general operation. AP_addi illustrates this approach:

⟨*functions* 335⟩+≡
```
    T AP_addi(T x, long int y) {
        ⟨declare and initialize t 347⟩
        return AP_add(x, set(&t, y));
    }
```

⟨*declare and initialize t* 347⟩≡
```
    unsigned char d[sizeof (unsigned long)];
    struct T t;
    t.size = sizeof d;
    t.digits = d;
```

The second chunk above allocates the temporary AP_T and its associated digits array on the stack by declaring the appropriate locals. This is possible because the size of the digits array is bounded by the number of bytes in an unsigned long.

Four of the remaining convenience functions have the same pattern:

⟨*functions*⟩+≡
```
T AP_subi(T x, long int y) {
    ⟨declare and initialize t 347⟩
    return AP_sub(x, set(&t, y));
}

T AP_muli(T x, long int y) {
    ⟨declare and initialize t 347⟩
    return AP_mul(x, set(&t, y));
}

T AP_divi(T x, long int y) {
    ⟨declare and initialize t 347⟩
    return AP_div(x, set(&t, y));
}

int AP_cmpi(T x, long int y) {
    ⟨declare and initialize t 347⟩
    return AP_cmp(x, set(&t, y));
}
```

AP_modi is the oddball, because it returns a long instead of an AP_T or int, and because it must discard the AP_T returned by AP_mod.

⟨*functions* 335⟩+≡
```
long int AP_modi(T x, long int y) {
    long int rem;
    T r;

    ⟨declare and initialize t 347⟩
    r = AP_mod(x, set(&t, y));
    rem = XP_toint(r->ndigits, r->digits);
    AP_free(&r);
    return rem;
}
```

18.3.7 Shifting

The two shift functions call their XP relatives to shift their operands. For AP_lshift, the result has $\lceil s/8 \rceil$ more digits than the operand and the same sign as the operand.

⟨*functions* 335⟩+≡

```
T AP_lshift(T x, int s) {
    T z;

    assert(x);
    assert(s >= 0);
    z = mk(x->ndigits + ((s+7)&~7)/8);
    XP_lshift(z->size, z->digits, x->ndigits,
        x->digits, s, 0);
    z->sign = x->sign;
    return normalize(z, z->size);
}
```

For AP_rshift, the result has $\lfloor s/8 \rfloor$ fewer bytes, and it is possible that the result is zero, in which case its sign must be positive.

```
T AP_rshift(T x, int s) {
    assert(x);
    assert(s >= 0);
    if (s >= 8*x->ndigits)
        return AP_new(0);
    else {
        T z = mk(x->ndigits - s/8);
        XP_rshift(z->size, z->digits, x->ndigits,
            x->digits, s, 0);
        normalize(z, z->size);
        z->sign = iszero(z) ? 1 : x->sign;
        return z;
    }
}
```

The if statement handles the case when s specifies a shift amount greater than or equal to the number of bits in x.

18.3.8 String and Integer Conversions

AP_toint(x) returns a long int with the same sign as x and with a magnitude equal to |x| mod (LONG_MAX+1).

⟨*functions* 335⟩+≡
```
long int AP_toint(T x) {
    unsigned long u;

    assert(x);
    u = XP_toint(x->ndigits, x->digits)%(LONG_MAX + 1UL);
    if (x->sign == -1)
        return -(long)u;
    else
        return  (long)u;
}
```

The rest of the AP functions convert AP_Ts to strings and vice versa. AP_fromstr converts a string to an AP_T; it accepts a signed number with the following syntax.

number = { *white* } [- | +] { *white* } *digit* { *digit* }

where *white* denotes a white-space character and *digit* is a digit character in the specified base, which must be from two to 36 inclusive. For bases that exceed 10, letters specify the digits that exceed nine. AP_fromstr calls XP_fromstr, and it stops scanning its string argument when it encounters an illegal character or the null character.

⟨*functions* 335⟩+≡
```
T AP_fromstr(const char *str, int base, char **end) {
    T z;
    const char *p = str;
    char *endp, sign = '\0';
    int carry;

    assert(p);
    assert(base >= 2 && base <= 36);
    while (*p && isspace(*p))
        p++;
    if (*p == '-' || *p == '+')
```

```
        sign = *p++;
⟨z ← 0 351⟩
    carry = XP_fromstr(z->size, z->digits, p,
        base, &endp);
    assert(carry == 0);
    normalize(z, z->size);
    if (endp == p) {
        endp = (char *)str;
        z = AP_new(0);
    } else
        z->sign = iszero(z) || sign != '-' ? 1 : -1;
    if (end)
        *end = (char *)endp;
    return z;
}
```

AP_fromstr passes the address of endp to XP_fromstr because it needs to know what terminated the scan so it can check for illegal inputs. If end is nonnull, AP_fromstr sets *end to endp.

The number of bits in z is $n \cdot \lg$ base where n is the number of digits in the string, and thus z's XP_T must have a digits array of at least $m = (n \cdot \lg$ base$)/8$ bytes. Suppose that base is 2^k; then $m = n \cdot \lg(2^k)/8 = k \cdot n/8$. Thus, if we choose k so that 2^k is the smallest power of two equal to or greater than base, z needs $\lceil k \cdot n/8 \rceil$ digits. k is a conservative estimate of the number of bits each digit in base represents. For example, when base is 10, each digit carries $\lg 10 \approx 3.32$ bits, and k is four. k ranges from one, when base is two, to six, when base is 36.

⟨z ← 0 351⟩≡
```
    {
        const char *start;
        int k, n = 0;
        for ( ; *p == '0' && p[1] == '0'; p++)
            ;
        start = p;
        for ( ; ⟨*p is a digit in base 352⟩; p++)
            n++;
        for (k = 1; (1<<k) < base; k++)
            ;
        z = mk(((k*n + 7)&~7)/8);
```

```
            p = start;
    }
```

⟨*p *is a digit in* base 352⟩≡
```
    (   '0' <= *p && *p <= '9' && *p < '0' + base
    || 'a' <= *p && *p <= 'z' && *p < 'a' + base - 10
    || 'A' <= *p && *p <= 'Z' && *p < 'A' + base - 10)
```

The first for loop in ⟨$z \leftarrow 0$ 351⟩ skips over leading zeros.

AP_tostr can use a similar trick to approximate the number of characters, n, needed for the string representation of x in base. The number of digits in x's digits array is $m = (n \cdot \lg \text{base})/8$. If we choose k so that 2^k is the largest power of two less than or equal to base, then $m = n \cdot \lg(2^k)/8 = k \cdot n/8$, and n is $\lceil 8 \cdot m/k \rceil$, plus one for the terminating null character. Here, k underestimates the number of bits each digit in base represents so that n will be a conservative estimate of the number of digits required. For example, when base is 10, the digits in x each yield $8/\lg 10 \approx 2.41$ decimal digits, and k is three, so space for $\lceil 8/3 \rceil = 3$ decimal digits is allocated for each digit in x. k ranges from five, when base is 36, to one, when base is two.

⟨size ← *number of characters in* str 352⟩≡
```
    {
        int k;
        for (k = 5; (1<<k) > base; k--)
            ;
        size = (8*x->ndigits)/k + 1 + 1;
        if (x->sign == 1)
            size++;
    }
```

AP_tostr lets XP_tostr compute the string representation of x:

⟨*functions* 335⟩+≡
```
    char *AP_tostr(char *str, int size, int base, T x) {
        XP_T q;

        assert(x);
        assert(base >= 2 && base <= 36);
        assert(str == NULL || size > 1);
        if (str == NULL) {
```

```
        ⟨size ← number of characters in str 352⟩
        str = ALLOC(size);
    }
    q = ALLOC(x->ndigits);
    memcpy(q, x->digits, x->ndigits);
    if (x->sign == -1) {
        str[0] = '-';
        XP_tostr(str + 1, size - 1, base, x->ndigits, q);
    } else
        XP_tostr(str, size, base, x->ndigits, q);
    FREE(q);
    return str;
}
```

The last AP function is AP_fmt, which is a Fmt-style conversion function for printing AP_Ts. It uses AP_tostr to format the value in decimal and calls Fmt_putd to emit it.

⟨*functions* 335⟩+≡
```
    void AP_fmt(int code, va_list *app,
        int put(int c, void *cl), void *cl,
        unsigned char flags[], int width, int precision) {
        T x;
        char *buf;

        assert(app && flags);
        x = va_arg(*app, T);
        assert(x);
        buf = AP_tostr(NULL, 0, 10, x);
        Fmt_putd(buf, strlen(buf), put, cl, flags,
            width, precision);
        FREE(buf);
    }
```

Further Reading

AP_Ts are similar to the "bignums" in some programming languages. Recent versions of Icon, for example have only one integer type, but use arbitrary-precision arithmetic as necessary to represent the values computed. Programmers don't need to distinguish between machine integers and arbitrary-precision integers.

Facilities for arbitrary-precision arithmetic are often provided as a standard library or package. LISP systems have long included bignum packages, for example, and there's a similar package for ML.

Most symbolic arithmetic systems do arbitrary-precision arithmetic, because that's their purpose. Mathematica (Wolfram 1988), for example, provides integers of arbitrary length and rationals in which the numerator and denominator are both arbitrary-length integers. Maple V (Char et al. 1992), another symbolic computation system, has similar facilities.

Exercises

18.1 `AP_div` and `AP_mod` allocate and deallocate temporary space every time they're called. Revise them so that they share `tmp`, allocate it once, keep track of its size, and expand it when necessary.

18.2 The recursive algorithm used in `AP_pow` is equivalent to the familliar iterative algorithm that computes $z = x^y$ by repeatedly squaring and multiplying (see Section 4.6.3 of Knuth 1981):

$z \leftarrow x, u \leftarrow 1$
while $y > 1$ do
  if y is odd then $u \leftarrow u \cdot z$
  $z \leftarrow z^2$
  $y \leftarrow y/2$
$z \leftarrow u \cdot z$

Iteration is usually faster than recursion, but the real advantage of this approach is that it allocates less space for intermediate values. Reimplement `AP_pow` using this algorithm and measure the time and space improvements. How large do x and y have to be before this algorithm is noticeably better than the recursive one?

18.3 Implement `AP_ceil(AP_T x, AP_T y)` and `AP_floor(AP_T x, AP_T y)`, which return the ceiling and floor of x/y. Be sure to specify what happens when x and y have different signs.

18.4 The AP interface is "noisy" — there are lots of parameters and it is easy to confuse the input and output parameters. Design and implement a new interface that uses a Seq_T as a stack from which the functions fetch operands and store results. Focus on making the interface as clean as possible, but don't omit important functionality.

18.5 Implement an AP function that generates random numbers, uniformly distributed in a specified range.

18.6 Design an interface whose functions do arithmetic modulo n for an arbitrary n, and thus accept and return values in the set of integers from zero to $n-1$. Be careful about division: It's defined only when this set is a finite field, which is when n is a prime.

18.7 Multiplying two n-digit numbers takes time proportional to n^2 (see page 308). A. Karatsuba showed (in 1962) how to multiply in time proportional to $n^{1.58}$ (see Section 4.3 in Geddes, Czapor, and Labahn 1992 and Section 4.3.3 in Knuth 1981). An n-digit number x can be split into a sum of its most significant and least significant $n/2$ bits; that is, $x = aB^{n/2} + b$. Thus, the product xy can be written as

$$xy = (aB^{n/2} + b)(cB^{n/2} + d) = acB^n + (ad + bc)B^{n/2} + bd,$$

which takes four multiplications and one addition. The coefficient of the middle term can be rewritten as

$$ad + bc = ac + bd + (a - b)(d - c).$$

The product xy thus requires only three multiplications (ac, bd, and $(a-b)(d-c)$), two subtractions, and two additions. When n is large, saving one $n/2$-digit multiplication reduces the execution time of multiplication at the expense of space for the intermediate values. Implement a recursive version of AP_mul that uses Karatsuba's algorithm, and determine for what value of n it is noticeably faster than the naive algorithm. Use XP_mul for the intermediate computations.

19

MULTIPLE-PRECISION ARITHMETIC

The last of the three arithmetic interfaces, MP, exports functions that implement *multiple*-precision arithmetic on unsigned and two's-complement integers. Like XP, MP reveals its representation for *n*-bit integers, and the MP functions operate on integers of a given size. Unlike XP, the lengths of MP's integers are given in bits, and MP's functions implement both signed and unsigned arithmetic. Like the AP functions, the MP functions enforce the usual suite of checked runtime errors.

MP is intended for applications that need extended-precision arithmetic, but want finer control over allocations, need both unsigned and signed operations, or must mimic two's-complement *n*-bit arithmetic. Examples include compilers and applications that use encryption. Some modern encryption algorithms involve manipulating fixed-precision integers with hundreds of digits.

Some compilers must use multiple-precision integers. A cross-compiler runs on platform *X* and generates code for platform *Y*. If *Y* has integers bigger than *X*, the compiler can use MP to manipulate *Y*-sized integers. Also, compilers must use multiple-precision arithmetic to convert floating-point constants to the closest floating-point values they specify.

19.1 Interface

The MP interface is large — 49 functions and two exceptions — because it exports a complete suite of arithmetic functions on n-bit signed and unsigned integers.

⟨*mp.h*⟩≡
```
#ifndef MP_INCLUDED
#define MP_INCLUDED
#include <stdarg.h>
#include <stddef.h>
#include "except.h"

#define T MP_T
typedef unsigned char *T;
```
⟨*exported exceptions* 359⟩
⟨*exported functions* 358⟩
```
#undef T
#endif
```

Like XP, MP reveals that an n-bit integer is represented by $\lceil n/8 \rceil$ bytes, stored least significant byte first. MP uses the two's-complement representation for signed integers; bit $n - 1$ is the sign bit.

Unlike the XP functions, the MP functions implement the usual checked runtime errors; for example, it is a checked runtime error to pass a null MP_T to any function in this interface. However, it is an unchecked runtime error to pass an MP_T that is too small to hold an n-bit integer.

MP is initialized automatically to do arithmetic on 32-bit integers. Calling

⟨*exported functions* 358⟩≡
```
extern int MP_set(int n);
```

changes MP so that subsequent calls do n-bit arithmetic. MP_set returns the previous size. It is a checked runtime error for n to be less than two. Once initalized, most applications use only one size of extended integer. For example, a cross-compiler might manipulate constants using 128-bit arithmetic. This design caters to these kinds of applications; it simplifies the use of the other MP functions, and simplifies their argument lists as well. Omitting n is the obvious simplification, but a more important simplification is that there are no restrictions on the source and destination arguments: The same MP_T can always appear as both a source and a destination. Eliminating these restrictions is possible because the temporary space needed by some of the functions depends only on n and thus can be allocated once by MP_set.

This design also avoids allocations. MP_set can raise Mem_Failed, but only four of the other 48 MP functions do allocations. One of those is

⟨*exported functions* 358⟩+≡
```
extern T MP_new(unsigned long u);
```

which allocates an MP_T of the appropriate size, initializes it to u, and returns it.

⟨*exported functions* 358⟩+≡
```
extern T MP_fromint (T z, long v);
extern T MP_fromintu(T z, unsigned long u);
```

set z to v or u and return z. MP_new, MP_fromint, and MP_fromintu raise

⟨*exported exceptions* 359⟩≡
```
extern const Except_T MP_Overflow;
```

if u or v don't fit in n bits. MP_new and MP_fromintu raise MP_Overflow when u exceeds $2^n - 1$, and MP_fromint raises MP_Overflow when v is less than -2^{n-1} or exceeds $2^{n-1} - 1$.

All of the MP functions compute their results *before* they raise an exception. The extraneous bits are simply discarded. For example,

```
MP_T z;
MP_set(8);
z = MP_new(0);
MP_fromintu(z, 0xFFF);
```

sets z to 0xFF and raises MP_Overflow. Clients can use a TRY-EXCEPT statement to ignore the exception when that is the appropriate action. For example,

```
MP_T z;
MP_set(8);
z = MP_new(0);
TRY
    MP_fromintu(z, 0xFFF);
EXCEPT(MP_Overflow) ;
END_TRY;
```

sets z to 0xFF and discards the overflow exception.

This convention does not apply to

⟨*exported functions* 358⟩+≡
```
extern unsigned long MP_tointu(T x);
extern           long MP_toint (T x);
```

which return the value of x as a signed or unsigned long. These functions raise MP_Overflow when x doesn't fit in the return type, and there's no way to capture the result when an exception occurs. Clients can use

⟨*exported functions* 358⟩+≡
```
extern T MP_cvt (int m, T z, T x);
extern T MP_cvtu(int m, T z, T x);
```

to convert x to an MP_T of the appropriate size. MP_cvt and MP_cvtu convert x to an m-bit signed or unsigned MP_T in z and return z. They raise MP_Overflow when x doesn't fit in the m-bit destination, but they set z before doing so. Thus,

```
unsigned char z[sizeof (unsigned)];
TRY
    MP_cvtu(8*sizeof (unsigned), z, x);
EXCEPT(MP_Overflow) ;
END_TRY;
```

sets z to the least significant $8 \cdot$ sizeof (unsigned) bits from x regardless of the size of x.

When m exceeds the number of bits in x, MP_cvtu extends the result with zeros, and MP_cvt extends the result with x's sign bit. It is a checked runtime error for m to be less than two, and it is an unchecked runtime error for z to be too small to hold an m-bit integer.

The arithmetic functions are

⟨*exported functions* 358⟩+≡
```
extern T MP_add (T z, T x, T y);
extern T MP_sub (T z, T x, T y);
extern T MP_mul (T z, T x, T y);
extern T MP_div (T z, T x, T y);
extern T MP_mod (T z, T x, T y);
extern T MP_neg (T z, T x);

extern T MP_addu(T z, T x, T y);
extern T MP_subu(T z, T x, T y);
extern T MP_mulu(T z, T x, T y);
extern T MP_divu(T z, T x, T y);
extern T MP_modu(T z, T x, T y);
```

Those with names ending in u do unsigned arithmetic; the others do two's-complement signed arithmetic. Overflow semantics are the only difference between the unsigned and signed operations, as detailed below. MP_add, MP_sub, MP_mul, MP_div, and MP_mod and their unsigned counterparts compute $z = x + y$, $z = x - y$, $z = x \cdot y$, $z = x/y$, and $z = x \bmod y$, respectively, and return z. Italics denote the values of x, y, and z. MP_neg sets to z to the negative of x and returns z. If x and y have different signs, MP_div and MP_mod truncate toward minus infinity; thus $x \bmod y$ is always positive.

All these functions, except MP_divu and MP_modu, raise MP_Overflow if the result does not fit. MP_subu raises MP_Overflow when $x < y$, and MP_sub raises MP_Overflow when x and y have different signs and the sign of the result is different from x's sign. MP_div, MP_divu, MP_mod, and MP_modu raise

⟨*exported exceptions* 359⟩+≡
```
extern const Except_T MP_Dividebyzero;
```

when y is zero.

⟨*exported functions* 358⟩+≡
```
extern T MP_mul2u(T z, T x, T y);
extern T MP_mul2 (T z, T x, T y);
```

return double-length products: They both compute $z = x \cdot y$, where z has $2n$ bits, and return z. Thus, the result cannot overflow. It is an unchecked runtime error for z to be too small to hold $2n$ bits. Note that since z must accommodate $2n$ bits, it cannot be allocated by MP_new.

The convenience functions accept an immediate unsigned long or long for their second operand:

⟨*exported functions* 358⟩+≡
```
extern T MP_addi (T z, T x, long y);
extern T MP_subi (T z, T x, long y);
extern T MP_muli (T z, T x, long y);
extern T MP_divi (T z, T x, long y);

extern T MP_addui(T z, T x, unsigned long y);
extern T MP_subui(T z, T x, unsigned long y);
extern T MP_mului(T z, T x, unsigned long y);
extern T MP_divui(T z, T x, unsigned long y);

extern          long MP_modi (T x,          long y);
extern unsigned long MP_modui(T x, unsigned long y);
```

These functions are equivalent to their more general counterparts when their second operands are initialized to y, and they raise similar exceptions. For example,

```
MP_T z, x;
long y;
MP_muli(z, x, y);
```

is equivalent to

```
MP_T z, x;
long y;
{
    MP_T t = MP_new(0);
    int overflow = 0;
    TRY
        MP_fromint(t, y);
    EXCEPT(MP_Overflow)
        overflow = 1;
    END_TRY;
    MP_mul(z, x, t);
    if (overflow)
```

```
        RAISE(MP_Overflow);
   }
```

The convenience functions do no allocations, however. Notice that these convenience functions, including MP_divui and MP_modui, raise MP_Overflow if *y* is too big, but they do so *after* computing *z*.

⟨*exported functions* 358⟩+≡
```
   extern int MP_cmp  (T x, T y);
   extern int MP_cmpi (T x, long y);

   extern int MP_cmpu (T x, T y);
   extern int MP_cmpui(T x, unsigned long y);
```

compare *x* and *y* and return a value less than zero, equal to zero, or greater than zero, if, respectively $x < y$, $x = y$, or $x > y$. MP_cmpi and MP_cmpui don't insist that *y* fit in an MP_T; they simply compare *x* and *y*.

The following functions treat their input MP_Ts as strings of *n* bits:

⟨*exported functions* 358⟩+≡
```
   extern T MP_and (T z, T x, T y);
   extern T MP_or  (T z, T x, T y);
   extern T MP_xor (T z, T x, T y);
   extern T MP_not (T z, T x);

   extern T MP_andi(T z, T x, unsigned long y);
   extern T MP_ori (T z, T x, unsigned long y);
   extern T MP_xori(T z, T x, unsigned long y);
```

MP_and, MP_or, MP_xor and their immmediate counterparts set *z* to the bitwise AND, inclusive OR, and exclusive OR of *x* and *y* and return z. MP_not sets *z* to the one's complement of *x* and returns z. These functions never raise exceptions, and the convenience variants ignore the overflow that would usually occur when *y* is too big. For example,

```
   MP_T z, x;
   unsigned long y;
   MP_andi(z, x, y);
```

is equivalent to

```
MP_T z, x;
unsigned long y;
{
    MP_T t = MP_new(0);
    TRY
        MP_fromintu(t, y);
    EXCEPT(MP_Overflow) ;
    END_TRY;
    MP_and(z, x, t);
}
```

None of these functions do any allocations, however.

The three shift functions

⟨*exported functions* 358⟩+≡
```
    extern T MP_lshift(T z, T x, int s);
    extern T MP_rshift(T z, T x, int s);
    extern T MP_ashift(T z, T x, int s);
```

implement logical and arithmetic shifts. MP_lshift sets z to x shifted left s bits, and MP_rshift sets z to x shifted right s bits. Both functions fill the vacated bits with zeros and return z. MP_ashift is like MP_rshift, but the vacated bits are filled with x's sign bit. It is a checked runtime error for s to be negative.

The following functions convert between MP_Ts and strings.

⟨*exported functions* 358⟩+≡
```
    extern T      MP_fromstr(T z, const char *str,
        int base, char **end);
    extern char *MP_tostr  (char *str, int size,
        int base, T x);
    extern void  MP_fmt    (int code, va_list *app,
        int put(int c, void *cl), void *cl,
        unsigned char flags[], int width, int precision);
    extern void  MP_fmtu   (int code, va_list *app,
        int put(int c, void *cl), void *cl,
        unsigned char flags[], int width, int precision);
```

MP_fromstr interprets the string in str as an unsigned integer in base, sets z to that integer, and returns z. It ignores leading white space, and consumes one or more digits in base. For bases greater than 10, the lowercase and uppercase letters specify the digits beyond nine. MP_fromstr is like strtoul: If end is nonnull, MP_fromstr sets *end to the address of the character that terminated the scan. If str does not specify a valid integer, MP_fromstr sets *end to str, if end is nonnull, and returns null. MP_fromstr raises MP_Overflow if the string in str specifies an integer that is too big. It is a checked runtime error for str to be null, or for base to be less than two or more than 36.

MP_tostr fills str[0..size-1] with a null-terminated string representing x in base, and returns str. If str is null, MP_tostr ignores size and allocates the necessary string; it is the client's responsibility to deallocate the string. It is a checked runtime error for str to be nonnull, for size to be too small to hold the null-terminated result, or for base to be less than two or more than 36. When str is null, MP_tostr can raise Mem_Failed.

MP_fmt and MP_fmtu are Fmt-style conversion functions for printing MP_Ts. Both consume an MP_T *and* a base; MP_fmt converts the signed MP_T to a string using the same conventions as printf's %d conversion, and MP_fmtu converts the unsigned MP_T using conventions of printf's %u conversion. Both functions can raise Mem_Failed. It is a checked runtime error for app or flags to be null.

19.2 Example: Another Calculator

mpcalc is like calc, except that it does signed and unsigned computations on *n*-bit integers. It illustrates the use of the MP interface. Like calc, mpcalc uses Polish suffix notation: Values are pushed onto a stack, and operators pop their operands from the stack and push their results. A value is one or more consecutive digits in the current input base, and the operators are as follows.

~	negation	&	AND
+	addition	|	inclusive OR
–	subtraction	^	exclusive OR
*	multiplication	<	left shift
/	division	>	right shift
%	remainder	!	not
i	set the input base	o	set the output base
k	set the precision	c	clear the stack

> d   duplicate the value at the top of the stack
>
> p   print the value at the top of the stack
>
> q   quit

White-space characters separate values but are otherwise ignored; other characters are announced as unrecognized operators. The size of the stack is limited only by available memory, but a diagnostic announces stack underflow.

The command *n*k, where *n* is at least two, specifies the size of the integers manipulated by mpcalc; the default is 32. The stack must be empty when the k operator is executed. The i and o operators specify the input and output bases; the defaults are both 10. When the input base exceeds 10, the leading digit of a value must be between zero and nine inclusive.

If the output base is two, eight, or 16, the + = * / and % operators do unsigned arithmetic, and the p and f operators print unsigned values. For all other bases, + = * / and % do signed arithmetic, and p and f print signed values. The ~ operator always does signed arithmetic, and the & | ^ ! < and > operators always interpret their operands as unsigned numbers.

mpcalc announces overflow and division by zero when they occur. For overflow, the result in this case is the *n* least significant bits of the value. For division by zero, the result is zero.

The overall structure of mpcalc is much like that of calc: It interprets the input, computes values, and manages a stack.

⟨*mpcalc.c*⟩≡
```
#include <ctype.h>
#include <stdio.h>
#include <string.h>
#include <stdlib.h>
#include <limits.h>
#include "mem.h"
#include "seq.h"
#include "fmt.h"
#include "mp.h"

⟨mpcalc data 367⟩
⟨mpcalc functions 367⟩
```

As the inclusion of seq.h suggests, mpcalc uses a sequence for its stack:

⟨*mpcalc data* 367⟩≡
```
  Seq_T sp;
```

⟨*initialization* 367⟩≡
```
  sp = Seq_new(0);
```

Values are pushed by calling `Seq_addhi`, and they're popped by calling `Seq_remhi`. mpcalc must not call `Seq_remhi` when the sequence is empty, so it wraps all pop operations in a function that checks for underflow:

⟨*mpcalc functions* 367⟩≡
```
  MP_T pop(void) {
      if (Seq_length(sp) > 0)
          return Seq_remhi(sp);
      else {
          Fmt_fprint(stderr, "?stack underflow\n");
          return MP_new(0);
      }
  }
```

Like calc's pop, mpcalc's pop always returns an MP_T, even when the stack is empty, because this simplifies error-checking.

Dealing with MP's exceptions makes mpcalc's main loop a bit more complicated than calc's. Like calc's main loop, mpcalc's reads the next value or operator and switches on it. But it also sets up some MP_Ts for operands and results, and it uses a TRY-EXCEPT statement to catch the exceptions.

⟨*mpcalc functions* 367⟩+≡
```
  int main(int argc, char *argv[]) {
      int c;

      ⟨initialization 367⟩
      while ((c = getchar()) != EOF) {
          MP_T x = NULL, y = NULL, z = NULL;
          TRY
              switch (c) {
              ⟨cases 368⟩
              }
          EXCEPT(MP_Overflow)
```

```
                    Fmt_fprint(stderr, "?overflow\n");
                EXCEPT(MP_Dividebyzero)
                    Fmt_fprint(stderr, "?divide by 0\n");
                END_TRY;
                if (z)
                    Seq_addhi(sp, z);
                FREE(x);
                FREE(y);
            }
            ⟨clean up and exit 368⟩
    }
```

⟨*clean up and exit* 368⟩≡
  ⟨*clear the stack* 368⟩
```
  Seq_free(&sp);
  return EXIT_SUCCESS;
```

x and y are used for operands, and z is used for the result. If x and y are nonnull after switching on an operator, they hold operands that were popped from the stack and thus must be deallocated. If z is nonnull, it holds the result, which must be pushed. This approach permits the TRY-EXCEPT statement to appear only once, instead of around the code for each operator.

An input character is either white space, the first digit of a value, an operator, or something else, which is an error. Here are the easy cases:

⟨*cases* 368⟩≡
```
  default:
      if (isprint(c))
          Fmt_fprint(stderr, "?'%c'", c);
      else
          Fmt_fprint(stderr, "?'\\%03o'", c);
      Fmt_fprint(stderr, " is unimplemented\n");
      break;
  case ' ': case '\t': case '\n': case '\f': case '\r':
      break;
  case 'c': ⟨clear the stack 368⟩ break;
  case 'q': ⟨clean up and exit 368⟩
```

⟨*clear the stack* 368⟩≡
```
  while (Seq_length(sp) > 0) {
```

```
    MP_T x = Seq_remhi(sp);
    FREE(x);
}
```

A digit identifies the beginning of a value; `calc` gathers up the digits and calls `MP_fromstr` to convert them to an `MP_T`. `ibase` is the current input base.

⟨*cases* 368⟩≡
```
  case '0': case '1': case '2': case '3': case '4':
  case '5': case '6': case '7': case '8': case '9': {
      char buf[512];
      z = MP_new(0);
      ⟨gather up digits into buf 369⟩
      MP_fromstr(z, buf, ibase, NULL);
      break;
  }
```

⟨*gather up digits into* buf 369⟩≡
```
  {
      int i = 0;
      for ( ; ⟨c is a digit in ibase 369⟩; c = getchar(), i++)
          if (i < (int)sizeof (buf) - 1)
              buf[i] = c;
      if (i > (int)sizeof (buf) - 1) {
          i = (int)sizeof (buf) - 1;
          Fmt_fprint(stderr,
              "?integer constant exceeds %d digits\n", i);
      }
      buf[i] = '\0';
      if (c != EOF)
          ungetc(c, stdin);
  }
```

Excessively long values are announced and truncated. A character is a digit in `ibase` if

⟨*c is a digit in* ibase 369⟩≡
```
  strchr(&"zyxwvutsrqponmlkjihgfedcba9876543210"[36-ibase],
      tolower(c))
```

is nonnull.

The cases for most of the arithmetic operators have the same form:

⟨*cases* 368⟩+≡
```
  case '+': ⟨pop x & y, set z 370⟩ (*f->add)(z, x, y); break;
  case '-': ⟨pop x & y, set z 370⟩ (*f->sub)(z, x, y); break;
  case '*': ⟨pop x & y, set z 370⟩ (*f->mul)(z, x, y); break;
  case '/': ⟨pop x & y, set z 370⟩ (*f->div)(z, x, y); break;
  case '%': ⟨pop x & y, set z 370⟩ (*f->mod)(z, x, y); break;
  case '&': ⟨pop x & y, set z 370⟩    MP_and(z, x, y); break;
  case '|': ⟨pop x & y, set z 370⟩    MP_or (z, x, y); break;
  case '^': ⟨pop x & y, set z 370⟩    MP_xor(z, x, y); break;

  case '!': z = pop(); MP_not(z, z); break;
  case '~': z = pop(); MP_neg(z, z); break;
```

⟨*pop* x & y, *set* z 370⟩≡
```
  y = pop(); x = pop();
  z = MP_new(0);
```

f points to a structure that holds pointers to functions for those operations that depend on whether mpcalc is doing signed or unsigned arithmetic.

⟨*mpcalc data* 367⟩+≡
```
  int ibase = 10;
  int obase = 10;
  struct {
      char *fmt;
      MP_T (*add)(MP_T, MP_T, MP_T);
      MP_T (*sub)(MP_T, MP_T, MP_T);
      MP_T (*mul)(MP_T, MP_T, MP_T);
      MP_T (*div)(MP_T, MP_T, MP_T);
      MP_T (*mod)(MP_T, MP_T, MP_T);
  } s = { "%D\n",
      MP_add, MP_sub, MP_mul, MP_div, MP_mod },
    u = { "%U\n",
      MP_addu, MP_subu, MP_mulu, MP_divu, MP_modu },
   *f = &s;
```

obase is the output base. Initially, the bases are both 10, and f points to s, which holds pointers to the MP functions for signed arithmetic. The i operator changes ibase, the o operator changes obase, and both operators reaim f at either u or s:

⟨*cases* 369⟩+≡
```
  case 'i': case 'o': {
      long n;
      x = pop();
      n = MP_toint(x);
      if (n < 2 || n > 36)
          Fmt_fprint(stderr, "?%d is an illegal base\n",n);
      else if (c == 'i')
          ibase = n;
      else
          obase = n;
      if (obase == 2 || obase == 8 || obase == 16)
          f = &u;
      else
          f = &s;
      break;
      }
```

The base isn't changed if y can't be converted to a long (that is, if MP_toint raises MP_Overflow), or if the resulting integer isn't a legal base.

The s and u structures also hold a Fmt-style format string that is used to print MP_Ts. mpcalc registers MP_fmt with %D and MP_fmtu with %U:

⟨*initialization* 367⟩+≡
```
  Fmt_register('D', MP_fmt);
  Fmt_register('U', MP_fmtu);
```

f->fmt thus accesses the appropriate format string, which the p and f operators use to print MP_Ts. Note that p pops its operand into z — the code in the main loop pushes that value back onto the stack.

⟨*cases* 369⟩+≡
```
  case 'p':
      Fmt_print(f->fmt, z = pop(), obase);
      break;
```

```
case 'f': {
    int n = Seq_length(sp);
    while (--n > 0)
        Fmt_print(f->fmt, Seq_get(sp, n), obase);
    break;
}
```

Compare the code for f with calc's code on page 332; it's easy to print all of the values on the stack when it's represented with a Seq_T.

The shift operators guard against illegal shift amounts, and shift their operand in place:

⟨*cases* 369⟩+≡
```
  case '<': { ⟨get s & z 372⟩; MP_lshift(z, z, s); break; }
  case '>': { ⟨get s & z 372⟩; MP_rshift(z, z, s); break; }
```

⟨*get* s & z 372⟩≡
```
  long s;
  y = pop();
  z = pop();
  s = MP_toint(y);
  if (s < 0 || s > INT_MAX) {
      Fmt_fprint(stderr,
          "?%d is an illegal shift amount\n", s);
      break;
  }
```

If MP_toint raises MP_Overflow, or s is negative or exceeds the largest int, the operand, z, is simply pushed back onto the stack.

The remaining cases are for the k and d operators:

⟨*cases* 369⟩+≡
```
  case 'k': {
      long n;
      x = pop();
      n = MP_toint(x);
      if (n < 2 || n > INT_MAX)
          Fmt_fprint(stderr,
              "?%d is an illegal precision\n", n);
      else if (Seq_length(sp) > 0)
          Fmt_fprint(stderr, "?nonempty stack\n");
```

```
        else
            MP_set(n);
        break;
        }
    case 'd': {
        MP_T x = pop();
        z = MP_new(0);
        Seq_addhi(sp, x);
        MP_addui(z, x, 0);
        break;
        }
```

Again, setting z causes that value to be pushed by the code in the main loop.

19.3 Implementation

⟨*mp.c*⟩≡
```
    #include <ctype.h>
    #include <string.h>
    #include <stdio.h>
    #include <stdlib.h>
    #include <limits.h>
    #include "assert.h"
    #include "fmt.h"
    #include "mem.h"
    #include "xp.h"
    #include "mp.h"

    #define T MP_T
```

⟨*macros* 374⟩
⟨*data* 373⟩
⟨*static functions* 389⟩
⟨*functions* 374⟩

⟨*data* 373⟩≡
```
    const Except_T MP_Dividebyzero = { "Division by zero" };
    const Except_T MP_Overflow     = { "Overflow" };
```

XP represents an *n*-bit number as $\lceil n/8 \rceil = (n-1)/8 + 1$ bytes, least significant byte first (*n* is always positive). The following figure shows how MP interprets these bytes. The least significant byte is on the right, and addresses increase to the left.

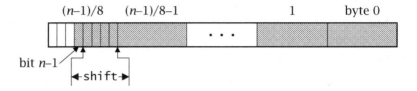

The sign bit is bit $n-1$, that is, bit $(n-1)$ mod 8 in byte $(n-1)/8$. Given *n*, MP computes three values of interest in addition to saving *n* as nbits: nbytes, the number of bytes required to hold *n* bits; shift, the number of bits the most significant byte must be shifted right to isolate the sign bit; and msb, a mask of shift+1 ones, which is used to detect overflow. When *n* is 32, these values are:

⟨*data* 373⟩+≡
```
static int nbits  =  32;
static int nbytes = (32-1)/8 + 1;
static int shift  = (32-1)%8;
static unsigned char msb = 0xFF;
```

As suggested above, MP uses nbytes and shift to access the sign bit:

⟨*macros* 374⟩≡
```
#define sign(x) ((x)[nbytes-1]>>shift)
```

These values are changed by MP_set:

⟨*functions* 374⟩≡
```
int MP_set(int n) {
    int prev = nbits;

    assert(n > 1);
    ⟨initialize 375⟩
    return prev;
}
```

⟨*initialize* 375⟩≡
```
  nbits  = n;
  nbytes = (n-1)/8 + 1;
  shift  = (n-1)%8;
  msb    = ones(n);
```

⟨*macros* 374⟩+≡
```
  #define ones(n)  (~(~0UL<<(((n)-1)%8+1)))
```

Shifting ~0 left (n-1)%8+1 bits forms a mask of ones followed by
$(n - 1) \bmod 8 + 1$ zeros; complementing it yields $(n - 1) \bmod 8 + 1$ ones
in the least significant bits. ones is defined this way because it is used
for other values of n besides the values passed to MP_set.

MP_set also allocates some temporary space for use in the arithmetic
functions, like MP_div. The allocation is thus done once in MP_set
instead of repeatedly in the arithmetic functions. MP_set allocates
enough space for one 2·nbyte+2 temporary and three nbyte
temporaries.

⟨*data* 373⟩+≡
```
  static unsigned char temp[16 + 16 + 16 + 2*16+2];
  static T tmp[] = {temp, temp+1*16, temp+2*16, temp+3*16};
```

⟨*initialize* 375⟩+≡
```
  if (tmp[0] != temp)
      FREE(tmp[0]);
  if (nbytes <= 16)
      tmp[0] = temp;
  else
      tmp[0] = ALLOC(3*nbytes + 2*nbytes + 2);
  tmp[1] = tmp[0] + 1*nbytes;
  tmp[2] = tmp[0] + 2*nbytes;
  tmp[3] = tmp[0] + 3*nbytes;
```

MP_set can use the statically allocated temp when nbytes doesn't
exceed 16, or when n doesn't exceed 128. Otherwise, it must allocate
space for the temporary. temp is necessary because MP must be initialized as if MP_set(32) had been executed.

Most of the MP functions call XP functions to do the actual arithmetic
on nbyte numbers, then check whether the result exceeds nbits bits.
MP_new and MP_fromintu illustrate this strategy.

⟨*functions* 374⟩+≡
```
T MP_new(unsigned long u) {
    return MP_fromintu(ALLOC(nbytes), u);
}

T MP_fromintu(T z, unsigned long u) {
    unsigned long carry;

    assert(z);
    ⟨set z to u 376⟩
    ⟨test for unsigned overflow 376⟩
    return z;
}
```

⟨*set z to u* 376⟩≡
```
carry = XP_fromint(nbytes, z, u);
carry |= z[nbytes-1]&~msb;
z[nbytes-1] &= msb;
```

If XP_fromint returns a nonzero carry, u doesn't fit in nbytes. If carry is zero, u fits in nbytes, but it might not fit in nbits bits. MP_fromintu must ensure that the 8-(shift+1) most significant bits in z's most significant byte are zeros. MP_set has arranged for msb to hold a mask of shift+1 ones, so ~msb isolates the desired bits, which are OR'ed into carry before they're discarded. The test for unsigned overflow simply tests carry:

⟨*test for unsigned overflow* 376⟩≡
```
if (carry)
    RAISE(MP_Overflow);
```

Notice that MP_fromintu sets z before testing for overflow; as specified by the interface, all of the MP functions must set their results before raising an exception.

Testing for signed overflow is a bit more complicated, because it depends on the operation involved. MP_fromint illustrates an easy case.

⟨*functions* 374⟩+≡
```
T MP_fromint(T z, long v) {
    assert(z);
    ⟨set z to v 377⟩
```

```
        if (⟨v is too big 377⟩)
            RAISE(MP_Overflow);
        return z;
    }
```

First, MP_fromint initializes z to the value of v, taking care to pass only positive values to XP_fromint:

⟨*set* z *to* v 377⟩≡
```
    if (v == LONG_MIN) {
        XP_fromint(nbytes, z, LONG_MAX + 1UL);
        XP_neg(nbytes, z, z, 1);
    } else if (v < 0) {
        XP_fromint(nbytes, z, -v);
        XP_neg(nbytes, z, z, 1);
    } else
        XP_fromint(nbytes, z, v);
    z[nbytes-1] &= msb;
```

The first two if clauses handle negative values: z is set to the absolute value of v, and then to its two's complement, which is accomplished by passing a one as the fourth argument to XP_neg. MP_fromint must treat the most negative integer specially, because it can't negate it. If v is negative, z's most significant bits will be ones, and the excess bits must be discarded. Many of the MP functions use the z[nbytes-1] &= msb idiom shown above to discard the excess bits in z's most significant byte.

For MP_fromint, signed overflow occurs when nbits is less than the number of bits in a long and v is outside z's range.

⟨v *is too big* 377⟩≡
```
    (nbits < 8*(int)sizeof (v) &&
        (v < -(1L<<(nbits-1)) || v >= (1L<<(nbits-1))))
```

The two shift expressions compute the most negative and most positive nbits-long signed integer.

19.3.1 Conversions

MP_toint and MP_cvt illustrate another instance of checking for signed overflow:

⟨*functions* 374⟩+≡
```
long MP_toint(T x) {
    unsigned char d[sizeof (unsigned long)];

    assert(x);
    MP_cvt(8*sizeof d, d, x);
    return XP_toint(sizeof d, d);
}
```

MP_cvt raises MP_Overflow if d can't hold x; if d can hold x, XP_toint returns the desired value.

MP_cvt does both kinds of conversions: It converts an MP_T to an MP_T with either fewer or more bits.

⟨*functions* 374⟩+≡
```
T MP_cvt(int m, T z, T x) {
    int fill, i, mbytes = (m - 1)/8 + 1;

    assert(m > 1);
    ⟨checked runtime errors for unary functions 378⟩
    fill = sign(x) ? 0xFF : 0;
    if (m < nbits) {
        ⟨narrow signed x 379⟩
    } else {
        ⟨widen signed x 379⟩
    }
    return z;
}
```

⟨*checked runtime errors for unary functions* 378⟩≡
```
assert(x); assert(z);
```

If m is less than nbits, MP_cvt "narrows" the value of x and assigns it to z. This case must check for signed overflow. x fits in m bits if bits m through nbits−1 in x are either all zeros or all ones; that is, if the excess bits in x are equal to the sign bit of x when it's treated as an m-bit integer. In the chunk below, fill is FF if x is negative and zero otherwise, so x[i]^fill should be zero if the bits x[m..nbits−1] are all ones or all zeros.

⟨*narrow signed* x 379⟩≡
```
   int carry = (x[mbytes-1]^fill)&~ones(m);
   for (i = mbytes; i < nbytes; i++)
       carry |= x[i]^fill;
   memcpy(z, x, mbytes);
   z[mbytes-1] &= ones(m);
   if (carry)
       RAISE(MP_Overflow);
```

If x is in range, carry will be zero; otherwise, some of carry's bits will be ones. The initial assignment to carry ignores the bits that will be part of z's nonsign bits.

If m is at least nbits, MP_cvt "widens" the value of x and assigns it to z. Overflow cannot occur in this case, but MP_cvt must propagate x's sign bit, which is given by fill.

⟨*widen signed* x 379⟩≡
```
   memcpy(z, x, nbytes);
   z[nbytes-1] |= fill&~msb;
   for (i = nbytes; i < mbytes; i++)
       z[i] = fill;
   z[mbytes-1] &= ones(m);
```

MP_tointu uses a similar approach: It calls MP_cvtu to convert x to an MP_T with the number of bits in an unsigned long, then calls XP_toint to return the value.

⟨*functions* 374⟩+≡
```
   unsigned long MP_tointu(T x) {
       unsigned char d[sizeof (unsigned long)];

       assert(x);
       MP_cvtu(8*sizeof d, d, x);
       return XP_toint(sizeof d, d);
   }
```

Again, MP_cvtu either narrows or widens the value of x and assigns it to z.

⟨*functions* 374⟩+≡
```
T MP_cvtu(int m, T z, T x) {
    int i, mbytes = (m - 1)/8 + 1;

    assert(m > 1);
    ⟨checked runtime errors for unary functions 378⟩
    if (m < nbits) {
        ⟨narrow unsigned x 380⟩
    } else {
        ⟨widen unsigned x 380⟩
    }
    return z;
}
```

When m is less than nbits, overflow occurs if any of x's bits m through nbits−1 are ones, which is checked with code that is similar to, but simpler than, the code in MP_cvt:

⟨*narrow unsigned* x 380⟩≡
```
int carry = x[mbytes-1]&~ones(m);
for (i = mbytes; i < nbits; i++)
    carry |= x[i];
memcpy(z, x, mbytes);
z[mbytes-1] &= ones(m);
⟨test for unsigned overflow 376⟩
```

When m is at least nbits, overflow cannot occur, and the excess bits in z are set to zeros:

⟨*widen unsigned* x 380⟩≡
```
memcpy(z, x, nbytes);
for (i = nbytes; i < mbytes; i++)
    z[i] = 0;
```

19.3.2 Unsigned Arithmetic

As the code for MP_cvtu and MP_cvt suggests, the unsigned arithmetic functions are easier to implement than their signed counterparts, because they don't need to handle signs and testing for overflow is simpler. Unsigned addition illustrates an easy case; XP_add does all the work.

⟨*functions* 374⟩+≡
```
  T MP_addu(T z, T x, T y) {
      int carry;

      ⟨checked runtime errors for binary functions 381⟩
      carry = XP_add(nbytes, z, x, y, 0);
      carry |= z[nbytes-1]&~msb;
      z[nbytes-1] &= msb;
      ⟨test for unsigned overflow 376⟩
      return z;
  }
```

⟨*checked runtime errors for binary functions* 381⟩≡
```
    assert(x); assert(y); assert(z);
```

Subtraction is just as easy, but MP_Overflow is raised when there's an outstanding borrow:

⟨*functions* 374⟩+≡
```
  T MP_subu(T z, T x, T y) {
      int borrow;

      ⟨checked runtime errors for binary functions 381⟩
      borrow = XP_sub(nbytes, z, x, y, 0);
      borrow |= z[nbytes-1]&~msb;
      z[nbytes-1] &= msb;
      ⟨test for unsigned underflow 381⟩
      return z;
  }
```

⟨*test for unsigned underflow* 381⟩≡
```
    if (borrow)
        RAISE(MP_Overflow);
```

MP_mul2u is the simplest of the multiplication functions, because overflow cannot occur.

⟨*functions* 374⟩+≡
```
  T MP_mul2u(T z, T x, T y) {
      ⟨checked runtime errors for binary functions 381⟩
      memset(tmp[3], '\0', 2*nbytes);
```

```
          XP_mul(tmp[3], nbytes, x, nbytes, y);
          memcpy(z, tmp[3], (2*nbits - 1)/8 + 1);
          return z;
    }
```

MP_mul2u computes the result into tmp[3] and copies tmp[3] to z so that x or y can be used as z, which would not work if MP_mul2u computed the result directly into z. Allocating the temporary space in MP_set thus not only isolates the allocations, but avoids restrictions on x and y.

MP_mul also calls XP_mul to compute a double-length result in tmp[3], and then narrows that result to nbits and assigns it to z.

⟨*functions* 374⟩+≡
```
    T MP_mulu(T z, T x, T y) {
        ⟨checked runtime errors for binary functions 381⟩
        memset(tmp[3], '\0', 2*nbytes);
        XP_mul(tmp[3], nbytes, x, nbytes, y);
        memcpy(z, tmp[3], nbytes);
        z[nbytes-1] &= msb;
        ⟨test for unsigned multiplication overflow 382⟩
        return z;
    }
```

The product overflows if any of the bits nbits through $2 \cdot$ nbits-1 in tmp[3] are ones. This condition can be tested much the way the similar condition in MP_cvtu is tested:

⟨*test for unsigned multiplication overflow* 382⟩≡
```
    {
        int i;
        if (tmp[3][nbytes-1]&~msb)
            RAISE(MP_Overflow);
        for (i = 0; i < nbytes; i++)
            if (tmp[3][i+nbytes] != 0)
                RAISE(MP_Overflow);
    }
```

MP_divu avoids XP_div's restrictions on its arguments by copying y to a temporary:

⟨*functions* 374⟩+≡
```
   T MP_divu(T z, T x, T y) {
       ⟨checked runtime errors for binary functions 381⟩
       ⟨copy y to a temporary 383⟩
       if (!XP_div(nbytes, z, x, nbytes, y, tmp[2], tmp[3]))
           RAISE(MP_Dividebyzero);
       return z;
   }
```

⟨*copy y to a temporary* 383⟩≡
```
   {
       memcpy(tmp[1], y, nbytes);
       y = tmp[1];
   }
```

tmp[2] holds the remainder, which is discarded; tmp[1] holds y, and y is reaimed at tmp[1]. tmp[3] is the 2·nbyte+2 temporary needed by XP_div. MP_modu is similar, but it uses tmp[2] to hold the quotient:

⟨*functions* 374⟩+≡
```
   T MP_modu(T z, T x, T y) {
       ⟨checked runtime errors for binary functions 381⟩
       ⟨copy y to a temporary 383⟩
       if (!XP_div(nbytes, tmp[2], x, nbytes, y, z, tmp[3]))
           RAISE(MP_Dividebyzero);
       return z;
   }
```

19.3.3 Signed Arithmetic

AP's sign-magnitude representation forces AP_add to consider the signs x of y. The properties of the two's-complement representation permit MP_add to avoid this case analysis and simply call XP_add regardless of the signs of x and y. Thus, signed addition is nearly identical to unsigned addition; the only important difference is the test for overflow.

⟨*functions* 374⟩+≡
```
   T MP_add(T z, T x, T y) {
       int sx, sy;
```

```
⟨checked runtime errors for binary functions 381⟩
sx = sign(x);
sy = sign(y);
XP_add(nbytes, z, x, y, 0);
z[nbytes-1] &= msb;
⟨test for signed overflow 384⟩
return z;
}
```

Overflow occurs in addition when x and y have the same signs. When the sum overflows, its sign is different from that of x and y:

```
⟨test for signed overflow 384⟩≡
    if (sx == sy && sy != sign(z))
        RAISE(MP_Overflow);
```

Signed subtraction has the same form as addition, but the test for overflow is different.

```
⟨functions 374⟩+≡
    T MP_sub(T z, T x, T y) {
        int sx, sy;

        ⟨checked runtime errors for binary functions 381⟩
        sx = sign(x);
        sy = sign(y);
        XP_sub(nbytes, z, x, y, 0);
        z[nbytes-1] &= msb;
        ⟨test for signed underflow 384⟩
        return z;
    }
```

For subtraction, underflow occurs when x and y have different signs. When x is positive and y is negative, the result should be positive; when x is negative and y is positive, the result should be negative. Thus, if x and y have different signs, and the result has the same sign as y, underflow has occurred.

```
⟨test for signed underflow 384⟩≡
    if (sx != sy && sy == sign(z))
        RAISE(MP_Overflow);
```

Negating x is equivalent to subtracting it from zero: Overflow can occur only when x is negative, and when the result overflows, it's still negative.

⟨*functions* 374⟩+≡
```
T MP_neg(T z, T x) {
    int sx;

    ⟨checked runtime errors for unary functions 378⟩
    sx = sign(x);
    XP_neg(nbytes, z, x, 1);
    z[nbytes-1] &= msb;
    if (sx && sx == sign(z))
        RAISE(MP_Overflow);
    return z;
}
```

MP_neg must clear the excess bits in z's most significant byte because they will be ones when x is positive.

The easiest way to implement signed multiplication is to negate negative operands, do an unsigned multiplication, and negate the result when the operands have different signs. For MP_mul2, overflow can never occur because it computes a double-length result, and the details are easy to fill in:

⟨*functions* 374⟩+≡
```
T MP_mul2(T z, T x, T y) {
    int sx, sy;

    ⟨checked runtime errors for binary functions 381⟩
    ⟨tmp[3] ← x·y 385⟩
    if (sx != sy)
        XP_neg((2*nbits - 1)/8 + 1, z, tmp[3], 1);
    else
        memcpy(z, tmp[3], (2*nbits - 1)/8 + 1);
    return z;
}
```

⟨tmp[3] ← x·y 385⟩≡
```
sx = sign(x);
sy = sign(y);
```

⟨*if x < 0, negate x* 386⟩
⟨*if y < 0, negate y* 386⟩
```
memset(tmp[3], '\0', 2*nbytes);
XP_mul(tmp[3], nbytes, x, nbytes, y);
```

The product has $2 \cdot$ nbits, which needs only $(2 \cdot \text{nbits} - 1)/8 + 1$ bytes of z. x and y are negated, when necessary, by forming the negated values in an appropriate temporary, and reaiming x or y at that temporary.

⟨*if x < 0, negate x* 386⟩≡
```
if (sx) {
    XP_neg(nbytes, tmp[0], x, 1);
    x = tmp[0];
    x[nbytes-1] &= msb;
}
```

⟨*if y < 0, negate y* 386⟩≡
```
if (sy) {
    XP_neg(nbytes, tmp[1], y, 1);
    y = tmp[1];
    y[nbytes-1] &= msb;
}
```

By convention, x and y are negated or copied, when necessary, into tmp[0] and tmp[1] by the MP functions.

MP_mul is similar to MP_mul2, but only the least significant nbits of the $2 \cdot$ nbit result are copied to z, and overflow occurs when the result doesn't fit in nbits, or when the operands have the same signs and the result is negative.

⟨*functions* 374⟩+≡
```
T MP_mul(T z, T x, T y) {
    int sx, sy;

    ⟨checked runtime errors for binary functions 381⟩
    ⟨tmp[3] ← x·y 385⟩
    if (sx != sy)
        XP_neg(nbytes, z, tmp[3], 1);
    else
        memcpy(z, tmp[3], nbytes);
    z[nbytes-1] &= msb;
```

⟨*test for unsigned multiplication overflow* 382⟩
```
    if (sx == sy && sign(z))
        RAISE(MP_Overflow);
    return z;
}
```

Signed division is much like unsigned division when the operands have the same signs, because both the quotient and the remainder are nonnegative. Overflow occurs only when the dividend is the most negative *n*-bit value and the divisor is −1; in this case, the quotient will be negative.

⟨*functions* 374⟩+≡
```
  T MP_div(T z, T x, T y) {
      int sx, sy;

      ⟨checked runtime errors for binary functions 381⟩
      sx = sign(x);
      sy = sign(y);
      ⟨if x < 0, negate x 386⟩
      ⟨if y < 0, negate y 386⟩ else ⟨copy y to a temporary 383⟩
      if (!XP_div(nbytes, z, x, nbytes, y, tmp[2], tmp[3]))
          RAISE(MP_Dividebyzero);
      if (sx != sy) {
          ⟨adjust the quotient 388⟩
      } else if (sx && sign(z))
          RAISE(MP_Overflow);
      return z;
  }
```

MP_div either negates *y* into its temporary or copies it there, because y and z might the same MP_T, and it uses tmp[2] to hold the remainder.

The complicated case for signed division and modulus is when the operands have different signs. In this case, the quotient is negative but must be truncated toward minus infinity, and the remainder is positive. The required adjustments are the same ones that AP_div and AP_mod do: The quotient is negated and, if the remainder is nonzero, the quotient is decremented. Also, if the unsigned remainder is nonzero, *y* minus that remainder is the correct value.

⟨*adjust the quotient* 388⟩≡
```
  XP_neg(nbytes, z, z, 1);
  if (!iszero(tmp[2]))
      XP_diff(nbytes, z, z, 1);
  z[nbytes-1] &= msb;
```

⟨*macros* 374⟩+≡
```
  #define iszero(x) (XP_length(nbytes,(x))==1 && (x)[0]==0)
```

MP_div doesn't bother adjusting the remainder, because it's discarded. MP_mod does just the opposite: It adjusts only the remainder, and uses tmp[2] to hold the quotient.

⟨*functions* 374⟩+≡
```
  T MP_mod(T z, T x, T y) {
      int sx, sy;

      ⟨checked runtime errors for binary functions 381⟩
      sx = sign(x);
      sy = sign(y);
      ⟨if x < 0, negate x 386⟩
      ⟨if y < 0, negate y 386⟩ else ⟨copy y to a temporary 383⟩
      if (!XP_div(nbytes, tmp[2], x, nbytes, y, z, tmp[3]))
          RAISE(MP_Dividebyzero);
      if (sx != sy) {
          if (!iszero(z))
              XP_sub(nbytes, z, y, z, 0);
      } else if (sx && sign(tmp[2]))
          RAISE(MP_Overflow);
      return z;
  }
```

19.3.4 Convenience Functions

The arithmetic convenience functions take a long or unsigned long immediate operand, convert it to an MP_T, if necessary, and perform the corresponding arithmetic operation. When y is a single digit in base 2^8, these functions can use the single-digit functions exported by XP. But there are two opportunities for overflow: y might be too big, and the operation itself might overflow. If y is too big, these functions must complete the operation and the assignment to z before raising an exception. MP_addui illustrates the approach used by all the convenience functions:

⟨*functions* 374⟩+≡
```
    T MP_addui(T z, T x, unsigned long y) {
        ⟨checked runtime errors for unary functions 378⟩
        if (y < BASE) {
            int carry = XP_sum(nbytes, z, x, y);
            carry |= z[nbytes-1]&~msb;
            z[nbytes-1] &= msb;
            ⟨test for unsigned overflow 376⟩
        } else if (applyu(MP_addu, z, x, y))
            RAISE(MP_Overflow);
        return z;
    }
```

⟨*macros* 374⟩+≡
```
    #define BASE (1<<8)
```

If y is one digit, XP_sum can compute $x + y$. This code also detects overflow when nbits is less than eight and y is too big, because the sum will be too big for any value of x. Otherwise, MP_addui calls applyu to convert y to an MP_T and to apply the more general function MP_addu. applyu returns a one if y is too big, but only after it computes z:

⟨*static functions* 389⟩≡
```
    static int applyu(T op(T, T, T), T z, T x,
        unsigned long u) {
        unsigned long carry;

        { T z = tmp[2]; ⟨set z to u 376⟩ }
        op(z, x, tmp[2]);
        return carry != 0;
    }
```

applyu uses the code from MP_frommtu to convert the unsigned long operand into tmp[2]. It saves the carry from the conversion because the conversion might overflow. It then calls the function specified by its first argument, and returns one if the saved carry is nonzero, or zero otherwise. The function op might raise an exception, too, but only after it sets z.

The convenience functions for unsigned subtraction and multiplication are similar. When y is less than 2^8, MP_subui calls MP_diff.

⟨*functions* 381⟩+≡
```
T MP_subui(T z, T x, unsigned long y) {
    ⟨checked runtime errors for unary functions 381⟩
    if (y < BASE) {
        int borrow = XP_diff(nbytes, z, x, y);
        borrow |= z[nbytes-1]&~msb;
        z[nbytes-1] &= msb;
        ⟨test for unsigned underflow 381⟩
    } else if (applyu(MP_subu, z, x, y))
        RAISE(MP_Overflow);
    return z;
}
```

When y is too big, $x - y$ underflows for all x, so MP_subui doesn't need to check whether y is too big before calling XP_diff.

MP_mului calls MP_product, but MP_mului must explicitly check whether y is too big when nbits is less than eight, because XP_product won't catch that error when x is zero. This check is made *after* computing z.

```
T MP_mului(T z, T x, unsigned long y) {
    ⟨checked runtime errors for unary functions 381⟩
    if (y < BASE) {
        int carry = XP_product(nbytes, z, x, y);
        carry |= z[nbytes-1]&~msb;
        z[nbytes-1] &= msb;
        ⟨test for unsigned overflow 376⟩
        ⟨check if unsigned y is too big 390⟩
    } else if (applyu(MP_mulu, z, x, y))
        RAISE(MP_Overflow);
    return z;
}
```

⟨*check if unsigned y is too big* 390⟩≡
```
if (nbits < 8 && y >= (1U<<nbits))
    RAISE(MP_Overflow);
```

MP_divui and MP_modui use XP_quotient, but they must test for a zero divisor themselves (because XP_quotient accepts only nonzero, single-digit divisors), and they must test for overflow when nbits is less than eight and *y* is too big.

⟨*functions* 381⟩+≡
```
T MP_divui(T z, T x, unsigned long y) {
    ⟨checked runtime errors for unary functions 381⟩
    if (y == 0)
        RAISE(MP_Dividebyzero);
    else if (y < BASE) {
        XP_quotient(nbytes, z, x, y);
        ⟨check if unsigned y is too big 390⟩
    } else if (applyu(MP_divu, z, x, y))
        RAISE(MP_Overflow);
    return z;
}
```

MP_modui calls XP_quotient, but only to compute the remainder. It discards the quotient computed into tmp[2]:

⟨*functions* 381⟩+≡
```
unsigned long MP_modui(T x, unsigned long y) {
    assert(x);
    if (y == 0)
        RAISE(MP_Dividebyzero);
    else if (y < BASE) {
        int r = XP_quotient(nbytes, tmp[2], x, y);
        ⟨check if unsigned y is too big 390⟩
        return r;
    } else if (applyu(MP_modu, tmp[2], x, y))
        RAISE(MP_Overflow);
    return XP_toint(nbytes, tmp[2]);
}
```

The signed arithmetic convenience functions use the same approach, but call a different apply function, which uses MP_fromint's code to convert a long to a signed MP_T in tmp[2], calls the desired function, and returns one if the immediate operand is too big, or zero otherwise.

⟨*static functions* 389⟩+≡
```
static int apply(T op(T, T, T), T z, T x, long v) {
    { T z = tmp[2]; ⟨set z to v 377⟩ }
    op(z, x, tmp[2]);
    return ⟨v is too big 377⟩;
}
```

When $|y|$ is less than 2^8, the signed convenience functions have a bit more work to do than their unsigned counterparts, because they must deal with signed operands. The single-digit XP functions take only positive single-digit operands, so the signed convenience functions must use the signs of their operands to determine which function to call. The analysis is similar to that done by the AP functions (see page 338), but MP's two's-complement representation simplifies the details. Here are the cases for addition.

	$y < 0$	$y \geq 0$
$x < 0$	$-(|x| + |y|) = x - |y|$	$-(|x| - |y|) = x + |y|$
$x \geq 0$	$|x| - |y| = x - |y|$	$|x| + |y| = x + |y|$

When y is negative, $x + y$ is equal to $x - |y|$ for any x, so MP_addi can use XP_diff to compute the sum; it can use XP_sum when y is nonnegative.

⟨*functions* 381⟩+≡
```
T MP_addi(T z, T x, long y) {
    ⟨checked runtime errors for unary functions 381⟩
    if (-BASE < y && y < BASE) {
        int sx = sign(x), sy = y < 0;
        if (sy)
            XP_diff(nbytes, z, x, -y);
        else
            XP_sum (nbytes, z, x,  y);
        z[nbytes-1] &= msb;
        ⟨test for signed overflow 384⟩
        ⟨check if signed y is too big 393⟩
    } else if (apply(MP_add, z, x, y))
        RAISE(MP_Overflow);
    return z;
}
```

⟨*check if signed* y *is too big* 393⟩≡
```
    if (nbits < 8
    && (y < -(1<<(nbits-1)) || y >= (1<<(nbits-1))))
        RAISE(MP_Overflow);
```

The cases for signed subtraction are just the opposite of those for addition (see page 340 for AP_sub's case):

	$y < 0$	$y \geq 0$
$x < 0$	$-(\|x\| - \|y\|) = x + \|y\|$	$-(\|x\| + \|y\|) = x - \|y\|$
$x \geq 0$	$\|x\| + \|y\| = x + \|y\|$	$\|x\| - \|y\| = x - \|y\|$

So, MP_subi calls XP_sum to add $\|y\|$ to any x when y is negative, and calls XP_diff when y is nonnegative.

⟨*functions* 381⟩+≡
```
    T MP_subi(T z, T x, long y) {
        ⟨checked runtime errors for unary functions 381⟩
        if (-BASE < y && y < BASE) {
            int sx = sign(x), sy = y < 0;
            if (sy)
                XP_sum (nbytes, z, x, -y);
            else
                XP_diff(nbytes, z, x,  y);
            z[nbytes-1] &= msb;
            ⟨test for signed underflow 384⟩
            ⟨check if signed y is too big 393⟩
        } else if (apply(MP_sub, z, x, y))
            RAISE(MP_Overflow);
        return z;
    }
```

MP_muli uses MP_mul's strategy: It negates negative operands, computes the product by calling XP_product, and negates the product when the operands have different signs.

⟨*functions* 381⟩+≡
```
    T MP_muli(T z, T x, long y) {
        ⟨checked runtime errors for unary functions 381⟩
```

```
        if (-BASE < y && y < BASE) {
            int sx = sign(x), sy = y < 0;
            ⟨if x < 0, negate x 386⟩
            XP_product(nbytes, z, x, sy ? -y : y);
            if (sx != sy)
                XP_neg(nbytes, z, x, 1);
            z[nbytes-1] &= msb;
            if (sx == sy && sign(z))
                RAISE(MP_Overflow);
            ⟨check if signed y is too big 393⟩
        } else if (apply(MP_mul, z, x, y))
            RAISE(MP_Overflow);
        return z;
    }
```

MP_divi and MP_modi must check for a zero divisor, because they call XP_quotient to compute the quotient and remainder. MP_divi discards the remainder, and MP_modi discards the quotient:

```
⟨functions⟩+≡
    T MP_divi(T z, T x, long y) {
        ⟨checked runtime errors for unary functions 381⟩
        if (y == 0)
            RAISE(MP_Dividebyzero);
        else if (-BASE < y && y < BASE) {
            int r;
            ⟨z ← x/y, r ← x mod y 395⟩
            ⟨check if signed y is too big 393⟩
        } else if (apply(MP_div, z, x, y))
            RAISE(MP_Overflow);
        return z;
    }

    long MP_modi(T x, long y) {
        assert(x);
        if (y == 0)
            RAISE(MP_Dividebyzero);
        else if (-BASE < y && y < BASE) {
            T z = tmp[2];
            int r;
            ⟨z ← x/y, r ← x mod y 395⟩
```

```
        ⟨check if signed y is too big 393⟩
            return r;
    } else if (apply(MP_mod, tmp[2], x, y))
        RAISE(MP_Overflow);
    return MP_toint(tmp[2]);
}
```

`MP_modi` calls `MP_toint` instead of `XP_toint` to ensure that the sign is extended properly.

The chunk common to both `MP_divi` and `MP_modi` computes the quotient and the remainder, and adjusts the quotient and remainder when x and y have different signs and the remainder is nonzero.

⟨$z \leftarrow x/y$, $r \leftarrow x$ *mod* y 395⟩≡
```
    int sx = sign(x), sy = y < 0;
    ⟨if x < 0, negate x 386⟩
    r = XP_quotient(nbytes, z, x, sy ? -y : y);
    if (sx != sy) {
        XP_neg(nbytes, z, z, 1);
        if (r != 0) {
            XP_diff(nbytes, z, z, 1);
            r = y - r;
        }
        z[nbytes-1] &= msb;
    } else if (sx && sign(z))
        RAISE(MP_Overflow);
```

19.3.5 Comparisons and Logical Operations

Unsigned comparison is easy — `MP_cmp` can just call `XP_cmp`:

⟨*functions* 381⟩+≡
```
    int MP_cmpu(T x, T y) {
        assert(x);
        assert(y);
        return XP_cmp(nbytes, x, y);
    }
```

When x and y have different signs, `MP_cmp(x,y)` simply returns the difference of the signs of y and x:

⟨*functions* 381⟩+≡
```
int MP_cmp(T x, T y) {
    int sx, sy;

    assert(x);
    assert(y);
    sx = sign(x);
    sy = sign(y);
    if (sx != sy)
        return sy - sx;
    else
        return XP_cmp(nbytes, x, y);
}
```

When x and y have the same signs, MP_cmp can treat them as unsigned numbers and call XP_cmp to compare them.

The comparison convenience functions can't use applyu and apply, because they compute integer results, and because they don't insist that their long or unsigned long operands fit in an MP_T. These functions simply compare an MP_T with an immediate value; when the value is too big, that will be reflected in the outcome of the comparison. When an unsigned long has at least nbits bits, MP_cmpui converts the MP_T to an unsigned long and uses the usual C comparisons. Otherwise, it converts the immediate value to an MP_T in tmp[2] and calls XP_cmp.

⟨*functions* 381⟩+≡
```
int MP_cmpui(T x, unsigned long y) {
    assert(x);
    if ((int)sizeof y >= nbytes) {
        unsigned long v = XP_toint(nbytes, x);
        ⟨return −1, 0, +1, if v < y, v = y, v > y 396⟩
    } else {
        XP_fromint(nbytes, tmp[2], y);
        return XP_cmp(nbytes, x, tmp[2]);
    }
}
```

⟨*return −1, 0, +1, if* v < y, v = y, v > y 396⟩≡
```
if (v < y)
    return -1;
else if (v > y)
```

```
            return 1;
      else
            return 0;
```

MP_cmpui doesn't have to check for overflow after it calls XP_fromint, because that call is made only when *y* has fewer bits than an MP_T.

MP_cmpi can avoid comparisons altogether when *x* and *y* have different signs. Otherwise, it uses MP_cmpui's approach: If the immediate value has at least as many bits as an MP_T, the comparison can be done with C comparisons.

⟨*functions* 374⟩+≡
```
  int MP_cmpi(T x, long y) {
      int sx, sy = y < 0;

      assert(x);
      sx = sign(x);
      if (sx != sy)
          return sy - sx;
      else if ((int)sizeof y >= nbytes) {
          long v = MP_toint(x);
          ⟨return −1, 0, +1, if v < y, v = y, v > y 396⟩
      } else {
          MP_fromint(tmp[2], y);
          return XP_cmp(nbytes, x, tmp[2]);
      }
  }
```

When *x* and *y* have the same signs and *y* has fewer bits than an MP_T, MP_cmpi can safely convert *y* to an MP_T in tmp[2], and then call XP_cmp to compare *x* and tmp[2]. MP_cmpi calls MP_fromint instead of XP_fromint in order to handle negative values of *y* correctly.

The binary logical functions — MP_and, MP_or, and MP_xor — are the easiest MP functions to implement because each byte of the result is a bitwise operation on the corresponding bytes in the operands:

⟨*macros* 374⟩+≡
```
  #define bitop(op) \
      int i; assert(z); assert(x); assert(y); \
      for (i = 0; i < nbytes; i++) z[i] = x[i] op y[i]; \
      return z
```

⟨*functions* 374⟩+≡
```
T MP_and(T z, T x, T y) { bitop(&); }
T MP_or (T z, T x, T y) { bitop(|); }
T MP_xor(T z, T x, T y) { bitop(^); }
```

MP_not is the oddball that doesn't fit bitop's pattern:

⟨*functions* 374⟩+≡
```
T MP_not(T z, T x) {
    int i;

    ⟨checked runtime errors for unary functions 378⟩
    for (i = 0; i < nbytes; i++)
        z[i] = ~x[i];
    z[nbytes-1] &= msb;
    return z;
}
```

There's little to be gained from writing special-case code for single-digit operands to the three logical convenience functions, and immediate operands to these functions don't cause an exception. applyu can still be used; its return value is simply ignored.

⟨*macros* 374⟩+≡
```
#define bitopi(op) assert(z); assert(x); \
    applyu(op, z, x, y); \
    return z
```

⟨*functions* 374⟩+≡
```
T MP_andi(T z, T x, unsigned long y) { bitopi(MP_and); }
T MP_ori (T z, T x, unsigned long y) { bitopi(MP_or);  }
T MP_xori(T z, T x, unsigned long y) { bitopi(MP_xor); }
```

The three shift functions call XP_lshift or XP_rshift, after enforcing their checked runtime errors, and after checking for the easy case when s exceeds or is equal to nbits, in which case, the result is all zeroes or all ones. XP_ashift fills with ones and thus implements an arithmetic right shift.

⟨*macros* 374⟩+≡
```
#define shft(fill, op) \
```

```
    assert(x); assert(z); assert(s >= 0); \
    if (s >= nbits) memset(z, fill, nbytes); \
    else op(nbytes, z, nbytes, x, s, fill); \
    z[nbytes-1] &= msb; \
    return z
```

⟨*functions* 374⟩+≡
```
    T MP_lshift(T z, T x, int s) { shft(0, XP_lshift); }
    T MP_rshift(T z, T x, int s) { shft(0, XP_rshift); }
    T MP_ashift(T z, T x, int s) { shft(sign(x),XP_rshift); }
```

19.3.6 String Conversions

The last four functions convert between strings and MP_Ts. MP_fromstr is like strtoul; it interprets the string as an unsigned number in a base between two and 36, inclusive. Letters specify the digits above nine in bases that exceed 10.

⟨*functions* 374⟩+≡
```
    T MP_fromstr(T z, const char *str, int base, char **end){
        int carry;

        assert(z);
        memset(z, '\0', nbytes);
        carry = XP_fromstr(nbytes, z, str, base, end);
        carry |= z[nbytes-1]&~msb;
        z[nbytes-1] &= msb;
        ⟨test for unsigned overflow 376⟩
        return z;
    }
```

XP_fromstr does the conversion and sets *end to the address of the character that terminated the conversion, if end is nonnull. z is initialized to zero because XP_fromint adds the converted value to z.

MP_tostr performs the opposite conversion: It takes an MP_T and fills a string with the string representation of the MP_T's value in a base between two and 36, inclusive.

⟨*functions* 374⟩+≡
```
    char *MP_tostr(char *str, int size, int base, T x) {
        assert(x);
```

```
        assert(base >= 2 && base <= 36);
        assert(str == NULL || size > 1);
        if (str == NULL) {
            ⟨size ← number of characters to represent x in base 400⟩
            str = ALLOC(size);
        }
        memcpy(tmp[1], x, nbytes);
        XP_tostr(str, size, base, nbytes, tmp[1]);
        return str;
    }
```

If `str` is null, `MP_tostr` allocates a string long enough to hold x's representation in `base`. `MP_tostr` uses `AP_tostr`'s trick for computing the size of the string: `str` must have at least $\lceil nbits/k \rceil$ characters, where k is chosen so that 2^k is the largest power of two less than or equal to `base` (see page 352), plus one for the terminating null character.

⟨size ← *number of characters to represent x in* base 400⟩≡
```
    {
        int k;
        for (k = 5; (1<<k) > base; k--)
            ;
        size = nbits/k + 1 + 1;
    }
```

The Fmt-style conversion functions format an unsigned or signed `MP_T`. Each consumes *two* arguments: an `MP_T` and a base between two and 36, inclusive. `MP_fmtu` calls `MP_tostr` to convert its `MP_T`, and calls `Fmt_putd` to emit the converted result. Recall that `Fmt_putd` emits a number in the style of `printf`'s %d conversion.

⟨*functions* 374⟩+≡
```
    void MP_fmtu(int code, va_list *app,
        int put(int c, void *cl), void *cl,
        unsigned char flags[], int width, int precision) {
        T x;
        char *buf;

        assert(app && flags);
        x = va_arg(*app, T);
        assert(x);
```

```
          buf = MP_tostr(NULL, 0, va_arg(*app, int), x);
          Fmt_putd(buf, strlen(buf), put, cl, flags,
              width, precision);
          FREE(buf);
      }
```

MP_fmt has a bit more work to do, because it interprets an MP_T as a signed number, but MP_tostr accepts only unsigned MP_Ts. Thus, MP_fmt itself allocates the buffer, so that it can include a leading sign, if necessary.

⟨*functions* 374⟩+≡
```
  void MP_fmt(int code, va_list *app,
      int put(int c, void *cl), void *cl,
      unsigned char flags[], int width, int precision) {
      T x;
      int base, size, sx;
      char *buf;

      assert(app && flags);
      x = va_arg(*app, T);
      assert(x);
      base = va_arg(*app, int);
      assert(base >= 2 && base <= 36);
      sx = sign(x);
      ⟨if x < 0, negate x 386⟩
      ⟨size ← number of characters to represent x in base 400⟩
      buf = ALLOC(size+1);
      if (sx) {
          buf[0] = '-';
          MP_tostr(buf + 1, size, base, x);
      } else
          MP_tostr(buf, size + 1, base, x);
      Fmt_putd(buf, strlen(buf), put, cl, flags,
          width, precision);
      FREE(buf);
  }
```

Further Reading

Multiple-precision arithmetic is often used in compilers, and sometimes it must be used. For example, Clinger (1990) shows that converting floating-point literals to their corresponding IEEE floating-point representations sometimes requires multiple-precision arithmetic to achieve the best accuracy.

Schneier (1996) is a comprehensive survey of cryptography. This book is practical, and includes C implementations for some of the algorithms it describes. It also has extensive bibliography that is a good starting point for deeper investigations.

As shown on page 308, multiplying two n-digit numbers takes time proportional to n^2. Section 20.6 in Press et al. (1992) shows how to use the fast Fourier transform to implement multiplication in time proportional to $n \lg n \lg \lg n$. It also implements x/y by computing the reciprocal $1/y$ and multiplying it by x. This approach requires multiple-precision numbers with fractional parts.

Exercises

19.1 The MP functions do a lot of unnecessary work when nbits is a multiple of eight. Can you revise the MP implementation to avoid this work when nbits mod 8 is zero? Implement your scheme and measure its benefits — or costs.

19.2 For many applications, once chosen, nbits never changes. Implement a program generator that, given a specific value for nbits, generates an interface and an implementation for nbits-bit arithmetic, MP_*nbits*, that is otherwise identical to MP.

19.3 Design and implement an interface for arithmetic on fixed-point, multiple-precision numbers; that is, numbers with a whole part and a fractional part. Clients should be able to specify the number of digits in both parts. Be sure to specify the details of rounding. Section 20.6 in Press et al. (1992) includes some useful algorithms for this exercise.

19.4 Design and implement an interface for arithmetic on floating-point numbers in which clients can specify the number of bits in the exponent and in the significand. Read Goldberg (1991) before attempting this exercise.

19.5   The XP and MP functions do not use const-qualified parameters for the reasons detailed on page 300. There are, however, other definitions for XP_T and MP_T that work correctly with const. For example, if T is defined by

```
typedef unsigned char T[];
```

then "const T" means "array of constant unsigned char," and, for example, MP_add could be declared by

```
unsigned char *MP_add(T z, const T x, const T y);
```

In MP_add, x and y have type "pointer to constant unsigned char," because array types in formal parameters "decay" to the corresponding pointer types. Of course, const doesn't prevent accidental aliasing, because the same array may be passed to both z and x, for example. This declaration for MP_add illustrates the disadvantage of defining T as an array type: T cannot be used as a return type, and clients cannot declare variables of type T. This kind of array type is useful only for parameters. This problem can be avoided by defining T as a typedef for unsigned char:

```
typedef unsigned char T;
```

With this definition, the declaration for MP_add can be either of:

```
T *MP_add(T z[], const T x[], const T y[]);
T *MP_add(T *z, T *x, T *y);
```

Reimplement XP and its clients, AP, MP, calc, and mpcalc, using both these definitions for T. Compare the readability of the results with the originals.

20
THREADS

The typical C program is a sequential, or *single-threaded*, program. That is, there is one locus of control in the program. A program's location counter gives the address of each instruction as it is executed. Most of the time, the location is advanced sequentially, one instruction at a time. Occasionally, a jump or call instruction causes the location counter to change to the jump destination or to the address of the function called. The values of the location counter trace out a path through the program that describes its execution, and this path looks like a thread through the program.

A concurrent or multithreaded program has more than one thread, and, in the most general case, these threads are all executing at the same time, at least conceptually. This concurrent execution is what makes writing multithreaded applications so much more complicated than writing single-threaded applications, because the threads can interact with one another in potentially nondeterministic ways. The three interfaces in this chapter export functions to create and manage threads, to synchronize the actions of cooperating threads, and to communicate among threads.

Threads are useful for applications that have inherent concurrent activities. Graphical user interfaces are a prime example; keyboard inputs, mouse movements and clicks, and display output all occur simultaneously. In multithreaded systems, a thread can be dedicated to each of these activities without concern for the others. This approach helps simplify the implementation of a user interface because each of these threads can be designed and written as if it were a sequential program, except in the few places where they must communicate or synchronize with other threads.

On multiprocessor computers, threads can improve performance in applications that can be decomposed naturally into relatively independent subtasks. Each subtask is run in a separate thread, and they all run concurrently and thus finish sooner than if the subtasks were done sequentially. Section 20.2 describes a sorting program that uses this approach.

Threads can also help structure sequential programs because they have *state*: A thread includes enough associated information for it to be stopped, and then subsequently resumed where it left off. A typical UNIX C compiler, for example, consists of a separate preprocessor, a compiler proper, and an assembler. The preprocessor reads the source code, includes headers and expands macros, and emits the resulting source; the compiler reads and parses the expanded source, generates code, and emits assembly language; and the assembler reads the assembly language and emits object code. These phases usually communicate with one another by reading and writing temporary files. With threads, each phase could run as a separate thread in a single application, eliminating the temporary files and the overhead of reading, writing, and deleting them. The compiler itself might also use separate threads for the lexical analyzer and for the parser. Section 20.2 illustrates this use of threads in a pipeline that computes prime numbers.

Some systems were not designed for multithreaded applications, which limits the usefulness of threads. For example, most UNIX systems have blocking I/O primitives. That is, when a thread issues a read request, the UNIX process and all the threads in it wait for that request to be filled. On these systems, threads cannot overlap useful computation with I/O. Similar comments apply to signal handling. Most UNIX systems associate signals and signal handlers with the process, not with the individual threads in the process.

Thread systems support either *user-level* or *kernel-level* threads, or perhaps both. User-level threads are implemented completely in user mode, without help from the operating system. User-level thread packages often have some of the drawbacks described above. On the bright side, user-level threads can be very efficient. The `Thread` interface described in the next section provides user-level threads.

Kernel-level threads use operating system facilities to provide, for example, nonblocking I/O and per-thread signal handling. Newer operating systems have kernel-level threads and use them to provide thread interfaces. Some operations in these interfaces require system calls, however, which usually cost more than similar operations in user-level threads.

Even on systems with kernel-level threads, standard libraries may not be reentrant or thread-safe. A *reentrant* function changes only locals and parameters. A function that changes global variables or uses static variables to hold intermediate results is *nonreentrant*. Typical implementations of some of the functions in the standard C library are nonreentrant. If two or more activations of a nonreentrant function exist at the same time, they can modify these intermediate values in unpredictable ways. In a single-threaded program, multiple activations can exist simultaneously because of direct and indirect recursion. In a multi-threaded program, multiple activations occur because different threads can call the same function simultaneously. Two threads calling a nonreentrant function at the same time will thus modify the same storage with undefined results.

A *thread-safe* function uses synchronization mechanisms to manage access to shared data, and thus may or may not be reentrant. A thread-safe function can be called by more than one thread simultaneously without concern for synchronization. This makes them easier for multi-threaded clients to use, but comes with the cost of the synchronization, even for single-threaded clients.

Standard C doesn't require that the library functions be reentrant or thread-safe, so programmers must assume the worst and use synchronization primitives to ensure that only one thread at a time executes a nonreentrant library function.

Most of the functions in this book are not thread-safe, but are reentrant. A few, like `Text_map`, are nonreentrant, and multithreaded clients must make their own synchronization arrangements. For example, if several threads share a `Table_T`, they must ensure that only one of them at a time calls the functions in the `Table` interface with that `Table_T`, as explained below.

Some thread interfaces are designed for both user-level and kernel-level threads. The Open Software Foundation's Distributed Computing Environment, DCE for short, is available on most variants of UNIX, Open-VMS, OS/2, Windows NT, and Windows 95. Typically, DCE threads use kernel-level threads when the host operating system supports them; otherwise, DCE threads are implemented as user-level. With more than 50 functions, the DCE thread interface is considerably larger than the three interfaces in this chapter combined, but the DCE interface does more. For example, its implementations support thread-level signals and protect calls to the standard library functions with appropriate synchronization.

Sun Microsystems's Solaris 2 operating system has a two-level thread facility. Kernel-level threads are called lightweight processes, or LWPs. Every UNIX "heavyweight" process has at least one LWP, and Solaris runs a UNIX process by running one or more of its LWPs. Kernel support for LWPs includes nonblocking I/O and per-LWP signals. User-level threads are provided by an interface similar to, but larger than, Thread, and its implementation runs user-level threads on LWPs. One LWP can service one or more user-level threads. Solaris multiplexes the processors between the LWPs, which multiplex themselves between user-level threads.

The POSIX (Portable Operating Systems Interface) thread interface — pthreads for short — is emerging as the leading standard thread interface. Most vendors now offer a pthreads implementation, perhaps based on their own thread interfaces. For example, Sun Microsystems uses Solaris 2 LWPs to implement pthreads. The pthreads facilities are a superset of those exported by Thread and Sem. The larger POSIX interface handles per-thread signals, includes several synchronization mechanisms, and specifies which standard C library functions must be thread-safe.

20.1 Interfaces

Each of the three interfaces in this chapter is small. They're divided into separate interfaces because each has a related but distinct purpose.

In theory, all running threads execute concurrently, but in practice, there are usually more threads than real processors. The processors are thus multiplexed between the running threads according to a scheduling policy. With *nonpreemptive* scheduling, a running thread may execute a function that causes it to become blocked or to otherwise relinquish its processor. With *preemptive* scheduling, a running thread gives up its processor implicitly. This policy is usually implemented with a clock interrupt, which periodically interrupts the running thread and gives its processor to another running thread. A *quantum* is the amount of time a running thread runs before it is preempted, at which point a *context switch* suspends the current thread and resumes another (perhaps the same) running thread. Context switches also occur with nonpreemptive scheduling when a running thread blocks. The Thread interface uses preemption when its implementation supports it.

Atomic actions execute without preemption. A thread that starts executing an atomic action will complete that action without interruption by another thread. If a thread calls an atomic function, the call is executed without interruption. Most of the functions described in this chapter must be atomic so that their results and effects are predictable. Atomic functions may block, however; the synchronization functions in the Sem interface are examples.

As the last two paragraphs show, concurrent programming comes with its own jargon, and different terms are often used for the same concepts. For example, threads may be called lightweight processes, tasks, subtasks, or microtasks; synchronization mechanisms may be called events, condition variables, synchronizing resources, and messages.

20.1.1 Threads

The Thread interface exports an exception and the functions that support thread creation.

⟨*thread.h*⟩≡
```
#ifndef THREAD_INCLUDED
#define THREAD_INCLUDED
#include "except.h"

#define T Thread_T
typedef struct T *T;

extern const Except_T Thread_Failed;
extern const Except_T Thread_Alerted;

extern int  Thread_init (int preempt, ...);
extern T    Thread_new  (int apply(void *),
               void *args, int nbytes, ...);
extern void Thread_exit (int code);
extern void Thread_alert(T t);
extern T    Thread_self (void);
extern int  Thread_join (T t);
extern void Thread_pause(void);

#undef T
#endif
```

Calls to all of the functions in this interface are atomic.

Thread_init initializes the thread system, and must be called before any of the other functions. It is a checked runtime error to call any other function in this interface, or in the Sem and Chan interfaces, before calling Thread_init, or to call Thread_init more than once.

If preempt is zero, Thread_init initializes the thread system to support only nonpreemptive scheduling, and returns one. If preempt is one, the thread system is initialized for preemptive scheduling. If preemption is supported, Thread_init returns one. Otherwise, the system is initialized for nonpreemptive scheduling, and Thread_init returns zero.

Typical clients initialize the thread system in main. For example, for a client that needs preemption, main usually has the following form.

```
int main(int argc, char *argv[]) {
    int preempt;
    ...
    preempt = Thread_init(1, NULL);
    assert(preempt == 1);
    ...
    Thread_exit(EXIT_SUCCESS);
    return EXIT_SUCCESS;
}
```

Thread_init may also accept additional implementation-dependent arguments, often specified with name-value pairs. For example, for implementations that support priorities,

```
preempt = Thread_init(1, "priorities", 4, NULL);
```

might initialize the thread system with four priority levels. Unknown optional arguments are usually ignored. Implementations that use this approach usually expect a null pointer as the terminating argument.

As the code template above suggests, threads must terminate execution by calling Thread_exit. The integer argument is an exit code, much like the one passed to the standard library's exit function. This value is made available to other threads that may be waiting for the calling thread's demise, as explained below. If there is only one thread in the system, calling Thread_exit is equivalent to calling exit.

Thread_new creates a new thread and returns its *thread handle*, which is an opaque pointer. Thread handles are passed to Thread_join and Thread_alert, and are returned by Thread_self. The new thread runs independently of the thread that created it. When the new thread begins execution, it executes the equivalent of

```
void *p = ALLOC(nbytes);
memcpy(p, args, nbytes);
Thread_exit(apply(p));
```

That is, apply is called with a *copy* of the nbytes bytes pointed to by args, which is presumed to point to argument data for the new thread. args is often a pointer to a structure whose fields hold apply's arguments, and nbytes is the size of that structure. The new thread starts execution with an empty exception stack: It does *not* inherit the exception state set up by TRY-EXCEPT statements in the calling thread. Exceptions are thread-specific; TRY-EXCEPT statements executed in one thread cannot affect the exceptions in another one.

If args is nonnull and nbytes is zero, the new thread executes the equivalent of

```
Thread_exit(apply(args));
```

That is, args is passed to apply unmodified. If args is null, the new thread executes the equivalent of

```
Thread_exit(apply(NULL));
```

It is a checked runtime error for apply to be null, or for args to be non-null and nbytes to be negative. If args is null, nbytes is ignored.

Like Thread_init, Thread_new may take additional implementation-specific arguments, often specified as name-value pairs. An example is

```
Thread_T t;
t = Thread_new(apply, args, nbytes, "priority", 2, NULL);
```

which creates a new thread with priority two. As this example suggests, optional arguments should be terminated with a null pointer.

Thread creation is *synchronous*: Thread_new returns after the new thread has been created and has received its argument, but perhaps before the new thread begins execution. Thread_new raises Thread_Failed if it cannot create the new thread because of resource limitations. For example, implementations may limit the number of threads that can exist simultaneously; when this limit is exceeded, Thread_new raises Thread_Failed.

Thread_exit(code) terminates execution of the calling thread. Threads waiting for the termination of the calling thread (by virtue of Thread_join) are resumed, and the value of code is returned as the result of calling Thread_join in each of the resumed threads. When the last thread calls Thread_exit, the entire program terminates by calling exit(code).

Thread_join(t) causes the calling thread to suspend execution until thread t terminates by calling Thread_exit. When thread t terminates, the calling thread is resumed, and Thread_join returns the integer that was passed to Thread_exit by t. If t names a nonexistent thread, Thread_join returns -1 immediately. As a special case, the call Thread_join(NULL) waits for *all* threads to terminate, including those that might be created by other threads. In this case, Thread_join returns zero. It is a checked runtime error for a nonnull t to name the calling thread, or for more than one thread to specify a null t. Thread_join can raise Thread_Alerted.

Thread_self returns the thread handle of the calling thread.

Thread_pause causes the calling thread to relinquish the processor to another thread that's ready to run, if there is one. Thread_pause is used primarily in nonpreemptive scheduling; there's no need to call Thread_pause with preemptive scheduling.

Threads have three states: running, blocked, and dead. A new thread begins as running. If it calls Thread_join, it becomes blocked, waiting for another thread to terminate. When a thread calls Thread_exit, it becomes dead. Threads may also become blocked when they call a communications function exported by Chan or a synchronization function exported by Sem. It is a checked runtime error for there to be no running threads.

Thread_alert(t) sets t's "alert-pending" flag. If t is blocked, Thread_alert makes t runnable, and arranges for it to clear its alert-pending flag and to raise Thread_Alerted the next time it runs. If t is already running, Thread_alert arranges for t to clear its flag and to raise Thread_Alerted the next time it calls Thread_join or a blocking communications or synchronization function. It is a checked runtime error to pass to Thread_alert a null handle or to a handle of a nonexistent thread.

There is no way to terminate a running thread; threads must terminate themselves, either by calling Thread_exit or by responding to Thread_Alerted. If a thread doesn't catch Thread_Alerted, the entire program will terminate with an uncaught exception error. The most common response to an alert is to terminate the thread, which can be accomplished with `apply` functions that have the following general form.

```
int apply(void *p) {
    TRY
        ...
    EXCEPT(Thread_Alerted)
        Thread_exit(EXIT_FAILURE);
    END_TRY;
    Thread_exit(EXIT_SUCCESS);
}
```

The TRY-EXCEPT statement must be executed by the thread itself. Code like

```
Thread_T t;
TRY
    t = Thread_new(...);
EXCEPT(Thread_Alerted)
    Thread_exit(EXIT_FAILURE);
END_TRY;
Thread_exit(EXIT_SUCCESS);
```

is incorrect, because the TRY-EXCEPT applies to the calling thread, not to the new thread.

20.1.2 General Semaphores

General, or counting, semaphores are low-level synchronization primitives. Abstractly, a semaphore is a protected integer that can be incremented and decremented atomically. The two operations on a semaphore s are `wait` and `signal`. `signal(s)` is logically equivalent to incrementing it atomically. `wait(s)` waits for s to become positive, then decrements it atomically:

```
while (s <= 0)
    ;
s = s - 1;
```

Of course, actual implementations block the calling thread; they don't loop as this explanation suggests.

The Sem interface wraps the counter in a structure, and exports an initialization function and the two synchronization functions:

⟨*sem.h*⟩≡
```
#ifndef SEM_INCLUDED
#define SEM_INCLUDED

#define T Sem_T
typedef struct T {
    int count;
    void *queue;
} T;

⟨exported macros 416⟩

extern void Sem_init  (T *s, int count);
extern T    *Sem_new   (int count);
extern void Sem_wait  (T *s);
extern void Sem_signal(T *s);

#undef T
#endif
```

A semaphore is a pointer to an instance of a Sem_T structure. This interface reveals the innards of Sem_Ts, but only so that they can be allocated statically or embedded in other structures. Clients must treat Sem_T as an opaque type and access fields of Sem_T values only via the functions in this interface; it is an unchecked runtime error to access the fields of a Sem_T directly. It is a checked runtime error to pass a null Sem_T pointer to any function in this interface.

Sem_init accepts a pointer to a Sem_T and an initial value for its counter; it then initializes the semaphore's data structures and sets its counter to the specified initial value. Once initialized, a pointer to the Sem_T can be passed to the two synchronization functions. It is an unchecked runtime error to call Sem_init on the same semaphore more than once.

Sem_new is the atomic equivalent of

```
Sem_T *s;
NEW(s);
Sem_init(s, count);
```

Sem_new can raise Mem_Failed.

Sem_wait accepts a pointer to a Sem_T, waits for its counter to become positive, decrements the counter by one, and returns. This operation is atomic. If the calling thread's alert-pending flag is set, Sem_wait raises Thread_Alerted immediately and does not decrement the counter. If the alert-pending flag is set while the thread is blocked, the thread stops waiting and raises Thread_Alerted without decrementing the counter. It is a checked runtime error to call Sem_wait before calling Thread_init.

Sem_signal accepts a pointer to a Sem_T and increments its counter atomically. If other threads are waiting for the counter to become positive and the Sem_signal operation causes it to become positive, one of those threads will complete its call to Sem_wait. It is a checked runtime error to call Sem_wait before calling Thread_init.

It is an unchecked runtime error to pass an uninitialized semaphore to Sem_wait or to Sem_signal.

The queuing implicit in the Sem_wait and Sem_signal operations is first-in, first-out, and it's fair. That is, a thread t blocked on a semaphore s will be resumed before other threads that call Sem_wait(&s) after t.

A binary semaphore, or *mutex*, is a general semaphore whose counter is zero or one. A mutex is used for mutual exclusion. For example,

```
Sem_T mutex;
Sem_init(&mutex, 1);
...
Sem_wait(&mutex);
statements
Sem_signal(&mutex);
```

creates and initializes a binary semaphore, and uses it to ensure that only one thread at a time executes *statements*, which is an example of a *critical region*.

This idiom is so common that Sem exports macros for it that implement a LOCK-END_LOCK statement with the syntax:

```
LOCK(mutex)
    statements
END_LOCK
```

where *mutex* is a binary semaphore initialized to one. The LOCK statement helps avoid the common and disastrous errors of omitting the call
to Sem_signal at the end of a critical region, and of calling Sem_signal
with the wrong semaphore.

⟨*exported macros* 416⟩≡
```
#define LOCK(mutex) do { Sem_T *_yymutex = &(mutex); \
    Sem_wait(_yymutex);
#define END_LOCK Sem_signal(_yymutex); } while (0)
```

If *statements* can raise an exception, then LOCK-END_LOCK must *not* be
used, because if an exception occurs, the mutex will not be released. In
this case, the proper idiom is

```
TRY
    Sem_wait(&mutex);
    statements
FINALLY
    Sem_signal(&mutex);
END_TRY;
```

The FINALLY clause ensures that the mutex is released whether or not an
exception occurred. A reasonable alternative is to incorporate this idiom
in the definitions for LOCK and END_LOCK, but then every use of LOCK-
END_LOCK incurs the overhead of the TRY-FINALLY statement.

Mutexes are often embedded in ADTs to make accessing them thread-
safe. For example,

```
typedef struct {
    Sem_T mutex;
    Table_T table;
} Protected_Table_T;
```

associates a mutex with a table. The code

```
Protected_Table_T tab;
tab.table = Table_new(...);
Sem_init(&tab.mutex, 1);
```

creates a protected table, and

```
LOCK(tab.mutex)
    value = Table_get(tab.table, key);
END_LOCK;
```

fetches the value associated with key atomically. Notice that LOCK takes the mutex, not its address. Since Table_put can raise Mem_Failed, additions to tab should be made with code like

```
TRY
    Sem_wait(&tab.mutex);
    Table_put(tab.table, key, value);
FINALLY
    Sem_signal(&tab.mutex);
END_TRY;
```

20.1.3 Synchronous Communication Channels

The Chan interface provides synchronous communication channels that can be used to pass data between threads.

⟨*chan.h*⟩≡
```
#ifndef CHAN_INCLUDED
#define CHAN_INCLUDED

#define T Chan_T
typedef struct T *T;

extern T   Chan_new     (void);
extern int Chan_send    (T c, const void *ptr, int size);
extern int Chan_receive(T c,       void *ptr, int size);

#undef T
#endif
```

Chan_new creates, initializes, and returns a new channel, which is a pointer. Chan_new can raise Mem_Failed.

Chan_send accepts a channel, a pointer to a buffer that holds the data to be sent, and the number of bytes that buffer holds. The calling thread waits until another thread calls Chan_receive with the same channel; when this rendezvous occurs, the data is copied from the sender to the receiver and both calls return. Chan_send returns the number of bytes accepted by the receiver.

Chan_receive accepts a channel, a pointer to a buffer that is to receive the data, and the maximum number of bytes that buffer can hold. The caller waits until another thread calls Chan_send with the same channel; when this rendezvous occurs, the data is copied to the receiver from the sender, and both calls return. If the sender supplies more than size bytes, the excess bytes are discarded. Chan_receive returns the number of bytes accepted.

Chan_send and Chan_receive both accept a size of zero. It is a checked runtime error to pass a null Chan_T, a null ptr, or a negative size to either function. If the calling thread's alert-pending flag is set, Chan_send and Chan_receive raise Thread_Alerted immediately. If the alert-pending flag is set while the thread is blocked, the thread stops waiting and raises Thread_Alerted. In this case, the data may or may not have been transmitted.

It is a checked runtime error to call any function in this interface before calling Thread_init.

20.2 Examples

The three programs in this section illustrate simple uses of threads and channels, and the use of semaphores for mutual exclusion. Chan's implementation, detailed in the next section, is an example of the use of semaphores for synchronization.

20.2.1 Sorting Concurrently

With preemption, threads execute concurrently, at least conceptually. A group of cooperating threads can work on independent parts of a problem. On a system with multiple processors, this approach uses concurrency to reduce overall execution time. Of course, on a single-processor system, the program will actually run a bit slower, because of the overhead of switching between threads. This approach does, however, illustrate the use of the `Thread` interface.

Sorting is a problem that can be easily decomposed into independent subparts. `sort` generates a specified number of random integers, sorts them concurrently, and checks that the result is sorted:

⟨*sort.c*⟩≡
```c
#include <stdlib.h>
#include <stdio.h>
#include <time.h>
#include "assert.h"
#include "fmt.h"
#include "thread.h"
#include "mem.h"

⟨sort types 421⟩
⟨sort data 422⟩
⟨sort functions 420⟩

main(int argc, char *argv[]) {
    int i, n = 100000, *x, preempt;

    preempt = Thread_init(1, NULL);
    assert(preempt == 1);
    if (argc >= 2)
        n = atoi(argv[1]);
    x = CALLOC(n, sizeof (int));
    srand(time(NULL));
    for (i = 0; i < n; i++)
        x[i] = rand();
    sort(x, n, argc, argv);
    for (i = 1; i < n; i++)
        if (x[i] < x[i-1])
            break;
    assert(i == n);
    Thread_exit(EXIT_SUCCESS);
    return EXIT_SUCCESS;
}
```

`time`, `srand`, and `rand` are standard C library functions. `time` returns some integral encoding of the calendar time, which `srand` uses to set the seed for generating a sequence of pseudo-random numbers. Subsequent calls to rand return the numbers in this sequence. sort begins by filling x[0..n-1] with n random numbers.

The function sort is an implementation of quicksort. The textbook implementation partitions the array into two subarrays separated by a "pivot" value, and then calls itself recursively to sort each subarray. The recursion bottoms out when the subarrays are empty.

```
void quick(int a[], int lb, int ub) {
    if (lb < ub) {
        int k = partition(a, lb, ub);
        quick(a, lb, k - 1);
        quick(a, k + 1, ub);
    }
}

void sort(int *x, int n, int argc, char *argv[]) {
    quick(x, 0, n - 1);
}
```

partition(a, i, j) arbitrarily picks a[i] as the pivot value. It rearranges a[i..j] so that all the values in a[i..k-1] are less than or equal to the pivot, v; all the values in a[k+1..j] are greater than v; and a[k] holds v.

⟨*sort functions* 420⟩≡
```
int partition(int a[], int i, int j) {
    int v, k, t;

    j++;
    k = i;
    v = a[k];
    while (i < j) {
        i++; while (a[i] < v && i < j) i++;
        j--; while (a[j] > v          ) j--;
        if (i < j) { t = a[i]; a[i] = a[j]; a[j] = t; }
    }
    t = a[k]; a[k] = a[j]; a[j] = t;
    return j;
}
```

The last exchange in partition leaves v in a[k], and partition returns k.

The recursive calls to quick can be executed concurrently by separate threads. First, quick's arguments must be packaged in a structure so that quick can be passed to Thread_new:

⟨*sort types* 421⟩≡
```
struct args {
    int *a;
    int lb, ub;
};
```

⟨*sort functions* 420⟩+≡
```
int quick(void *cl) {
    struct args *p = cl;
    int lb = p->lb, ub = p->ub;

    if (lb < ub) {
        int k = partition(p->a, lb, ub);
        ⟨quick 421⟩
    }
    return EXIT_SUCCESS;
}
```

The recursive calls are executed in a separate thread, but only if there are enough elements in the subarray to make it worthwhile. For example, a[lb..k-1] is sorted by

⟨*quick* 421⟩≡
```
p->lb = lb;
p->ub = k - 1;
if (k - lb > cutoff) {
    Thread_T t;
    t = Thread_new(quick, p, sizeof *p, NULL);
    Fmt_print("thread %p sorted %d..%d\n", t, lb, k - 1);
} else
    quick(p);
```

where cutoff gives the minimum number of elements required to sort the subarray in a separate thread. Similarly, a[k+1..ub] is sorted by

⟨*quick* 421⟩+≡
```
    p->lb = k + 1;
    p->ub = ub;
    if (ub - k > cutoff) {
        Thread_T t;
        t = Thread_new(quick, p, sizeof *p, NULL);
        Fmt_print("thread %p sorted %d..%d\n", t, k + 1, ub);
    } else
        quick(p);
```

sort makes the initial call to quick, which spawns many threads as the sort progresses; sort then calls Thread_join to wait for all of these threads to terminate:

⟨*sort data* 422⟩≡
```
    int cutoff = 10000;
```

⟨*sort functions* 420⟩+≡
```
    void sort(int *x, int n, int argc, char *argv[]) {
        struct args args;

        if (argc >= 3)
            cutoff = atoi(argv[2]);
        args.a = x;
        args.lb = 0;
        args.ub = n - 1;
        quick(&args);
        Thread_join(NULL);
    }
```

Executing sort with the default values of n and cutoff, 100,000 and 10,000, spawns 18 threads:

```
% sort
thread 69f08 sorted 0..51162
thread 6dfe0 sorted 51164..99999
thread 72028 sorted 51164..73326
thread 76070 sorted 73328..99999
thread 6dfe0 sorted 51593..73326
thread 72028 sorted 73328..91415
thread 7a0b8 sorted 51593..69678
```

```
thread 7e100 sorted 73328..83741
thread 82148 sorted 3280..51162
thread 69f08 sorted 73328..83614
thread 7e100 sorted 51593..67132
thread 6dfe0 sorted 7931..51162
thread 69f08 sorted 14687..51162
thread 6dfe0 sorted 14687..37814
thread 72028 sorted 37816..51162
thread 69f08 sorted 15696..37814
thread 6dfe0 sorted 15696..26140
thread 76070 sorted 26142..37814
```

Different executions sort different values, so the number of threads created and the traces printed by quick will be different for each execution.

sort has an important bug: It fails to protect the calls to Fmt_print in quick. Fmt_print is not guaranteed to be reentrant, and many of the routines in the C library are nonreentrant. There's no guarantee that printf or any other library routine will work correctly if it's interrupted and later resumed.

20.2.2 Critical Regions

Any data that can be accessed by more than one thread in a preemptive system must be protected. Access must be limited to a critical region in which only one thread at a time is permitted. spin is a simple example of the right way and wrong way to access shared data.

⟨*spin.c*⟩≡
```
#include <stdio.h>
#include <stdlib.h>
#include "assert.h"
#include "fmt.h"
#include "thread.h"
#include "sem.h"

#define NBUMP 30000

⟨spin types 425⟩
⟨spin functions 424⟩

int n;
```

```
int main(int argc, char *argv[]) {
    int m = 5, preempt;

    preempt = Thread_init(1, NULL);
    assert(preempt == 1);
    if (argc >= 2)
        m = atoi(argv[1]);
    n = 0;
    ⟨increment n unsafely 424⟩
    Fmt_print("%d == %d\n", n, NBUMP*m);
    n = 0;
    ⟨increment n safely 425⟩
    Fmt_print("%d == %d\n", n, NBUMP*m);
    Thread_exit(EXIT_SUCCESS);
    return EXIT_SUCCESS;
}
```

spin spawns m threads that each increment n NBUMP times. The first m
threads don't ensure that n is incremented atomically:

⟨*increment* n *unsafely* 424⟩≡
```
    {
        int i;
        for (i = 0; i < m; i++)
            Thread_new(unsafe, &n, 0, NULL);
        Thread_join(NULL);
    }
```

main fires off m threads, each of which calls unsafe with a pointer to a
pointer to n:

⟨*spin functions* 424⟩≡
```
    int unsafe(void *cl) {
        int i, *ip = cl;

        for (i = 0; i < NBUMP; i++)
            *ip = *ip + 1;
        return EXIT_SUCCESS;
    }
```

unsafe is wrong because the execution of *ip = *ip + 1 might be interrupted. If it's interrupted just after *ip is fetched, and other threads increment *ip, the value assigned to *ip will be incorrect.

Each of the second m threads call

⟨*spin types* 425⟩≡
```
struct args {
    Sem_T *mutex;
    int *ip;
};
```

⟨*spin functions* 424⟩+≡
```
int safe(void *cl) {
    struct args *p = cl;
    int i;

    for (i = 0; i < NBUMP; i++)
        LOCK(*p->mutex)
            *p->ip = *p->ip + 1;
        END_LOCK;
    return EXIT_SUCCESS;
}
```

safe ensures that only one thread at a time executes the critical region, which is statement *ip = *ip + 1. main initializes one binary semaphore that all the threads use to enter the critical region in safe:

⟨*increment* n *safely* 425⟩≡
```
{
    int i;
    struct args args;
    Sem_T mutex;
    Sem_init(&mutex, 1);
    args.mutex = &mutex;
    args.ip = &n;
    for (i = 0; i < m; i++)
        Thread_new(safe, &args, sizeof args, NULL);
    Thread_join(NULL);
}
```

Preemption can occur at any time, so each execution of spin can produce different results for the threads that use unsafe:

```
% spin
87102 == 150000
150000 == 150000
% spin
148864 == 150000
150000 == 150000
```

20.2.3 Generating Primes

The last example illustrates a pipeline implemented by communication channels. sieve N computes and prints the prime numbers less than or equal to N. For example:

```
% sieve 100
2 3 5 7 11 13 17 19 23 29 31 37 41 43 47 53 59 61 67 71 73
79 83 89 97
```

sieve is an implementation of the well-known Sieve of Eratosthenes for computing primes, in which each "sieve" is a thread that discards multiples of its primes. Channels connect these threads to form a pipeline, as depicted in Figure 20.1. The source thread (the white box) generates two followed by the odd integers, and fires them down the pipe. The filters (the light gray boxes) between the source and the sink (the dark gray box) discard numbers that are multiples of their primes, and pass the others down the pipe. The sink also filters out its primes, but if a number gets by the sink's filter, it is a prime. Each box in Figure 20.1 is a thread; the numbers in each box are the primes associated with that

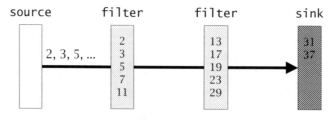

Figure 20.1 A prime-number sieve

thread, and the lines between the boxes that form the pipeline are channels.

There are n primes attached to the sink and to each filter. When the sink has accumulated n primes — 5 in Figure 20.1 — it spawns a fresh copy of itself and turns itself into a filter. Figure 20.2 shows how the sieve expands as it computes the primes up to and including 100.

After sieve initializes the thread system, it creates threads for the source and for the sink, connects them with a new channel, and exits:

⟨*sieve.c*⟩≡
```
#include <stdio.h>
#include <stdlib.h>
#include "assert.h"
#include "fmt.h"
#include "thread.h"
#include "chan.h"

struct args {
    Chan_T c;
    int n, last;
};

⟨sieve functions 429⟩

int main(int argc, char *argv[]) {
    struct args args;

    Thread_init(1, NULL);
    args.c = Chan_new();
    Thread_new(source, &args, sizeof args, NULL);
    args.n    = argc > 2 ? atoi(argv[2]) : 5;
    args.last = argc > 1 ? atoi(argv[1]) : 1000;
    Thread_new(sink,   &args, sizeof args, NULL);
    Thread_exit(EXIT_SUCCESS);
    return EXIT_SUCCESS;
}
```

source emits integers on its "output" channel, which is passed in the c field of the args structure, which is the only field source needs:

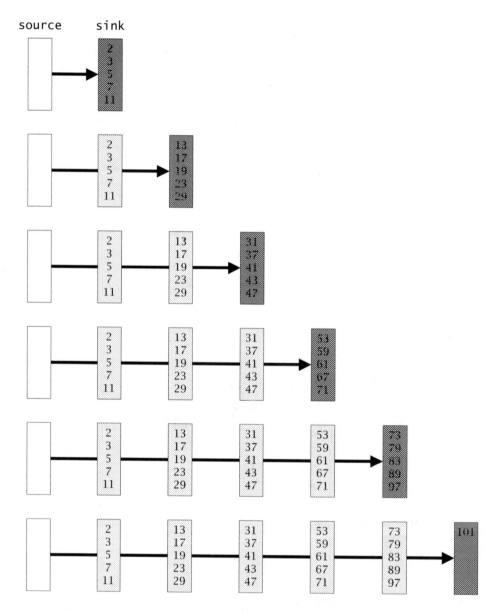

Figure 20.2 Evolution of the sieve for the primes up to 100

⟨*sieve functions* 429⟩≡
```
int source(void *cl) {
    struct args *p = cl;
    int i = 2;

    if (Chan_send(p->c, &i, sizeof i))
        for (i = 3; Chan_send(p->c, &i, sizeof i); )
            i += 2;
    return EXIT_SUCCESS;
}
```

source sends two and the succeeding odd integers as long as a receiver accepts them. Once the sink has printed all the primes, it reads zero bytes from its input channel, which signals its upstream filter that the job is done, and terminates. Each filter does likewise, until source hears that its receiver read zero bytes, at which point it terminates.

A filter reads integers from its input channel and writes potential primes to its output channel, until the thread consuming the potential primes has had its fill:

⟨*sieve functions* 429⟩+≡
```
void filter(int primes[], Chan_T input, Chan_T output) {
    int j, x;

    for (;;) {
        Chan_receive(input, &x, sizeof x);
        ⟨x is a multiple of primes[0...] 429⟩
        if (primes[j] == 0)
            if (Chan_send(output, &x, sizeof x) == 0)
                break;
    }
    Chan_receive(input, &x, 0);
}
```

primes[0..n-1] hold the primes associated with a filter. This array is terminated with a zero, so the search loop zips down primes until it either determines that x is not a prime or bumps into the terminator:

⟨x is a multiple of primes[0...] 429⟩≡
```
for (j = 0; primes[j] != 0 && x%primes[j] != 0; j++)
    ;
```

As suggested by the code above, the search fails when it ends at the terminating zero. In this case, x *might* be a prime, so it is sent down the output channel to another filter or to the sink.

All of the action is in the sink; the c field of args holds the sink's input channel, the n field gives the number of primes per filter, and the last field holds *N*, which gives the range of the primes desired. sink initializes its primes array and listens to its input:

⟨*sieve functions* 429⟩+≡
```
int sink(void *cl) {
    struct args *p = cl;
    Chan_T input = p->c;
    int i = 0, j, x, primes[256];

    primes[0] = 0;
    for (;;) {
        Chan_receive(input, &x, sizeof x);
        ⟨x is a multiple of primes[0...] 429⟩
        if (primes[j] == 0) {
            ⟨x is prime 430⟩
        }
    }
    Fmt_print("\n");
    Chan_receive(input, &x, 0);
    return EXIT_SUCCESS;
}
```

If x isn't a multiple of one of the nonzero values in primes, then it is a prime, and sink prints it and adds it to primes.

⟨*x is prime* 430⟩≡
```
if (x > p->last)
    break;
Fmt_print(" %d", x);
primes[i++] = x;
primes[i] = 0;
if (i == p->n)
    ⟨spawn a new sink and call filter 431⟩
```

When x exceeds p->last, all of the desired primes have been printed, and sink can terminate. Before doing so, it waits for one more integer from its input channel, but reads zero bytes, which signals the upstream threads that the computation is complete.

After sink accumulates n primes, it clones itself and becomes a filter, which requires a new channel:

⟨*spawn a new* sink *and call* filter 431⟩≡

```
{
    p->c = Chan_new();
    Thread_new(sink, p, sizeof *p, NULL);
    filter(primes, input, p->c);
    return EXIT_SUCCESS;
}
```

The new channel becomes the clone's input channel and the filter's output channel. The sink's input channel is the filter's input channel. When filter returns, its thread exits.

All of the switching between threads in sieve occurs in Chan_send and Chan_receive, and there's always at least one thread ready to run. Thus, sieve works with either preemptive or nonpreemptive scheduling, and it's a simple example of using threads primarily for structuring an application. Nonpreemptive threads are often called *coroutines*.

20.3 Implementations

The Chan implementation can be built entirely on top of the Sem implementation, so it's machine-independent. Sem is machine-independent, too, but it depends on the innards of the Thread implementation, so Thread also implements Sem. A uniprocessor Thread implementation can be made largely independent of both the host machine and its operating system. As detailed below, machine and operating-system dependencies creep into the code for only context switching and preemption.

20.3.1 Synchronous Communication Channels

A Chan_T is a pointer to a structure that holds three semaphores, a pointer to the message, and a byte count:

⟨*chan.c*⟩≡

```
#include <string.h>
#include "assert.h"
```

```
#include "mem.h"
#include "chan.h"
#include "sem.h"

#define T Chan_T
struct T {
    const void *ptr;
    int *size;
    Sem_T send, recv, sync;
};
```

⟨*chan functions* 432⟩

When a new channel is created, the `ptr` and `size` fields are undefined, and the counters for the semaphores `send`, `recv`, and `sync` are initialized to one, zero, and zero, respectively:

⟨*chan functions* 432⟩≡

```
T Chan_new(void) {
    T c;

    NEW(c);
    Sem_init(&c->send, 1);
    Sem_init(&c->recv, 0);
    Sem_init(&c->sync, 0);
    return c;
}
```

The `send` and `recv` semaphores control access to `ptr` and `size`, and the `sync` semaphore ensures that the message transmission is synchronous as specified by the `Chan` interface. A thread sends a message by filling in the `ptr` and `size` fields, but only when it is safe to do so. `send` is one when a sender can set `ptr` and `size`, and zero otherwise — for example, before a receiver takes the messsage. Similarly, `recv` is one when `ptr` and `size` hold valid pointers to a message and its size, and zero otherwise — for example, before a sender has set `ptr` and `size`. `send` and `recv` oscillate: `send` is one when `recv` is zero and vice versa. `sync` is one when a receiver has successfully copied a message into its private buffer.

Chan_send sends a message by waiting on `send`, filling in `ptr` and `size`, signalling `recv`, and waiting on `sync`:

⟨*chan functions* 432⟩+≡
```
int Chan_send(Chan_T c, const void *ptr, int size) {
    assert(c);
    assert(ptr);
    assert(size >= 0);
    Sem_wait(&c->send);
    c->ptr = ptr;
    c->size = &size;
    Sem_signal(&c->recv);
    Sem_wait(&c->sync);
    return size;
}
```

`c->size` holds a pointer to the byte count so that the receiver can modify that count, thereby notifying the sender of how many bytes were transmitted. `Chan_receive` performs the three steps that complement those done by `Chan_send`. `Chan_receive` receives a message by waiting on `recv`, copying the message into its argument buffer and modifying the byte count, and signalling `sync` then `send`:

⟨*chan functions* 432⟩+≡
```
int Chan_receive(Chan_T c, void *ptr, int size) {
    int n;

    assert(c);
    assert(ptr);
    assert(size >= 0);
    Sem_wait(&c->recv);
    n = *c->size;
    if (size < n)
        n = size;
    *c->size = n;
    if (n > 0)
        memcpy(ptr, c->ptr, n);
    Sem_signal(&c->sync);
    Sem_signal(&c->send);
    return n;
}
```

`n` is the number of bytes actually received, which might be zero. This code handles all three cases: when the sender's `size` exceeds the receiver's size, when the two sizes are equal, and when the receiver's size exceeds the sender's size.

20.3.2 Threads

The Thread implementation, thread.c, implements the Thread and Sem interfaces:

⟨*thread.c*⟩≡

```
#include <stdio.h>
#include <stdlib.h>
#include <string.h>
#include </usr/include/signal.h>
#include <sys/time.h>
#include "assert.h"
#include "mem.h"
#include "thread.h"
#include "sem.h"

void _MONITOR(void) {}
extern void _ENDMONITOR(void);

#define T Thread_T
⟨macros 436⟩
⟨types 435⟩
⟨data 435⟩
⟨prototypes 439⟩
⟨static functions 436⟩
⟨thread functions 438⟩
#undef T

#define T Sem_T
⟨sem functions 457⟩
#undef T
```

The vacuous function _MONITOR and the external function _ENDMONITOR are used only for their addresses. As described below, these addresses encompass critical sections — thread code that must not be interrupted. A little of this code is written in assembly language, and _ENDMONITOR is defined at the end of the assembly language file so that the critical section includes this assembly code. Its name starts with an underscore because that's the convention for implementation-defined assembly language names used here.

A thread handle is an opaque pointer to a Thread_T structure, which carries all of the information necessary to determine the state of the thread. This structure is often called a *thread control block.*

⟨*types* 435⟩≡
```
struct T {
    unsigned long *sp;        /* must be first */
    ⟨fields 435⟩
};
```

The initial fields hold machine- and operating system–dependent values. These fields appear first in Thread_T structures because they're accessed by assembly-language code. Placing them first makes these fields easier to access, and new fields can be added without changing existing assembly-language code. Only one field, sp, which holds the thread's stack pointer, is needed on most machines.

Most thread manipulations revolve around putting threads on queues and removing them from queues. The Thread and Sem interfaces are designed to maintain a simple invariant: A thread is on no queue or it is on exactly one queue. This design makes it possible to avoid allocating any space for queue entries. Instead of using, say, Seq_Ts to represent queues, queues are represented by circularly linked lists of Thread_T structures. The ready queue, which holds running threads that do not have processors, is an example:

⟨*data* 435⟩≡
```
static T ready = NULL;
```

⟨*fields* 435⟩≡
```
T link;
T *inqueue;
```

Figure 20.3 shows three threads on the ready queue in the order *A, B,* and *C.* ready points to the *last* thread in the queue, *C,* and the queue is linked through the link fields. The inqueue field of each Thread_T structure points to the queue variable — here, ready — and is used to remove a thread from a queue. A queue is empty when the queue variable is null, as suggested by ready's initial value and tested by the macro

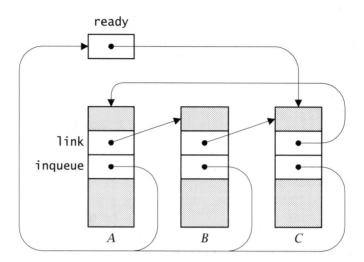

Figure 20.3 Three threads in the ready queue

⟨*macros* 436⟩≡
```
#define isempty(q) ((q) == NULL)
```

If a thread t is on a queue, then t->link and t->inqueue are nonnull; otherwise both fields are null. The queue functions below use assertions involving the link and inqueue fields to ensure that the invariant mentioned above holds. For example, put appends a thread to an empty or nonempty queue:

⟨*static functions* 436⟩≡
```
static void put(T t, T *q) {
    assert(t);
    assert(t->inqueue == NULL && t->link == NULL);
    if (*q) {
        t->link = (*q)->link;
        (*q)->link = t;
    } else
        t->link = t;
    *q = t;
    t->inqueue = q;
}
```

Thus, put(t, &ready) appends t to the ready queue. put takes the address of the queue variable so that it can modify it: After calling put(t, &q), q equals t and t->inqueue equals &q.

get removes the first element from a given queue:

⟨*static functions* 436⟩+≡
```
static T get(T *q) {
    T t;

    assert(!isempty(*q));
    t = (*q)->link;
    if (t == *q)
        *q = NULL;
    else
        (*q)->link = t->link;
    assert(t->inqueue == q);
    t->link = NULL;
    t->inqueue = NULL;
    return t;
}
```

The code uses the inqueue field to ensure that the thread was indeed in q, and it clears the link and inqueue fields to mark the thread as not being in any queue.

The third and last queue function removes a queued thread from the queue in which appears:

⟨*static functions* 436⟩+≡
```
static void delete(T t, T *q) {
    T p;

    assert(t->link && t->inqueue == q);
    assert(!isempty(*q));
    for (p = *q; p->link != t; p = p->link)
        ;
    if (p == t)
        *q = NULL;
    else {
        p->link = t->link;
        if (*q == t)
            *q = p;
```

```
        }
        t->link = NULL;
        t->inqueue = NULL;
    }
```

The first assertion ensures that t is in q, and the second ensures that the queue is nonempty, which it must be since t is in it. The if statement handles the case in which t is the only thread on q.

Thread_init creates the "root" thread (the Thread_T structure for the root thread is allocated statically):

⟨*thread functions* 438⟩≡
```
    int Thread_init(int preempt, ...) {
        assert(preempt == 0 || preempt == 1);
        assert(current == NULL);
        root.handle = &root;
        current = &root;
        nthreads = 1;
        if (preempt) {
            ⟨initialize preemptive scheduling 454⟩
        }
        return 1;
    }
```

⟨*data* 435⟩+≡
```
    static T current;
    static int nthreads;
    static struct Thread_T root;
```

⟨*fields* 435⟩+≡
```
    T handle;
```

current is the thread that currently holds the processor, and nthreads is the number of existing threads. Thread_new increments nthreads and Thread_exit decrements it. The handle field simply points to the thread handle and helps check the validity of handles: t identifies an existing thread only if t is equal to t->handle.

If current is null, Thread_init has not been called, so testing for a null current, as shown above, implements the checked runtime error that Thread_init must be called only once. Checking for a nonnull current in the other Thread and Sem functions implements the checked runtime error that Thread_init must be called before any other Thread, Sem, or Chan function. An example is Thread_self, which simply returns current:

⟨*thread functions* 438⟩+≡
```
T Thread_self(void) {
    assert(current);
    return current;
}
```

Switching between threads requires some machine-dependent code, because each thread has its own stack and exception state, for example. There are numerous possible designs for the context-switch primitives, all of which are relatively simple because they're written in whole or in part in assembly language. The Thread implementation uses the single, implementation-specific primitive,

⟨*prototypes* 439⟩≡
```
extern void _swtch(T from, T to);
```

which switches contexts from thread from to thread to, where from and to are pointers to Thread_T structures. _swtch is like setjmp and longjmp: When thread *A* calls _swtch, control transfers to, say, thread *B*. When *B* calls _swtch to resume *A*, *A*'s call to _swtch returns. Thus, *A* and *B* treat _swtch as just another function call. This simple design also takes advantage of the machine's calling sequence, which, for example, helps save *A*'s state when it switches to *B*. The only disadvantage is that a new thread must be created with a state that looks as if the thread called _swtch, because the first time it runs will be as a result of a *return* from _swtch.

_swtch is called in only one place, the static function run:

⟨*static functions* 436⟩+≡
```
static void run(void) {
    T t = current;

    current = get(&ready);
    t->estack = Except_stack;
    Except_stack = current->estack;
    _swtch(t, current);
}
```

⟨*fields* 435⟩+≡
```
Except_Frame *estack;
```

run switches from the currently executing thread to the thread at the head of the ready queue. It dequeues the leading thread from ready, sets current, and switches to the new thread. The estack field holds the pointer to the exception frame at the top of a thread's exception stack, and run takes care of updating Except's global Except_stack, which is described on page 53.

All of the Thread and Sem functions that can cause a context switch call run, and they put the current thread on ready or another appropriate queue before calling run. Thread_pause is the simplest example: It puts current on ready and calls run.

⟨*thread functions* 438⟩+≡
```
void Thread_pause(void) {
    assert(current);
    put(current, &ready);
    run();
}
```

If there's only one running thread, Thread_pause puts it on ready and run removes it and switches to it. Thus, _swtch(t, t) must work properly. Figure 20.4 depicts the context switches between threads *A*, *B*, and *C* that execute the following calls, assuming that *A* holds the processor initially and ready holds *B* and *C* in that order.

A	*B*	*C*
Thread_pause()	Thread_pause()	Thread_pause()
Thread_join(*C*)	Thread_exit(0)	Thread_exit(0)
Thread_exit(0)		

The vertical solid arrows in Figure 20.4 show when each thread has the processor, and the horizontal dashed arrows are the context switches; the ready queue is shown in brackets beside the solid arrows. The Thread function and the call to _swtch it causes appear under each context switch.

When *A* calls Thread_pause, it's added to ready, and *B* is removed and gets the processor. While *B* is running, ready holds *C A*. When *B* calls Thread_pause, *C* is removed from ready and gets the processor,

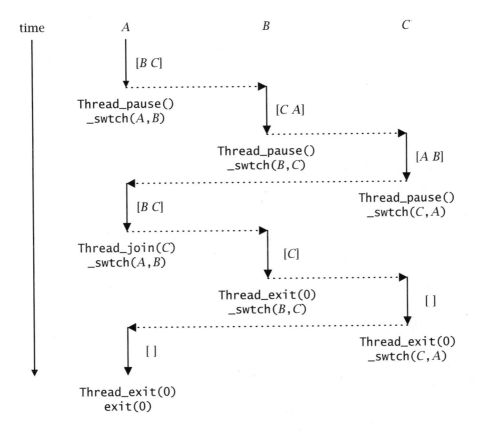

Figure 20.4 Context-switching between three threads

and `ready` holds *A B*. After *C* calls `Thread_pause`, `ready` again holds *B C* while *A* is executing. When *A* calls `Thread_join(C)`, it blocks on *C*'s termination, so the processor is given to *B*, the leading thread in `ready`.

At this point, `ready` holds only *C*, because *A* is in a queue associated with *C*. When *B* calls `Thread_exit`, `run` switches to *C* and `ready` becomes empty. *C* terminates by calling `Thread_exit`, which causes *A* to be put back in `ready` as a result of *C*'s termination. Thus, when `Thread_exit` calls `run`, *A* gets the processor. *A*'s call to `Thread_exit` does not cause a context switch, however: *A* is the only thread in the system, so `Thread_exit` calls `exit`.

Deadlock occurs when `ready` is empty and `run` is called; that is, there are no running threads. Deadlock is a checked runtime error, and it's detected in `get` when it's called with an empty ready queue.

Thread_join and Thread_exit illustrate the queue manipulations involving "join queues" and the ready queue. There are two flavors of Thread_join: Thread_join(t) waits for thread t to terminate and returns t's exit code — the value t passed to Thread_exit; t must not be the calling thread. Thread_join(NULL) waits for all threads to terminate and returns zero; only one thread can call Thread_join(NULL).

⟨*thread functions* 438⟩+≡
```
int Thread_join(T t) {
    assert(current);
    testalert();
    if (t) {
        ⟨wait for thread t to terminate 442⟩
    } else {
        ⟨wait for all threads to terminate 443⟩
        return 0;
    }
}
```

As described below, testalert raises Thread_Alerted if the calling thread has been alerted. When t is nonnull and refers to an existing thread, the calling thread puts itself on t's join queue to wait for its demise; otherwise, Thread_join returns –1 immediately.

⟨*wait for thread* t *to terminate* 442⟩≡
```
    if (t->handle == t) {
        put(current, &t->join);
        run();
        testalert();
        return current->code;
    } else
        return -1;
```

⟨*fields* 435⟩+≡
```
    int code;
    T join;
```

t is an existing thread only if t->handle is equal to t. As shown below, Thread_exit clears the handle field when a thread terminates. When t terminates, Thread_exit stores its argument in the code field of each of the Thread_Ts in t->join as it moves those threads to the ready queue.

Thus, when those threads execute again, that exit code is readily available, and it is returned by Thread_join in each resumed thread.

When t is null, the calling thread is put on join0, which holds the one and only thread waiting for all others to terminate:

⟨*wait for all threads to terminate* 443⟩≡
```
assert(isempty(join0));
if (nthreads > 1) {
    put(current, &join0);
    run();
    testalert();
}
```

⟨*data* 435⟩+≡
```
static T join0;
```

The next time the calling thread runs, it will be the only existing thread. This code also handles the case when the calling thread is the only thread in the system, which occurs when nthreads is equal to one.

Thread_exit has numerous jobs to do: It must deallocate the resources associated with the calling thread, resume the threads waiting for the calling thread to terminate and arrange for them to get the exit code, and check whether the calling thread is the second to last or last thread in the system.

⟨*thread functions* 438⟩+≡
```
void Thread_exit(int code) {
    assert(current);
    release();
    if (current != &root) {
        current->next = freelist;
        freelist = current;
    }
    current->handle = NULL;
    ⟨resume threads waiting for current's termination 444⟩
    ⟨run another thread or exit 444⟩
}
```

⟨*fields* 435⟩+≡
```
T next;
```

⟨*data* 435⟩+≡
```
static T freelist;
```

The call to `release` and the code that appends `current` to `freelist` collaborate to deallocate the calling thread's resources, as detailed below. If the calling thread is the root thread, its storage must not be deallocated, because that storage is allocated statically.

Clearing the `handle` field marks the thread as nonexistent, and those threads waiting for its demise can now be resumed:

⟨*resume threads waiting for* current's *termination* 444⟩≡
```
while (!isempty(current->join)) {
    T t = get(&current->join);
    t->code = code;
    put(t, &ready);
}
```

The calling thread's exit code is copied to the `code` field in the `Thread_T` structures of the waiting threads so that `current` can be deallocated.

If only two threads exist and one of them is in `join0`, that waiting thread can now be resumed.

⟨*resume threads waiting for* current's *termination* 444⟩+≡
```
if (!isempty(join0) && nthreads == 2) {
    assert(isempty(ready));
    put(get(&join0), &ready);
}
```

The assertion helps detect errors in maintaining `nthreads` and `ready`: If `join0` is nonempty and `nthreads` is two, `ready` must be empty, because one of the two existing threads is in `join0` and the other one is executing `Thread_exit`.

`Thread_exit` concludes by decrementing `nthreads` and either calling the library function `exit` or running another thread:

⟨*run another thread or exit* 444⟩≡
```
if (--nthreads == 0)
    exit(code);
else
    run();
```

Thread_alert marks a thread as "alerted" by setting a flag in its Thread_T structure and removing it from the queue, if it's in one.

⟨*thread functions* 438⟩+≡
```
void Thread_alert(T t) {
    assert(current);
    assert(t && t->handle == t);
    t->alerted = 1;
    if (t->inqueue) {
        delete(t, t->inqueue);
        put(t, &ready);
    }
}
```

⟨*fields* 435⟩+≡
```
int alerted;
```

Thread_alert itself cannot raise Thread_Alerted, because the calling thread has a different state than t. Threads must raise Thread_Alerted and deal with it themselves, which is the purpose of testalert:

⟨*static functions* 436⟩+≡
```
static void testalert(void) {
    if (current->alerted) {
        current->alerted = 0;
        RAISE(Thread_Alerted);
    }
}
```

⟨*data* 435⟩+≡
```
const Except_T Thread_Alerted = { "Thread alerted" };
```

testalert is called whenever a thread is about to block, or when it is resumed after being blocked. The former case is illustrated by the call to testalert at the beginning of Thread_join on page 442. The latter case always occurs after a call to run, and it's illustrated by the calls to testalert in the chunks ⟨*wait for thread* t *to terminate* 442⟩ and ⟨*wait for all threads to terminate* 443⟩. Similar usage appears in Sem_wait and Sem_signal; see page 458.

20.3.3 Thread Creation and Context-Switching

The last Thread function is Thread_new. Some of Thread_new is machine-dependent, because it interacts with _swtch, but most of it is nearly machine-independent. Thread_new has four tasks: allocate the resources for a new thread, initialize the new thread's state so that it can be started by a return from _swtch, increment nthreads, and append the new thread to ready.

⟨*thread functions* 438⟩+≡
```
T Thread_new(int apply(void *), void *args,
    int nbytes, ...) {
    T t;

    assert(current);
    assert(apply);
    assert(args && nbytes >= 0 || args == NULL);
    if (args == NULL)
        nbytes = 0;
    ⟨allocate resources for a new thread 446⟩
    t->handle = t;
    ⟨initialize t's state 449⟩
    nthreads++;
    put(t, &ready);
    return t;
}
```

In this uniprocessor implementation of Thread, the only resources a thread needs are the Thread_T structure and a stack. The Thread_T structure and a 16K byte stack are allocated with a single call to Mem's ALLOC:

⟨*allocate resources for a new thread* 446⟩≡
```
{
    int stacksize = (16*1024+sizeof (*t)+nbytes+15)&~15;
    release();
    ⟨begin critical region 447⟩
    TRY
        t = ALLOC(stacksize);
        memset(t, '\0', sizeof *t);
    EXCEPT(Mem_Failed)
```

```
        t = NULL;
    END_TRY;
    ⟨end critical region 447⟩
    if (t == NULL)
        RAISE(Thread_Failed);
    ⟨initialize t's stack pointer 448⟩
}
```

⟨*data* 435⟩+≡
```
const Except_T Thread_Failed =
    { "Thread creation failed" };
```

This code is complex because it must maintain several invariants, the most important of which is that a call to a Thread function must not be interrupted. Two mechanisms collaborate to maintain this invariant: one deals with interrupts that occur when control is in a Thread function, and is described below. The other mechanism handles interrupts when control is in a routine that is called by a Thread function, which is illustrated by the calls to ALLOC and memset. These kinds of calls are bracketed by chunks that identify critical regions by incrementing and decrementing the value of critical:

⟨*begin critical region* 447⟩≡
```
do { critical++;
```

⟨*end critical region* 447⟩≡
```
critical--; } while (0);
```

⟨*data* 435⟩+≡
```
static int critical;
```

As shown on page 455, interrupts that occur when critical is nonzero are ignored.

Thread_new must catch Mem_Failed itself, and raise its exception, Thread_failed, after it has completed the critical section. If it didn't catch the exception, control would pass to the caller's exception handler, with critical set to a positive value that would never be decremented.

Thread_new assumes that stacks grow toward lower addresses, and it initializes the sp field as depicted in Figure 20.5; the shaded box at the top is the Thread_T structure, and the ones at the bottom are the copy of args and the initial frames, as described below.

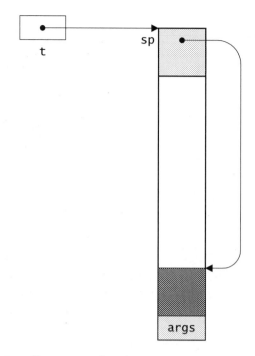

Figure 20.5 Allocation of a Thread_T structure and a stack

⟨*initialize* t*'s stack pointer* 448⟩≡
```
t->sp = (void *)((char *)t + stacksize);
while (((unsigned long)t->sp)&15)
    t->sp--;
```

As suggested by the assignment to stacksize and by this chunk, Thread_new initializes the stack pointer so that it's aligned on a 16-byte boundary, which accommodates most platforms. Most machines require either a four-byte or eight-byte stack alignment, but the DEC ALPHA requires a 16-byte alignment.

Thread_new starts by calling release, which Thread_exit also calls. Thread_exit can't deallocate the current thread's stack because it's using it. So it adds the thread handle to freelist, and delays the deallocation until the next call to release:

⟨*static functions* 436⟩+≡
```
static void release(void) {
    T t;
```

```
⟨begin critical region 447⟩
while ((t = freelist) != NULL) {
    freelist = t->next;
    FREE(t);
}
⟨end critical region 447⟩
}
```

release is more general than necessary: freelist has only one element, because release is called by both Thread_exit and Thread_new. If only Thread_new had called release, dead Thread_Ts could accumulate on freelist. release uses a critical section because it calls Mem's FREE.

Next, Thread_new initializes the new thread's stack so that it holds a copy of the nbytes bytes starting at args, and the frames needed to make it appear as if the thread had called _swtch. This latter initialization is machine-dependent:

```
⟨initialize t's state 449⟩≡
    if (nbytes > 0) {
        t->sp -= ((nbytes + 15U)&~15)/sizeof (*t->sp);
        ⟨begin critical region 447⟩
        memcpy(t->sp, args, nbytes);
        ⟨end critical region 447⟩
        args = t->sp;
    }
    #if alpha
    { ⟨initialize an ALPHA stack 463⟩ }
    #elif mips
    { ⟨initialize a MIPS stack 461⟩ }
    #elif sparc
    { ⟨initialize a SPARC stack 452⟩ }
    #else
    Unsupported platform
    #endif
```

The bottom of the stack shown in Figure 20.5 depicts the result of these initializations: The darker shading identifies the machine-dependent frames and the lighter shading is the copy of args. thread.c and swtch.s are the only modules in this book that use conditional compilation.

The stack initialization is easier to understand after digesting an assembly-language implementation of _swtch:

⟨*swtch.s*⟩≡
```
#if alpha
⟨ALPHA swtch 462⟩
⟨ALPHA startup 463⟩
#elif sparc
⟨SPARC swtch 450⟩
⟨SPARC startup 452⟩
#elif mips
⟨MIPS swtch 460⟩
⟨MIPS startup 461⟩
#else
Unsupported platform
#endif
```

_swtch(from, to) must save from's state, restore to's state, and continue executing to by returning from to's most recent call to _swtch. Calling conventions save much of the state, because they usually dictate that the values of some registers must be saved across calls, and that some machine-state information, such as condition codes, is not saved. So _swtch saves only the state it needs that is not preserved by the calling conventions — the return address, for example — and it can save these values on the calling thread's stack.

The SPARC _swtch is perhaps the easiest one because the SPARC calling convention saves all of the registers by giving each function its own "register window"; the only registers it must preserve are the frame pointer and the return address.

⟨*SPARC swtch* 450⟩≡
```
        .global __swtch
        .align  4
        .proc   4
1   __swtch:save    %sp,-(8+64),%sp
2           st      %fp,[%sp+64+0]   ! save from's frame pointer
3           st      %i7,[%sp+64+4]   ! save from's return address
4           ta      3                ! flush from's registers
5           st      %sp,[%i0]        ! save from's stack pointer
6           ld      [%i1],%sp        ! load to's stack pointer
7           ld      [%sp+64+0],%fp   ! restore to's frame pointer
```

8	ld	[%sp+64+4],%i7	! restore **to**'s return address
9	ret		! continue execution of **to**
10	restore		

The line numbers above identify the nonboilerplate lines for the explanation below, and they are not part of the assembly-language code. By convention, assembly-language names are prefixed with an underscore, so _swtch is known as __swtch in assembly language on the SPARC.

Figure 20.6 shows the layout of a frame for _swtch; all SPARC frames have at least 64 bytes at the top of the frame into which the operating system stores the function's register window, when necessary. The other two words in _swtch's 72-byte frame hold the saved frame pointer and the return address.

Line 1 in _swtch allocates a stack frame for _swtch. Lines 2 and 3 save from's frame pointer (%fp) and return address (%i7) at the seventeenth and eighteenth 32-bit words in the new frame (at offsets 64 and 68). Line 4 makes a system call to "flush" from's register windows to the stack, which is necessary in order to continue execution with to's register windows. This call is unfortunate: one of the presumed advantages of user-level threads is that context-switching does not require kernel intervention. On the SPARC, however, only the kernel can flush the register windows.

Line 5 saves from's stack pointer in the sp field of its Thread_T structure. This instruction shows why that field is first: This code is independent of the size of a Thread_T and the locations of the other fields. Line 6 is italicized because it is the actual context switch. This instruction loads to's stack pointer into %sp, the stack pointer register. Henceforth, _swtch is executing on to's stack. Lines 7 and 8 restore to's frame

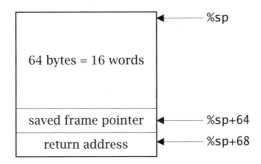

Figure 20.6 Layout of a stack frame for _swtch

pointer and return address, because %sp now points at the top of to's stack. Lines 9 and 10 comprise the normal function return sequence, and control continues at the address saved the last time to called _swtch.

Thread_new must create a frame for _swtch so that some other call to _swtch can return properly and start execution of the new thread, and this execution must call apply. Figure 20.7 shows what Thread_new builds: The frame for _swtch is on the top of the stack, and the frame under it is for the following startup code.

⟨SPARC startup 452⟩≡
```
        .global __start
        .align  4
        .proc   4
1    __start:ld       [%sp+64+4],%o0
2            ld       [%sp+64],%o1
3            call     %o1; nop
4            call     _Thread_exit; nop
5            unimp    0
        .global __ENDMONITOR
        __ENDMONITOR:
```

The return address in the _swtch frame points to _start, and the startup frame holds apply and args, as shown in Figure 20.7. On the first return from _swtch, control lands at _start (which is __start in the assembly code). Line 1 in the startup code loads args into %o0, which, following the SPARC calling conventions, is used to pass the first argument. Line 2 loads the address of apply into %o1, which is otherwise unused, and line 3 makes an indirect call to apply. If apply returns, its exit code will be in %o0, and thus that value will be passed to Thread_exit, which never returns. Line 5 should never be executed, and will cause a fault if it is. _ENDMONITOR is explained below.

The 15 lines of assembly language in _swtch and _start are all that's necessary on the SPARC; initializing the stack for a new thread as shown in Figure 20.7 can be done entirely in C. The two frames are built bottom-up, as follows.

⟨initialize a SPARC stack 452⟩≡
```
1    int i; void *fp; extern void _start(void);
2    for (i = 0; i < 8; i++)
3        *--t->sp = 0;
4    *--t->sp = (unsigned long)args;
```

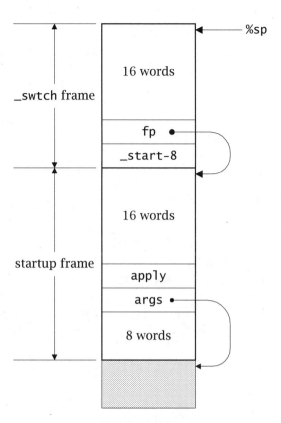

Figure 20.7 Startup and initial _swtch frames on the SPARC

```
5   *--t->sp = (unsigned long)apply;
6   t->sp -= 64/4;
7   fp = t->sp;
8   *--t->sp = (unsigned long)_start - 8;
9   *--t->sp = (unsigned long)fp;
10  t->sp -= 64/4;
```

Lines 2 and 3 create the eight words at the bottom of the startup frame. Lines 4 and 5 push the value of args and apply onto the stack, and line 6 allocates the 64 bytes at the top of the startup frame. The stack pointer at this point is the frame pointer that must be restored by _swtch, so line 7 saves this value in fp. Line 8 pushes the return address — the saved value of %i7. The return address is eight bytes before _start because the SPARC ret instruction adds eight to the address in %i7 when it returns. Line 9 pushes the saved value of %fp, and line 10 concludes with the 64 bytes at the top of the _swtch frame.

If apply is a function that takes a variable number of arguments, its entry sequence stores the values in %o0 through %o5 into the stack at offsets 64 through 88 in its caller's frame, that is, in the startup frame. Lines 2 and 3 allocate this space and an additional eight bytes so that the stack pointer remains aligned on an eight-byte boundary, as dictated by the SPARC hardware.

The MIPS and ALPHA versions of _swtch and _start appear in Section 20.3.6.

20.3.4 Preemption

Preemption is equivalent to periodic, implicit calls to Thread_pause. The UNIX-dependent implementation of preemption in Thread arranges for a "virtual" timer interrupt every 50 milliseconds, and the interrupt handler executes code equivalent to Thread_pause. The timer is virtual, because it ticks only while the process is executing. Thread_init uses the UNIX signal facility to initialize timer interrupts. The first step associates the interrupt handler with the virtual timer signal, SIGVTALRM:

⟨*initialize preemptive scheduling* 454⟩≡
```
{
    struct sigaction sa;
    memset(&sa, '\0', sizeof sa);
    sa.sa_handler = (void (*)())interrupt;
    if (sigaction(SIGVTALRM, &sa, NULL) < 0)
        return 0;
}
```

A sigaction structure has three fields: sa_handler is the address of the function that's to be called when the SIGVTALRM signal occurs, sa_mask is a signal set that specifies other signals that should be blocked while an interrupt is being handled in addition to SIGVTALRM, and sa_flags provides signal-specific options. Thread_init sets sa_handler to interrupt, described below, and clears the other fields.

The sigaction function is the POSIX standard function for associating handlers with signals. The POSIX standard is supported by most UNIX variants and by some other operating systems, such as Windows NT. The three arguments give the symbolic name for the signal number, a pointer to the sigaction structure that modifies the action of that signal, and a pointer to another `sigaction` structure that's filled in with the previous action for the signal. When the third argument is null, information about the previous action is not returned.

The `sigaction` function returns zero when the signal's action has been modified as specified by the second argument; it returns –1 otherwise. `Thread_init` returns zero when `sigaction` returns –1, to indicate that the thread system cannot support preemptive scheduling.

Once the signal handler is in place, the virtual timer is initialized:

⟨*initialize preemptive scheduling* 454⟩+≡
```
{
    struct itimerval it;
    it.it_value.tv_sec    =  0;
    it.it_value.tv_usec   = 50;
    it.it_interval.tv_sec    =  0;
    it.it_interval.tv_usec = 50;
    if (setitimer(ITIMER_VIRTUAL, &it, NULL) < 0)
        return 0;
}
```

The `it_value` field in an `itimerval` structure specifies the amount of time in seconds (`tv_sec`) and milliseconds (`tv_msec`) to the next timer interrupt. The values in the `it_interval` field are used to reset the `it_value` field when the timer expires. `Thread_init` arranges for the timer interrupt to occur every 50 milliseconds.

The `setitimer` function is much like the `sigaction` function: Its first argument specifies which timer's action is to be affected (there's also a timer for real time), the second argument is a pointer to the `itimerval` structure that holds the new timer values, and the third argument is a pointer to the `itimerval` structure that gets the previous timer values, or null if the previous values are not needed. `setitimer` returns zero when the timer is set successfully, and returns –1 otherwise.

The signal handler, `interrupt`, is called when the virtual timer expires. When the interrupt is dismissed, which occurs when `interrupt` returns, the timer begins anew. `interrupt` executes the equivalent of `Thread_pause`, unless the current thread is in a critical region or is somewhere in a `Thread` or `Sem` function.

⟨*static functions* 436⟩+≡
```
static int interrupt(int sig, int code,
    struct sigcontext *scp) {
```

```
      if (critical ||
          scp->sc_pc >= (unsigned long)_MONITOR
      && scp->sc_pc <= (unsigned long)_ENDMONITOR)
              return 0;
      put(current, &ready);
      sigsetmask(scp->sc_mask);
      run();
      return 0;
  }
```

The sig argument carries the signal number, and code supplies additional data for some signals. The scp argument is a pointer to a sigcontext structure that, among other values, contains the location counter at the time of the interrupt in the sc_pc field. thread.c begins with the vacuous function _MONITOR, and the assembly-language code in swtch.s ends with a definition for the global symbol _ENDMONITOR. If the object files are loaded into the program so that the object code for swtch.s follows the object code for thread.c, then the interrupted thread is executing a Thread or Sem function if its location counter is between _MONITOR and _ENDMONITOR. Thus, if critical is nonzero, or scp->sc_pc is between _MONITOR and _ENDMONITOR, interrupt returns and thus ignores this timer interrupt. Otherwise, interrupt puts the current thread on ready and runs another one.

The call to sigsetmask restores the signals disabled by the interrupt, which are given in the signal set scp->sc_mask; this set usually holds the SIGVTALRM signal only. This call is necessary because the next thread to run may not have been suspended by an interrupt. Suppose, for example, that thread A calls Thread_pause explicitly, and execution continues with thread B. When a timer interrupt occurs, control lands in interrupt with SIGVTALRM signals disabled. B reenables SIGVTALRM, and gives up the processor to A.

If the call to sigsetmask is omitted, A would be resumed with SIGVTALRM *disabled*, because A was suspended by Thread_pause, not by interrupt. When the next timer interrupt occurs, A is suspended and B continues. In this case, calling sigsetmask is redundant, because B dismisses the interrupt, which restores the signal mask. A flag in the Thread_T structure could be used to avoid the unnecessary calls to sigsetmask.

The second and succeeding arguments to interrupt handlers are system-dependent. Most UNIX variants support the code and scp arguments shown above, but other POSIX-compliant systems may supply different arguments to handlers.

20.3.5 General Semaphores

Creating and initializing semaphores are the easy two of the four Sem functions:

⟨*sem functions* 457⟩≡
```
T *Sem_new(int count) {
    T *s;

    NEW(s);
    Sem_init(s, count);
    return s;
}

void Sem_init(T *s, int count) {
    assert(current);
    assert(s);
    s->count = count;
    s->queue = NULL;
}
```

Sem_wait and Sem_signal are short, but it is tricky to write implementations that are both correct and fair. The semaphore operations are semantically equivalent to:

```
Sem_wait(s):    while (s->count <= 0)
                     ;
                --s->count;

Sem_signal(s):  ++s->count;
```

These semantics lead to the concise and correct, but unfair, implementations shown below; these implementations also ignore alerts and checked runtime errors.

```
void Sem_wait(T *s) {
    while (s->count <= 0) {
        put(current, &s->queue);
```

```
            run();
        }
        --s->count;
    }

    void Sem_signal(T *s) {
        if (++s->count > 0 && !isempty(s->queue))
            put(get(&s->queue), &ready);
    }
```

These implementations are unfair because they permit "starvation." Assume s is initialized to one and threads A and B both execute

```
    for (;;) {
        Sem_wait(s);
        ...
        Sem_signal(s);
    }
```

Suppose A is in the critical region denoted by the ellipsis, and B is in s->queue. When A calls Sem_signal, B is moved to the ready queue. If B executes next, its call to Sem_wait will return and B will enter the critical region. But A might call Sem_wait first and grab the critical region. If A is preempted inside the region, B resumes but finds that s->count is zero, and is moved back onto s->queue. Without some intervention, B could cycle between ready and s->queue indefinitely, and more threads competing for s make starvation more likely.

One solution is to ensure that when a thread is moved from s->queue to ready, it's guaranteed to get the semaphore. This scheme can be implemented by moving a thread from s->queue to ready when s->count is about to be incremented from zero to one, but not actually incrementing it. Similarly, s->count isn't decremented when a blocked thread is resumed inside of Sem_wait.

⟨*sem functions* 457⟩+≡
```
    void Sem_wait(T *s) {
        assert(current);
        assert(s);
        testalert();
        if (s->count <= 0) {
            put(current, (Thread_T *)&s->queue);
```

```
            run();
            testalert();
        } else
            --s->count;
    }

    void Sem_signal(T *s) {
        assert(current);
        assert(s);
        if (s->count == 0 && !isempty(s->queue)) {
            Thread_T t = get((Thread_T *)&s->queue);
            assert(!t->alerted);
            put(t, &ready);
        } else
            ++s->count;
    }
```

When s->count is zero and thread C is moved to the ready queue, C is guaranteed to get the semaphore, because other threads that call Sem_wait block since s->count is zero. For general semaphores, however, C may not get the semaphore first: If D calls Sem_signal before C runs again, that opens the door for another thread to get the semaphore before C, though C will get it too.

Alerts make Sem_wait hard to understand. If a thread blocked on s is alerted, its call to run in Sem_wait returns with its alerted flag set. In this case, the thread was moved to ready by Thread_Alert, not by Sem_signal, so its resumption is unrelated to the value of s->count. The thread must leave s undisturbed, clear its alerted flag, and raise Thread_Alerted.

20.3.6 Context-Switching on the MIPS and ALPHA

The MIPS and ALPHA versions of _swtch and _start are similar in design to the SPARC versions but the details are different.

The MIPS version of _swtch appears below. The frame size is 88 bytes. The store instructions through the sw $31,48+36($sp) save the "caller-saved" floating-point and integer registers; register 31 holds the return address. The italicized instruction switches contexts by loading to's stack pointer, and the load instructions that follow restore to's caller-saved registers.

⟨*MIPS swtch* 460⟩≡

```
    .text
    .globl  _swtch
    .align  2
    .ent    _swtch
    .set    reorder
_swtch: .frame  $sp,88,$31
        subu    $sp,88
        .fmask  0xfff00000,-48
        s.d     $f20,0($sp)
        s.d     $f22,8($sp)
        s.d     $f24,16($sp)
        s.d     $f26,24($sp)
        s.d     $f28,32($sp)
        s.d     $f30,40($sp)
        .mask   0xc0ff0000,-4
        sw      $16,48+0($sp)
        sw      $17,48+4($sp)
        sw      $18,48+8($sp)
        sw      $19,48+12($sp)
        sw      $20,48+16($sp)
        sw      $21,48+20($sp)
        sw      $22,48+24($sp)
        sw      $23,48+28($sp)
        sw      $30,48+32($sp)
        sw      $31,48+36($sp)
        sw      $sp,0($4)
        lw      $sp,0($5)
        l.d     $f20,0($sp)
        l.d     $f22,8($sp)
        l.d     $f24,16($sp)
        l.d     $f26,24($sp)
        l.d     $f28,32($sp)
        l.d     $f30,40($sp)
        lw      $16,48+0($sp)
        lw      $17,48+4($sp)
        lw      $18,48+8($sp)
        lw      $19,48+12($sp)
        lw      $20,48+16($sp)
        lw      $21,48+20($sp)
        lw      $22,48+24($sp)
```

```
lw      $23,48+28($sp)
lw      $30,48+32($sp)
lw      $31,48+36($sp)
addu    $sp,88
j       $31
```

Here's the MIPS startup code:

⟨*MIPS startup* 461⟩≡
```
.globl  _start
_start: move    $4,$23          # register 23 holds args
        move    $25,$30         # register 30 holds apply
        jal     $25
        move    $4,$2           # Thread_exit(apply(p))
        move    $25,$21         # register 21 holds Thread_exit
        jal     $25
        syscall
.end    _swtch
.globl  _ENDMONITOR
_ENDMONITOR:
```

This code collaborates with the MIPS-dependent portion of Thread_new, which arranges for Thread_exit, args, and apply to appear in registers 21, 23, and 30, respectively, by storing them in the right places in the frame. apply's first argument is passed in register 4, and returns its result in register 2. The startup code doesn't need a frame, so Thread_new builds only a _swtch frame, but it does allocate four words on the stack under that frame in case apply takes a variable number of arguments.

⟨*initialize a MIPS stack* 461⟩≡
```
extern void _start(void);
t->sp -= 16/4;
t->sp -= 88/4;
t->sp[(48+20)/4] = (unsigned long)Thread_exit;
t->sp[(48+28)/4] = (unsigned long)args;
t->sp[(48+32)/4] = (unsigned long)apply;
t->sp[(48+36)/4] = (unsigned long)_start;
```

The address of Thread_exit is passed in register 21 because the MIPS startup code must be position-independent. The startup code copies the

address of args to register 4 and the addresses of apply and
Thread_exit to register 25 before the calls (the jal instructions)
because that's what is demanded by the MIPS position-independent calling sequence.

The ALPHA chunks are similar to the corresponding MIPS chunks.

⟨ALPHA swtch 462⟩≡

```
    .globl  _swtch
    .ent    _swtch
    _swtch: lda     $sp,-112($sp)       # allocate _swtch's frame
            .frame  $sp,112,$26
            .fmask  0x3f0000,-112
            stt     $f21,0($sp)         # save from's registers
            stt     $f20,8($sp)
            stt     $f19,16($sp)
            stt     $f18,24($sp)
            stt     $f17,32($sp)
            stt     $f16,40($sp)
            .mask   0x400fe00,-64
            stq     $26,48+0($sp)
            stq     $15,48+8($sp)
            stq     $14,48+16($sp)
            stq     $13,48+24($sp)
            stq     $12,48+32($sp)
            stq     $11,48+40($sp)
            stq     $10,48+48($sp)
            stq     $9,48+56($sp)
            .prologue 0
            stq     $sp,0($16)          # save from's stack pointer
            ldq     $sp,0($17)          # restore to's stack pointer
            ldt     $f21,0($sp)         # restore to's registers
            ldt     $f20,8($sp)
            ldt     $f19,16($sp)
            ldt     $f18,24($sp)
            ldt     $f17,32($sp)
            ldt     $f16,40($sp)
            ldq     $26,48+0($sp)
            ldq     $15,48+8($sp)
            ldq     $14,48+16($sp)
            ldq     $13,48+24($sp)
            ldq     $12,48+32($sp)
```

```
        ldq      $11,48+40($sp)
        ldq      $10,48+48($sp)
        ldq      $9,48+56($sp)
        lda      $sp,112($sp)      # deallocate frame
        ret      $31,($26)
  .end  _swtch
```

⟨*ALPHA startup* 463⟩≡
```
  .globl  _start
  .ent    _start
  _start: .frame  $sp,0,$26
          .mask   0x0,0
          .prologue 0
          mov     $14,$16          # register 14 holds args
          mov     $15,$27          # register 15 holds apply
          jsr     $26,($27)        # call apply
          ldgp    $26,0($26)       # reload the global pointer
          mov     $0,$16           # Thread_exit(apply(args))
          mov     $13,$27          # register 13 has Thread_exit
          jsr     $26,($27)
          call_pal0
  .end    _start
  .globl  _ENDMONITOR
  _ENDMONITOR:
```

⟨*initialize an ALPHA stack* 463⟩≡
```
  extern void _start(void);
  t->sp -= 112/8;
  t->sp[(48+24)/8] = (unsigned long)Thread_exit;
  t->sp[(48+16)/8] = (unsigned long)args;
  t->sp[(48+ 8)/8] = (unsigned long)apply;
  t->sp[(48+ 0)/8] = (unsigned long)_start;
```

Further Reading

Andrews (1991) is a comprehensive text about concurrent programming. It describes most of the problems specific to programming concurrent systems and their solutions, including synchronization mechanisms, message-passing systems, and remote procedure calls. It also describes features designed specifically for concurrent programming in four programming languages.

Thread is based on Modula-3's thread interface, which is derived from experience with the Modula-2+ thread facilities at Digital's System Research Center (SRC). Chapter 4 in Nelson (1991), by Andrew Birrell, is a guide to programming with threads; anyone who writes thread-based applications will benefit from this article. The thread facilities in most modern operating systems are based in some way on the SRC interfaces.

Tanenbaum (1995) surveys the design issues for user-level and kernel-level threads and outlines their implementations. His case studies describe the thread packages in three operating systems (Amoeba, Chorus, and Mach), and threads in the Open Software Foundation's Distributed Computing Environment. Originally, DCE, as this environment is known, ran on the OSF/1 variant of UNIX, but it is now available for most operating systems, including OpenVMS, OS/2, Windows NT, and Windows 95.

POSIX threads (Institute for Electrical and Electronic Engineers 1995) and Solaris 2 threads are described in detail by Kleiman, Shah, and Smaalders (1996). This practically oriented book includes a chapter on the interaction of threads and libraries, numerous examples using threads to parallelize algorithms, including sorting, and thread-safe implementations for lists, queues, and hash tables.

sieve is adapted from a similar example that McIlroy (1968) used to illustrate programming with coroutines, which are like nonpreemptive threads. Coroutines appear in several languages, sometimes under different names. Icon's coexpressions are an example (Wampler and Griswold 1983). Marlin (1980) surveys many of the original coroutine proposals and describes model implementations in Pascal variants.

Channels are based on CSP — communicating sequential processes (Hoare 1978). Threads and channels also appear in Newsqueak, an applicative concurrent language. Channels in CSP and Newsqueak are more powerful than those provided by Chan, because both languages have facilities to wait nondeterministically on more than one channel. Pike (1990) tours the highlights of the implementation of an interpreter for Newsqueak, and describes using random numbers to vary the preemption frequency, which makes thread scheduling nondeterministic (but fair). McIlroy (1990) details a Newsqueak program that manipulates power series by treating them as data streams; his approach is similar in spirit to sieve.

Newsqueak has been used to implement window systems, which exemplify the kinds of interactive applications that benefit the most from threads. The NeWS window system (Gosling, Rosenthal, and Arden 1989) is another example of a window system written in a language with threads. The heart of the NeWS system is a PostScript interpreter, which renders text and images. Most of the NeWS window system itself is written in its variant of PostScript, which includes extensions for nonpreemptive threads.

The functional language Concurrent ML (Reppy 1997) supports threads and synchronous channels much like those provided by Chan. It is often easier to implement threads in nonimperative languages than in stack-based, imperative languages. In Standard ML, for example, there's no stack, because activations can outlive their callers, so no special arrangements are needed to support threads. As a result, Concurrent ML is implemented entirely in Standard ML.

Using _MONITOR and _ENDMONITOR functions to delimit the code in the Thread and Sem implementation is from Cormack (1988), which describes a similar but slightly different interface for UNIX threads. Chapter 10 in Stevens (1992) is a comprehensive treatment of signals and signal-handling procedures; it describes the differences among the UNIX variants and the POSIX standard.

Exercises

20.1 Binary semaphores — usually called locks or mutexes — are the most prevalent type of semaphore. Design a separate interface for locks whose implementation is simpler than the one for general semaphores. Be careful about alerts.

20.2 Suppose thread *A* locks x and then attempts to lock y, and *B* locks y and then attempts to lock x. These threads are deadlocked: *A* can't continue until *B* unlocks y, and *B* can't continue until *A* unlocks x. Extend your implementation of locks in the previous exercise to detect these kinds of simple deadlocks.

20.3 Reimplement the Chan interface in thread.c without using semaphores. Design a suitable representation for channels, and use the internal queue and thread functions directly instead of the semaphore functions. Be careful about alerts. Devise a test suite that measures the benefits of this presumably more efficient implementation. Quantify the level of message activity that an application must have for this revised implementation to make a measurable difference in runtime.

20.4 Design and implement an interface for asynchronous, buffered communications — an interthread message facility in which the sender doesn't wait for the message to be received, and messages are buffered until they're received. Your design should permit messages to outlive their sending threads; that is, for a thread to send a message and then exit before that message is received. Asynchronous communication is more complicated than Chan's synchronous communication, because it must cope with storage management for the buffered messages and with more error conditions, for example, providing a way for a thread to determine whether a message has been received.

20.5 Modula-3 supports *condition variables*. A condition variable c is associated with a lock m. The atomic operation sleep(m, c) causes the calling thread to unlock m and wait on c. The calling thread must have m locked. wakeup(c) causes one or more threads waiting on c to resume execution; one of those relocks m and returns from its call to sleep. broadcast(c) is like wakeup(c), but *all* threads sleeping on c resume execution. Alerts don't affect threads blocked on a condition variable, unless they called alertsleep instead of sleep. When a thread that has called alertsleep is alerted, it locks m and raises Thread_Alerted. Design and implement an interface that supports condition variables; use your locks from Exercise 20.1.

20.6 If your system supports nonblocking I/O system calls, use them to build a thread-safe implementation of C's standard I/O library. That is, when one thread calls fgetc, for example, other threads can execute while that thread waits for input.

20.7 Devise a way to make the Thread and Sem functions atomic without using _MONITOR and _ENDMONITOR. Hints: A single global critical flag isn't enough. You'll need a critical flag for each thread, and the assembly-language code will need to modify this flag. Be careful — it is incredibly easy to make subtle errors using this approach.

20.8 Extend `Thread_new` so that it accepts optional arguments that specify the stack size. For example,

```
t = Thread_new(..., "stacksize", 4096, NULL);
```

would create a thread with a 4K byte stack.

20.9 Add support for a small number of priorities to `Thread`'s implementation as suggested in Section 20.1. Modify `Thread_init` and `Thread_new` so they accept priority specifications as optional arguments. Tanenbaum (1995) describes how to implement a fair scheduling policy that supports priorities.

20.10 DCE supports templates, which are essentially associative tables of thread attributes. When a thread is created with DCE's `pthread_create`, a template supplies attributes such as stack size and priority. Templates avoid repeating the same arguments in thread-creation calls, and let thread attributes be specified other than at the creation site. Design a template facility for `Thread` using `Table_Ts`, and revise `Thread_new` so that it accepts a template as one of its optional arguments.

20.11 Implement `Thread` and `Sem` on a multiprocessor with shared memory, such as a Sequent. This implementation is more complicated than the implementation detailed in Section 20.3 because threads really do execute concurrently on a multiprocessor. Implementing atomic operations will require some form of low-level spin locks that ensure exclusive access to short critical regions that access shared data structures, like those in the `Thread` and `Sem` functions.

20.12 Implement `Thread`, `Sem`, and `Chan` on a massively parallel processor (MPP) with many processors, like the Cray T3D, which is composed of 2^n DEC ALPHA processors. On MPPs, each processor has its own memory, and there's some low-level mechanism (usually implemented in hardware) for one processor to access the memory of another. One of the challenges in this exercise is deciding how to map the shared-memory model favored by the `Thread`, `Sem`, and `Chan` interfaces onto the distributed-memory model provided by MPPs.

20.13 Implement `Thread`, `Sem`, and `Chan` using DCE threads. Be sure to specify what system-dependent optional parameters your implementation of `Thread_new` accepts.

20.14 Implement `Thread`, `Sem`, and `Chan` using LWPs on Solaris 2, providing optional parameters for `Thread_new` as necessary.

20.15 Implement `Thread`, `Sem`, and `Chan` using POSIX threads (see Kleiman, Shah, and Smaalders 1996).

20.16 Implement `Thread`, `Sem`, and `Chan` using Microsoft's Win32 threads interface (see Richter 1995).

20.17 If you have access to a C compiler for the SPARC, such as `lcc` (Fraser and Hanson 1995), modify the compiler so that it doesn't use the SPARC register windows, which eliminates the `ta 3` system call in `_swtch`. You'll have to recompile any libraries you use, too. Measure the resulting improvements in runtime. Warning: This exercise is a large project.

20.18 `Thread_new` must allocate a stack because most compilation systems assume that a contiguous stack has already been allocated when a program begins execution. A few systems, such as the Cray-2, allocate the stack in chunks, on the fly. The function entry sequence allocates the frame in the current chunk, if it fits; otherwise, it allocates a new chunk of sufficient size and links it to the current chunk. The exit sequence unlinks and deallocates a chunk when its last frame is removed. This approach not only simplifies thread creation, but also checks for stack overflow automatically. Modify a C compiler to use this approach, and measure its benefits. As with the previous exercise, you'll need to recompile any libraries you use; this exercise, too, is a large project.

APPENDIX

INTERFACE SUMMARY

Interface summaries are listed below in alphabetical order; the sub-sections name each interface and its primary type, if it has one. The notation "T is opaque X_T" indicates that interface X exports an opaque pointer type X_T, abbreviated as T in the descriptions. The representation for X_T is given, if the interface reveals its primary type.

The summary for each interface lists, in alphabetical order, the exported variables, excluding exceptions, followed by the exported functions. The prototype for each function is followed by the exceptions it can raise and a concise description. The abbreviations c.r.e. and u.r.e. stand for checked and unchecked runtime error(s).

The following table summarizes the interfaces by category and gives the pages on which the summaries begin.

Fundamentals		ADTs		Strings		Arithmetic		Threads	
Arena	471	Array	472	Atom	474	AP	470	Chan	476
Arith	472	ArrayRep	473	Fmt	477	MP	480	Sem	484
Assert	474	Bit	474	Str	487	XP	494	Thread	493
Except	476	List	478	Text	491				
Mem	479	Ring	483						
		Seq	485						
		Set	486						
		Stack	487						
		Table	490						

AP

T is opaque AP_T

It is a c.r.e. to pass a null T to any AP function.

`T AP_add(T x, T y)`	Mem_Failed
`T AP_addi(T x, long int y)`	Mem_Failed

   return the sum x + y.

`int AP_cmp(T x, T y)`
`int AP_cmpi(T x, long int y)`
   return an int <0, =0, or >0 if x<y, x=y, or x>y.

`T AP_div(T x, T y)`	Mem_Failed
`T AP_divi(T x, long int y)`	Mem_Failed

   return the quotient x/y; see `Arith_div`. It is a c.r.e. for y=0.

`void AP_fmt(int code, va_list *app,`   Mem_Failed
    `int put(int c, void *cl), void *cl,`
    `unsigned char flags[], int width, int precision)`
a Fmt conversion function: consumes a T and formats it like printf's %d. It is a c.r.e. for `app` or `flags` to be null.

`void AP_free(T *z)`
   deallocates and clears *z. It is a c.r.e. for *z or *z to be null.

`T AP_fromstr(const char *str, int base,`   Mem_Failed
    `char **end)`
interprets `str` as an integer in `base` and returns the resulting T. Ignores leading white space and accepts an optional sign followed by one or more digits in `base`. For 10<base≤36, lowercase or uppercase letters are interpreted as digits greater than 9. If end≠null, *end points to the character in `str` that terminated the scan. If `str` does not specify an integer in `base`, AP_fromstr returns null and sets *end to `str`, if end is nonnull. It is c.r.e. for str=null or for base<2 or base>36.

`T AP_lshift(T x, int s)`   Mem_Failed
   returns x shifted left by s bits; vacated bits are filled with zeros, and the result has the same sign as x. It is a c.r.e. for s<0.

`T AP_mod(T x, T y)`	Mem_Failed
`long AP_modi(T x, long int y)`	Mem_Failed

   return x mod y; see `Arith_mod`. It is a c.r.e. for y=0.

`T AP_mul(T x, T y)`	Mem_Failed
`T AP_muli(T x, long int y)`	Mem_Failed

   return the product x·y.

T AP_neg(T x)   Mem_Failed
    returns −x.

T AP_new(long int n)   Mem_Failed
    allocates and returns a new T initialized to n.

T AP_pow(T x, T y, T p)   Mem_Failed
    returns x^y mod p. If p=null, returns x^y. It is a c.r.e for y<0 or for a non-null p<2.

T AP_rshift(T x, int s)   Mem_Failed
    returns x shifted right by s bits; vacated bits are filled with zeros, and the result has the same sign as x. It is a c.r.e. for s<0.

T AP_sub(T x, T y)   Mem_Failed
T AP_subi(T x, long int y)   Mem_Failed
    return the difference x − y.

long int AP_toint(T x)
    returns a long with same sign as x and magnitude |x| mod LONG_MAX+1.

char *AP_tostr(char *str, int size,   Mem_Failed
    int base, T x)
    fills str[0..size-1] with the character representation of x in base and returns str. If str=null, AP_tostr allocates it. Uppercase letters are used for digits that exceed 9 when base>10. It is c.r.e. for a non-null str to be too small or for base<2 or base>36.

Arena

T **is opaque** Arena_T

It is a c.r.e. to pass nbytes≤0 or a null T to any Arena function.

void *Arena_alloc(T arena, long nbytes,   Arena_Failed
    const char *file, int line)
    allocates nbytes bytes in arena and returns a pointer to the first byte. The bytes are uninitialized. If Arena_alloc raises Arena_Failed, file and line are reported as the offending source coordinates.

void *Arena_calloc(T arena, long count,   Arena_Failed
    long nbytes, const char *file, int line)
    allocates space in arena for an array of count elements, each occupying nbytes, and returns a pointer to the first element. It is a c.r.e. for count≤0. The elements are uninitialized. If Arena_calloc raises Arena_Failed, file and line are reported as the offending source coordinates.

```
void Arena_dispose(T *ap)
```
deallocates *all* of the space in `*ap`, deallocates the arena itself, and clears `*ap`. It is a c.r.e. for `ap` or `*ap` to be null.
```
void Arena_free(T arena)
```
deallocates *all* of the space in `arena` — all of the space allocated since the last call to `Arena_free`.
```
T Arena_new(void)                                    Arena_NewFailed
```
allocates, initializes, and returns a new arena.

Arith

```
int Arith_ceiling(int x, int y)
```
returns the least integer not less than the real quotient of x/y. It is a u.r.e. for y=0.
```
int Arith_div(int x, int y)
```
returns x/y, the maximum integer that does not exceed the real number z such that $z \cdot y = x$. Truncates toward $-\infty$; e.g., `Arith_div`(–13, 5) returns –3. It is a u.r.e. for y=0.
```
int Arith_floor(int x, int y)
```
returns the greatest integer not exceeding the real quotient of x/y. It is a u.r.e. for y=0.
```
int Arith_max(int x, int y)
```
returns max(x, y).
```
int Arith_min(int x, int y)
```
returns min(x, y).
```
int Arith_mod(int x, int y)
```
returns $x - y \cdot$`Arith_div`(x, y); e.g., `Arith_mod`(–13, 5) returns 2. It is a u.r.e. for y=0.

Array   T **is opaque** Array_T

Array indices run from zero to *N*–1, where *N* is the length of the array. The empty array has no elements. It is a c.r.e. to pass a null T to any Array function.

T Array_copy(T array, int length)   Mem_Failed
  creates and returns a new array that holds the initial length elements
  from array. If length exceeds the length of array, the excess elements are cleared.

void Array_free(T *array)
  deallocates and clears *array. It is a c.r.e. for array or *array to be
  null.

void *Array_get(T array, int i)
  returns a pointer to the ith element in array. It is a c.r.e. for i<0 or
  i≥N, where N is the length of array.

int Array_length(T array)
  returns the number of elements in array.

T Array_new(int length, int size)   Mem_Failed
  allocates, initializes, and returns a new array of length elements each
  of size bytes. The elements are cleared. It is a c.r.e. for length<0 or
  size≤0.

void *Array_put(T array, int i, void *elem)
  copies Array_size(array) bytes from elem into the ith element in
  array and returns elem. It is a c.r.e. for elem=null or for i<0 or i≥N,
  where N is the length of array.

void Array_resize(T array, int length)   Mem_Failed
  changes the number of elements in array to length. If length
  exceeds the original length, the excess elements are cleared. It is a
  c.r.e. for length<0.

int Array_size(T array)
  returns the size in bytes of the elements in array.

ArrayRep   T is Array_T

```
typedef struct T {
    int length; int size; char *array; } *T;
```

It is a u.r.e. to change the fields in a T.

void ArrayRep_init(T array, int length,
    int size, void *ary)
  initializes the fields in array to the values of length, size, and ary.
  It is a c.r.e. for length≠0 and ary=null, length=0 and ary≠null, or
  size≤0. It is a u.r.e. to initialize a T by other means.

Assert

assert(e)
   raises Assert_Failed if e is zero. Syntactically, assert(e) is an expression. If NDEBUG is defined when assert.h is included, assertions are disabled.

Atom

It is a c.r.e. to pass a null str to any Atom function. It is a u.r.e. to modify an atom.

int Atom_length(const char *str)
   returns the length of the atom str. It is a c.r.e. for str not to be an atom.
const char *Atom_new(const char *str, int len)   Mem_Failed
   returns the atom for str[0..len-1], creating one if necessary. It is a c.r.e. for len<0.
const char *Atom_string(const char *str)   Mem_Failed
   returns Atom_new(str, strlen(str)).
const char *Atom_int(long n)   Mem_Failed
   returns the atom for the decimal string representation of n.

Bit   T **is opaque** Bit_T

The bits in a bit vector are numbered zero to $N-1$, where N is the length of the vector. It is a c.r.e to pass a null T to any Bit function, except for Bit_union, Bit_inter, Bit_minus, and Bit_diff.

void Bit_clear(T set, int lo, int hi)
   clears bits lo..hi in set. It is a c.r.e. for lo>hi, or for lo<0 or lo$\geq N$ where N is the length of set; likewise for hi.
int Bit_count(T set)
   returns the number of ones in set.

T Bit_diff(T s, T t)   Mem_Failed
    returns the symmetric difference s / t: the exclusive OR of s and t. If
    s=null or t=null, it denotes the empty set. It is a c.r.e. for s=null and
    t=null, or for s and t to have different lengths.

int Bit_eq(T s, T t)
    returns 1 if s = t and zero otherwise. It is a c.r.e. for s and t to have
    different lengths.

void Bit_free(T *set)
    deallocates and clears *set. It is a c.r.e. for set or *set to be null.

int Bit_get(T set, int n)
    returns bit n. It is a c.r.e. for n<0 or n≥N where N is the length of set.

T Bit_inter(T s, T t)   Mem_Failed
    returns s ∩ t: the logical AND of s and t. See Bit_diff for c.r.e.

int Bit_length(T set)
    returns the length of set.

int Bit_leq(T s, T t)
    returns 1 if s ⊆ t and zero otherwise. See Bit_eq for c.r.e.

int Bit_lt(T s, T t)
    returns 1 if s ⊂ t and zero otherwise. See Bit_eq for c.r.e.

void Bit_map(T set,
    void apply(int n, int bit, void *cl), void *cl)
    calls apply(n, bit, cl) for each bit in set from zero to $N–1$, where N
    is the length of set. Changes to set by apply affect subsequent val-
    ues of bit.

T Bit_minus(T s, T t)   Mem_Failed
    returns s – t: the logical AND of s and ~t. See Bit_diff for c.r.e.

T Bit_new(int length)   Mem_Failed
    creates and returns a new bit vector of length zeros. It is a c.r.e. for
    length<0.

void Bit_not(T set, int lo, int hi)
    complements bits lo..hi in set. See Bit_clear for c.r.e.

int Bit_put(T set, int n, int bit)
    sets bit n to bit and returns the previous value of bit n. It is a c.r.e. for
    bit<0 or bit>1, or for n<0 or n≥N, where N is the length of set.

void Bit_set(T set, int lo, int hi)
    sets bits lo..hi in set. See Bit_clear for c.r.e.

T Bit_union(T s, T t)   Mem_Failed
    returns s ∪ t: the inclusive OR of s and t. See Bit_diff for c.r.e.

Chan

T **is opaque** Chan_T

It is a c.r.e. to pass a null T to any Chan function, or to call any Chan function before calling Thread_init.

T Chan_new(void)   Mem_Failed
    creates, initializes, and returns a new channel.

int Chan_receive(T c, void *ptr, int size)   Thread_Alerted
    waits for a corresponding Chan_send, then copies up to size bytes from the sender to ptr, and returns the number copied. It is a c.r.e. for ptr=null or size<0.

int Chan_send(T c, const void *ptr, int size Thread_Alerted
    waits for a corresponding Chan_receive, then copies up to size bytes from ptr to the receiver, and returns the number copied. See Chan_receive for c.r.e.

Except

T **is** Except_T

```
typedef struct T { char *reason; } T;
```

The syntax of TRY statements is as follows; S and e denote statements and exceptions. The ELSE clause is optional.

    TRY S EXCEPT(e_1) S_1 ... EXCEPT(e_n) S_n ELSE S_0 END_TRY

    TRY S FINALLY S_1 END_TRY

void Except_raise(const T *e, const char *file, int line)
    raises exception *e at source coordinate file and line. It is a c.r.e. for e=null. Uncaught exceptions cause program termination.
RAISE(e)
    raises e.
RERAISE
    reraises the exception that caused execution of a handler.
RETURN
RETURN *expression*
    is a return statement used within TRY statements. It is a u.r.e. to use a C return statement in TRY statements.

Fmt

T **is** Fmt_T

```
typedef void (*T)(int code,
    va_list *app, int put(int c, void *cl), void *cl,
    unsigned char flags[256], int width, int precision)
```

defines the type of a conversion function, which is called by the Fmt functions when the associated conversion specifier appears in a format string. Here and below, put(c, cl) is called to emit each formatted character c. Table 14.1 (page 220) summarizes the initial set of conversion specifiers. It is a c.r.e to pass a null put, buf, or fmt to any Fmt function, or for a format string to use a conversion specifier that has no associated conversion function.

```
char *Fmt_flags = "-+ 0"
```
points to the flag characters that can appear in conversion specifiers.
```
void Fmt_fmt(int put(int c, void *cl), void *cl,
    const char *fmt, ...)
```
formats and emits the "..." arguments according to the format string fmt.
```
void Fmt_fprint(FILE *stream, const char *fmt, ...)
void Fmt_print(const char *fmt, ...)
```
format and emit the "..." arguments according to fmt; Fmt_fprint writes to stream, and Fmt_print writes to stdout.
```
void Fmt_putd(const char *str, int len,
    int put(int c, void *cl), void *cl,
    unsigned char flags[256], int width, int precision)
void Fmt_puts(const char *str, int len,
    int put(int c, void *cl), void *cl,
    unsigned char flags[256], int width, int precision)
```
format and emit the converted numeric (Fmt_putd) or string (Fmt_puts) in str[0..len-1] according to Fmt's defaults (see Table 14.1, page 220) and the values of flags, width, and precision. It is a c.r.e for str=null, len<0, or flags=null.
```
T Fmt_register(int code, T cvt)
```
associates cvt with the format character code, and returns the previous conversion function. It is a c.r.e. for code<0 or code>255.

```
int Fmt_sfmt(char *buf, int size,                    Fmt_Overflow
    const char *fmt, ...)
```
formats the "..." arguments into buf[1..size-1] according to fmt, appends a null character, and returns the length of buf. It is a c.r.e. for size≤0. Raises Fmt_Overflow if more than size−1 characters are emitted.

```
char *Fmt_string(const char *fmt, ...)
```
formats the "..." arguments into a null-terminated string according to fmt and returns that string.

```
void Fmt_vfmt(int put(int c, void *cl), void *cl,
    const char *fmt, va_list ap)
```
See Fmt_fmt; takes arguments from the list ap.

```
int Fmt_vsfmt(char *buf, int size,                   Fmt_Overflow
    const char *fmt, va_list ap)
```
See Fmt_sfmt; takes arguments from the list ap.

```
char *Fmt_vstring(const char *fmt, va_list ap)
```
See Fmt_string; takes arguments from the list ap.

List   T is List_T

```
typedef struct T *T;
struct T { T rest; void *first; };
```

All List functions accept a null T for any list argument and interpret it as the empty list.

```
T List_append(T list, T tail)
```
appends tail to list and returns list. If list=null, List_append returns tail.

```
T List_copy(T list)                                  Mem_Failed
```
creates and returns a top-level copy of list.

```
void List_free(T *list)
```
deallocates and clears *list. It is a c.r.e. for list=null.

```
int List_length(T list)
```
returns the number of elements in list.

```
T List_list(void *x, ...)                            Mem_Failed
```
creates and returns a list whose elements are the "..." arguments up to the first null pointer.

```
void List_map(T list,
    void apply(void **x, void *cl), void *cl)
```
calls apply(&p->first, cl) for each element p in list. It is a u.r.e. for apply to change list.

```
T List_pop(T list, void **x)
```
assigns list->first to *x, if x is nonnull, deallocates list, and returns list->rest. If list=null, List_pop returns null and does not change *x.

```
T List_push(T list, void *x)                    Mem_Failed
```
adds a new element that holds x onto the front of list and returns the new list.

```
T List_reverse(T list)
```
reverses the elements in list in place and returns the reversed list.

```
void **List_toArray(T list, void *end)          Mem_Failed
```
creates an *N*+1-element array of the *N* elements in list and returns a pointer to its first element. The *N*th element in the array is end.

Mem

It is a c.r.e. to pass nbytes≤0 to any Mem function or macro.

```
ALLOC(nbytes)                                   Mem_Failed
```
allocates nbytes bytes and returns a pointer to the first byte. The bytes are uninitialized. See Mem_alloc.

```
CALLOC(count, nbytes)                           Mem_Failed
```
allocates space for an array of count elements, each occupying nbytes bytes, and returns a pointer to the first element. It is a c.r.e. for count≤0. The elements are cleared. See Mem_calloc.

```
FREE(ptr)
```
deallocates ptr, if ptr is nonnull, and clears ptr. ptr is evaluated more than once. See Mem_free.

```
void *Mem_alloc(long nbytes,                    Mem_Failed
    const char *file, int line)
```
allocates nbytes bytes and returns a pointer to the first byte. The bytes are uninitialized. If Mem_alloc raises Mem_Failed, file and line are reported as the offending source coordinates.

```
void *Mem_calloc(long count, long nbytes,          Mem_Failed
    const char *file, int line)
```
allocates space for an array of count elements, each occupying nbytes bytes, and returns a pointer to the first element. It is a c.r.e. for count≤0. The elements are cleared, which does not necessarily initialize pointers to null or floating-point values to 0.0. If Mem_calloc raises Mem_Failed, file and line are reported as the offending source coordinate.

```
void Mem_free(void *ptr, const char *file, int line)
```
deallocates ptr, if ptr is nonnull. It is a u.r.e. for ptr to be a pointer that was not returned by a previous call to a Mem allocation function. Implementations may use file and line to report memory-usage errors.

```
void *Mem_resize(void *ptr, long nbytes,          Mem_Failed
    const char *file, int line)
```
changes the size of the block at ptr to hold nbytes bytes, and returns a pointer to the first byte of the new block. If nbytes exceeds the size of the original block, the excess bytes are uninitialized. If nbytes is less than the size of the original block, only nbytes of its bytes appear in the new block. If Mem_resize raises Mem_Failed, file and line are reported as the offending source coordinates. It is a c.r.e. for ptr=null, and it is a u.r.e. for ptr to be a pointer that was not returned by a previous call to a Mem allocation function.

```
NEW(p)                                             Mem_Failed
NEWO(p)                                            Mem_Failed
```
allocate a block large enough to hold *p, set p to the address of the block, and return that address. NEWO clears the bytes, and NEW leaves them uninitialized. Both macros evaluate ptr once.

```
RESIZE(ptr, nbytes)                                Mem_Failed
```
changes the size of the block at ptr to hold nbytes bytes, reaims ptr at the resized block, and returns the address of the block. ptr is evaluated more than once. See Mem_resize.

MP   T is MP_T

```
typedef unsigned char *T
```

MP functions do *n*-bit signed and unsigned arithmetic, where *n* is initially 32 and can be changed by MP_set. Function names that end in u or ui do unsigned arithmetic; others do signed arithmetic. MP functions compute their results before raising `MP_Overflow` or `MP_DivideByZero`. It is a c.r.e. to pass a null T to any MP function. It is a u.r.e. to pass a T that is too small to any MP function.

```
T MP_add(T z, T x, T y)                    MP_Overflow
T MP_addi(T z, T x, long y)                MP_Overflow
T MP_addu(T z, T x, T y)                   MP_Overflow
T MP_addui(T z, T x, unsigned long y)      MP_Overflow
    set z to x + y and return z.
T MP_and(T z, T x, T y)
T MP_andi(T z, T x, unsigned long y)
    set z to x AND y and return z.
T MP_ashift(T z, T x, int s)
    sets z to x shifted right by s bits and returns z. Vacated bits are filled
    with x's sign bit. It is a c.r.e. for s<0.
int MP_cmp(T x, T y)
int MP_cmpi(T x, long y)
int MP_cmpu(T x, T y)
int MP_cmpui(T x, unsigned long y)
    return an int <0, =0, or >0 if x<y, x=y, or x>y.
T MP_cvt(int m, T z, T x)                  MP_Overflow
T MP_cvtu(int m, T z, T x)                 MP_Overflow
    narrow or widen x to an m-bit signed or unsigned integer in z and
    return z. It is a c.r.e. for m<2.
T MP_div(T z, T x, T y)        MP_Overflow, MP_DivideByZero
T MP_divi(T z, T x, long y)    MP_Overflow, MP_DivideByZero
T MP_divu(T z, T x, T y)                    MP_DivideByZero
T MP_divui(T z, T x,          MP_Overflow, MP_DivideByZero
        unsigned long y)
    set z to x/y and return z. The signed functions truncate toward −∞; see
    Arith_div.
void MP_fmt(int code, va_list *app,
    int put(int c, void *cl), void *cl,
    unsigned char flags[], int width, int precision)
void MP_fmtu(int code, va_list *app,
    int put(int c, void *cl), void *cl,
    unsigned char flags[], int width, int precision)
```
are Fmt conversion functions. They consume a T and a base b and format it like `printf`'s %d and %u. It is a c.r.e. for the $b<2$ or $b>36$, and for `app` or `flags` to be null.

```
T MP_fromint(T z, long v)                        MP_Overflow
T MP_fromintu(T z, unsigned long u)              MP_Overflow
```
set z to v or u and return z.
```
T MP_fromstr(T z, const char *str, int base,     MP_Overflow
    char **end)
```
interprets str as an integer in base, sets z to that integer, and returns z. See AP_fromstr.
```
T MP_lshift(T z, T x, int s)
```
set z to x shifted left by s bits and return z. Vacated bits are filled with zeros. It is a c.r.e. for s<0.
```
T MP_mod(T z, T x, T y)           MP_Overflow, MP_DivideByZero
```
sets z to x mod y and returns z. Truncates toward $-\infty$; see Arith_mod.
```
long MP_modi(T x, long y)         MP_Overflow, MP_DivideByZero
```
returns x mod y. Truncates toward $-\infty$; see Arith_mod.
```
T MP_modu(T z, T x, T y)                       MP_DivideByZero
```
sets z to x mod y and returns z.
```
unsigned long MP_modui(T x,       MP_Overflow, MP_DivideByZero
    unsigned long y)
```
returns x mod y.
```
T MP_mul(T z, T x, T y)                          MP_Overflow
```
sets z to x·y and returns z.
```
T MP_mul2(T z, T x, T y)                         MP_Overflow
T MP_mul2u(T z, T x, T y)                        MP_Overflow
```
set z to the *double-length* result of x·y and return z, which has $2n$ bits.
```
T MP_muli(T z, T x, long y)                      MP_Overflow
T MP_mulu(T z, T x, T y)                         MP_Overflow
T MP_mului(T z, T x, unsigned long y)            MP_Overflow
```
set z to x·y and return z.
```
T MP_neg(T z, T x)                               MP_Overflow
```
sets z to –x and returns z.
```
T MP_new(unsigned long u)           Mem_Failed, MP_Overflow
```
creates and returns a T initialized to u.
```
T MP_not(T z, T x)
```
sets z to ~x and returns z.
```
T MP_or(T z, T x, T y)
T MP_ori(T z, T x, unsigned long y)
```
set z to x OR y and return z.
```
T MP_rshift(T z, T x, int s)
```
sets z to x shifted right by s bits and returns z. Vacated bits are filled with zeros. It is a c.r.e. for s<0.

```
int MP_set(int n)                              Mem_Failed
```
   resets MP to do n-bit arithmetic. It is a c.r.e. for n<2.
```
T MP_sub(T z, T x, T y)                        MP_Overflow
T MP_subi(T z, T x, long y)                    MP_Overflow
T MP_subu(T z, T x, T y)                        MP_Overflow
T MP_subui(T z, T x, unsigned long y)          MP_Overflow
```
   set z to x – y and return z.
```
long int MP_toint(T x)                         MP_Overflow
unsigned long MP_tointu(T x)                   MP_Overflow
```
   return x as a long int or unsigned long.
```
char *MP_tostr(char *str, int size,            Mem_Failed
    int base, T x)
```
   fills str[0..size-1] with a null-terminated string representing x in
   base, and returns str. If str=null, MP_tostr ignores size and allocates the string. See AP_tostr.
```
T MP_xor(T z, T x, T y)
T MP_xori(T z, T x, unsigned long y)
```
   set z to x XOR y and return z.

Ring   T **is opaque** Ring_T

Ring indices run from zero to $N-1$, where N is the length of the ring. The
empty ring has no elements. Pointers can be added or removed anywhere; rings expand automatically. Rotating a ring changes its origin. It
is a c.r.e. to pass a null T to any Ring function.

```
void *Ring_add(T ring, int pos, void *x)       Mem_Failed
```
   inserts x at *position* pos in ring and returns x. Positions identify
   points between elements; see Str. It is a c.r.e. for $pos < -N$ or
   $pos > N+1$, where N is the length of ring.
```
void *Ring_addhi(T ring, void *x)              Mem_Failed
void *Ring_addlo(T ring, void *x)              Mem_Failed
```
   adds x to the high (index $N-1$) or low (index 0) end of ring and
   returns x.
```
void Ring_free(T *ring)
```
   deallocates and clears *ring. It is a c.r.e. for ring or *ring to be null.
```
int Ring_length(T ring)
```
   returns the number of elements in ring.

void *Ring_get(T ring, int i)

returns the ith element in ring. It is a c.r.e. for i<0 or i≥N, where *N* is the length of ring.

T Ring_new(void)   Mem_Failed

creates and returns an empty ring.

void *Ring_put(T ring, int i, void *x)   Mem_Failed

changes the ith element in ring to x and returns the previous value. See Ring_get for c.r.e.

void *Ring_remhi(T ring)
void *Ring_remlo(T ring)

removes and returns the element at the high end (index *N*–1) or low end (index 0) of ring. It is a c.r.e. for ring to be empty.

void *Ring_remove(T ring, int i)

removes and returns element i from ring. It is a c.r.e. for i<0 or i≥N, where *N* is the length of ring.

T Ring_ring(void *x, ...)   Mem_Failed

creates and returns a ring whose elements are the "..." arguments up to the first null pointer.

void Ring_rotate(T ring, int n)

rotates the origin of ring n elements left (n<0) or right (n≥0). It is a c.r.e. for |n|<0 or |n|>N, where *N* is the length of ring.

Sem   T **is opaque** Sem_T

    typedef struct T { int count; void *queue; } T;

It is a u.r.e. to read or write the fields in a T directly, or to pass an uninitialized T to any Sem function. It is a c.r.e. to pass a null T to any Sem function, or to call any Sem function before calling Thread_init.

The syntax of the LOCK statement is as follows; *S* and *m* denote statements and a T.

    LOCK(*m*) *S* END_LOCK

m is locked, statements *S* are executed and *m* is unlocked. LOCK can raise Thread_Alerted.

void Sem_init(T *s, int count)
  sets s->count to count. It is a u.r.e. to call Sem_init more than once
  on the same T.

Sem_T *Sem_new(int count)   Mem_Failed
  creates and returns a T with its count field initialized to count.

void Sem_wait(T *s)   Thread_Alerted
  waits until s->count>0, then decrements s->count.

void Sem_signal(T *s)   Thread_Alerted
  increments s->count.

Seq   T **is opaque** Seq_T

Sequence indices run from zero to $N-1$, where N is the length of the
sequence. The empty sequence has no elements. Pointers can be added
or removed from the low end (index zero) or the high end (index $N-1$);
sequences expand automatically. It is a c.r.e. to pass a null T to any Seq
function.

void *Seq_addhi(T seq, void *x)   Mem_Failed
void *Seq_addlo(T seq, void *x)   Mem_Failed
  adds x to the high or low end of seq and returns x.

void Seq_free(T *seq)
  deallocates and clears *seq. It is a c.r.e. for seq or *seq to be null.

int Seq_length(T seq)
  returns the number of elements in seq.

void *Seq_get(T seq, int i)
  returns the ith element in seq. It is a c.r.e. for i<0 or i≥N, where N is
  the length of seq.

T Seq_new(int hint)   Mem_Failed
  creates and returns an empty sequence. hint is an estimate of the
  maximum size of the sequence. It is a c.r.e for hint<0.

void *Seq_put(T seq, int i, void *x)
  changes the ith element in seq to x and returns the previous value.
  See Seq_get for c.r.e.

void *Seq_remhi(T seq)
void *Seq_remlo(T seq)
  remove and return the element at the high or low end of seq. It is a
  c.r.e. for seq to be empty.

```
T Seq_seq(void *x, ...)                          Mem_Failed
```
creates and returns a sequence whose elements are the "..." arguments up to the first null pointer.

Set

T is opaque `Set_T`

It is a c.r.e. to pass a null `member` or T to any `Set` function, except for `Set_diff`, `Set_inter`, `Set_minus`, and `Set_union`, which interpret a null T as the empty set.

```
T Set_diff(T s, T t)                             Mem_Failed
```
returns the symmetric difference s / t: a set whose members appear in only one of s or t. It is a c.r.e. for both s=null and t=null, or for non-null s and t to have different `cmp` and `hash` functions.

```
void Set_free(T *set)
```
deallocates and clears *set. It is a c.r.e. for `set` or *set to be null.

```
T Set_inter(T s, T t)                            Mem_Failed
```
returns s ∩ t: a set whose members appears in s and t. See `Set_diff` for c.r.e.

```
int Set_length(T set)
```
returns the number of elements in `set`.

```
void Set_map(T set,
    void apply(const void *member, void *cl), void *cl)
```
calls `apply(member, cl)` for each member ∈ `set`. It is a c.r.e. for `apply` to change `set`.

```
int Set_member(T set, const void *member)
```
returns one if member ∈ set and zero otherwise.

```
T Set_minus(T s, T t)                            Mem_Failed
```
returns the difference s – t: a set whose members appear in s but not in t. See `Set_diff` for c.r.e.

```
T Set_new(int hint,                              Mem_Failed
    int cmp(const void *x, const void *y),
    unsigned hash(const void *x))
```
creates, initializes, and returns an empty set. See `Table_new` for an explanation of `hint`, `cmp`, and `hash`.

```
void Set_put(T set, const void *member)          Mem_Failed
```
adds member to set, if necessary.

void *Set_remove(T set, const void *member)
> removes member from set, if member ∈ set, and returns the removed member; otherwise, Set_remove returns null.

void **Set_toArray(T set, void *end)   Mem_Failed
> creates a N+1-element array that holds the N members in set in an unspecified order and returns a pointer to the first element. Element N is end.

T Set_union(T s, T t)   Mem_Failed
> returns s ∪ t: a set whose members appear in s or t. See Set_diff for c.r.e.

Stack

T **is opaque** Stack_T

It is a c.r.e. to pass null T to any Stack function.

int Stack_empty(T stk)
> returns one if stk is empty and zero otherwise.

void Stack_free(T *stk)
> deallocates and clears *stk. It is a c.r.e. for stk or *stk to be null.

T Stack_new(void)   Mem_Failed
> returns a new, empty T.

void *Stack_pop(T stk)
> pops and returns the top element on stk. It is a c.r.e. for stk to be empty.

void Stack_push(T stk, void *x)   Mem_Failed
> pushes x onto stk.

Str

The Str functions manipulate null-terminated strings. Positions identify points between characters; for example, the positions in STRING are:

$$_{-6}^{1}S_{-5}^{2}T_{-4}^{3}R_{-3}^{4}I_{-2}^{5}N_{-1}^{6}G_{0}^{7}$$

Any two positions can be given in either order. Str functions that create strings allocate space for their results. In the descriptions below, s[i:j] denotes the substring of s between positions i and j. It is a c.r.e. to pass a nonexistent position or a null character pointer to any Str function, except as specified for Str_catv and Str_map.

```
int Str_any(const char *s, int i, const char *set)
```
returns the positive position in s after s[i:i+1] if that character appears in set, or zero otherwise. It is a c.r.e. for set=null.

```
char *Str_cat(const char *s1, int i1, int j1,        Mem_Failed
        const char *s2, int i2, int j2)
```
returns s1[i1:j1] concatenated with s2[i2:j2].

```
char *Str_catv(const char *s, ...)                   Mem_Failed
```
returns a string consisted of the triples in "..." up to a null pointer. Each triple specifies an s[i:j].

```
int Str_chr(const char *s, int i, int j, int c)
```
returns the position in s before the leftmost occurrence of c in s[i:j], or zero otherwise.

```
int Str_cmp(const char *s1, int i1, int j1,
        const char *s2, int i2, int j2)
```
returns an integer <0, =0, or >0 if s1[i1:j1]<s2[i2:j2], s1[i1:j1]=s2[i2:j2], or s1[i1:j1]>s2[i2:j2].

```
char *Str_dup(const char *s, int i, int j,          Mem_Failed
        int n)
```
returns n copies of s[i:j]. It is a c.r.e. for n<0.

```
int Str_find(const char *s, int i, int j, const char *str)
```
returns the position in s before the leftmost occurrence of str in s[i:j], or zero otherwise. It is a c.r.e. for str=null.

```
void Str_fmt(int code, va_list *app,
        int put(int c, void *cl), void *cl,
        unsigned char flags[], int width, int precision)
```
is a Fmt conversion function. It consumes three arguments — a string and two positions — and formats the substring in the style of printf's %s. It is a c.r.e. for app or flags to be null.

```
int Str_len(const char *s, int i, int j)
```
returns the length of s[i:j].

```
int Str_many(const char *s, int i, int j, const char *set)
```
returns the positive position in s after a nonempty run of characters from set at the beginning of s[i:j], or zero otherwise. It is a c.r.e. for set=null.

`char *Str_map(const char *s, int i, int j,`   `Mem_Failed`
    `const char *from, const char *to)`
  returns the string obtained from mapping the characters in `s[i:j]` according to `from` and `to`. Each character from `s[i:j]` that appears in `from` is mapped to the corresponding character in `to`. Characters that do not appear in `from` map to themselves. If `from`=null and `to`=null, their previous values are used. If `s`=null, `from` and `to` establish a default mapping. It is a c.r.e. for only one of `from` or `to` to be null, for `strlen(from)`≠`strlen(to)`, for `s`, `from`, and `to` to all be null, or for `from`=null and `to`=null on the first call.

`int Str_match(const char *s, int i, int j, const char *str)`
  returns the positive position in `s` if `s[i:j]` starts with `str`, or zero otherwise. It is a c.r.e. for `str`=null.

`int Str_pos(const char *s, int i)`
  returns the positive position corresponding to `s[i:i]`; subtracting one yields the index of `s[i:i+1]`.

`int Str_rchr(const char *s, int i, int j, int c)`
  is the rightmost variant of `Str_chr`.

`char *Str_reverse(const char *s, int i, int j)`   `Mem_Failed`
  returns a copy of `s[i:j]` with the characters in the opposite order.

`int Str_rfind(const char *s, int i, int j, const char *str)`
  is the rightmost variant of `Str_find`.

`int Str_rmany(const char *s, int i, int j, const char *set)`
  returns the positive position in `s` before a nonempty run of characters from `set` at the end of `s[i:j]`, or zero otherwise. It is a c.r.e. for `set`=null.

`int Str_rmatch(const char *s, int i, int j,`
    `const char *str)`
  returns the positive position in `s` before `str` if `s[i:j]` ends with `str`, or zero otherwise. It is a c.r.e. for `str`=null.

`int Str_rupto(const char *s, int i, int j, const char *set)`
  is the rightmost variant of `Str_upto`.

`char *Str_sub(const char *s, int i, int j)`   `Mem_Failed`
  returns `s[i:j]`.

`int Str_upto(const char *s, int i, int j, const char *set)`
  returns the position in `s` before the leftmost occurrence in `s[i:j]` of any character in `set`, or zero otherwise. It is a c.r.e. for `set`=null.

Table

T is opaque `Table_T`

It is a c.r.e. to pass a null T or a null `key` to any `Table` function.

`void Table_free(T *table)`
    deallocates and clears `*table`. It is a c.r.e. for `table` or `*table` to be null.

`void *Table_get(T table, const void *key)`
    returns the value associated with `key` in `table`, or null if `table` does not hold `key`.

`int Table_length(T table)`
    returns the number of key-value pairs in `table`.

`void Table_map(T table,`
        `void apply(const void *key, void **value, void *cl),`
        `void *cl)`
    calls `apply(key, &value, cl)` for each key-value in `table` in an unspecified order. It is a c.r.e. for `apply` to change `table`.

`T Table_new(int hint,`   Mem_Failed
        `int cmp(const void *x, const void *y),`
        `unsigned hash(const void *key))`
    creates, initializes, and returns a new, empty table that can hold an arbitrary number of key-value pairs. `hint` is an estimate of the number of such pairs expected. It is a c.r.e. for hint<0. `cmp` and `hash` are functions for comparing and hashing keys. For keys x and y, `cmp(x,y)` must return an int <0, =0, or >0 if x<y, x=y, or x>y. If `cmp(x,y)` returns zero, then `hash(x)` must equal `hash(y)`. If cmp=null or hash=null, `Table_new` uses a function suitable for `Atom_T` keys.

`void *Table_put(T table,`   Mem_Failed
        `const void *key, void *value)`
    changes the value associated with `key` in `table` to `value` and returns the previous value, or adds `key` and `value` if `table` does not hold `key`, and returns null.

`void *Table_remove(T table, const void *key)`
    removes the key-value pair from `table` and returns the removed value. If `table` does not hold `key`, `Table_remove` has no effect and returns null.

`void **Table_toArray(T table, void *end)`   Mem_Failed
    creates a 2N+1-element array that holds the N key-value pairs in `table` in an unspecified order and returns a pointer to the first ele-

ment. The keys appear in the even-numbered array elements and the corresponding values appear in the following odd-numbered elements; element $2N$ is end.

Text

T **is** Text_T

```
typedef struct T { int len; const char *str; } T;
typedef struct Text_save_T *Text_save_T;
```

A T is a descriptor; clients can read the fields of a descriptor, but it is a u.r.e. to write them. Text functions accept and return descriptors *by value*; it is a c.r.e. to pass a descriptor with str=null or len<0 to any Text function.

Text manages the memory for its immutable strings; it is a u.r.e. to write this string space or deallocate it by external means. Strings in string space can contain null characters, so are not terminated by them.

Some Text functions accept positions, which identify points between characters; see Str. In the descriptions below, s[i:j] denotes the substring in s between positions i and j.

```
const T Text_cset   = { 256, "\000\001…\376\377" }
const T Text_ascii  = { 128, "\000\001…\176\177" }
const T Text_ucase  = {  26, "ABCDEFGHIJKLMNOPQRSTUVWXYZ" }
const T Text_lcase  = {  26, "abcdefhijklmnopqrtuvwxyz" }
const T Text_digits = {  10, "0123456789" }
const T Text_null   = {   0, "" }
```
are static descriptors initialized as shown.

int Text_any(T s, int i, T set)
    returns the positive position in s after s[i:i+1] if that character appears in set, or zero otherwise.

T Text_box(const char *str, int len)
    builds and returns a descriptor for the client-allocated string str of length len. It is a c.r.e. for str=null or len<0.

T Text_cat(T s1, T s2)   Mem_Failed
    returns s1 concatenated with s2.

int Text_chr(T s, int i, int j, int c)
    See Str_chr.

int Text_cmp(T s1, T s2)
    returns an int <0, =0, or >0 if s1<s2, s1=s2, or s1>s2.

T Text_dup(T s, int n)   Mem_Failed
    returns n copies of s. It is a c.r.e. for n<0.
int Text_find(T s, int i, int j, T str)
    See Str_find.
void Text_fmt(int code, va_list *app,
        int put(int c, void *cl), void *cl,
        unsigned char flags[], int width, int precision)
    is a Fmt conversion function. It consumes a pointer to a descriptor and
    formats the string in the style of printf's %s. It is a c.r.e. for the
    descriptor pointer, app, or flags to be null.
char *Text_get(char *str, int size, T s)
    copies s.str[0..str.len-1] to str[0..size-1], appends a null, and
    returns str. If str=null, Text_get allocates the space. It is a c.r.e. for
    str≠null and size<s.len+1.
int Text_many(T s, int i, int j, T set)
    See Str_many.
T Text_map(T s, const T *from, const T *to)   Mem_Failed
    returns the string obtained from mapping the characters in s accord-
    ing to from and to; see Str_map. If from=null and to=null, their previ-
    ous values are used. It is a c.r.e for only one of from or to to be null, or
    for from->len≠to->len.
int Text_match(T s, int i, int j, T str)
    See Str_match.
int Text_pos(T s, int i)
    See Str_pos.
T Text_put(const char *str)   Mem_Failed
    copies the null-terminated str into string space and returns its
    descriptor. It is a c.r.e. for str=null.
int Text_rchr(T s, int i, int j, int c)
    See Str_rchr.
void Text_restore(Text_save_T *save)
    pops the string space to the point denoted by save. It is a c.r.e. for
    save=null. It is a u.r.e. to use other Text_save_T values that denote
    locations higher than save after calling Text_restore.
T Text_reverse(T s)   Mem_Failed
    returns a copy of s with the characters in the opposite order.
int Text_rfind(T s, int i, int j, T str)
    See Str_rfind.
int Text_rmany(T s, int i, int j, T set)
    See Str_rmany.

```
int Text_rmatch(T s, int i, int j, T str)
    See Str_rmatch.
int Text_rupto(T s, int i, int j, T set)
    See Str_rupto.
Text_save_T Text_save(void)                          Mem_Failed
    returns an opaque pointer that encodes the current top of the string
    space.
T Text_sub(T s, int i, int j)
    returns s[i:j].
int Text_upto(T s, int i, int j, T set)
    See Str_upto.
```

Thread

T **is opaque** Thread_T

It is a c.r.e. to call any Thread function before calling Thread_init.

```
void Thread_alert(T t)
```
sets t's alert-pending flag and makes t runnable. The next time t runs, or calls a blocking Thread, Sem, or Chan primitive, it clears its flag and raises Thread_Alerted. It is a c.r.e. for t=null or to name a nonexistent thread.

```
void Thread_exit(int code)
```
terminates the calling thread and passes code to any threads waiting for the calling thread to terminate. When the last thread calls Thread_exit, the program terminates with exit(code).

```
int Thread_init(int preempt, ...)
```
initializes the Thread for nonpreemptive (preempt=0) or preemptive (preempt=1) scheduling and returns preempt or zero if preempt=1 and preemptive scheduling is not supported. Thread_init may accept additional implementation-defined parameters; the argument list must be terminated with a null. It is a c.r.e. to call Thread_init more than once.

```
int Thread_join(T t)                               Thread_Alerted
```
suspends the calling thread until thread t terminates. When t terminates, Thread_join returns t's exit code. If t=null, the calling thread waits for all other threads to terminate, and then returns zero. It is a c.r.e. for t to name the calling thread or for more than one thread to pass a null t.

```
T Thread_new(int apply(void *),                    Thread_Failed
    void *args, int nbytes, ...)
```
creates, initializes, and starts a new thread, and returns its handle. If
nbytes=0, the new thread executes Thread_exit(apply(args)); otherwise, it executes Thread_exit(apply(p)), where p points to a *copy*
of the nbytes block starting at args. The new thread starts with its
own empty exception stack. Thread_new may accept additional implementation-defined parameters; the argument list must be terminated
with a null. It is a c.r.e. for apply=null, or for args=null and
nbytes<0.

```
void Thread_pause(void)
```
relinquishes the processor to another thread, perhaps the caller.

```
T Thread_self(void)
```
returns the calling thread's handle.

XP   T **is** XP_T

```
typedef unsigned char *T;
```

An extended-precision unsigned integer is represented in base 2^8 by an
array of n digits, least significant digit first. Most XP functions take n as
an argument along with source and destination Ts; it is a u.r.e. for $n<1$ or
for n not to be the length of the corresponding Ts. It is a u.r.e. to pass a
null T or a T that is too small to any XP function.

```
int XP_add(int n, T z, T x, T y, int carry)
```
sets z[0..n-1] to $x + y +$ carry and returns the carry out of z[n-1].
carry must be zero or one.

```
int XP_cmp(int n, T x, T y)
```
returns an int <0, =0, or >0 if x<y, x=y, or x>y.

```
int XP_diff(int n, T z, T x, int y)
```
sets z[0..n-1] to $x - y$, where y is a single digit, and returns the borrow into z[n-1]. It is a u.r.e. for $y>2^8$.

```
int XP_div(int n, T q, T x, int m, T y, T r, T tmp)
```
sets q[0..n-1] to x[0..n-1]/y[0..m-1], r[0..m-1] to x[0..n-1] mod
y[0..m-1], and returns one, if y≠0. If y=0, XP_div returns zero and
leaves q and r unchanged. tmp must hold at least n+m+2 digits. It is a
u.r.e. for q or r to be one of x or y, for q and r to be the same T, or for
tmp to be too small.

```
unsigned long XP_fromint(int n, T z, unsigned long u)
```
sets z[0..n-1] to u mod 2^{8n} and returns u/2^{8n}.
```
int XP_fromstr(int n, T z, const char *str,
    int base, char **end)
```
interprets str as an unsigned integer in base using z[0..n-1] as the initial value in the conversion, and returns the first nonzero carry-out of the conversion step. If end≠null, *end points to the character in str that terminated the scan or produced a nonzero carry. See AP_fromstr.
```
int XP_length(int n, T x)
```
returns the length of x; that is, the index plus one of the most significant nonzero digit in x[0..n-1].
```
void XP_lshift(int n, T z, int m, T x, int s, int fill)
```
sets z[0..n-1] to x[0..m-1] shifted left by s bits, and fills the vacated bits with fill, which must be zero or one. It is a u.r.e. for s<0.
```
int XP_mul(T z, int n, T x, int m, T y)
```
adds x[0..n-1]·y[0..m-1] to z[0..n+m-1] and returns the carry-out of z[n+m-1]. If z=0, XP_mul computes x·y. It is a u.r.e. for z to be the same T as x or y.
```
int XP_neg(int n, T z, T x, int carry)
```
sets z[0..n-1] to ~x + carry, where carry is zero or one, and returns the carry-out of z[n-1].
```
int XP_product(int n, T z, T x, int y)
```
sets z[0..n-1] to x·y, where y is a single digit, and returns the carry-out of z[n-1]. It is a u.r.e. for y≥2^8.
```
int XP_quotient(int n, T z, T x, int y)
```
sets z[0..n-1] to x/y, where y is a single digit, and returns x mod y. It is a u.r.e. for y=0 or y≥2^8.
```
void XP_rshift(int n, T z, int m, T x, int s, int fill)
```
shifts right; see XP_lshift. If n>m, the excess bits are treated as if they were equal to fill.
```
int XP_sub(int n, T z, T x, T y, int borrow)
```
sets z[0..n-1] to x − y − borrow and returns the borrow into z[n-1]. borrow must be zero or one.
```
int XP_sum(int n, T z, T x, int y)
```
sets z[0..n-1] to x + y, where y is a single digit, and returns the carry-out of z[n-1]. It is a u.r.e. for y>2^8.
```
unsigned long XP_toint(int n, T x)
```
returns x mod (ULONG_MAX+1).

`char *XP_tostr(char *str, int size, int base, int n, T x)`
fills `str[0..size-1]` with the character representation of `x` in `base`, sets `x` to zero, and returns `str`. It is a c.r.e. for `str=null`, `size` to be too small, or for `base<2` or `base>36`.

BIBLIOGRAPHY

Each entry is followed by the page numbers on which the entry is cited.

Abelson, H., and G. J. Sussman. 1985. *Structure and Interpretation of Computer Programs.* Cambridge, Mass.: MIT Press. (114)

Adobe Systems Inc. 1990. *PostScript Language Reference Manual* (second edition). Reading, Mass.: Addison-Wesley. (133)

Andrews, G. R. 1991. *Concurrent Programming: Principles and Practice.* Menlo Park, Calif.: Addison-Wesley. (463)

Aho, A. V., B. W. Kernighan, and P. J. Weinberger. 1988. *The AWK Programming Language.* Reading, Mass.: Addison-Wesley. (13, 132, 265)

Aho, A. V., R. Sethi, and J. D. Ullman. 1986. *Compilers: Principles, Techniques, and Tools.* Reading, Mass.: Addison-Wesley. (43)

American National Standards Institute. 1990. *American National Standard for Information Systems — Programming Language — C.* ANSI X3.159-1989. New York. (12)

Appel, A. W. 1991. Garbage collection. In P. Lee (ed.), *Topics in Advanced Language Implementation Techniques*, 89–100. Cambridge, Mass.: MIT Press. (100)

Austin, T. M., S. E. Breach, and G. S. Sohi. 1994. Efficient detection of all pointer and array access errors. *Proceedings of the SIGPLAN'94 Conference on Programming Language Design and Implementation, SIGPLAN Notices* 29 (7), 290–301. July. (85)

Barrett, D. A., and B. G. Zorn. 1993. Using lifetime predictors to improve allocation performance. *Proceedings of the SIGPLAN'93 Conference on Programming Language Design and Implementation, SIGPLAN Notices* 28 (6), 187–196. June. (98)

Bentley, J. L. 1982. *Writing Efficient Programs*. Englewood Cliffs, N.J.: Prentice-Hall. (13)

Boehm, H., R. Atkinson, and M. Plass. 1995. Ropes: An alternative to strings. *Software — Practice and Experience* 25 (12), 1315–30. December. (294)

Boehm, H., and M. Weiser. 1988. Garbage collection in an uncooperative environment. *Software — Practice and Experience* 18 (9), 807–20. September. (100)

Briggs, P., and L. Torczon. 1993. An efficient representation for sparse sets. *ACM Letters on Programming Languages and Systems* 2 (1–4), 59–69. March–December. (213, 213)

Brinch-Hansen, P. 1994. Multiple-length division revisited: A tour of the minefield. *Software — Practice and Experience* 24 (6), 579–601. June. (321)

Budd, T. A. 1991. *An Introduction to Object-Oriented Programming*. Reading, Mass.: Addison-Wesley. (31)

Char, B. W., K. O. Geddes, G. H. Gonnet, B. L. Leong, M. B. Monagan, and S. M. Watt. 1992. *First Leaves: A Tutorial Introduction to Maple V*. New York: Springer-Verlag. (354)

Clinger, W. D. 1990. How to read floating-point numbers accurately. *Proceedings of the SIGPLAN'90 Conference on Programming Language Design and Implementation, SIGPLAN Notices* 25 (6), 92–101. June. (239, 402)

Cohen, J. 1981. Garbage collection of linked data structures. *ACM Computing Surveys* 13 (3), 341–67. September. (100)

Cormack, G. V. 1988. A micro-kernel for concurrency in C. *Software — Practice and Experience* 18 (5), 485–91. May. (465)

Ellis, M. A., and B. Stroustrup. 1990. *The Annotated C++ Reference Manual*. Reading, Mass.: Addison-Wesley. (31, 63)

Evans, D. 1996. Static detection of dynamic memory errors. *Proceedings of the SIGPLAN'96 Conference on Programming Language Design and Implementation, SIGPLAN Notices* 31 (5), 44–53. May. (14, 85)

Fraser, C. W., and D. R. Hanson. 1995. *A Retargetable C Compiler: Design and Implementation.* Menlo Park, Calif.: Addison-Wesley. (xi, xiii, 13, 42, 65, 98, 468)

Geddes, K. O., S. R. Czapor, and G. Labahn. 1992. *Algorithms for Computer Algebra.* Boston: Kluwer Academic. (355)

Gimpel, J. F. 1974. The minimization of spatially-multiplexed character sets. *Communications of the ACM* 17 (6), 315–18. June. (213)

Goldberg, D. 1991. What every computer scientist should know about floating-point arithmetic. *ACM Computing Surveys* 23 (1), 5-48. March. (238, 403)

Gosling, J., D. S. H. Rosenthal, and M. J. Arden. 1989. *The NeWS Book.* New York: Springer-Verlag. (465)

Griswold, R. E. 1972. *The Macro Implementation of SNOBOL4.* San Francisco: W. H. Freeman (out of print). (42, 132, 293)

———. 1980. Programming techniques using character sets and character mappings in Icon. *The Computer Journal* 23 (2), 107-14. (264)

Griswold, R. E., and M. T. Griswold. 1986. *The Implementation of the Icon Programming Language.* Princeton, N.J.: Princeton University Press. (133, 158)

———. 1990. *The Icon Programming Language* (second edition). Englewood Cliffs, N.J.: Prentice-Hall. (xii, 132, 158, 169, 180, 264, 266, 293)

Grunwald, D., and B. G. Zorn. 1993. CustoMalloc: Efficient synthesized memory allocators. *Software — Practice and Experience* 23 (8), 851-69. August. (85)

Hansen, W. J. 1992. Subsequence references: First-class values for substrings. *ACM Transactions on Programming Languages and Systems* 14 (4), 471-89. October. (294, 295)

Hanson, D. R. 1980. A portable storage management system for the Icon programming language. *Software — Practice and Experience* 10 (6), 489-500. June. (294, 295)

———. 1987. Printing common words. *Communications of the ACM* 30 (7), 594-99. July. (13)

————. 1990. Fast allocation and deallocation of memory based on object lifetimes. *Software — Practice and Experience* 20 (1), 5-12. January. (98)

Harbison, S. P. 1992. *Modula-3*. Englewood Cliffs, N.J.: Prentice-Hall. (31)

Harbison, S. P., and G. L. Steele Jr. 1995. *C: A Reference Manual* (fourth edition). Englewood Cliffs, N.J.: Prentice-Hall. (12)

Hastings, R., and B. Joyce. 1992. Purify: Fast detection of memory leaks and access errors. *Proceedings of the Winter USENIX Technical Conference*, San Francisco, 125-36. January. (85)

Hennessy, J. L., and D. A. Patterson. 1994. *Computer Organization and Design: The Hardware/Software Interface*. San Mateo, Calif.: Morgan Kaufmann. (238, 321, 322)

Hoare, C. A. R. 1978. Communicating sequential processes. *Communications of the ACM* 21 (8), 666-77. August. (464)

Horning, J., B. Kalsow, P. McJones, and G. Nelson. 1993. Some Useful Modula-3 Interfaces. Research Report 113, Palo Alto, Calif.: Systems Research Center, Digital Equipment Corp. December. (31, 180)

International Organization for Standardization. 1990. *Programming Languages — C*. ISO/IEC 9899:1990. Geneva. (12)

Institute for Electrical and Electronic Engineers. 1995. *Information Technology — Portable Operating Systems Interface (POSIX) — Part 1: System Application Programming Interface (API) — Amendment 2: Threads Extension [C Language]*. IEEE Standard 1003.1c-1995. New York. Also ISO/IEC 9945-2:1990c. (464)

Jaeschke, R. 1991. *The Dictionary of Standard C*. Horsham, Penn.: Professional Press Books. (12)

Kernighan, B. W., and R. Pike. 1984. *The UNIX Programming Environment*. Englewood Cliffs, N.J.: Prentice-Hall. (13, 13)

Kernighan, B. W., and P. J. Plauger. 1976. *Software Tools*. Reading, Mass.: Addison-Wesley. (12, 295)

————. 1978. *The Elements of Programming Style* (second edition). Englewood Cliffs, N.J.: Prentice-Hall. (13)

Kernighan, B. W., and D. M. Ritchie. 1988. *The C Programming Language* (second edition). Englewood Cliffs, N.J.: Prentice-Hall. (12, 13, 85, 86)

Kleiman, S., D. Shah, and B. Smaalders. 1996. *Programming with Threads.* Upper Saddle River, N.J.: Prentice-Hall. (464, 468)

Knuth, D. E. 1973a. *The Art of Computer Programming: Volume 1, Fundamental Algorithms* (second edition). Reading, Mass.: Addison-Wesley. (13, 85, 100, 113, 196)

———. 1973b. *The Art of Computer Programming: Volume 3, Searching and Sorting.* Reading, Mass.: Addison-Wesley. (42, 42)

———. 1981. *The Art of Computer Programming: Volume 2, Seminumerical Algorithms* (second edition). Reading, Mass.: Addison-Wesley. (321, 354, 355)

———. 1992. *Literate Programming.* CSLI Lecture Notes Number 27. Stanford, Calif.: Center for the Study of Language and Information, Stanford Univ. (12)

Koenig, A. 1989. *C Traps and Pitfalls.* Reading, Mass.: Addison-Wesley. (13)

Larson, P. 1988. Dynamic hash tables. *Communications of the ACM* 31 (4), 446–57. April. (133, 134)

Ledgard, H. F. 1987. *Professional Software Volume II. Programming Practice.* Reading, Mass.: Addison-Wesley. (13)

Maguire, S. 1993. *Writing Solid Code.* Redmond, Wash.: Microsoft Press. (13, 31, 64, 85, 86)

Marlin, C. D. 1980. *Coroutines: A Programming Methodology, a Language Design and an Implementation.* Lecture Notes in Computer Science 95, New York: Springer-Verlag. (464)

McConnell, S. 1993. *Code Complete: A Practical Handbook of Software Construction.* Redmond, Wash.: Microsoft Press. (13)

McIlroy, M. D. 1968. Coroutines. Unpublished Report, Murray Hill, N.J.: Bell Telephone Laboratories. May. (464)

———. 1990. Squinting at power series. *Software — Practice and Experience* 20 (7), 661–83. July. (464)

McKeeman, W. M., J. J. Horning, and D. B. Wortman. 1970. *A Compiler Generator*, Englewood Cliffs, N.J.: Prentice-Hall (out of print). (294)

Meyer, B. 1992. *Eiffel: The Language.* London: Prentice-Hall International. (31, 63)

Musser, D. R., and A. Saini. 1996. *STL Tutorial and Reference Guide: C++ Programming with the Standard Template Library.* Reading, Mass.: Addison-Wesley. (31)

Nelson, G. 1991. *Systems Programming with Modula-3.* Englewood Cliffs, N.J.: Prentice-Hall. (31, 63, 169, 464)

Parnas, D. L. 1972. On the criteria to be used in decomposing systems into modules. *Communications of the ACM* 5 (12), 1053–58. December. (30)

Pike, R. 1990. The implementation of Newsqueak. *Software — Practice and Experience* 20 (7), 649–59. July. (464)

Plauger, P. J. 1992. *The Standard C Library.* Englewood Cliffs, N.J.: Prentice-Hall. (12, 30, 238, 264)

Press, W. H., S. A. Teukolsky, W. T. Vetterling, and B. P. Flannery. 1992. *Numerical Recipes in C: The Art of Scientific Computing* (second edition). Cambridge, England: Cambridge University Press. (402, 402)

Pugh, W. 1990. Skip lists: A probabilistic alternative to balanced trees. *Communications of the ACM* 33 (6), 668–76. June. (181)

Ramsey, N. 1994. Literate programming simplified. *IEEE Software* 13 (9), 97–105. September. (13)

Reppy, J. H. 1997. *Concurrent Programming in ML.* Cambridge, England: Cambridge University Press. (465)

Richter, J. 1995. *Advanced Windows: The Developer's Guide to the Win32 API for Windows NT 3.5 and Windows 95.* Redmond, Wash.: Microsoft Press. (468)

Roberts, E. S. 1989. Implementing Exceptions in C. Research Report 40, Palo Alto, Calif.: Systems Research Center, Digital Equipment Corp. March. (63, 64)

————. 1995. *The Art and Science of C: An Introduction to Computer Science.* Reading, Mass.: Addison-Wesley. (31, 264)

Schneier, B. 1996. *Applied Cryptography: Protocols, Algorithms, and Source Code in C* (second edition). New York: John Wiley. (402)

Sedgewick, R. 1990. *Algorithms in C.* Reading, Mass.: Addison-Wesley. (xii, xiv, 13, 42, 134, 196)

Sewell, W. 1989. *Weaving a Program: Literate Programming in WEB.* New York: Van Nostrand Reinhold. (13)

Steele, Jr., G. L., and J. L. White. 1990. How to print floating-point numbers accurately. *Proceedings of the SIGPLAN'90 Conference on Programming Language Design and Implementation, SIGPLAN Notices* 25 (6), 112–26. June. (239, 239)

Stevens, W. R. 1992. *Advanced Programming in the UNIX Environment.* Reading, Mass.: Addison-Wesley. (465)

Tanenbaum, A. S. 1995. *Distributed Operating Systems.* Englewood Cliffs, N.J.: Prentice-Hall. (464, 467)

Ullman, J. D. 1994. *Elements of ML Programming.* Englewood Cliffs, N.J.: Prentice-Hall. (114)

Vo, K. 1996. Vmalloc: A general and efficient memory allocator. *Software — Practice and Experience* 26 (3), 357–74. March. (99)

Wampler, S. B., and R. E. Griswold. 1983. Co-expressions in Icon. *Computer Journal* 26 (1), 72–78. January. (464)

Weinstock, C. B., and W. A. Wulf. 1988. Quick fit: An efficient algorithm for heap storage management. *SIGPLAN Notices* 23 (10), 141–48. October. (85)

Wolfram, S. 1988. *Mathematica: A System for Doing Mathematics by Computer.* Menlo Park, Calif.: Addison-Wesley. (354)

Zorn, B. G. 1993. The measured cost of conservative garbage collection. *Software — Practice and Experience* 23 (7), 733–56. July. (100)

INDEX

Entries for many program identifiers include bold, italic, roman, and underlined page numbers. Bold numbers refer to the definitions of the identifiers; italic numbers refer to their significant uses in interfaces, implementations, or examples; and roman numbers refer to their uses in the text. Underlined page numbers refer to the interface specifications for the identifiers.

A

Abelson, Harold, 114, 497
abort, *59*
abstract data types, 21
   naming conventions for, 22
Aho, Alfred V., 13, 43, 132, 265, 497
alerts, implementing thread, 459
alignment, 32, 83, 94, 162
ALLOC, 39, <u>70</u>, **70**, *71, 113, 126, 132, 149, 154, 175, 252–255, 265, 280, 343, 353, 375, 376, 400, 401,* 411, *446*
Amoeba operating system, 464
Andrews, Gregory R., 463, 497
AP_add, <u>326</u>, *330,* **339**, *347,* 383
AP_addi, <u>326</u>, *332, 345, 346,* **347**
AP_cmp, <u>327</u>, **346**, *348*
AP_cmpi, <u>327</u>, *331,* **348**
AP_div, <u>326</u>, *331,* **342**, *348*
AP_divi, <u>326</u>, **348**
AP_fmt, <u>325</u>, *332,* **353**
AP_free, <u>325</u>, *330, 333, 337, 343–348*
AP_fromstr, <u>324</u>, 329, *330,* **350**
AP_lshift, <u>326</u>, **349**

AP_mod, <u>326</u>, *331,* **343**, *346, 348*
AP_modi, <u>326</u>, **348**
AP_mul, <u>326</u>, *330,* **338**, *345, 348*
AP_muli, <u>326</u>, **348**
AP_neg, <u>326</u>, *333,* **337**
AP_new, <u>324</u>, *328, 331,* **335**, *344, 349*
AP_pow, <u>326</u>, *331,* **344**, *345, 346*
AP_rshift, <u>326</u>, *345, 346,* **349**
AP_sub, <u>326</u>, *330,* **341**, *348, 393*
AP_subi, <u>326</u>, **348**
AP_T, **334**
AP_toint, <u>325</u>, **350**
AP_tostr, <u>325</u>, **352**, *353*
Appel, Andrew W., xv, xvii, 100, 497
applicative algorithms, 90, 106
arbitrary-precision integers. *See*
   multiple-precision integers
Arden, Michelle J., 465, 499
Arena_alloc, <u>91</u>, *94, 97*
Arena_calloc, <u>91</u>, *97*
Arena_dispose, <u>91</u>, **94**
Arena_Failed, <u>90</u>, **92**, *97*
Arena_free, <u>91</u>, *94,* **97**
Arena_new, <u>91</u>, **93**
Arena_NewFailed, <u>90</u>, **92**, *94*

Arena_T, **92**
arena-based allocation, 89
Arith_ceiling, <u>17</u>, **21**
Arith_div, <u>17</u>, **19**, *21*, 31
Arith_floor, <u>17</u>, **20**
Arith_max, <u>16</u>, **19**, *154*
Arith_min, <u>16</u>, **19**, *156, 157*
Arith_mod, <u>17</u>, **20**, 31
arithmetic shift, 302, 364
Array_copy, <u>164</u>, **169**
Array_free, <u>163</u>, **167**, *176*
Array_get, <u>163</u>, **167**
Array_length, <u>163</u>, **168**
Array_new, <u>162</u>, **166**, *169*
Array_put, <u>163</u>, **167**
Array_resize, <u>164</u>, **168**, 179, *179*
Array_size, <u>163</u>, **168**
Array_T, 162, **164**, 174
ArrayRep_init, <u>165</u>, *166*, **166**, *175*
arrays
    descriptors for, 164
    dope vectors for, 164
    dynamic, 161
    vs. pointers, 10
    reshaping, 170
    sequences as, 171
    sparse, 170
assert (function), **61**
assert (macro), 26, **60**
Assert_Failed, <u>60</u>, **61**, *79*
assertions, 26, 31, 59
    compiler pragmas for, 64
    as exceptions, 60
    in Modula-3 and Eiffel, 31
    overhead of, 61
    in production programs, 61, 62
associative tables, 115
    hash-table representation of, 125
Astfalk, Greg, xvii
Atkinson, Russell R., 294, 498
Atom_int, <u>34</u>, **35**

Atom_length, <u>34</u>, **41**
Atom_new, <u>34</u>, *35*, **37**
Atom_string, <u>34</u>, **35**, *122, 145*
atomic actions, 408
atoms, comparing, 33
Austin, Todd M., 85, 497
AWK, 13, 132, 265

B

bags, 158
Barrett, David A., 98, 497
Bentley, Jon L., 13, 498
bignums, 353
binary search trees, 134
Birrell, Andrew D., 464
bit vectors, 158, 199
    word-at-time operations on, 203
Bit_clear, <u>201</u>, **208**
Bit_count, **204**
Bit_diff, <u>202</u>, **213**
Bit_eq, <u>201</u>, **209**
Bit_free, **204**
Bit_get, <u>200</u>, **205**
Bit_inter, <u>202</u>, **212**
Bit_leq, <u>201</u>, **210**
Bit_lt, <u>201</u>, **210**
Bit_map, <u>201</u>, **209**
Bit_minus, <u>202</u>, **212**
Bit_new, <u>200</u>, **203**, *211, 212*
Bit_not, <u>201</u>, **208**
Bit_put, <u>200</u>, **205**
Bit_set, <u>201</u>, **206**
Bit_size, <u>200</u>, **204**
Bit_T, **202**, 239
Bit_union, <u>202</u>, **211**
Boehm, Hans-Jurgen, 42, 100, 294, 498
Breach, Scott E., 85, 497
Briggs, Preston, 213, 498
Brinch-Hansen, Per, 321, 322, 498

Budd, Timothy A., 31, 498

C

C++, xi, 31, 63, 100
callbacks. *See* closures
CALLOC, <u>70</u>, **70**, *71*, *166*, *203*, *335*, *419*
calloc, 67, *75*
carries and borrows, 299
casts, 217, 300
   in variable length argument lists,
     105, 172, 184
Chan_new, <u>418</u>, *427*, *431*, **432**
Chan_receive, <u>418</u>, *429*, *430*, **433**
Chan_send, <u>418</u>, *429*, **433**
Chan_T, *427*, *430*, **432**
channels, communication, 417, 426
Char, Bruce W., 354, 498
characters
   plain, 40
   signed vs. unsigned, 40, 237, 258
checked runtime errors, 24, 25, 45
   for AP, 324-327
   for Arena, 91, 92
   for Array, 163, 164
   for ArrayRep, 165
   for Atom, 34
   for Bit, 200-202
   for Chan, 410, 418
   for Except, 48
   for Fmt, 217-221
   for List, 106
   for Mem, 70, 72, 73
   for MP, 358, 360, 364, 365
   omitting, 299
   for Ring, 184-187
   for Sem, 410, 414, 415
   for Seq, 172, 173
   for Set, 139, 140
   for Stack, 25
   for Str, 244-249

   for Table, 116-118
   for Text, 270-276
   for Thread, 410-412
   for XP, 302, 303
Chorus operating system, 464
chunks, literate program, 2
   concatenating, 6
   navigating, 4, 6
circular buffers, 174
clients, 15
Clinger, William D., 239, 402, 498
closures, 87, 106, 113, 118, 139, 201
Cohen, Jacques, 100, 498
communicating sequential processes,
   464
communication channels, 417, 426
comparison functions
   for sets, 138
   for tables, 116
Concurrent ML, 465
concurrent programs. *See*
   multithreaded programs
condition variables, 466
conditional compilation, 12, 22
const qualifier, 29, 300, 403
context-switching, 408, 439
conversion functions, 216, 219
   for AP, 325, 353
   example, 222
   floating-point, 237
   for MP, 365, 400
   numeric, 232
   octal and hexadecimal, 235
   for pointers, 236
   for Str, 249, 263
   table of, 229
   for Text, 276, 293
conversion specifiers, 217
   default, 218
   for floating-point values, 220
   parsing, 229

for pointers, 220
syntax of, 230
table of default, 220
Cormack, Gordon V., 465, 498
coroutines, 431, 464
coupling, 15
`critical`, 447, **447**, *456*
critical regions, 415, 423, 434, 447
cross-compilers, 357
cryptography, 402
`cvt_c`, **237**
`cvt_d`, **232**
`cvt_f`, **238**
`cvt_o`, **235**
`cvt_p`, **236**
`cvt_s`, **222**
`cvt_u`, **235**
`cvt_x`, **236**, 242
Czapor, Stephen R., 355, 499

D

dangerous interfaces, 299
dangling pointers, 23, 27, 72
data types, 21
Davidson, Jack W., xvii
DBL_MAX, 237
DBL_MAX_10_EXP, 237
deadlock, 441
declaration-before-use rule, 6
distributed computing environment
    (DCE), 407, 464
`div`, 17, 18
division
    estimating quotient digits for, 313
    influence on choosing a base, 314
    long, 311
    scaling operands of, 321
    shift and subtract algorithm for,
        322
    signed vs. unsigned, 35

single-digit, 310
`doubleword`, 5, **7**, *8*
dynamic arrays. *See* arrays
dynamic hash tables, 133

E

Eiffel, 31, 63
Ellis, John R., xvii
Ellis, Margaret A., 31, 63, 498
`ELSE`, <u>49</u>, **57**
`END_LOCK`, <u>416</u>, **416**, *425*
`END_TRY`, <u>49</u>, **58**
`_ENDMONITOR`, 434, **452**, 456, **461**,
        463, 465, 466
errors
    checked runtime, 24, 45
    unchecked runtime, 24
    user, 45
Evans, David E., 14, 85, 498
`EXCEPT`, <u>48</u>, **56**, *367*, *368*, *446*
`Except_entered`, **54**, *57*
`Except_finalized`, **54**, *57*
`Except_Frame`, **53**, 53, *54*, *440*
`Except_handled`, **54**, *57*
`Except_raise`, *51*, 53, **58**, *79*, *97*
`Except_raised`, **54**
`Except_stack`, 53, *56*, *58*, *439*
`Except_T`, **48**, <u>48</u>
exceptions, 24, 45
    for AP, 324–327
    for Arena, 91
    for Array, 163, 164
    for Atom, 34
    for Bit, 200, 202
    for Chan, 418
    for Fmt, 219
    for List, 105–107
    for Mem, 70, 73
    for MP, 359–365
    raising and handling, 25

reraising, 51
for Ring, 184–186
scope of, 46
for Sem, 415
for Seq, 172, 173
for Set, 138–140
for Stack, 25
for Str, 244
for Table, 116–118
for Text, 271–276
for Thread, 411, 412
unhandled, 59
extended-precision integers. *See*
    multiple-precision integers

F

Fernández, Maria F., xvii
field width, 217
FINALLY, 51, **57**
first, **123**
first and rest sets, 119, 146
first-fit allocation, 82, 89
Flannery, Brian P., 402, 502
floating-point values, xvi
    conversion specifiers for, 220
    Fmt conversion functions for, 237
    initializing with Mem_calloc, 70
Fmt_flags, 218, **230**
Fmt_fmt, 217, **225**
Fmt_fprint, 219, **226**
Fmt_Overflow, **225**
Fmt_print, 219, **225**, 249, *250, 332,*
    333, 371, 372
Fmt_putd, 221, *232,* **233,** *235, 236,*
    353, 400, *401*
Fmt_puts, 221, *222,* **222,** 263, *264,*
    293
Fmt_register, 221, **230,** 249, *250,*
    332, 371
Fmt_sfmt, 219, **226**

Fmt_string, 219, **227**
Fmt_T, **216,** 221
Fmt_vfmt, 217, *225, 226, 227, 228,*
    229
Fmt_vsfmt, 219, *226,* **227**
Fmt_vstring, 219, *227,* **228**
fputc, 217
fragmentation, internal, 95
Fraser, Christopher W., xi, xvii, 13, 42,
    65, 98, 468, 499
FREE, 27, **72,** *72, 111, 112, 123, 125,*
    131, 132, 143, 144, 152, 153, 167,
    168, 189, 194, 204, 287, 337, 343,
    353, 368, 375, 401, 449
free, 1, 67, *75,* 89, *94, 98*
ftp, xvi

G

garbage collection, 99
    conservative, 100
    of strings, 294
Geddes, Keith O., 354, 355, 498, 499
getword, **5,** 119, **120,** *122, 145,* 146
Gimpel, James F., 14, 213, 499
Goldberg, David, 238, 403, 499
Gonnet, Gaston H., 354, 498
Gosling, James, 465, 499
Gounares, Alex, xvii
graphical user interfaces, using
    threads for, 405
Griswold, Madge T., xii, 132, 133, 158,
    169, 180, 264, 266, 293, 499
Griswold, Ralph E., xii, 42, 132, 133,
    158, 169, 180, 264, 266, 293, 464,
    499, 503
Grunwald, Dirk, 85, 499

H

Hansen, Wilfred J., 294, 295, 499

Hanson, David R., 13, 42, 65, 98, 294, 295, 468, 499, 500
Hanson, Jennifer E., 248
Harbison, Samuel P., 12, 31, 500
hash functions, 39, 116, 148
hash tables, 36, 77, 125, 148
  dynamic, 133
  load factors of, 133
Hastings, Reed, 85, 500
header files, 16
  conventions for, 22
Hennessy, John L., 238, 321, 322, 500
hints, 44, 116, 138, 150, 172
Hoare, Charles Anthony R., 464, 500
Horning, James J., 31, 180, 294, 500, 502

I

Icon (programming language), xii, 100, 132, 158, 169, 180, 264, 293, 464
#ifdef, 22
implementation-defined behaviors, 18
implementations, multiple, 72
indices
  for bit vectors, 200
  for bytes in bit vectors, 205
  for characters in strings, 244, 278
  converting to positions, 251
  for dynamic arrays, 162
  for rings, 184
  for sequences, 173
information hiding, 15, 21
interrupt, *454*, **455**
ITIMER_VIRTUAL, *455*

J

Jaeschke, Rex, xvii, 12, 500

jmp_buf, *46*, *53*
join queues, 442
Joyce, Bob, 85, 500

K

Kalsow, Bill, xvii, 31, 180, 500
Karatsuba, Anatoly A., 355
Kernighan, Brian W., xvii, 12, 13, 85, 86, 132, 265, 295, 497, 500, 501
Khattra, Taj, xvii
Kleiman, Steve R., 464, 468, 501
Knuth, Donald E., xiii, 12, 13, 42, 85, 100, 113, 196, 321, 354, 355, 501
Koenig, Andrew, 13, 501

L

Labahn, George, 355, 499
Larson, Per-Åke, 133, 134, 501
layered interfaces. *See* two-level interfaces
lcc, xi, 42, 98
LCLint, 14, 85
ldiv, 17
Ledgard, Henry F., 13, 501
Leong, Benton L., 354, 498
Li, Kai, xv, xvii
lightweight processes in Solaris, 408
LISP, 42, 100, 103, 114, 354
List_append, 105, **110**
List_copy, 106, **110**
List_free, 106, **112**
List_length, 106, **112**
List_list, 104, **108**
List_map, 106, **113**
List_pop, 105, **110**
List_push, 105, **108**
List_reverse, 106, **111**
List_T, **103**, 104
List_toArray, 107, **113**

lists
  arrays of doubly linked, 197
  circularly linked, 114, 435
  deleting an element from a doubly
    linked, 194
  doubly linked, 183, 187
  empty, 104
  inserting elements in doubly
    linked, 190
  singly linked, 103, 127
literate programming, 2
location counters, 405
LOCK, <u>416</u>, **416**, *425*
LOCK-END_LOCK statements, 415
LONG_MAX, *35*, 36, *377*
LONG_MIN, *35*, *377*
longjmp, 46, *58*, 65

M

Mach operating system, 464
macros, 12, 30
Maguire, Steve, 13, 31, 64, 85, 86, 501
malloc, 1, 39, 67, *74*, *82*, *84*, 89, *93*,
    96
Maple V, 354
Marlin, Christopher D., 464, 501
Mathematica, 354
McConnell, Steve, 13, 501
McIlroy, M. Douglas, 464, 501
McJones, Paul, 31, 180, 500
McKeeman, William M., 294, 502
Mem_alloc, <u>70</u>, **74**, *80*, *81*, **82**
Mem_calloc, <u>70</u>, **75**, **81**
Mem_Failed, *34*, <u>70</u>, 73, **74**, 105
Mem_free, <u>72</u>, **75**, **79**, *80*
Mem_resize, <u>72</u>, **75**, **80**
memchr, *288–291*
memcmp, 258, 289, *290*

memcpy, *169*, *179*, *212*, *280–283*, *310*,
    313, *337*, *353*, *379–386*, *400*, 411,
    433, *449*
memory leaks, 68, 87
memset, *229*, *310*, *311*, *381*, *382*, *386*,
    399, *446*, *454*
Meyer, Bertrand, 31, 63, 502
ML, 100, 103, 114, 354, 465
Modula-2+, 464
Modula-3, xi, 31, 63, 100, 161, 169,
    180, 464, 466
modular arithmetic, 18
Monagan, Michael B., 354, 498
_MONITOR, **434**, 434, 456, 465, 466
MP_add, <u>361</u>, *370*, **383**, *392*
MP_addi, <u>362</u>, **392**
MP_addu, <u>361</u>, *370*, **381**, *389*
MP_addui, <u>362</u>, *373*, **389**
MP_and, <u>363</u>, 364, *370*, **398**
MP_andi, <u>363</u>, **398**
MP_ashift, <u>364</u>, **399**
MP_cmp, <u>363</u>, **396**
MP_cmpi, <u>363</u>, **397**
MP_cmpu, <u>363</u>, **395**
MP_cmpui, <u>363</u>, **396**
MP_cvt, <u>360</u>, *378*, **378**
MP_cvtu, <u>360</u>, *379*, **380**
MP_div, <u>361</u>, *370*, **387**, *394*
MP_divi, <u>362</u>, **394**
MP_Dividebyzero, <u>361</u>, *368*, **373**,
    383, *387–391*, **394**
MP_divu, <u>361</u>, *370*, **383**, *391*
MP_divui, <u>362</u>, **391**
MP_fmt, <u>365</u>, *371*, **401**
MP_fmtu, <u>365</u>, *371*, **400**
MP_fromint, <u>359</u>, 362, *376*
MP_fromintu, <u>359</u>, 364, **376**
MP_fromstr, <u>364</u>, *369*, **399**
MP_lshift, <u>364</u>, *372*, **399**
MP_mod, <u>361</u>, *370*, **388**, *391*, *395*
MP_modi, <u>362</u>, **394**

`MP_modu`, <u>361</u>, *370*, **383**

`MP_modui`, <u>362</u>, **391**

`MP_mul`, <u>361</u>, 362, *370*, **386**, *394*

`MP_mul2`, **385**

`MP_mul2u`, **381**

`MP_muli`, <u>362</u>, **393**

`MP_mulu`, <u>361</u>, *370*, **382**, *390*

`MP_mului`, <u>362</u>, **390**

`MP_neg`, <u>361</u>, *370*, **385**

`MP_new`, <u>359</u>, 362, 364, *367*, *369*, *370*, *373*, **376**

`MP_not`, <u>363</u>, *370*, **398**

`MP_or`, <u>363</u>, *370*, **398**

`MP_ori`, <u>363</u>, **398**

`MP_Overflow`, <u>359</u>, 360, *367*, **373**, *376–395*

`MP_rshift`, <u>364</u>, *372*, **399**

`MP_set`, <u>358</u>, 359, *373*, **374**

`MP_sub`, <u>361</u>, *370*, **384**, *393*

`MP_subi`, <u>362</u>, **393**

`MP_subu`, <u>361</u>, *370*, **381**, *390*

`MP_subui`, <u>362</u>, **390**

`MP_T`, **358**

`MP_toint`, <u>360</u>, *371*, *372*, **378**, *395*, *397*

`MP_tointu`, <u>360</u>, **379**

`MP_tostr`, <u>365</u>, **399**, *401*

`MP_xor`, <u>363</u>, *370*, **398**

`MP_xori`, <u>363</u>, **398**

Muller, Eric, xvii

multiple-precision integers
  adding, 305, 338, 380, 383
  choosing a base for, 298, 314
  comparing, 346, 395
  conversion functions for, 353, 365, 400
  converting long ints to, 324, 336
  converting strings to, 302, 319, 324, 350, 364, 399
  converting to long ints, 324, 350
  converting to strings, 320, 325, 352, 365, 399
  converting to unsigned longs, 304
  converting unsigned longs to, 303
  creating temporary, 347
  dividing, 309, 342, 382, 387
  exponentiating, 343
  fast algorithms for multiplying, 355, 402
  of fixed size, 357
  in floating-point conversions, 402
  logical operations on, 363, 397
  managing allocation of, 330
  masking excess bits in, 377
  modulus of, 343
  multiplying, 307, 337, 381, 382, 385
  narrowing and widening, 360, 378
  n-bit arithmetic on, 358
  negating, 307, 337, 385
  normalized, 335
  number of characters in strings for, 352, 400
  number of digits in, 351
  overflow of, 361
  representing, 297, 374
  shifting, 349, 364, 398
  signed, 323
  signed overflow of, 376
  signed underflow and overflow of, 384
  sign-magnitude representation of, 334, 383
  subtracting, 306, 340, 381, 384
  unsigned overflow of, 376
  using larger bases for, 322

multisets. *See* bags

multithreaded programs, 405

Musser, David R., 31, 502

mutexes, 415, 465

mutual exclusion, 415

N

name spaces, 16, 21
names
    collisions of, 16
    conventions for abstract data type, 22
    conventions for identifier, 9
    defining symbolic, 36
Navia, Jacob, xvii
NDEBUG, <u>59</u>, *60*, 61
NELEMS, **37**, 39, *41*
Nelson, Greg, xvii, 31, 63, 169, 180, 464, 500, 502
NEW, 26, *27*, 39, **71**, <u>71</u>, *108, 110, 122, 129, 151, 166, 191, 193, 203, 287, 432, 457*
NEWO, **71**, <u>71</u>, *175*, 176, *188*
NeWS window system, 465
Newsqueak (programming language), 464
nibbles, 204
Noah, Elma Lee, xvii
nonblocking I/O, 406
nonpreemptive scheduling, 412
noweb, 13

O

Objective-C, 133
O'Keefe, Richard A., xvii
one's-complement, 301
OpenVMS operating system, 464
OS/2, 464
OSF/1 operating system, 464
Ousterhout, John K., xv

P

Parnas, David L., 30, 502
pattern matching, 264

Patterson, David A., 238, 321, 322, 500
PC-Lint, 14, 85
performance, 30
    average-case, 11
    using threads to improve, 406
    worst-case, 11
Pike, Rob, xvii, 13, 464, 500, 502
pipelines, 406
Plass, Michael F., 294, 498
Plauger, Phillip J., xvii, 12, 13, 30, 238, 264, 295, 500, 502
pointers
    vs. arrays, 10
    conversion specifiers for, 220
    converting between, 28
    dangling. *See* dangling pointers
    detecting invalid, 32
    Fmt conversion function for, 236
    function vs. object, 28
    generic, 28
    initializing with Mem_calloc, 70
    to integers, 122, 144
    opaque, 22, 30
    to pointers, 124, 131, 145, 151
    to Text_Ts, 293
    use with qsort, 123
    to variable length argument lists, 221
    void, 28, 217
Polish suffix notation, 327, 365
positions
    and avoiding allocations, 251
    converting to indices, 251, 278
    nonpositive, 185, 243, 271
    in rings, 185
    specifying substrings with, 244, 245
    in strings, 243, 271
POSIX threads, 408, 464
PostScript, 133

precision specifications, 217
preemptive scheduling, 408
Press, William H., 402, 502
primes
    computing in pipeline, 426
    as hash-table sizes, 127, 150
printf, shortcomings of, 215
programming-in-the-small, 2
pthreads. *See* POSIX threads
Pugh, William, 181, 502
Purify, 85

Q

qsort, *123, 143, 144*
queues
    using circularly linked lists for, 435
    using sequences for, 171
quick-fit allocation, 85
quicksort, 420

R

RAISE, 48, **48**, 49, 53, *61, 74, 94, 97,*
    227, 376–395, 445, 447
Ramsey, Norman, xvii, 13, 502
rand, 40
ready queue, 435, 440
realloc, 2, 67, *75*
red-black trees, 134
reentrant functions, 407
regular expressions, 265, 295
rendezvous, 418
Reppy, John H., xvii, 465, 502
RERAISE, 51, **51**, 51, 53
RESIZE, **73**, 73, *168, 228*, 239
rest, **123**
RETURN (macro), **52**, 52
reverse polish notation, 327, 365
Richter, Jeffrey, 468, 502
right shifts, 317

Ring_add, 185, **193**
Ring_addhi, 186, *188*, **191**, *193*
Ring_addlo, 186, **193**
Ring_free, 184, **189**
Ring_get, 185, **190**
Ring_length, 184, **189**
Ring_new, 184, *188*
Ring_put, 185, **190**
Ring_remhi, 186, **195**, *196*
Ring_remlo, 186, **196**
Ring_remove, 186, **194**
Ring_ring, 184, **188**
Ring_rotate, 186, **196**
Ring_T, **187**
Ritchie, Dennis M., 12, 13, 85, 86, 501
Roberts, Eric S., 31, 63, 64, 264, 502,
    503
Rogers, Anne M., xvii
root thread, 438
Rosenthal, David S. H., 465, 499

S

Saini, Atul, 31, 502
Scheme, 103, 114
Schneier, Bruce, 402, 503
Sedgewick, Robert, xii, 13, 42, 134,
    196, 503
Sem_init, 414, *425, 432*, **457**
Sem_new, 414, **457**
Sem_signal, 415, *433*, **459**
Sem_T, **414**, 414, *425, 432*
Sem_wait, 415, *433*, **458**
semaphores, 413
    avoiding starvation, 458
    binary, 465
    implementing, 457
    implementing channels with, 431
Seq_addhi, 173, *176*, **178**, *368, 373*
Seq_addlo, 173, **178**
Seq_free, 172, **176**, *368*

Seq_get, <u>173</u>, **177**, *372*
Seq_length, <u>172</u>, **176**, *367, 368, 372*
Seq_new, <u>172</u>, **175**, *176, 367*
Seq_put, <u>173</u>, **177**
Seq_remhi, <u>173</u>, **177**, *367, 369*
Seq_remlo, <u>173</u>, **178**
Seq_seq, <u>172</u>, **176**
Seq_T, **174**, *367*
sequences
   as queues, 171
   as stacks, 366
Set_diff, <u>140</u>, **157**
Set_free, <u>138</u>, <u>139</u>, **152**
Set_inter, <u>140</u>, **156**, *156*
Set_length, <u>139</u>, *144*, **152**
Set_map, <u>139</u>, **153**
Set_member, <u>139</u>, *148*, **150**
Set_minus, <u>140</u>, **156**
Set_new, <u>138</u>, *147*, **149**, *155-157*
Set_put, <u>139</u>, *148*, **151**
Set_remove, <u>139</u>, **152**
Set_T, *145*, 149, **149**
Set_toArray, <u>139</u>, *144*
Set_union, <u>140</u>, **154**
Sethi, Ravi, 13, 43, 497
setitimer, *455*
setjmp, 46, *47*, *54*, 65
SETL, 158
sets
   bit-vector representation of, 158, 199
   comparing, 201
   hash-table representation of, 149
   implementing comparisons of, 209
   implementing difference, 156, 212
   implementing intersection, 155, 212
   implementing symmetric difference, 157, 212
   implementing union, 154, 211
   operations on, 137, 201

   spatially multiplexed, 214
   testing membership in, 150, 205
   universes for, 137, 199
Sewell, William, 13, 503
Shah, Devang, 464, 468, 501
Sieve of Eratosthenes, 426
sigaction, *454*, 454
sigcontext, *455*
signals, 46, 64
signed ints vs. unsigned ints, 71
sigsetmask, *456*
SIGVTALRM, *454*
single-threaded programs, 405
size_t, 71
sizeof, *37*, 37
Smaalders, Bart, 464, 468, 501
SmallTalk, 100, 133
SNOBOL4, 42, 132, 293
Sohi, Gurindar S., 85, 497
Solaris operating system, 408
sprintf, *237*
Spuler, David, xvii
Stack interface, shortcomings of, 332
Stack_empty, <u>23</u>, **26**, *328, 332, 333*
Stack_free, <u>23</u>, **27**, *329, 333*
Stack_new, <u>23</u>, **26**, 32, *328, 332*
Stack_pop, <u>23</u>, **27**, *328, 333*
Stack_push, <u>23</u>, **27**, *330-333*
Stack_T, 21, **25**, *328*
stack-based allocation, 89
standard I/O, 30
_start, **452**, 452, *453*, **461**, **463**
Steele Jr., Guy L., 12, 239, 500, 503
Stevens, W. Richard, xvii, 465, 503
Str_any, <u>247</u>, **261**
Str_cat, <u>245</u>, **253**
Str_catv, <u>245</u>, **254**
Str_chr, <u>247</u>, **258**
Str_cmp, <u>246</u>, **257**
Str_dup, <u>245</u>, **252**
Str_find, <u>247</u>, **259**

Str_fmt, <u>249</u>, **264**
Str_len, <u>246</u>, **257**
Str_many, <u>247</u>, *250*, **261**
Str_map, <u>245</u>, **256**, 283, 284
Str_match, <u>248</u>, **262**
Str_pos, <u>246</u>, **256**
Str_rchr, <u>247</u>, **258**
Str_reverse, <u>245</u>, **253**
Str_rfind, <u>247</u>, **260**
Str_rmany, <u>248</u>, **262**
Str_rmatch, <u>248</u>, **263**
Str_rupto, <u>247</u>, **259**
Str_sub, <u>245</u>, **252**, 265
Str_upto, <u>247</u>, *250*, **259**
string.h, shortcomings of functions
    in, 242
strings
    analyzing, 246, 274
    boxing in descriptors, 271
    comparing, 257, 285
    converting integers to, 320, 325,
        352, 365, 399
    converting to integers, 302, 319,
        324, 350, 364, 399
    descriptor representation of, 269
    immutable, 269
    null characters in, 270
    passing descriptors by value, 270
    vs. pointers to characters, 241
    predefined, 274
    sharing, 272
    shortcomings of C, 269
    special allocation for, 279, 285
    special cases for concatenating,
        282
    special cases for duplicating, 281
    substrings of, 272
strncmp, 258, 289
Stroustrup, Bjarne, 31, 63, 498
strtol, *324*
strtoul, *302*, 365

structures
    passing and returning, 270
    tags for, 21
substrings, 244
Sussman, Gerald J., 114, 497
_swtch, 439, 450, **450**, **460**, **462**
symbol tables, 115
synchronous communication
    channels, 417

T

T (type names), 22
Table_free, <u>117</u>, *124*, **132**
Table_get, <u>117</u>, *122*, **127**, *147*
Table_length, <u>117</u>, *123*, **129**, *143*,
    144
Table_map, 117, <u>118</u>, *124*, **130**, 153,
    201
Table_new, <u>116</u>, *122*, **126**, *142*, *147*,
    149
Table_put, <u>117</u>, *122*, **129**, *147*
Table_remove, <u>117</u>, **130**
Table_T, **125**, *145*
Table_toArray, <u>118</u>, *123*, **131**, *143*,
    144, 159, 161
tables of tables, 141
Tanenbaum, Andrew S., 464, 467, 503
Tcl/Tk, xv
templates, DCE, 467
Teukolsky, Saul A., 402, 502
Text_any, <u>275</u>, **290**
Text_ascii, <u>274</u>, **277**
Text_box, <u>271</u>, **278**
Text_cat, <u>273</u>, **282**
Text_chr, <u>275</u>, **288**
Text_cmp, <u>274</u>, **285**
Text_cset, <u>274</u>, **277**
Text_digits, <u>274</u>, **278**
Text_dup, <u>273</u>, **281**
Text_find, <u>275</u>, **289**

Text_fmt, <u>276</u>, **293**
Text_get, <u>271</u>, **280**
Text_lcase, <u>274</u>, **278**
Text_many, <u>275</u>, **291**
Text_map, <u>273</u>, **284**
Text_match, <u>275</u>, **292**
Text_null, <u>274</u>, **278**, *283, 284*
Text_pos, <u>273</u>, **278**
Text_put, <u>271</u>, 272, **280**
Text_rchr, <u>275</u>, **288**
Text_restore, <u>276</u>, **287**
Text_reverse, <u>273</u>, **283**
Text_rfind, <u>275</u>, **290**
Text_rmany, <u>275</u>, **291**
Text_rmatch, <u>275</u>, **292**
Text_rupto, <u>275</u>, **289**
Text_save, <u>276</u>
Text_save_T, <u>276</u>, **287**
Text_sub, <u>272</u>, **279**
Text_T, **270**, <u>270</u>
Text_ucase, <u>274</u>, **277**
Text_upto, <u>275</u>, **288**
Thread_alert, <u>412</u>, 445, **445**
Thread_Alerted, 413, **445**
Thread_exit, 410, <u>412</u>, 413, *419,
     424, 427*, 442, **443**, 461, *463*
Thread_Failed, <u>412</u>, **447**
Thread_init, <u>410</u>, *419, 424, 427*, **438**
Thread_join, <u>412</u>, *422, 424, 425,*
     442, **442**
Thread_new, 413, *421–431*, **446**
Thread_pause, <u>412</u>, *440*
Thread_self, <u>412</u>, **439**
Thread_T, **435**, *458, 459*
threads
     alerting, 412, 445, 459
     ALPHA startup code, 463
     ALPHA _swtch, 462
     and atomic actions, 408
     communicating, 417
computing primes with a pipeline
     of, 426
concurrent sorting with, 418
context-switching of, 408, 439
control blocks for, 435
creating, 410, 411
and exceptions, 411
handles for, 410
handling timer interrupts, 454
implementation-dependent
     arguments for, 410
initializing stacks for, 447
join queues for, 442
kernel, 406, 408
killing, 412
managing resources for, 443, 446
MIPS startup code, 461
MIPS _swtch, 459
nonpreemptive scheduling of, 408,
     412
passing arguments to new, 449
POSIX. *See* POSIX threads
preemptive scheduling of, 408, 454
priorities for, 467
queues for, 435
rendezvous of, 418
and signals, 407, 408
SPARC startup code, 452
SPARC _swtch, 450
specifying scheduling of, 410
stack pointers for, 435
and standard libraries, 407
states of, 412
suspending, 412
terminating, 412
user-level, 406
waiting for, 412
thread-safe ADTs, 416
thread-safe functions, 407
tokens, 266, 328, 369
Torczon, Linda, 213, 498

trees, 117
TRY, <u>48</u>, **54**, 360, *367*, 413, *446*
TRY-EXCEPT statements, <u>48</u>
    volatile variables in, 50
TRY-FINALLY statements, 50
two's-complement, 35, 301, 358
two-level interfaces, 162
typedefs, 21, 24

U

Ullman, Jeffrey D., 43, 114, 497, 503
unchecked runtime errors, 24, 28, 32
    for Arith, 24
    for Array, 163
    for ArrayRep, 165
    for Atom, 34
    for Except, 52
    for Fmt, 222
    for List, 105, 107
    for Mem, 72
    for MP, 358, 360, 362
    for Sem, 414, 415
    for Text, 270, 271, 276
    for XP, 299-301
#undef, 23
undefined behaviors, 18
underscores, leading, 22, 434
unreachable memory, 333
unsigned vs. signed arithmetic, 35, 233
user errors, 45

V

va_arg, 222, *222-237*, *254*, *255*, *264*, *293*, *353*, *400*, *401*
va_end, *188*, *225-228*, *254*
va_list, *188*, *216-238*, *254*, *264*, *276*, *293*, *353*, *400*, *401*
va_start, *176*, *188*, *225-227*, *254*

variable length argument lists, 105, 172, 176
    pointers to, 221
version-control tools, 12
Vetterling, William T., 402, 502
virtual timer, 454
Vo, Kiem-Phong, 99, 503
volatile qualifier, 50, *54*

W

Wampler, Steven B., 464, 503
Watt, Stephen M., 354, 498
WEB, 12
Weinberger, Peter J., 132, 265, 497
Weinstock, Charles B., 85, 503
Weiser, Mark, 100, 498
wf, *121*, **122**, 142
White, Jon L., 239, 503
Windows 95, 407, 464
Windows NT, 407, 464
Wolfram, Stephen, 354, 503
Wortman, David B., 294, 502
Wulf, William A., 85, 503

X

XP_add, <u>299</u>, **305**, *339*, *381*, 383, *384*
XP_cmp, <u>301</u>, **315**, *347*, *395*, *396*, *397*
XP_diff, <u>301</u>, **307**, *342*, *388-395*
XP_div, <u>300</u>, **310**, *343*, *383*, *387*, *388*
XP_fromint, <u>302</u>, **304**, *336*, *376*, *377*, *396*
XP_fromstr, <u>302</u>, **319**, *351*, *399*
XP_length, <u>302</u>, **304**, *310*, *388*
XP_lshift, <u>302</u>, **315**, *349*, *399*
XP_mul, <u>300</u>, **308**, 338, *382*, *386*
XP_neg, <u>301</u>, **307**, *377*, *385-388*, *394*, *395*
XP_product, <u>301</u>, **309**, *314*, *317*, *319*, *390*, *394*

XP_quotient, <u>301</u>, **310**, *311*, *318*,
    391, *395*
XP_rshift, <u>302</u>, **317**, *349*, *399*
XP_sub, <u>300</u>, **306**, *315*, *341*, *343*, *381*,
    384, *388*
XP_sum, <u>301</u>, **306**, *319*, *339*, *342*, *389*,
    392, *393*
XP_T, **299**, <u>299</u>

XP_toint, <u>302</u>, **304**, *348*, *350*, *378*,
    391, *396*
XP_tostr, <u>303</u>, **320**, 352, *353*, *400*
XPL compiler generator, 294
xref, *142*, **145**

Z

Zorn, Benjamin G., 85, 98, 100, 497,
    499, 503